EYEWITNESS TRAVEL

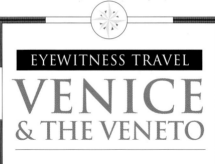

VENICE
& THE VENETO

EYEWITNESS TRAVEL

VENICE
& THE VENETO

MAIN CONTRIBUTORS:
SUSIE BOULTON
CHRISTOPHER CATLING

DK

LONDON, NEW YORK, MELBOURNE, MUNICH AND DELHI
www.dk.com

PRODUCED BY Pardoe Blacker Publishing Limited, Lingfield, Surrey
PROJECT Editor Caroline Ball
ART EDITOR Simon Blacker
EDITORS Jo Bourne, Molly Perham, Linda Williams
DESIGNERS Kelvin Barratt, Dawn Brend, Jon Eland,
Nick Raven, Steve Rowling
MAP CO-ORDINATORS Simon Farbrother, David Pugh
PICTURE RESEARCH Jill De Cet

CONTRIBUTOR (TRAVELLERS' NEEDS) Sally Roy

MAPS
Phil Rose, Jennifer Skelley, Jane Hanson
(Lovell Johns Ltd, Oxford UK)
Street Finder maps based upon digital data, adapted
with permission from L.A.C. (Italy)

PHOTOGRAPHERS
John Heseltine (Venice), Roger Moss (Veneto)

ILLUSTRATORS
Arcana Studios, Donati Giudici Associati srl,
Robbie Polley, Simon Roulstone

Reproduced by Colourscan, Singapore
Printed and bound in China by L. Rex Printing Co. Ltd

First American edition 1995
12 13 14 15 10 9 8 7 6 5 4 3 2 1

Published in the United States by DK Publishing,
375 Hudson Street, New York, New York 10014

**Reprinted with revisions 1995, 1997 (twice), 1998, 1999,
2000, 2001, 2002, 2003, 2004, 2006, 2008, 2010, 2012**

Copyright 1995, 2012 © Dorling Kindersley Limited, London
A Penguin Company

Published in Great Britain by Dorling Kindersley Limited.

A CATALOG RECORD FOR THIS BOOK IS AVAILABLE FROM THE LIBRARY OF CONGRESS.

ISSN: 1542–1554
ISBN: 978-0-75668-410-5

FLOORS ARE REFERRED TO THROUGHOUT IN ACCORDANCE WITH AMERICAN
USAGE; IE THE "FIRST FLOOR" IS THE FLOOR AT GROUND LEVEL.

*Front cover main image: Santa Maria della Salute
and the Grand Canal, Venice*

MIX
Paper from
responsible sources
FSC
www.fsc.org   FSC™ C018179

**The information in this
Dorling Kindersley Travel Guide is checked regularly.**
Every effort has been made to ensure that this book is as up-to-date
as possible at the time of going to press. Some details, however, such
as telephone numbers, opening hours, prices, gallery hanging
arrangements and travel information are liable to change. The
publishers cannot accept responsibility for any consequences arising
from the use of this book, nor for any material on third party
websites, and cannot guarantee that any website address in this book
will be a suitable source of travel information. We value the views
and suggestions of our readers very highly. Please write to: Publisher,
DK Eyewitness Travel Guides, Dorling Kindersley, 80 Strand,
London, WC2R 0RL, Great Britain, or email travelguides@dk.com.

CONTENTS

HOW TO USE THIS GUIDE 6

The Venetian explorer Marco Polo

INTRODUCING VENICE AND THE VENETO

FOUR GREAT DAYS IN VENICE AND THE VENETO 10

PUTTING VENICE AND THE VENETO ON THE MAP 12

A PORTRAIT OF THE VENETO 16

VENICE AND THE VENETO THROUGH THE YEAR 32

THE HISTORY OF VENICE AND THE VENETO 36

Palazzo Pisani Moretta on the Grand Canal

The medieval Palio dei Dieci Comuni at Montagnana

The Rialto Bridge, on the
Grand Canal

Veronese's *Passion and Virtue* in
the Villa Barbaro at Masèr

Asparagus stalks

The Doge's Palace
in Piazza San Marco

HOW TO USE THIS GUIDE

This guide helps you get the most from your stay in Venice and the Veneto. It provides both expert recommendations and detailed practical information. *Introducing Venice and the Veneto* maps the region and sets it in its historical and cultural context. *Venice Area by Area* and *The Veneto*

Area by Area describe the important sights, with maps, pictures and detailed illustrations. Suggestions for food, drink, accommodation, shopping and entertainment are in *Travellers' Needs*, and the *Survival Guide* has tips on everything from the Italian telephone system to travelling around Venice by *vaporetto*.

VENICE AREA BY AREA

The city has been divided into five sightseeing areas. The lagoon islands make up a sixth area. Each area has its own chapter, which opens with a list of the sights described. All the sights are numbered and plotted on an *Area Map*. The detailed information for each sight is presented in numerical order, making it easy to locate within the chapter.

Sights at a Glance lists the chapter's sights by category: Churches; Museums and Galleries; Historic Buildings; Palaces; Streets, Bridges and Squares.

Each area of Venice can be quickly identified by its colour coding.

A locator map shows where you are in relation to other areas of the city.

1 Area Map
For easy reference, the sights are numbered and located on a map. The sights are also shown on the Venice Street Finder *on pages 288–97.*

2 Street-by-Street Map
This gives a bird's eye view of the heart of each sightseeing area.

Stars indicate the sights that no visitor should miss.

A suggested route for a walk covers the more interesting streets in the area.

3 Detailed information on each sight
All the sights in Venice are described individually. Addresses, telephone numbers, nearest vaporetto stop, opening hours and information on admission charges are also provided.

THE VENETO PLAIN

The great arc of land that forms the Veneto Plain is one of tremendous contrast, and has much to offer the visitor. Its ancient cities are rich in history and their magnificent architecture is world-renowned. The source of the region's wealth is manifest in the industrial landscapes around the towns, but these are never far from beautiful countryside, which includes the green Euganean Hills, calm lagoons and the undulating foothills of the Dolomites.

1 Introduction

The landscape, history and character of each region is described here, showing how the area has developed over the centuries and what it offers to the visitor today.

THE VENETO AREA BY AREA

In this book, the Veneto has been divided into three regions, each of which has a separate chapter. The most interesting sights to visit have been numbered on a *Regional Map*.

Each area of the Veneto can be quickly identified by its colour coding.

2 Regional Map

This shows the road network and gives an illustrated overview of the whole region. All the sights are numbered and there are also useful tips on getting around the region by car, bus and train.

3 Detailed information on each sight

All the important towns and other places to visit are described individually. They are listed in order, following the numbering on the Regional Map. Within each town or city, there is detailed information on important buildings and other sights.

Stars indicate the best features and works of art.

For all the top sights, a Visitors' Checklist provides the practical information you will need to plan your visit.

Vicenza: Teatro Olimpico

4 The top sights

These are given two or more full pages. Historic buildings are dissected to reveal their interiors; museums and galleries have colour-coded floorplans to help you locate the most interesting exhibits.

CIVITAS VENECIAF

Ecclia   Ici Marc

INTRODUCING VENICE AND THE VENETO

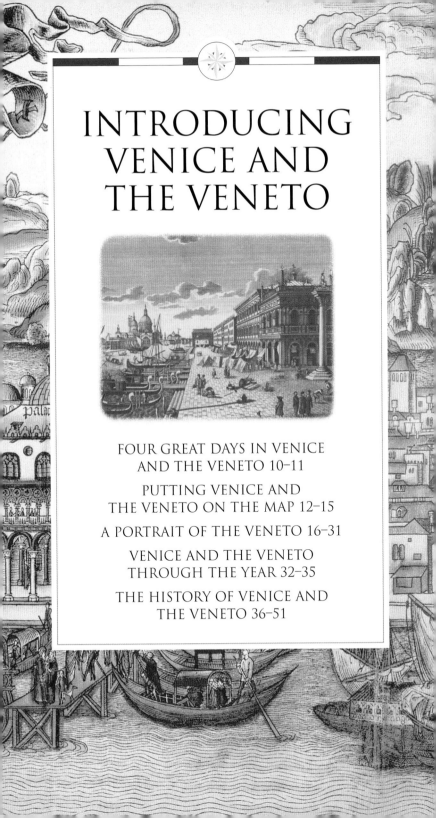

FOUR GREAT DAYS IN VENICE AND THE VENETO

Visitors are simply spoiled for choice in this part of Italy. There are scores of museums, churches and art galleries in Venice which demand attention, preferably with stops along the way for a meal at a waterside café or a ride on a gondola. Then there are the historic towns of the Veneto, each with its own special story to tell, dotted across the beautiful hinterland. The four itineraries outlined here are designed to show the variety of activities this region has to offer. The Venice and Verona days can be enjoyed using public transport alone, whereas Lake Garda is best explored by car and ferry. The price guides give an indication of the overall cost, including travel, food and admission charges.

Gondola, Venice

THE TREASURES AND STYLE OF ST MARK'S

- Early morning in the Basilica
- See how the Doges lived
- Fashion shopping along the Calle XXII Marzo
- View from a gondola

TWO ADULTS allow at least €120

Morning
It is worth getting to the **Basilica** *(see pp78–83)* as early as possible to enjoy the glittering mosaics and solemn Byzantine interior in the morning light. Don't forget to climb the narrow steps to the balconies that overlook St Mark's Square. Once back at ground level, wander around the busy *piazza*, bustling with people and pigeons, before taking a (pre-booked) guided tour of the **Torre dell'Orologio** *(see p76)*, with its magnificent astronomical clock, or the adjoining **Museo Correr** *(see p77)*. Nearby is the **Doge's Palace** *(see pp84–9)*, which offers the chance to visit

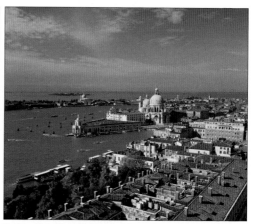

Rooftop view of Santa Maria della Salute and Punta della Dogana

the state apartments for a glimpse into how the city's former rulers once lived. A light lunch in the converted stables below is a good way to round off the morning.

Afternoon
A 5-minute walk away is the exclusive shopping street **Calle XXII Marzo** *(see p91)*, lined with top fashion boutiques with enticing window displays. A perfect, if expensive, way to end the day is with a relaxing **gondola ride** *(see p283)* over St Mark's basin and along the labyrinth of quiet back canals. Another option is to visit the historic **Caffè Florian** *(see p250)* and watch the world go by while sipping an aperitif to the sounds of its lively orchestra.

Feeding the pigeons in front of the Basilica on St Mark's Square

ART AND WATERBUSES

- Art at the Accademia
- A lunchtime *gelato*
- Get caught up in modern art
- Relax on a *vaporetto*

TWO ADULTS allow at least €120

Morning
The renowned **Accademia** art gallery *(see pp130–33)* is crammed with paintings illustrating Venice's glorious history as the Serenissima Republic. Canvases by great masters such as Titian, Bellini and Veronese adorn this converted monastery, and an audio gallery guide is a great help in navigating your way around. When you

have had your fill, walk over to the broad, sun-blessed **Zattere** waterfront *(see pp128–9)* for views of the Giudecca and passing waterborne traffic. Lunch can be enjoyed at any one of the outdoor restaurants here, finished off with a classic Italian *gelato* (ice cream) *(see pp250–51)*.

Afternoon
The afternoon can be well spent at the nearby **Peggy Guggenheim Collection** *(see p134)*, a landmark collection of Modern art. The works by Mirò, Picasso and Pollock, to name but a few, occupy a light-filled single-storey *palazzo* on the Grand Canal. A pleasant place to stop for a drink is the lovely terrace café. Once outside wander back to the Zattere and catch *vaporetto* **n.52** *(see pp284–5)*, which circumnavigates the city giving a panoramic conclusion to the day.

THE ROMANCE OF VERONA

- **A visit to Juliet's house**
- **The awe-inspiring Arena**
- **Sightseeing from a horse-drawn carriage**
- **A walk around the tranquil Giardini Giusti gardens**

TWO ADULTS allow at least €150

Morning
One of the most romantic cities in the world, Verona is the setting of the tragic tale of Romeo and Juliet.

The perfect way to start your visit is at the **Casa di Giulietta** (Juliet's house) *(see p199)*, although the building is not authentic it is still atmospheric. A short stroll away is the beautiful Piazza Brà, home to the awe-inspiring **Roman Arena** *(see pp194–5)*, where opera is performed outdoors in the summer months. It is well worth taking the time to climb up the immense tiers of stone seats to admire the massive structure and views of the surrounding city. A great place to stop for lunch is the family-run **Ristorante Greppia** *(see p249)*, the menu features plenty of delicious local specialities.

Afternoon
Returning to Piazza Brà, a nice way to view the sights, while resting your feet, is a gently paced horse-drawn carriage ride, which takes in many of the sights of the town, including the spectacular **Castelvecchio** museum *(see p193)* and the photogenic Pontevecchio bridge. Across the river is the **Giardino Giusti** *(see p203)*, a lovely example of a Renaissance garden dotted with aged cedar trees and clipped hedges. A lovely way to spend the early evening is with an apéritif in **Piazza delle Erbe** *(see p198)*. Try a glass of Valpolicella wine while watching the square empty of its daytime clutter, allowing the central fountain to once again make its presence felt.

The pretty town of Malcesine overlooks Lake Garda

A FAMILY DAY ON GLORIOUS LAKE GARDA

- **The tunnels of Gardesana**
- **View from the water**
- **Ride the revolving cable-car to Monte Baldo**
- **An evening swim off the rocks at Sirmione**

FAMILY OF 4 allow at least €150

Morning
From Desenzano drive up the western side of the lake on the exciting **Gardesana** *(see p205)*. This road hugs the shore and passes through numerous road tunnels. For a more relaxing ride choose one of the ferries that ply these waters. Take a break at **Riva del Garda** *(see p209)* to enjoy the beautiful views of the lake. On the way back down the eastern shore **Malcesine** *(see p209)*, with its castle sitting proudly on a rocky promontory, is a good place to stop for lunch.

Afternoon
From Malcesine you can take a spectacular revolving cable car up the side of Monte Baldo, a haven for lovers of wild flowers and spectacular views. Back down at lake level, proceed south towards the **Sirmione Peninsula** *(see pp206–7)*. Park at the entrance and explore the photogenic Rocca Scaligera. Nearby is the lakeside walk; the vast slabs of rock are a stunning place to take a swim.

The maze of carefully clipped hedges in Giardini Giusti

Putting Venice and the Veneto on the Map

The Veneto lies in the northernmost sector of Italy, and stretches from the Dolomite mountains in the north to the flatlands of the Venetian lagoon in the south. One of the most prosperous regions of Italy, the Veneto covers an area of 47,562 sq km (18,364 sq miles), and has a population of 4.5 million. Rail and road links with the rest of Europe are excellent, and three international airports serve the region: Valerio Catullo in Verona, Marco Polo on the edge of the lagoon, and Treviso.

EUROPE

NORWAY
FINLAND
SWEDEN
UNITED KINGDOM
REP. OF IRELAND
DENMARK
ESTONIA
RUSSIAN FEDERATION
LATVIA
LITHUANIA
NETHERLANDS
BELORUSSIA
POLAND
BELGIUM
GERMANY
LUXEMBOURG
CZECH REP.
UKRAINE
FRANCE
SLOVAKIA
SWITZERLAND
AUSTRIA
HUNGARY
ITALY
SLOVENIA
ROMANIA
CROATIA
Venezia (Venice)
SERBIA
BOSNIA & HERZEGOVINA
MONTENEGRO
KOSOVO
BULGARIA
ALBANIA
MACEDONIA
SPAIN
GREECE

Mulhouse
Basel (Basle)
Bodensee
Zurich
Doubs
LIECHTENSTEIN
BERNE
N12
10
S W I T Z E R L A N D
Genève (Geneva)
N9
Rhône
N2
L. Maggiore
Mt Blanc
A5
N6-E70
E70
Milano (Milan)
A4
A7
A4-E2
Torino (Turin)
A21
A26
A6
Genova (Genoa)
A12-E
Savona
Verdon
A10
A8-E80
Nice
A54
A9
Marseille
A57
Toulon

Ligurian Sea

Bastia
Calvi

C O R S I C A

Porto Torres
Olbia

S A R D I N I A
S131

Satellite image of the Veneto, with the Venetian lagoon bottom right

Piazza San Marco in Venice

KEY

☐	The Veneto
✈	Airport
⛴	Ferry port
═	Motorway
═	Major road
—	Railway line

0 kilometres   100

0 miles   100

Central Venice

Venice is divided into six ancient administrative districts or *sestieri*. The areas described in this book for the most part follow the *sestieri* boundaries, with San Polo and Santa Croce combined. Visitors usually start with the Piazza San Marco, heading for the Doge's Palace and the breath-taking basilica, but each district has its own distinct character, and time spent exploring each will be fully rewarded.

San Polo and Santa Croce: a pretty stone bridge by the Fondamenta del Megio linking streets unchanged for centuries

Dorsoduro: the mouth of the Grand Canal

0 metres   250

0 yards   250

Cannaregio: view along the picturesque Rio Madonna dell'Orto

Castello: façade detail of the Scuola Grande di San Marco

San Marco: the Campanile in Piazza San Marco

KEY

	Major sight
	Ferry boarding point
	Vaporetto boarding point
	Traghetto crossing
	Gondola waiting point
	Tourist information
	Hospital
	Police station
	Church
	Synagogue
	Post office

A PORTRAIT OF THE VENETO

*V*enice and the Veneto form, on the face of it, an unlikely partnership. Venice is a romantic tourist city frozen in time, the Veneto a forward-thinking and cosmopolitan part of modern Europe. Yet the commercial dynamism of the mainland cities is a direct legacy of the Old Lady of the Lagoon who, in her prime, ruled much of the Mediterranean.

Venice is one of the few cities in the world that can truly be described as unique. It survives against all the odds, built on a series of low mud banks amid the tidal waters of the Adriatic and regularly subject to floods. Once a powerful commercial and naval force in the Mediterranean, Venice has found a new role. Her *palazzi* have become shops, hotels and apartments, her warehouses have been transformed into museums and her convents have been turned into centres for art restoration. Yet little of the essential fabric of Venice has altered in 200 years. A prewar guide to the city is just as useful today as

The lion of St Mark, symbol of imperial Venice

when it was published, a rare occurrence on a continent scarred by the aerial bombing of World War II and the demands of postwar development. More than 14 million visitors a year succumb to the magic of this improbable city where the past has more meaning than the present.

For all this Venice has had a price to pay. So desirable is a Venetian apartment that rents are beyond the means of the Venetians themselves. Many of the city's apartments are owned by wealthy foreigners who use them perhaps for two or three weeks a year – unlit windows at night are indicative of absent owners.

Children attending their first communion at Monte Berico, outside Vicenza

◁ A traditional Carnival clown takes a break from the celebrations

An elderly Venetian in an ageing Venice

In 1997 the population of the city was 68,600 (compared with 150,000 in 1950), but in 2001 the numbers rose for the first time since the 1950s. The average age of the Venetian population is nearly 50. One reason the city shuts down so early at night is that the waiters, cooks and shop assistants all have to catch the last train home across the causeway to Mestre.

Mestre, by contrast, is a bustling city of 180,000 inhabitants, with a busy oil terminal and an expanding industrial base, as well as some of the liveliest discos in Italy. Governed by the same mayor and city council, Mestre and Venice have been described as the ugliest city in the world married to the most beautiful. Yet Mestre, founded by Venetians who foresaw a day when development land would run out in the lagoon, is simply an extension of the same entrepreneurial spirit that characterized mercantile Venice in her heyday, a spirit that is now typical of the region as a whole.

Fruit seller in Sirmione, on Lake Garda

One move to inject new life into Venice entails reconverting former industrial sites – the abattoir and the cotton mill have become university premises, while a former flour mill has been transformed into a convention centre.

THE INDUSTRIOUS NORTH

The creativity and industry of the people of the Veneto contradict all the clichés about the irrationality and indolence of the Italian character. For a tiny area, with a population of 4.5 million, the Veneto is remarkably productive. Many world-renowned companies have manufacturing bases in the area, from Jacuzzi Europe and Zanussi, to

Benetton shop in Treviso

Benetton, Olivetti and Iveco Ford. As a result, poverty is rare, and the region has progressed from its prewar agricultural base to a modern manufacturing and distribution economy.

Unencumbered by the rest of Italy, the three northern regions of Piedmont, Lombardy and Veneto alone would qualify for membership of the G10 group of the world's richest nations, a fact exploited by the region's politicians in separatist calls for independence from Rome. Cold-shouldering the rest of the Italian peninsula, the Veneto looks east to Slovenia for an example of a small state that has achieved independence, and north to Germany as a model of political federalism and sound economic management.

Valle di Cadore in the Dolomites, close to the Austrian border

Despite the ferocity of battles fought against them down the ages, the people in the north of the Veneto have a close relationship with their Teutonic neighbours. Today, German signs, food and language can be easily found in the towns around Lake Garda and the Dolomites. Here, the pretty Tyrolean farmsteads and onion-domed churches are a marked contrast to the isolated fishing communities of the lagoon, where Venice's maritime heritage is still evident. Between these two extremes, however, the cities of the Veneto plain, with their wealth of culture, provide a more typical view of Italian life.

Traditional Venetian rowing

café provides a meeting place for intellectual discourse and entertainment.

It is not just the Paduans who treat their streets and squares like so many corridors and rooms in one vast communal palace. After 5pm crowds throng Verona's Via Mazzini, taking part in the evening stroll, the *passeggiata*. Against the backdrop of the Roman arena or medieval *palazzi* they argue, swap gossip, forge alliances and strike deals. Younger strollers dress to impress, while young mothers bring their babies out to be admired. For all their modernity, the people of the Veneto still understand the powerful part played by ancient rituals such as this in cementing a strong sense of community.

ITALIAN TRADITION

Padua is a perfect example of the *città salotto*, a city built like a salon on a human scale, where the streets are an extension of the home and where the doorless Caffè Pedrocchi is treated like the city's main square. Here Paduans come to drink coffee or write a letter, read a newspaper or talk to friends. Just like the salons of old, the

Wedding Ferrari decorated with typical Italian style

The Building of Venice

Venice is built on a patchwork of more than 100 low-lying islands in the middle of a swampy lagoon. To overcome these extremely challenging conditions, early Venetian builders evolved construction techniques unique to the city, building with impermeable stone supported by larchwood rafts and timber piles. This method proved effective and most Venetian buildings are remarkably robust, many having stood for at least 400 years. By 1500 the city had taken on much of its present shape and only since the 20th century has further building begun to alter the outline.

Campo Santa Maria Mater Domini *is a typical medieval square, with its central wellhead and its business-like landward façades – decoration on buildings was usually reserved for the canal façades.*

Campaniles often lean because of compaction of the underlying subsoil.

Pinewood piles *were driven 7.5 m (25 ft) into the ground before building work could begin. They rest on the solid caranto (compressed clay) layer at the bottom of the lagoon.*

Istrian stone, a type of marble, was used to create damp-proof foundations.

Bricks

Closely packed piles do not rot in the waterlogged subsoil because there is no free oxygen, vital for microbes that cause decay.

Water grilles

Sand acting as a filter

The well was the source of the fresh water supply. Rainwater was channelled through pavement grilles into a clay-lined cistern filled with sand to act as a filter.

Ornate wellheads, *such as this one in the Doge's Palace courtyard photographed in the late 19th century, indicate the importance of a reliable water supply for the survival of the community. Strict laws protected the purity of the source, prohibiting "beasts, unwashed pots and unclean hands".*

THE CAMPANILE FOUNDATIONS

When the Campanile in the Piazza San Marco *(see p76)* collapsed in 1902, the ancient pilings, underpinning the 98.5-m high (323-ft) landmark, were found to be in excellent condition, after 1,000 years in the ground. Like the Campanile, all buildings in Venice are supported on slender oak and pine piles, harvested in the forests of the northern Veneto and floated downriver to the Venetian lagoon. Once driven through the lagoon subsoil, they create an immensely strong and flexible foundation. Even so, there is a limit to how much weight the piles can carry – the Campanile, its height having been increased several times, simply grew too tall and collapsed. When the tower was rebuilt, timber foundations were again used, but this time more than double the size.

Strengthening the Campanile foundations

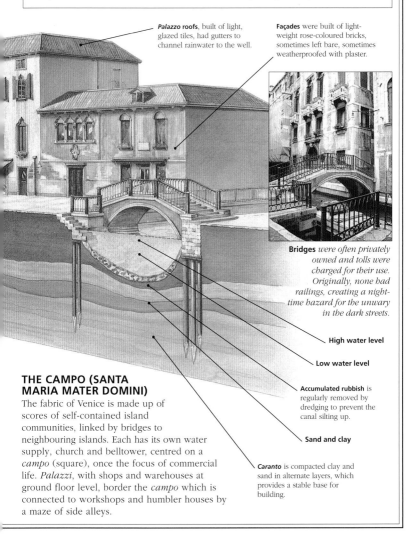

Palazzo **roofs**, built of light, glazed tiles, had gutters to channel rainwater to the well.

Façades were built of light-weight rose-coloured bricks, sometimes left bare, sometimes weatherproofed with plaster.

Bridges *were often privately owned and tolls were charged for their use. Originally, none had railings, creating a night-time hazard for the unwary in the dark streets.*

High water level

Low water level

Accumulated rubbish is regularly removed by dredging to prevent the canal silting up.

Sand and clay

Caranto is compacted clay and sand in alternate layers, which provides a stable base for building.

THE CAMPO (SANTA MARIA MATER DOMINI)

The fabric of Venice is made up of scores of self-contained island communities, linked by bridges to neighbouring islands. Each has its own water supply, church and belltower, centred on a *campo* (square), once the focus of commercial life. *Palazzi*, with shops and warehouses at ground floor level, border the *campo* which is connected to workshops and humbler houses by a maze of side alleys.

The Venetian Palazzo

Baroque statue

Venetian houses evolved to meet the needs of a city without roads. Visitors usually arrived by boat, so the façade facing the canal was given lavish architectural treatment, while the landward side, which was accessible from a square or alley, was rarely so ornate. Most Venetian houses were built with three storeys, with kitchens located on the ground floor for ready access to water, or in the attic to enable cooking smells to escape. Typically, a *palazzo* served as a warehouse and business premises, as well as a family home, reflecting the city's mercantile character.

Renaissance doorcase with lion

BYZANTINE (12TH AND 13TH CENTURIES)

The earliest surviving private *palazzi* in Venice date from the 13th century and reflect the architectural influence of the Byzantine world. Façades are recognizable by their ground-floor arcades and arched open galleries which run the entire length of the first floor. Simple motifs feature leaves or palm trees.

Byzantine roundel, Fondaco dei Turchi

The Byzantine arcades of the Fondaco dei Turchi (built 1225)

Façade carvings feature the owner's coat of arms and the Lion of St Mark.

Byzantine horseshoe-shaped arches

Cushion capitals have only simple motifs.

Palazzo Loredan (see p64) *has an elegant ground floor arcade and first floor gallery typical of a 13th-century Byzantine palace.*

GOTHIC (13TH TO MID-15TH CENTURIES)

Elaborate Gothic *palazzi* are more numerous than any other style in Venice. Most famous of all is the Doge's Palace (*see pp82–3*), with elegant arches in Istrian stone and fine tracery which give the façade a delicate, lace-like appearance. This style, emulated throughout the city, can be identified through its use of pointed arches and carved window heads.

Palazzo Foscari (see p66) *is a fine example of the 15th-century Venetian Gothic style, with its finely carved white Istrian stone façade and pointed arches.*

The interlacing ribs of pointed ogee arches create a delicate tracery.

Trefoil "three leaved" window heads are typically Gothic.

Quatrefoil patterns on elegant gallery windows

Gothic capitals are adorned with foliage, animals and faces.

Gothic capitals (Doge's Palace)

RENAISSANCE (15TH AND 16TH CENTURIES)

Houses of the Renaissance period were often built in sandstone rather than traditional Venetian brick. The style was based on Classical architecture, with emphasis on harmonious proportions and symmetry. The decorative language, borrowing motifs from ancient Rome and Greece, typically incorporated fluted columns, Corinthian capitals and semi-circular arches.

Palazzo Grimani (see p64) *has lavish stone carving which none but the wealthy could afford; massive foundations were constructed to bear the incredible weight.*

Corinthian pilasters on the portal to San Giovanni Evangelista

Bold projecting roof cornices are a feature of Renaissance architecture.

Theatrical masks serve as keystones to window arches.

The Venetian door, a very popular Renaissance motif, has a rounded central arch flanked by narrower side openings. This combination was also used for windows.

BAROQUE (17TH CENTURY)

Venetian Baroque has its roots in the Renaissance Classical style but is far more exuberant. Revelling in bold ornamentation that leaves no surface uncarved, garlands, swags, cherubs, grotesque masks and rosettes animate the main façades of buildings such as the 17th-century Ca' Pesaro.

Baroque cartouche

Semi-circular window head of Palazzo Balbi with two lights and spandrel decorated with a circle.

Massive blocks with deep ridges give solidity to the lower walls.

Ca' Pesaro (see p62) *is an example of Baroque experimentation, with its flat façade broken into a three-dimensional stone pattern of deep recesses and strong projections.*

Cherubs and plumed heads are carved into Baroque stone window heads.

Recessed windows and column clusters create an interesting play of light and shadow.

THE VENETIAN HOUSE

The layout of a typical *palazzo* (often called Ca', short for *casa,* or house) has changed little over the centuries, despite the very different styles of external decoration.

Offices, used for storing business records, evolved into libraries.

Attic rooms were reserved for servants.

Courtyards took the place of gardens.

The upper floor housed the family.

The *piano nobile* (grand floor), often lavishly decorated, was used to entertain visitors.

The ground floor storerooms and offices were used for the transaction of business.

The Villas of Palladio

Andrea Palladio

When it became fashionable in the 16th century for wealthy Venetians to acquire rural estates on the mainland, many turned to the prolific architect, Andrea Palladio (1508–80) for the design of their villas. Inspired by ancient Roman prototypes, described by authors such as Vitruvius and Virgil, Palladio provided his clients with elegant buildings in which the pursuit of pleasure could be combined with the functions of a working farm. Palladio's designs were widely imitated and continue to inspire architects to this day.

The façade *is symmetrical; dovecotes and stables in the wings balance the central block.*

The Room of the Little Dog *is ornate and lavishly decorated with frescoes by Veronese. Look closely to see the detail of a spaniel in one of the panels.*

The Nymphaeum *combines utility with art; the same spring that feeds the statue-lined pool also supplies water to the villa.*

KEY

☐ Crociera	☐ Room of the Little Dog
☐ Bacchus Room	☐ Room of the Oil Lamp
☐ Room of the Tribunal of Love	☐ Nymphaeum
☐ Hall of Olympus	☐ Non-exhibition space

THE VILLA BARBARO

Palladio and Veronese worked closely to create this splendid villa (commissioned in 1555, *see p167*). Lively frescoes of false balconies, doors, windows and rural views create the illusion of greater space, perfectly complementing Palladio's light, airy rooms.

DEVELOPMENT OF THE VILLA

Palladio experimented with many different designs which he published in his influential *Quattro Libri (Four Books)* in 1570, illustrating the astonishing fertility of his mind and his ability to create endless variations on the Classical Roman style.

The portico statues reflect Palladio's study of ancient Roman buildings.

The pedimented pavilion is all that survives of Palladio's ambitious design; the main residence was never built.

Stables and storerooms

Villa Thiene (1546), now the town hall, Quinto Vicentino

The Hall of Olympus *shows Giustiniana, mistress of the house and wife of Venetian ambassador Marcantonio Barbaro, with her youngest son, wetnurse and family pets.*

In the Crociera, *the cross-shaped central hall, servants peer round false doors, while imaginary landscapes blur the boundary between the house interior and the garden.*

The Room of the Oil Lamp *symbolizes virtuous behaviour; here Strength, with the club, leans on Truth, with the mirror.*

The Bacchus Room, *with its winemaking scenes and chimneypiece carved with the figure of Abundance, reflects the bucolic ideal of the villa as a place of good living and plenty.*

Arcades resemble triumphal arches.

***Palazzo*-style central hall**

Service wing

The domed cross plan was adapted by Palladio from church architecture.

The façades face the four points of the compass.

Villa Pisani (1555), Montagnana *(see p184)*

Villa Capra "La Rotonda" (1569), Vicenza *(see p171)*

Styles in Venetian Art

Venetian art grew out of the Byzantine tradition of iconographic art, designed to inspire religious awe. Because of the trade links between Venice and Constantinople, capital of Byzantium, the Eastern influence lasted longer here than elsewhere in Italy. Andrea Mantegna introduced the Renaissance style to the Veneto in the 1460s, and his brother-in-law Giovanni Bellini became Venice's leading painter. In the early 16th century Venetian artists began to develop their own style, in which soft shading and dramatic use of light distinguishes the works of Venetian masters Titian, Giorgione, Tintoretto and Veronese. The development of this characteristic Venetian style, which the prolific but lesser known artists of the Baroque and Rococo periods continued, can be seen in the chronological arrangement of the Accademia *(see p130–33)*.

Detail from Veneziano's Coronation of the Virgin

The Last Judgment *(12th century) from Torcello: in the damp climate, mosaics, not frescoes, were used to decorate Venetian churches.*

BYZANTINE GOTHIC

Paolo Veneziano is credited with the move from grand-scale mosaics to more intimate altarpieces. His painting mixes idealized figures with the hairstyles, costumes and textiles familiar to 14th-century Venetians. The typically lavish use of jewel colours and gold, symbol of purity, can also be seen in the work of Veneziano's pupil (and namesake) Lorenzo, and in the gilded warrior angels of Guariento *(see p179)*.

Veneziano's entire dazzling polyptych *(1325) of which this is the centrepiece, is in the Accademia* (see p132).

Paolo Veneziano's *Coronation of the Virgin*

The Madonna's gentle face *reinforces the courtly refinement of Veneziano's work.*

The composition and colours reflect the style of the early Byzantine icons which influenced the artist.

Arabesque patterns on the tunics reflect Moorish influence.

Musicians like these played at grand ceremonies in San Marco.

TIMELINE OF VENETIAN ARTISTS

1300	1350	1400	1450
	1356–72 (active) Lorenzo Veneziano	**1430–1516** Giovanni Bellini / **1431–1506** Andrea Mantegna	**1483–1539** Giovanni Pordenone
	1338–c.1368 Guariento	**1415–84** Antonio Vivarini	**1450– 1526** Vittore Carpaccio / **1480–1528** Palma il Vecchio / **1480–1556** Lorenzo Lotto
	1395–1455 Antonio Pisanello	**1429–1507** Gentile Bellini	**1467–1510** "Il Morto da Feltre"
	1400–71 Jacopo Bellini		**1477–1510** Giorgione
1321–62 (active) Paolo Veneziano		**1432–99** Bartolomeo Vivarini	
		1441–1507 Alvise Vivarini	**1487–1576** Titian

EARLY RENAISSANCE

Renaissance artists were fascinated by Classical sculpture and developed new techniques of perspective and shading to give their figures a three-dimensional look. Using egg-based tempera gave crisp lines and bold blocks of colour, but with little tonal gradation. The Bellini family dominated art in Renaissance Venice, and Giovanni, who studied anatomy for greater accuracy in his work, portrays the feelings of his subjects through their facial expressions.

In Bellini's 1488 Frari altarpiece, *the Madonna is flanked by Saints Peter, Nicholas, Benedict and Mark (see p102).*

Illusionistic details *fool the eye: the real moulding copies the painted one.*

St Benedict carries the Benedictine book of monastic rule.

Musical cherubs playing at the feet of the Virgin are a Bellini trademark; music was a symbol of order and harmony.

Giovanni Bellini's *Madonna and Child with Saints*

HIGH RENAISSANCE

Oil-based paints, developed in the late 15th century, liberated artists. This medium enabled them to create more fluid effects, an advantage Titian exploited fully. The increasingly expressive use of light by Titian and contemporaries resulted in a distinctive Venetian style, leading to Tintoretto's masterly combination of light and shade *(see p106–7).*

Titian began this Madonna *in 1519 for the Pesaro family altar in the great Frari church* (see p102), *after his Assumption was hung above the high altar.*

Titian's *Madonna di Ca' Pesaro*

The Virgin is placed off-centre, contrary to a centuries-old rule, but Titian's theatrical use of light ensures that she remains the focus of attention.

Saint Peter looks down at Venetian nobleman Jacopo Pesaro, who kneels to give thanks to the Virgin.

Members of the Pesaro family, *Titian's patrons, attend the Virgin; Lunardo Pesaro, gazing outwards, was heir to the family fortune.*

1500	1550	1600	1650	1700
1500–71 Paris Bordone	**1600–38** Francesco Maffei		**1712–93** Francesco Guardi	
1518–94 Tintoretto			**1707–88** Francesco Zuccarelli **1708–85** Pietro Longhi	
			1696–1770 Giambattista Tiepolo	
	1548–1628 Palma il Giovane		**1675–1758** Rosalba Carriera **1676–1729** Marco Ricci	
	1528–88 Paolo Veronese	**1581–1644** Bernardo Strozzi	**1697–1768** Canaletto	
	1517–92 Jacopo Bassano		**1727–1804** Giandomenico Tiepolo	

Gondolas and Gondoliers

Hippocampus (sea horse) ornament

Gondoliers are part of the symbolism and mythology of Venice. Local legend has it that they are born with webbed feet to help them walk on water. Their intimate knowledge of the city's waterways is passed down from father to son (this is still very much a male preserve). The gondola, with its slim hull and flat underside, is perfectly adapted to negotiating narrow, shallow canals. Once essential for the transport of goods from the markets to the *palazzi*, gondolas today are largely pleasure craft and a trip on one is an essential part of the Venetian experience *(see p284)*. It gives an entirely different perspective on the city, gliding past grand palatial homes, using a form of transport that dates back over 1,000 years.

Squero San Trovaso (see p129) *is the oldest of Venice's five surviving squeri (boatyards). Here, new wood is seasoned, while skilled craftsmen build new gondolas and repair some of the 400 craft in use.*

Traditional dress for a gondolier is a beribboned straw hat, striped vest and black trousers.

The gondolier, unusually for an oarsman, stands upright and pushes on the oar to row the boat in the direction he is facing.

Passengers sit on upholstered cushions and low stools.

The rowlock *(forcola)* can hold the oar in eight different positions for steering the craft.

The oar has a ribbed blade.

The asymmetrical shape *of the gondola counteracts the force of the oar. Without the leftward curve to the prow, 24 cm (9.5 inches) wider on the left than the right, the boat would go round in circles.*

CONTINUING A TRADITION

Gondolas are hand-crafted from nine woods – beech, cherry, elm, fir, larch, lime, mahogany, oak and walnut – using techniques established in the 1880s. A new gondola takes three months to build and costs £10,000.

GONDOLA DECORATION

Black pitch, or tar, was originally used to make gondolas watertight. In time this sombre colour gave way to bright paint-work and rich carpets, but such displays of wealth were banned in 1562. Today all except ceremonial gondolas are black, ornamented only with their *ferro*, and a golden hippocampus on either side. For special occasions such as weddings, the *felze* (the traditional black canopy) and garlands of flowers appear, while funeral craft, now seldom seen, have gilded angels.

Ceremonial gondolas

Upper Reaches of the Grand Canal *(c.1738) is one of many paintings by Canaletto to capture the everyday life of gondoliers and their craft. Since they were first recorded in 1094, gondolas have been a Venetian institution, inspiring writers, artists and musicians.*

Races and parades *are part of the fun during Venice regattas. Professional gondoliers race in pairs or in teams of six, using boats specially designed for competition. Many amateur gondoliers also participate in the events.*

The *ferro* serves to balance the weight of the rower. Its metal teeth symbolize the six *sestieri* of Venice, beneath a doge's cap.

Seven layers of black lacquer give the gondola its gloss.

The main frame is built of oak.

More than 280 separate pieces of wood are used in constructing a gondola.

Mooring posts *and channel markers feature prominently in the crowded waterways of Venice. The posts may be topped with a family crest, to indicate a private mooring.*

Funeral gondola approaching S Michele *(see p149)*

Wedding gondola

Venetian Masks and the Carnival

The Venetian gift for intrigue comes into its own during the Carnival, a vibrant, playful festival preceding the abstinence of Lent *(see p32)*. Masks and costume play a key role in this anonymous world; social divisions are dissolved, participants delight in playing practical jokes, and anything goes. The tradition of Carnival in Venice began in the 11th century and reached its peak of popularity and outrageousness in the 18th century. Industrialization left little leisure time and Carnival fell into decline, but was successfully revived in 1979.

Flamboyant Carnival costume

Modern Carnival Revellers
Since 1979, each year sees more lavish costumes and impromptu celebrations.

Laws forbidding the wearing of costly lace were suspended at Carnival.

The high spirits of Venetian women scandalized many foreign observers.

The Plague Doctor
This sinister Carnival garb is based on the medieval doctor's beaked face-protector and black gown, worn as a precaution against plague.

TRADITIONAL MASK CELEBRATION

Carnival in the 18th century began with a series of balls in the Piazza San Marco, as in this fresco on the walls of Quadri's famous café in the square *(see p74).*

Gambling at the Ridotto
Fortunes were squandered every night of Carnival at the state-run casino depicted in Guardi's painting (c.1768).

Street Entertainers
Musicians and comedians attract the crowds in the piazza San Marco.

The satyr-like profile of this dancer hints that he is the devil in disguise.

Columbine
A classic Carnival figure, Columbine wears lace and an apron, but no mask.

MAKING A MASK

Many masks, and the characters they represent, are deeply rooted in Venetian history. Though instantly recognizable by such features as the beaked nose of the Plague Doctor, each character can be interpreted in a style that is unique to its maker, making each piece a true work of art.

① **The form of the mask** *is first modelled out of clay. Then a plaster of Paris mould is made using the fired clay sculpture as a pattern.*

② **Papier mâché paste,** *made from a pulpy fibrous mixture of rags and paper dipped in glue, is used to make the mask itself.*

③ **To shape the mask,** *papier mâché paste is pushed into the plaster mould, then put aside to set. It becomes hard yet flexible as it dries.*

④ **The size, or glue,** *used to make the papier mâché gives the mask a smooth, shiny surface, similar to porcelain, when it is extracted.*

⑤ **An abrasive polish** *is used to buff the surface of the mask, which is then ready to receive the white base coat.*

⑥ **Cutting the eye holes** *and other features requires the mask maker to have a steady hand.*

⑦ **The features** *are painted on the mask and the final touches are added with a few clever brushstrokes.*

⑧ **The finished mask** *is ready to wear at the Carnival or to hang on a wall – the perfect Venetian souvenir.*

VENICE AND THE VENETO THROUGH THE YEAR

Venice is a city that can be enjoyed at all times of the year. Even winter's mists add to the city's romantic appeal, though clear blue skies and balmy weather make spring and autumn the best times to go. This is especially true if you combine a visit to Venice with a tour of the Veneto, where villa gardens and alpine meadows put on a colourful

Festive flag throwers in Feltre

display from the beginning of April. Autumn sees the beech, birch and chestnut trees of the region turn every shade of red and gold. In summer the waters of Lake Garda, fed by melted snow from the Alps, serve to moderate the heat. Winters are mild, allowing some of the crops typical of the southern Mediterranean, like lemons and oranges, to grow.

Winter in the delta of the River Po

WINTER

Once a quiet time of year, winter now brings an increasing number of visitors to the city of Venice, especially over Christmas, New Year and Carnival. Many a day that begins wet and overcast ends in a blaze of colour – the kind of sunset reflected off rain-washed buildings that Canaletto liked to paint. In the resorts of the Venetian Dolomites, popular for winter sports, the conditions are perfect for skiing from early December throughout the winter months.

DECEMBER

Nativity. Churches all over Venice and the Veneto mount elaborate Nativity scenes in the days leading up to Christmas. Attending mass is a moving experience at this time, even for non-Christians.

Canto della Stella. In Desenzano, on Lake Garda (see p204), Christmas is marked by open-air processions called *Canto della Stella*, literally "singing to the stars".

JANUARY

Epiphany (6 Jan). Children of the Veneto get another stocking full of presents at Epiphany, supposedly brought by the old witch Befania (also known as Befana, Refana or Berolon). She forgot about Christmas, according to the story, because she was too busy cleaning her house. Good children traditionally get sweets, but naughty children get cinders from her hearth. Images of the witch appear in cake-shop windows, along with evil-looking biscuits made to resemble charcoal.

FEBRUARY

Carnival (ten days up to Shrove Tuesday). The pre-Lent festival of Carnevale (see p30), which means "farewell to meat", is celebrated throughout the Veneto. First held in Venice in the 11th century, it consisted of two months of revelry every year. Carnival fell into decline during the 18th century, but was revived in 1979 with such success that the causeway has to be closed at times to prevent overcrowding in the city.

Today the ten-day festival is mainly an excuse for donning a mask and costume and parading around the city. Various events are organized for which the Tourist Board will have details, but anyone can buy a mask and participate while watching the gorgeous costumes on show in the Piazza San Marco (see pp74–5). **Bacanal del Gnoco** (last Fri of Carnival). Traditional masked procession in Verona, with groups from foreign countries and allegorical floats from the Verona area. Masked balls are held in the town's squares.

Masked revellers at the Carnival

AVERAGE DAILY HOURS OF SUNSHINE

Hours

10
8
6
4
2
0

Jan Feb Mar Apr May Jun Jul Aug Sep Oct Nov Dec

Sunshine Chart
Few days are entirely without sunshine in Venice and the Veneto. The amount of sunshine progressively builds up to mid-summer, when it is dangerous to venture out without adequate skin protection.

Spring wisteria in Verona's Giardini Giusti *(see p203)*

SPRING

This is the season when many fine gardens all over the Veneto and round Lake Garda come into their own. As the snow melts, there is time to catch the brief glory of the alpine meadows and the region's nature reserves, renowned for rare orchids and gentians. Verona holds its annual cherry market and many other towns celebrate the arrival of early crops.

MARCH

La Vecia *(mid-Lent).* Gardone and Gargnano, villages on Lake Garda *(see p204),* play host to festivals of great antiquity, when the effigy of an old woman is burnt on a bonfire. The so-called Hag's Trials are an echo of the darker side of medieval life.
Su e zo per i ponti *(second Sun in Mar).* A marathon-style race in Venice. Participants run or walk through the city's streets *su e zo per i ponti* (up and down the bridges).

APRIL

Festa di San Marco *(25 Apr).* The feast of St Mark, patron saint of Venice, is marked by a gondola race across St Mark's Basin between Sant' Elena *(see p121)* and Punta della Dogana *(see p135).* On this occasion, it is traditional for Venetian men to give their wives or lovers a red rose.

MAY

Festa della Sparesea *(1 May).* A delightful festival and regatta for the new season's asparagus is held on Cavallino, in the lagoon, where the crop is grown.

Spring produce in the Rialto's vegetable market

La Sensa *(Sun after Ascension Day).* The ceremony of Venice's Marriage with the Sea draws huge crowds, as it has every year since Doge Pietro Orseolo established the custom in AD 1000. Once the ceremony was marked with all the pomp that the doge and his courtiers could muster. Today the words: "We wed thee, O Sea, in token of true and lasting dominion" are spoken by a local dignitary who then casts a laurel crown and ring into the sea.

Celebrating La Sensa, Venice's annual Marriage with the Sea

Vogalonga *(Sun following La Sensa).* Hundreds of boats take part in the Vogalonga (the "Long Row") from the Piazza San Marco to Burano *(see p150)* and back – a distance of 32 km (20 miles).
Festa Medioevale del vino Soave Bianco Soave *(16 May).* Sumptuous medieval-style celebration of the investiture of the Castillian of Suavia. There is a procession with a historical theme, music in the town square, theatrical performances and displays of various sports.
Valpollicellore *(9 May).* Festival of local wine, with exhibitions, in Cellore d'Illasi.

AVERAGE MONTHLY TEMPERATURE (VENICE)

Temperature Chart
Summers in Venice can be unbearably humid, while winters can bring the occasional snowfall. Temperatures in the Dolomites are considerably lower, with snow and freezing conditions from November to March.

SUMMER

Summer brings the crowds to Venice. Queues for museums and popular sites are long, and hotels are frequently fully booked. Avoid visiting the city during the school holidays (mid-Jul–end Aug). Verona, too, will be full of opera lovers attending the famous festival, but elsewhere in the Veneto it is possible to escape the crowds and enjoy the spectacular countryside.

JUNE

Sagra di Sant'Antonio *(13 Jun).* The Feast of St Anthony has been celebrated in Padua for centuries. The day is marked by a lively fair in Prato della Valle *(see p183).*
Biennale *(Jun–Oct).* The world's biggest contemporary art exhibition takes place in Venice in odd-numbered years *(see p260).*
Festa di Santi Pietro e Paolo *(end Jun).* The feast day of Saints Peter and Paul is celebrated in many towns with fairs and musical festivals.
Regata dei 500 x 2 *(third Sun in Jun).* Adriatic Classic sailing regatta starting from Caorle *(see p175).*

Exhibit by Japanese artist Yayoi Kusama at the Biennale

Boats for hire at Sirmione on Lake Garda

JULY

Opera Festival *(Jul–Sep).* Verona's renowned opera festival overlaps with the equally famous **Shakespeare Festival**, providing culture lovers with a feast of music, drama, opera and dance in the stimulating setting of the Roman Arena and the city's churches *(see pp260–61).*
Festa del Redentore *(third Sun in Jul).* The city of Venice commemorates its deliverance from the plague of 1576. An impressive bridge of boats stretches across the Giudecca Canal so that people can walk to the Redentore church to attend mass. On the Saturday night, crowds line the Zattere or row their boats into the lagoon to watch a spectacular firework display *(see p154).*
Sardellata al Pal del Vo *(late Jul).* Moonlit sardine fishing displays on Lake Garda at Pal

del Vo. Boats are illuminated and decorated, and the catch is cooked and distributed to guests and participants.

AUGUST

Village Festivals. The official holiday month is marked by local festivals throughout the Veneto, giving visitors the chance to sample food and wines and see local costume and dance. Around Lake Garda these are often accompanied by firework displays and races in boats like large gondolas.
Palio di Feltre *(first weekend in Aug).* Medieval games, horse-racing and feasts commemorate Feltre's inclusion in the Venetian empire *(see p219).*
Festa dell'Assunta *(8–16 Aug).* Spectacular nine-day celebration in Vittorio Veneto *(see p219).* The colourful festivities feature dance, poetry, cabaret and music competitions.

AVERAGE MONTHLY RAINFALL

Rainfall Chart
The mountains and sea combine to give Venice and the Veneto higher rainfall than is normal in the rest of Italy, with the possibility of rain on just about any day of the year. The driest months are February and July.

AUTUMN

Expect to see a profusion of market stalls selling a huge range of wild fungi as soon as the climatic conditions are right for them to grow. Local people go on expeditions to harvest them, and mushroom dishes will also feature high on the restaurant menus along with game. Another feature of autumn is the grape harvest, a busy time of year in the wine-producing regions of Soave, Bardolino and Valpolicella *(see pp208–9).*

Grapes ripening in the Bardolino area

Medieval costume at Montagnana's Palio dei Dieci Comuni

SEPTEMBER

Venice Film Festival *(early Sep).* The International Film Festival attracts an array of filmstars and paparazzi to the Lido *(see p157).*
Regata Storica *(first Sun in Sep).* Gondoliers and other boatsmen compete in a regatta which starts with an historic pageant down the Grand Canal.

Partita a Scacchi *(second weekend in Sep, in even-numbered years).* Marostica's chequerboard main square hosts a human chess game in medieval costume *(see p166).*
Palio dei Dieci Comuni *(first Sun in Sep).* The liberation of the town of Montagnana is celebrated with a pageant and horse race *(see p184).*

OCTOBER

Bardolino Grape Festival *(first weekend in Oct).* A festival that celebrates the completion of the harvest.
Festa del Mosto *(first weekend in Oct).* The Feast of the Must on Sant'Erasmo, the market-garden island in the lagoon *(see p149).*
Venice Marathon *(mid-Oct).* This run starts on the Brenta Riviera and finishes in Venice.

NOVEMBER

Festa della Salute *(21 Nov).* Deliverance from the plague is celebrated with the erection of a pontoon bridge across the Grand Canal to La Salute *(see p135).* Venetians light candles in the church to give thanks for a year's good health.

PUBLIC HOLIDAYS
New Year (1 Jan)
Epiphany (6 Jan)
Easter Monday (variable)
Liberation Day (25 Apr)
Labour Day (1 May)
Republic Day (2 Jun)
Assumption (15 Aug)
All Saints (1 Nov)
Immaculate Conception (8 Dec)
Christmas Day (25 Dec)
Santo Stefano (26 Dec)

Rowers practising for the Regata Storica

THE HISTORY OF VENICE AND THE VENETO

The winged lion of St Mark is a familiar sight to anyone travelling in the Veneto. Mounted on top of tall columns in the central square of Vicenza, Verona, Chioggia and elsewhere, it is a sign that these cities were once part of the proud Venetian empire. The fact that the lion was never torn down as a hated symbol of oppression is a credit to the benign nature of Venetian authority.

Doge Giovanni
Mocenigo
(1478–85)

In the 6th century AD, Venice had been no more than a collection of small villages in a swampy lagoon. By the 13th century she ruled Byzantium and, in 1508, the pope, the kings of France and Spain and the Holy Roman Emperor felt compelled to join forces to stop the advances of this powerful empire. As the League of Cambrai, their combined armies sacked the cities of the Veneto, including those such as Vicenza which had initially sided with the League. Venetian territorial expansion was halted, but she continued to dominate the Eastern Mediterranean for another 200 years.

The Venetian system of government came as close to democracy as anyone was to devise until the 19th century, and it stood the city and its empire in good stead until the bumptious figure of Napoleon Bonaparte dared to intrude in 1797. But by then Venice had become a byword for decadence and decline, the essential mercantile instinct that had created and sustained the Serene Republic for so long having been extinguished. As though exhausted by 1,376 years of independent existence, the ruling doge and his Grand Council simply resigned, but their legacy lives on, to fascinate visitors with its extraordinary beauty and remarkable history.

A map dated 1550, showing how little Venice has changed in nearly 500 years

◁ Tintoretto's *Triumph of Doge Nicolò da Ponte* (1580–84), Sala del Maggior Consiglio, Doge's Palace

Roman Veneto

The Veneto takes its name from the Veneti, the pre-Roman inhabitants of the region, whose territory fell to the superior military might of the Romans in the 3rd century BC. Verona was then built as a base for the thrusting and ambitious Roman army which swept northwards over the Alps to conquer much of modern France and Germany. While the Roman empire remained intact the Veneto prospered, but the region bore the brunt of fierce and destructive barbarian attacks that began in the 4th century AD. Riddled by in-fighting and the split between Rome and Constantinople, the imperial administration began to crumble.

A Roman bust in Vicenza

Horsemen in Roman Army
Goths, Huns and Vandals served as mercenaries in the Roman cavalry but later turned to plunder.

Horse-Drawn Carriage
Finds from the region show the technological skills and luxurious lifestyles of the inhabitants.

The Forum (market square)

The Arena was completed in AD 30 to entertain the troops stationed in Verona. It could hold 30,000 spectators.

Chariot Racing
A pre-Roman chariot in Adria's museum (see p185) suggests the Romans adopted the sport from their predecessors.

VERONA
Securely fortified and moated by the River Adige, Roman Verona was divided into square blocks (*insulae* or "islands"). The Forum has since been filled in by medieval palaces, but several landmarks are still discernible today (*see p192*).

TIMELINE

6th century BC Veneto region occupied by the Euganei and the Veneti

89 BC The citizens of Verona, Padua, Vicenza, Este and Treviso granted full rights of Roman citizenship

87 BC Catullus, Roman love poet, born in Verona

600 BC	500	400	300	200	100

3rd century BC Veneto conquered by the Romans. The Veneti and Euganei adopt Roman culture and lose their separate identities

Catullus (87–c.54 BC)

Hunting in the Lagoon
The wild lagoon, future site of Venice, attracted fishermen and huntsmen in pursuit of game and wildfowl. It also became a place of refuge during raids by Huns and Goths.

The theatre, built in the 1st century BC, is still used for open-air performances *(see p260).*

Two arches of the Ponte Romano *(see p202)* survive intact.

Gladiators
Bloodthirsty citizens flocked to the gladiatorial contests in which prisoners of war, criminals and Christian martyrs were put to the sword.

WHERE TO SEE ROMAN VENETO

Verona *(p192)* has the highest concentration of Roman sites in the region; the archaeological museum *(p202)* is full of fine mosaics and sculptures, and Castelvecchio *(p193)* has some very rare early Christian glass and silver. Good museums can also be found at Este *(p184)*, Adria, Treviso *(p174)* and Portogruaro, situated near Concordia *(p175)*.

This fine mosaic *of a nightingale in Treviso Museum is from Trevisium, the town's Roman predecessor.*

Verona's Arena *is an awe-inspiring home for the city's opera festival, despite the loss of its outer wall to earthquakes.*

AD 100 The Arena, Verona's amphitheatre, is built. Near Eastern merchants bring Christianity to the region		**401** Led by Alaric, the Goths invade northern Italy; the Veneto bears the brunt of the attack			
		360 The Roman Empire's northern borders under attack from Slavic and Teutonic tribes			*Fierce Visigoth*
AD 1	**100**	**200**	**300**	**400**	
59 BC Livy, Roman historian, born in Padua		**313** Constantine the Great grants official status to Christianity	**395** Roman Empire splits into eastern and western halves	**410** Alaric succeeds in sacking Rome itself, but dies the same year	
		331 Constantinople takes over from Rome as capital of the Roman Empire			

The Birth of Venice

9th-century Venetian coin

Fleeing the Goths, who were systematically looting and burning their way southwards to Rome, the people of the Veneto sought refuge among the wild and uninhabited islands of their marshy coast. There they formed villages, and from the ashes of the Roman past rose the city of Venice (founded, as tradition has it, in AD 421). Exploiting its easily defended maritime position, important trade links with Byzantium were created. Venice proclaimed its brash self-confidence by brazenly stealing the relics of St Mark the Evangelist from Alexandria, in Egypt.

Early Venetian Settlements
The Rialto Bridge (from Rivo Alto, or "high bank") marks the spot of one of many early settlements.

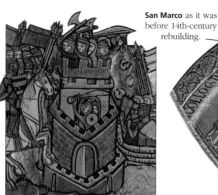

San Marco as it was before 14th-century rebuilding.

The First Crusade *(1095–9)*
Venice cunningly used the Crusades to her advantage, gaining valuable trading rights in captured cities such as Antioch and Tripoli.

The Bishop of Altino
The cathedral at Torcello was founded in AD 639, when Altino's bishop led a mass exodus to the lagoon island, fleeing Lombardic invaders.

THE ARRIVAL OF THE RELICS
This 13th-century mosaic from the façade of San Marco depicts the body of St Mark being carried into the newly built basilica for reburial in AD 832. By securing the relics of such an important saint, Venice signalled its ambition to be considered one of the foremost cities in Christendom, on a par with Rome.

TIMELINE

421 Venice founded, traditionally – and conveniently – on St Mark's Day, 25 April

452 Attila the Hun invades Italy and plunders the Veneto

570 The Lombards' first invasion of northern Italy; beginning of mass migration from the cities of the Veneto to lagoon islands

Charlemagne (742–814)

726 First documented doge, Orso Ipato

400	500	600	700	800

So-called "Attila's throne" in Torcello

639 Torcello cathedral founded

552 Totila the Goth invades Italy and destroys many towns in the Veneto

697 According to legend, Paoluccio Anafesta is elected first doge

774 Charlemagne invited to drive Lombards from Italy

800 Charlemagne is crowned first Holy Roman Emperor by Pope Leo III

Diplomacy
Strategically placed between the powers of Rome and Byzantium, Venice was continually exerting her powers of diplomacy. Here, Doge Ziani receives Holy Roman Emperor Frederick I, whom he reconciled with Pope Alexander III in 1177.

WHERE TO SEE EARLY VENICE

The cathedral at Torcello *(pp152–3)* is the oldest surviving building in Venice, and the Basilica San Marco *(pp78–83)* has many period treasures. Early Venetian coins are in the Correr Museum *(p77)*. The original statue of St Theodore is in the Doge's Palace courtyard.

Torcello cathedral's jewel-like mosaics (11th century) are masterpieces of Byzantine art, probably the work of craftsmen from Constantinople.

Looting the remains of St Mark from Alexandria was seen as an act of anti-Moslem piety.

The doge and his entourage are wearing Byzantine-style caps and robes.

St Theodore
The Byzantine emperor nominated Theodore as the patron saint of Venice. Venice chose St Mark instead, an act of defiance against Byzantine rule.

The Pala d'Oro, *St Mark's 10th-century altarpiece, shows merchants bringing St Mark's plundered relics to Venice.*

814 First Venetian coins minted; work begins on first Doge's Palace

832 First Basilica San Marco completed

1095 First Crusade; Venice provides ships and supplies

1120 Verona's San Zeno church begun

1171 Six districts *(sestieri)* of Venice established

1173 First Rialto Bridge built

1177 Emperor Frederick I Barbarossa agrees to peace terms with Pope Alexander III

900	1000	1100	1200

888 King Berengar I of Italy chooses Verona as his seat

828 Venetian merchants steal body of St Mark from Alexandria

1000 Doge Pietro Orseolo rids the Adriatic of pirates, commemorated by the first Marriage of Venice to the Sea ceremony

1128 First street lighting in Venice

1202 Venice diverts the Fourth Crusade to its own ends, the conquest of Byzantium

The Growth of the Empire

During the middle ages, Venice expanded in power and influence throughout the eastern Mediterranean, culminating in the conquest of Byzantium in 1204. At home, in contrast to the fractional strife of most of the area, Venice enjoyed a uniquely ordered administration head-ed by the doge, an elected leader whose powers were carefully defined by the Venetian constitution. Real power lay with the Council of Ten and the 2,000 or so members of the Grand Council, from whose number the doge and his advisers were elected.

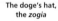

The doge's hat, the zogia

Bocca di Leone
Such letterboxes were used to report crimes anonymously and were often abused (p89).

Doge Enrico Dandolo boldly led the attack on Constantinople, despite being over 90 and completely blind.

Cangrande I
Founder of the Veronese Scaligeri dynasty (see p207), Cangrande I ("Big Dog") typified the totalitarian rule of most Italian cities.

Marco Polo in China
Renowned Venetian merchant, Marco Polo (see p143) spent over 20 years at the court of Kublai Khan.

SIEGE OF CONSTANTINOPLE
Facing financial difficulties, the leaders of the Fourth Crusade agreed to attack the capital of Byzantium, as payment for warships supplied by Venice. The city fell in 1204, leaving Venice ruler of Byzantium.

TIMELINE

The Four Horses of San Marco

1204 Conquest of Constantinople; Venice's plunder includes four bronze horses

1222 University of Padua founded

1260 Scaligeri family rules Verona

1271–95 Marco Polo's journey to China

1309 Present Doge's Palace begun

1325 The names of Venice's ruling families are fixed and inscribed in the Golden Book

1200	1250	1300	1350

1284 Gold ducats first minted in Venice

1301 Dante, exiled from his native Florence, is welcomed to Verona by the Scaligeri rulers

1310 The Venetian Constitution is passed; Council of Ten formed

1304–13 Giotto paints the Scrovegni Chapel frescoes (pp180–81) in Padua

1348–9 Black Death plague kills half Venice's population

Decapitation
Doge Marin Falier was beheaded in 1355 for plotting to become absolute ruler of Venice. His execution was a warning to future doges.

Imperial treasures and ancient buildings were lost when the 900-year-old city was looted and burned.

Electing the Doge
This pointer was used for counting votes during dogal elections, using a convoluted system designed to prevent candidates bribing their way to power.

Troops scaled the fortifications from galleys moored against the city walls.

Queen of Cyprus
Venice shamelessly gained Cyprus in 1489 by arranging for Caterina Cornaro, from one of Venice's noblest families, to marry the island's king, then poisoning him.

WHERE TO SEE IMPERIAL VENICE

The Doge's Palace combines ceremonial splendour and the grimmer business of imprisonment and torture (*pp84–9*). Aspects of the constitution are on display in the Correr Museum (*p77*). A *bocca di leone* survives on the Zattere (*p129*).

Many doges *are commemorated by Renaissance-style monuments in the church of Santi Giovanni e Paolo (pp116–17).*

Meetings of the Grand Council, *dominated by the merchant class, were held in the Sala del Maggior Consiglio (p87) in the Doge's Palace.*

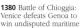

Battle of Chioggia	**1489** Cyprus ceded to Venice by Queen Caterina Cornaro	**1518** Titian's *Assumption* hung in Frari (*p102*)
1400	**1450**	**1500**
1380 Battle of Chioggia: Venice defeats Genoa to win undisputed maritime supremacy in the Adriatic and Mediterranean	**1453** Constantinople falls to the Turks; Venice's empire reaches its zenith	**1508** Andrea Palladio, architect, born in Padua
	1430 Giovanni Bellini born, greatest of the artistic family	*Titian (1487–1576)*

The Queen of the Adriatic

By the 16th century, Venice held a monopoly on Mediterranean trade and had colonized the whole of northeastern Italy, from the Adriatic to the Alps. Keeping hold of such a vast empire meant being in a constant state of war. The League of Cambrai, dedicated to destroying Venice, was formed in 1508 by the most powerful men in Europe, Pope Julius II and the Holy Roman Emperor Maximilian. Their troops sacked the cities of the Veneto, but the region remained loyal to Venice's relatively benign rule. Far more of a threat were the Turks. They carved out the Ottoman Empire from 1522, driving Venice from the eastern Mediterranean and eventually taking Cyprus in 1570.

16th-century armour from the Doge's Palace

Sails were a hazard in battle, but could be utilized for a swift escape.

Oarsmen sat in cramped conditions with less than 60 cm (2 ft) of space; each team was led by a foreman.

Galileo's Telescope
Galileo, professor at Padua University from 1592 to 1610, demonstrated his telescope to Doge Leonardo Donà in 1609.

Battle of Lepanto
Venice led the combined forces of the Christian world in this bloody victory over the Turks, fought in 1571.

TIMELINE

1514 Fire destroys the original timber Rialto Bridge	**1516** Jews confined to the Venetian Ghetto. End of League of Cambrai wars	**1585** First performance at Vicenza's Teatro Olimpico *(p172)*

1518 Tintoretto born

1528 Paolo Veronese born

1570 Cyprus lost to the Turks

1592 Galileo appointed professor of mathematics at Padua University

1500	1550	1600

1501 Doge Leonardo Loredan, great diplomat, begins 20-year rule

1529 Death of Luigi da Porto of Vicenza, author of the story of Romeo and Juliet

1571 Battle of Lepanto: decisive victory for the western fleet, led by Venice, over the Turks

1595 Shakespeare's *Romeo and Juliet*

1577 Palladio designs the Redentore church *(p154)* to mark the end of the plague that took 51,000 lives

Celebrating the End of the Plague

More deadly than any opposing army, plague hit Venice in 1575 and again in 1630, carrying off Titian among its 100,000 victims.

WHERE TO SEE MARITIME VENICE

The triumph of Venice over the sea is celebrated in the Museo Storico Navale *(p118)*. For a glimpse of the extensive and disused Arsenale shipyard in Castello, take a trip on *vaporetto* route No. 41, 42, 51 or 52 *(p283)*.

The Venice Arsenale

Venice was at the forefront of maritime construction. Her heavily defended shipyards were capable of turning out warships at the rate of one a day.

To synchronize the oarsmen, a drummer beat time at the stern.

Arsenale lions, *plundered from Piraeus in 1687, guard the forbidding gates of the Arsenale shipyard (p119).*

The trireme was so named because the oars were grouped in threes. Each trireme had up to 150 oars.

VENETIAN TRIREME

Venetian naval supremacy was based on the swift and highly manoeuvrable trireme, used to sink enemy ships by means of its pointed battering ram and its bow-mounted cannon.

Santa Maria della Salute *was built in thanksgiving for deliverance from the 1630 plague (p135).*

Monteverdi (1567–1643)

1678 Elena Piscopia receives doctorate from Padua University, the first woman in the world ever to be awarded a degree *(p178)*

1703 Vivaldi joins La Pietà as musical director

1718 Venetian maritime empire ends with the surrender of Morea to the Turks

1650

1700

1613 Monteverdi appointed choirmaster at Basilica San Marco

1630 Plague strikes Venice again, reducing the city's population to 102,243, its smallest for 250 years

1669 Venice loses Crete to the Turks

Elena Piscopia (1646–84)

1708 In a bitter winter, the lagoon freezes over and Venetians can walk to the mainland

Glorious Decadence

No longer a major power, 18th-century Venice became a byword for decadence, as aristocratic Venetians frittered away their inherited wealth in lavish parties and gambling. All this crumbled in 1797 when the city was besieged by Napoleon, who demanded the abdication of the doge. Napoleon granted the city to his opponents, the Austrians, whose often authoritarian rule drove many people of the Veneto to join the vanguard of the revolutionary Risorgimento. This movement, led in Venice by Daniele Manin, was dedicated to creating a free and united Italy, a dream not fully realized until 1870, four years after Venice was freed from Austrian rule.

Casanova, the Venetian libertine

The State-Run Casino
The notorious Ridotto, open to anyone wearing a mask, closed in 1774 as many Venetians had bankrupted themselves.

Gambling fever so gripped the city that gaming tables were set up between the columns in the Piazza.

Caffè Pedrocchi
Several intellectuals who had used this lavishly decorated café (see p178) in Padua as their base, were executed for leading a revolt against Austrian rule in 1831.

The Horses of St Mark
Among the art treasures looted by Napoleon were the Four Horses of St Mark, symbols of Venetian liberty. The horses were returned in 1815.

IMPERIAL RITUAL
Canaletto's *St Mark's Basin on Ascension Day* (c.1733) captures the empty splendour of Venice on the eve of her demise. The doge's gold and scarlet barge has been launched for the annual ceremony of Venice's Marriage to the Sea.

TIMELINE

1720 Caffè Florian opens in Venice *(p250)*

1725 Casanova born in Venice

1752 Completion of sea walls protecting the lagoon entrances

1755 Casanova imprisoned in Doge's Palace

1775 Caffè Quadri *(p250)* opens in Venice

1789 The Dolomites named after Déodat Dolomieu (1750–1801)

1720

1770

1757 Canova, Neo-Classical sculptor, born in Venice

Café Florian

1790 Venetian opera house, La Fenice, opens

1797 Napoleon invades the Veneto; Doge Lodovico Manin abdicates; Venetian Republic ends

1798 Napoleon grants Venice and its territories to his Austrian allies in return for Lombardy

Antonio Vivaldi
(1678–1741)
*Fashionable Venetians
flocked to hear the
red-haired priest's
latest compositions,
performed by the
orphan girls of La
Pietà. Vivaldi's most
famous work,* The
Four Seasons *(1725),
was a great success
throughout Europe.*

WHERE TO SEE
18TH-CENTURY VENICE

The Museo Storico Navale
(p118) displays a beautifully
crafted model of the Bucintoro and its original banner.
Vivaldi concerts are a regular
feature at La Pietà church
(p112). Paintings by Guardi,
Canaletto and Longhi capture
the spirit of the age and are
found in the Accademia
(pp130–3), Correr Museum
and Ca' Rezzonico *(p126)*.

**The Bucintoro, the doge's
ceremonial barge**

Sumptuary laws, passed in
1562, decreed that all Venetian
gondolas must be black to
prevent lavish
displays of
wealth.

Fortunes were spent *on opulent wigs, jewels and clothing
for costume balls and the
theatre. This high-heeled shoe
is in the Correr Museum (p77).*

The comic antics *of
Harlequin and Pantaloon at
La Fenice (p93) ensured the
popularity of the theatre
with Venetians.*

No Longer an Island
*Venice lost its isolation in 1846 when a causeway joined
the city to the mainland and the Italian rail network.*

1804 Napoleon crowned King
of Italy and takes back Venice

1814–15 Austrians drive French
from Venice; Congress of Vienna
returns the Veneto to Austria

*Daniele Manin
(1804–57)*

1859 Second War of Italian
Independence; after Battle of
Solferino, Red Cross founded

1861 Vittorio Emanuele
crowned King of Italy

1820

1870

1818 Byron
swims up
the Grand
Canal

1846 Venetian rail causeway links the city to the
mainland for the first time

1848 First Italian War of
Independence. Venice
revolts against Austrian rule

1853 Ruskin publishes
The Stones of Venice

1849 Hunger and
disease force Venetian
rebels, led by Daniele
Manin, to surrender

1866 Venice and
Veneto freed from
Austrian rule

Venice in Vogue

From being an introverted and unchanging city, Venice developed with remarkable speed. The opening of the Suez Canal in 1869 brought new prosperity; a new harbour was built for ocean-going ships and Venice became a favourite embarkation point for colonial administrators and rich Europeans travelling east. The fashion for sea-bathing and patronage by wealthy socialites reawakened interest in the city, and the founding of the Biennale attracted Europe's leading artists, who expressed their enthusiasm for the city in novels, paintings and music.

Peggy Guggenheim (1898–1979) *Patron of the avant garde, Peggy Guggenheim brought her outstanding art collection (see p134) to Venice in 1949.*

The Hotel Excelsior's Moorish exterior is distinctive.

Bathing huts, designed for modesty in the 1920s, are still a feature of the Lido.

Igor Stravinsky (1882–1971) *Along with Turgenev, Diaghilev and Ezra Pound, Stravinsky was one of many émigrés enchanted by the magic of Venice.*

Hotel Excelsior *When it was built in 1907, the Hotel Excelsior (see p233) was the world's largest hotel.*

THE LIDO

From the turn of the century, grand hotel developments along the sandy Adriatic shore turned the Lido into Europe's most stylish seaside resort. The island has since given its name to bathing establishments the world over.

TIMELINE

1883 Wagner dies in Palazzo Vendramin-Calergi

Richard Wagner (1813–83)

1902 Collapse of campanile in Piazza San Marco

1912 Opening of rebuilt campanile; Thomas Mann writes *Death in Venice*

1870	1880	1890	1900	1910

1881 Venice becomes second largest port in Italy after Genoa

1889 Poet Robert Browning dies in Ca' Rezzonico

1895 First Biennale art exhibition

1903 Patriarch Sarto of Venice becomes Pope Pius X

The International Exhibition of Modern Art

Venice became a showcase for all that was new in world art and architecture when the Biennale was launched. The first exhibition, in 1895, showed work by Renoir and Monet.

The manicured beaches of the Lido became a catwalk for style-conscious holidaymakers.

WHERE TO SEE TURN-OF-THE-CENTURY VENICE

Regular *vaporetto* services link Venice to the Lido *(p156)*, with its deluxe hotels, sports facilities and beaches. The pavilions of the Biennale *(p121)* are usually only open during the exhibition. A lift carries visitors to the top of the rebuilt Campanile *(p76)* for panoramic views of Venice.

San Michele, *the cemetery isle* (p151), *is the last resting place of eminent foreigners, such as Serge Diaghilev, Igor Stravinsky and Ezra Pound.*

The exclusive *Grand Hôtel des Bains* (p233) *on the Lido has retained its Art Deco style and private section of beach.*

The Campanile

After the appearance of ominous warning cracks, the 1,000-year-old bell tower crashed to the ground in 1902. It was rebuilt within a decade (see p76).

1917 Work starts on constructing the port of Marghera

1926 Mestre is formally granted town status

German travel poster from 1936

1954 Britten's *Turn of the Screw* premièred in Venice

1943–5 Mussolini rules a puppet state, the Salò Republic

1959 Patriarch Roncalli elected Pope John XXIII

1920	1930	1940	1950	1960

1918 Fierce fighting in mountain passes of the Veneto in the last weeks of World War I

1932 First Venice Film Festival

1931 Venice is linked to the mainland by a road causeway

1951 Stravinsky's *The Rake's Progress* premièred in Venice

1956 Cortina d'Ampezzo hosts Winter Olympics

1960 Venice airport opens

Venice Preserved

In November 1966 Venice was hit by the worst floods in its history, sparking worldwide concern for the future of the city's delicate and decaying fabric. Major steps have since been taken to protect Venice and its unique heritage, though some difficult issues remain, including the erosion and wave damage caused by public and private waterborne craft, and pollution from the mainland. However, the allure of Venice, set in its watery lagoon, is as compelling as ever.

Pink Floyd in Venice
Pink Floyd's 1989 rock concert threatened the city's equilibrium.

Venice as Film Set
Venice has served as the backdrop to countless films, including Fellini's Casanova *(1976) and* Indiana Jones and the Last Crusade *(1989).*

The Regata Storica, held in September, is an annual trial of strength and skill for gondoliers.

After the Flood
During the 1966 floods, the waters rose nearly 2 m (6 ft). Great damage was done by fuel oil, washed out of broken tanks. It is now banned from the city in favour of gas.

TOURISM

Venetian regattas are part of a rich tradition that enhances the city's attraction to tourists, providing employment for many on the mainland as well as in Venice itself. Even so, some complain that tourism has turned Venice from a living city into one vast museum.

TIMELINE

1966 Floods cause devastation in Venice. UNESCO launches its Save Venice appeal

1973 Laws passed to reduce pollution, subsidence and flooding

1978 Patriarch Luciani of Venice elected Pope John Paul I, but dies 33 days later

Carnival reveller

1988 First experimental stage of MOSE, the lagoon flood barrier, is completed

1960	1970	1980

1968 Protestors prevent part of the lagoon being drained to extend Marghera's industrial zone

1970 Luchino Visconti's film, *Death in Venice*

1979 Venetian Carnival is revived

Visconti and Dirk Bogarde on the set of Death in Venice

1983 Venice officially stops sinking after extraction of underground water prohibited

Benetton
The famous clothing firm, originating in Treviso, represents the modern face of Veneto industry.

Venice plays host to over 14 million visitors every year.

Glass Blowing
This age-old tradition still contributes to the economy.

Subsidence, caused by water extraction for use in Marghera, is being remedied by piping water into Venice.

The Acqua Alta
High tides can cause floods and paralyze the city. Plans for a flood barrier across the lagoon are subject to controversy.

RESTORATION IN VENICE

One positive result of the 1966 floods was a major international appeal for funds to pay for the cleaning of historic buildings, statues and paintings. Funds raised are coordinated under the auspices of UNESCO, with offices in Venice.

Restorers *learn how to repair and conserve fragile works of art at a European centre for conservation on San Servolo (p154).*

Madonna dell'Orto (p140) *was restored by the Italian Art and Archives Rescue Fund (later renamed Venice in Peril).*

1992 Venice rocked by corruption scandals. Metro network beneath lagoon proposed

1994 Voters decide against a divorce between Venice and Mestre, which share a mayor and city council

1995 Centenary of Biennale Exhibition

2006 Romano Prodi approves construction of the lagoon flood barrier

The fourth bridge over the Grand Canal

2008 The fourth bridge over the Grand Canal opens

1990	2000	2010	2020

1992 Venice Film Festival celebrates 60 years

1932–1992 Venice Film Festival poster

2002 Construction begins on the fourth bridge over the Grand Canal

2010 Floods in Vicenza and Paduan plains in November cause terrible damage; half of Vicenza was under water

A *traghetto* crossing the Grand Canal ▷

VENICE AREA
BY AREA

Venice at a Glance

Venice is small and most of the sights
can be comfortably visited on foot. The
heart of the city is the Piazza San
Marco, which is overlooked by the
great Basilica and the Doge's Palace.
For many, these are attractions enough,
but there are delights worth exploring
beyond the Piazza, such as the galleries
of the Accademia, Ca' Rezzonico and
the imposing Frari church. Unique to
Venice are the naval Arsenale to the
east and the Ghetto in the north.

Ghetto
*Established in the early 16th century, this
fascinating quarter was the world's first
ghetto (see p145).*

**Santa Maria Gloriosa
dei Frari**
*This soaring Gothic
edifice, founded by the
Franciscans in 1340,
is a rich repository of
Venetian painting
and sculpture
(see pp102–3).*

CANNAREGIO
Pages 136–45

**SAN POLO AND
SANTA CROCE**
Pages 96–107

DORSODURO
Pages 122–35

SAN MARC
Pages 72–9

0 metres	500
0 yards	500

Ca' Rezzonico
*The splendid rooms of
this palace, overlooking
the Grand Canal, are
decorated with 18th-
century furniture and
paintings (see p126).*

Accademia
*Carpaccio's St Ursula
cycle (1490–5) is one
of the treasures of the
Accademia, which
has a comprehensive
collection of Venetian
art (see pp130–3).*

Rialto Bridge
The bustling Rialto Bridge (see p100) was named after the ancient commercial seat of Venice, where the first inhabitants settled.

Ca' d'Oro
This ornate palace is the finest example of Venetian Gothic style (see p142).

Basilica San Marco
Magnificent mosaics sheathe the domes, walls and floor of the Byzantine Basilica (see pp78–83).

Arsenale
The great dockyard, first of its kind in Europe, was the naval nerve centre of the Venetian Empire (see p119).

CASTELLO
Pages 108–21

Doge's Palace
The colonnaded Gothic palace was the seat of government as well as home to the doge and his family (see pp84–89).

Santa Maria della Salute
Marking the southern end of the Grand Canal, this great Baroque church is one of the city's landmarks (see p135).

A VIEW OF THE GRAND CANAL

Known to the Venetians as the *Canalazzo*, the Grand Canal sweeps through the heart of Venice, following the course of an ancient river bed. Since the founding days of the empire it has served as the city's main thoroughfare. Once used by great galleys or trading vessels making their stately way to the Rialto, it is nowadays teeming with *vaporetti*, launches, barges and gondolas. Glimpses of its glorious past, however, are never far away. The annual re-enactment of historic pageants, preserving the traditions of the Venetian Republic, brings a blaze of colour to the canal. The most spectacular is the Regata Storica held in September *(see p35),* a huge procession of historic craft packed with crews in traditional costumes, followed by boat and gondola races down the Grand Canal.

Venetian gondolier

The parade of palaces bordering the winding waterway, built over a span of around 500 years, presents some of the finest architecture of the Republic. Historically it is like a roll-call of the old Venetian aristocracy, with almost every *palazzo* bearing the name of a once-grand family. Bright frescoes may have faded, precious marbles worn, and foundations frayed with the tides, but the Grand Canal is still, to quote Charles VIII of France's ambassador in 1495, "the most beautiful street in the world".

See pages 60–61

See pages 58–9

See pages 62–3

See pages 64–5

See pages 66–7

See pages 70–71

See pages 68–9

0 metres 250

0 yards 250

◁ **The Grand Canal at its most colourful, during the Regata Storica**

Santa Lucia to Palazzo Flangini

Vaporetto ticket office, Grand Canal

The Grand Canal is best admired from a gondola or a *vaporetto*. Several lines travel the length of the canal *(see p283)* but only the No. 1 goes slowly enough for you to take in any of the palaces. The journey from the station to San Zaccaria takes about 40 minutes. Nearly 4 km (2½ miles) long, the canal varies in width from 30 to 70 m (98 to 230 ft) and is spanned by four bridges, the Scalzi, the Rialto, the Accademia and the Constituzione. The modern Constituzione bridge links Piazzale Roma and Santa Lucia station.

LOCATOR MAP

Santa Maria di Nazareth *is known today as the Scalzi, after the supposedly "shoeless" Carmelites who founded it* (see p145). *Within is the tomb of Ludovico Manin, last of the doges.*

Santa Lucia railway station (see p280), *built in the mid-19th century and remodelled in the 1950s, links the city with the mainland.*

Ferro

Ferrovia

La Direzione Compartimentale, *the administration offices for the railway, was built at the same time as the station, on the site of the church of Santa Lucia and other ancient buildings.*

Palazzo Diedo, *also known as Palazzo Emo, is a Neo-Classical palace of the late 18th century. It is believed to be the birthplace of Angelo Emo (1731–92), the last admiral of the Venetian fleet. The palace was built by Andrea Tirali, an engineer who worked on the restoration of San Marco.*

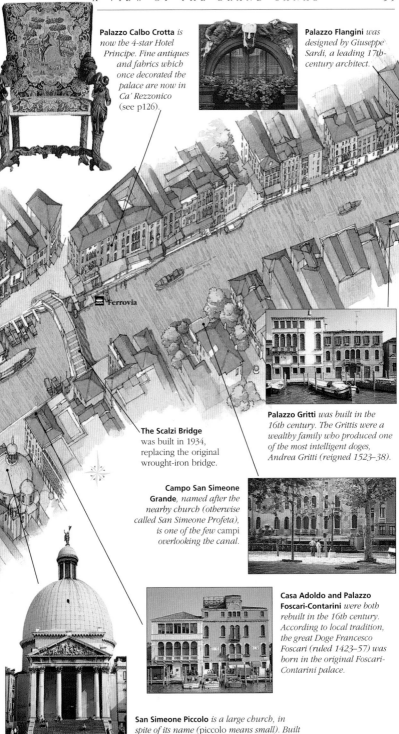

Palazzo Calbo Crotta *is now the 4-star Hotel Principe. Fine antiques and fabrics which once decorated the palace are now in Ca' Rezzonico (see p126).*

Palazzo Flangini *was designed by Giuseppe Sardi, a leading 17th-century architect.*

Ferrovia

The Scalzi Bridge was built in 1934, replacing the original wrought-iron bridge.

Palazzo Gritti *was built in the 16th century. The Grittis were a wealthy family who produced one of the most intelligent doges, Andrea Gritti (reigned 1523–38).*

Campo San Simeone Grande, *named after the nearby church (otherwise called San Simeone Profeta), is one of the few* campi *overlooking the canal.*

Casa Adoldo and Palazzo Foscari-Contarini *were both rebuilt in the 16th century. According to local tradition, the great Doge Francesco Foscari (ruled 1423–57) was born in the original Foscari-Contarini palace.*

San Simeone Piccolo *is a large church, in spite of its name (*piccolo *means small). Built in 1738, its design was based partly on the Pantheon in Rome. It is open for worship only.*

San Geremia to San Stae

This stretch sees the start of the great
palaces. The most remarkable is the
Vendramin Calergi, which
became a model for other
Venetian palaces.

San Geremia houses
the relics of St
Lucy, formerly
preserved in
Santa Lucia
where the
station now
stands.

Palazzo Labia, *frescoed with Tiepolo's
Venetian-style Story of Cleopatra, is
open to the public (see p143).*

Palazzo Querini
has the family
coat of arms on
the façade.

Ca' dei Cuori (House of
Hearts) was named after
the hearts in the family
coat of arms.

Riva di Biasio

Palazzo Giovanelli,
*a restored Gothic
palace, was acquired
by the Giovanellis in
1755. This titled non-
Venetian family had
been admitted into
the Great Council in
1668 for a fee of
100,000 ducats.*

Fondaco dei Turchi *was a splendid Veneto-
Byzantine building before last century's
brutal restoration. Today it houses the
Natural History Museum (see p105).*

**Palazzo Donà
Balbi,** *built in the
17th century, is
named after two
great Venetian
families who
intermarried.
The Donà family
produced four
doges.*

Deposito del Megio, *a crenellated building with a reconstructed Lion of St Mark,
was a granary in the 15th century.*

San Marcuola, *dedicated to St Ermagora and St Fortunatus, was built in 1728–36 by Giorgio Massari, but the façade was never completed.*

Palazzo Vendramin Calergi, *an early Renaissance palace, was designed by Mauro Coducci. The composer Richard Wagner died here in 1883. Today, Venice's casino is housed in the palace.*

Palazzo Marcello, rebuilt in the early 18th century, was the birthplace of composer Benedetto Marcello in 1686.

Palazzo Erizzo has two huge paintings depicting the feats of Paolo Erizzo, who died heroically fighting the Turks in 1469.

Palazzo Emo belonged to the family of a famous Venetian admiral *(see p58).*

San Marcuola

San Stae

Palazzo Tron, *built in the late 16th century, hosted a famous ball in 1775 in honour of Emperor Joseph II of Austria.*

Palazzo Belloni Battagia, *with its distinctive pinnacles, was built by Longhena in the mid-17th century for the Belloni family, who had bought their way into Venetian aristocracy.*

San Stae *is striking for its Baroque façade, graced by marble statues. It was funded by a legacy left by Doge Alvise Mocenigo in 1709 (see p105).*

Palazzo Barbarigo to the Markets

Here the canal is flanked by stately palaces, built over a period of five centuries. The most spectacular is the Gothic Ca' d'Oro, whose façade once glittered with gold.

LOCATOR MAP

Palazzo Barbarigo retains the vestiges of its 16th-century frescoed façade paintings.

Palazzo Gussoni-Grimani's façade once had frescoes by Tintoretto. It was home to the English ambassador in 1614–18.

Palazzo Fontana Rezzonico was the birthplace of Count Rezzonico (1693), the fifth Venetian pope.

San Stae

Ca' Foscarini, *a Gothic building of the 15th century, belonged to the Foscari family before it became the residence of the Duke of Mantua in 1520.*

Casa Favretto (Hotel San Cassiano) was the home of the painter Giacomo Favretto (1849–87).

Ca' Pesaro, *a huge and stately Baroque palace designed by Longhena (see p23), today houses the Gallery of Modern Art and the Oriental Museum (see p105). It was built for Leonardo Pesaro, a Procurator of San Marco.*

Palazzo Morosini Brandolin *belonged to the Morosini family, one of the Case Vecchie families, deemed to be noble before the 9th century.*

Ca' Corner della Regina *is named after Caterina Cornaro, Queen of Cyprus, who was born here in 1454. The present building (1724–7) was designed by Domenico Rossi.*

The Pescheria *has been the site of a busy fish market for six centuries. Today it takes place in the striking mock-Gothic market hall, built in 1907.*

Ca' d'Oro, *the most famous of Venetian Gothic palaces (see p144), houses paintings, frescoes and sculpture from the collection of Baron Giorgio Franchetti, who bequeathed the palace and all its contents to the State.*

CANALETTO

Antonio Canale (Canaletto) (1697–1768) is best known for his *vedute* or views of Venice. He studied in Rome, but lived here for most of his life. One of his patrons was Joseph Smith (*see below*). Sadly there are very few of his paintings left on view in the city.

Palazzo Sagredo *passed from the Morosini to the Sagredo family in the early 18th century. The façade shows characteristics of both Veneto-Byzantine and Gothic styles.*

Palazzo Foscarini *was the home of Marco Foscarini, a diplomat, orator and scholar who rose to the position of doge in 1762.*

Palazzo Mangili Valmarana *was designed by Antonio Visentini (above) in Classical style for Joseph Smith, who became the English consul in Venice. Smith (1682–1770) was a patron of both Visentini and Canaletto.*

Palazzo Michiel dalle Colonne was named after its distinctive colonnade.

Ca' D'Oro

Palazzo Michiel del Brusà was rebuilt and named after the great fire *(brusà)* that swept the city in 1774.

Ca' da Mosto *is a good example of 13th-century Veneto-Byzantine style. Alvise da Mosto, the 15th-century navigator, was born here in 1432.*

🚏 **Rialto Mercato**

Tribunale Fabbriche Nuove, Sansovino's market building (1555), is now the seat of the Assize Court.

The Rialto Quarter

The area around the rialto bridge is the oldest and busiest quarter of the city. Traditionally a centre of trade, crowded quaysides and colourful food markets still border the canal south of the bridge.

LOCATOR MAP

Palazzo Papadopoli, *formerly known as Coccina-Tiepolo, was built in 1560. Its splendid hall of mirrors has been preserved.*

Riva del Vin *is one of the few spots where you can sit and relax on the banks of the Grand Canal (see p98).*

Ca' Corner-Martinengo-Ravà *became the Leon Bianco Hotel in the 19th century. The American writer, James Fenimore Cooper, stayed here in 1838.*

Palazzo Barzizza, rebuilt in the 17th century, still preserves its early 13th-century façade.

San Silvestro

Palazzo Grimani, *a fine, if somewhat austere looking, Renaissance palace (see p23), was built in 1556 by Michele Sanmicheli for the Procurator, Girolamo Grimani. The State purchased the palace in 1807 and it is now occupied by the city's Court of Appeal.*

Palazzo Farsetti and Palazzo Loredan, *both occupied by the City Council, were built around 1200 and finally merged in 1868. Palazzo Farsetti became an academy for young artists, one of whom was Canova.*

Fondaco dei Tedeschi, *originally used as a warehouse and lodgings for German traders, has been bought by Benetton for redevelopment.*

Palazzo Camerlenghi, built in 1528, was once the offices of the city treasurers (*camerlenghi*). The ground floor was the State prison.

Rialto

Riva del Ferro is the quayside where German trading barges offloaded iron (*ferro*).

The Rialto Bridge (see p100) *was built to span the Grand Canal in what was, and still is, the most commercial quarter of the city.*

Casetta Dandolo's predecessor is said to have been the birthplace of Doge Enrico Dandolo (ruled 1192–1205).

Palazzo Manin-Dolfin *was built by Sansovino in 1538–40 but only his Classical stone façade survives. The interior was completely transformed for Ludovico Manin, last doge of Venice (died 1797). He intended to turn the house into a magnificent palace extending as far as Campo San Salvatore.*

Palazzo Bembo, *a 15th-century Gothic palace, was the birthplace of the Renaissance cardinal and scholar, Pietro Bembo, who wrote one of the earliest Italian grammars.*

THE DANDOLO FAMILY

The illustrious Dandolo family produced four doges, 12 procurators of San Marco, a patriarch of Grado and a queen of Serbia. The first of the doges was Enrico who, despite being old and blind, was the principal driving force in the Crusaders' plan to take Constantinople in 1204 (see p42). The other remarkable doge in the family was the humanist and historian, Andrea Dandolo (died 1354).

Doge Enrico Dandolo

La Volta del Canal

The point where the canal doubles back sharply on itself is known as La Volta – the bend. This splendid curve was long ago established as the finishing stretch for the annual Regata Storica (see p35).

(see p35)

LOCATOR MAP

Palazzo Marcello, *which belonged to an old Venetian family, is also called "dei Leoni" because of the lions either side of the doorway.*

Palazzo Persico, *on the corner of Rio San Polo, is a 16th-century house in Lombardesque style.*

Palazzo Civran-Grimani *is a Classical building of the early 17th century.*

Palazzo Balbi, *seat of the regional government, was built for Nicolò Balbi, who is said to have died of a chill surveying its construction. From here, Napoleon viewed the 1807 regatta, held in his honour.*

San Toma

Ca' Foscari *was built for Doge Francesco Foscari in 1437 (see p22). It is now part of the University of Venice.*

(see p22)

Palazzo Giustinian *was the residence of Wagner in 1858–9, when he was composing the second act of Tristan and Isolde.*

Ca' Rezzonico, *now the museum of 18th-century Venice (see p126), became the home of the poet Robert Browning and his son, Pen, in 1888.*

(see p126)

San Samuele

Ca' Rezzonico

Palazzo Barbarigo della Terrazza, built in the 1560s, was known for its roof terrace. It now houses the German Institute.

Palazzo Capello-Layard was the home of Sir Austen Henry Layard, excavator of Nineveh.

Sant' Angelo 🚤

Palazzo Corner Spinelli, Mauro Coducci's outstanding Renaissance palace, built in 1490–1510, became a proto-type for other mansions in Venice.

Palazzo Garzoni, *a renovated Gothic palace, is now part of the university. The* traghetto *service, which links the neighbouring Calle Garzoni to San Tomà on the other side of the canal, is one of the oldest in Venice.*

Palazzo Mocenigo, *formed by four palaces linked together, has a plaque to the poet Byron who stayed here in 1818.*

Palazzo Moro Lin, *also known as the "palace of the 13 windows", was created in the 17th century for the painter Pietro Liberi by merging two Gothic houses.*

Palazzo Grassi, *built in the 1730s, was bought by Fiat in 1984 and turned into a venue for art exhibitions.*

Palazzo Capello Malipiero, *a Gothic palace, was reconstructed in 1622. Beside it, in Campo di San Samuele, stands the church of San Samuele which has a 12th-century Veneto-Byzantine campanile.*

Ca' Rezzonico

Ca' Rezzonico to the Guggenheim

This southern stretch of the canal, widening after the Accademia, is lined by a rich and varied parade of palaces.

Palazzo del Duca, planned in the 15th century as a sumptuous palace but never finished, houses a collection of porcelain.

Palazzo Falier *was said to have been home to Doge Marin Falier, who was beheaded for treason in 1355 (see p43).*

Palazzo degli Scrigni, built in 1609, acquired its name from the coffers *(scrigni)* inherited by the Contarini in 1418.

Accademia

Palazzo Loredan, *home of Doge Francesco Loredan (1752–62), is one of many belonging to that family.*

The wooden Accademia Bridge *was built in 1932 as a temporary structure to replace a 19th-century iron bridge. By popular demand it has been retained.*

The Accademia *galleries, within the former church, monastery and Scuola della Carità, house the world's greatest collection of Venetian paintings (see pp130–33).*

Palazzo Contarini del Zaffo, *a magnificent Renaissance palace of the late 1400s, was built for a branch of the ubiquitous Contarini family. Early this century it was acquired by the Polignac family.*

LOCATOR MAP

Ca' Grande, *a huge Classical palace, was designed in 1545 by Sansovino for Giacomo Cornaro, nephew of the Queen of Cyprus. The family was one of the richest in Venice and spared no expense in the palace's decoration. This family tree illustrates the extent of the Cornaro's wealth and influence in Venice.*

Palazzo Franchetti Cavalli belonged to Archduke Frederick of Austria, who died here in 1836.

Palazzo Barbaro *comprises two palaces, one of which was bought by the Curtis family in 1885. Monet and Whistler painted here and Henry James (right) wrote* The Aspern Papers.

Casetta delle Rose, *one of the smallest houses on the canal, was the home of Italian poet Gabriele d'Annunzio during World War I. Canova (above) had his studio here in 1770.*

Palazzo Barbarigo, *beside the Campo San Vio, stands out for the harsh mosaics, added in 1887.*

Peggy Guggenheim *established her collection of modern art in Venice in 1951 (see p134). She chose as her venue the Palazzo Venier dei Leoni, which had been built in 1749 and never finished.*

Palazzo Dario, *built in 1487, is a charming but strangely ill-fated palace (see p135).*

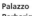

To La Salute and San Marco

The view along the final stretch of the canal is one of
the finest – and most familiar – in Venice. Near the
mouth rises the magnificent church of La Salute with
busy St Mark's Basin beyond.

LOCATOR MAP

The Palazzo Gritti-Pisani, *where
Ruskin stayed in 1851, is better
known today as the luxurious 5-star
Hotel Gritti Palace (see p228).*

Palazzo Contarini Fasan, *a tiny
15th-century palace with an
elegant façade, is popularly
known as the House of
Desdemona from Shakespeare's*
Othello.

**Santa
Maria Del
Giglio**

Salute

**The mock-Gothic
mansion**, Ca'
Genovese, was built
in 1892 in the place
of the second Gothic
cloister of the San
Gregorio monastery.

Palazzo Salviati *was the headquarters of the Salviati glass-
producing company, hence the
glass mosaics on the façade.*

**The deconsecrated Gothic
brick church** *of Abbazia San
Gregorio and a little cloister
are all that survive of what
was for centuries a powerful
monastic centre. The church
is now used as a laboratory
for the renovation of large-
scale paintings.*

Palazzo Tiepolo, *the Hotel Europa and Regina, was formerly owned by the Tiepolo family, associated with an unsuccessful uprising in 1310.*

Harry's Bar (see p92) *was popular with Hemingway and other writers. This was the very first Harry's Bar in the world.*

Palazzo Giustinian, head-quarters of the Biennale, used to be a hotel, where Turner, Verdi and Proust stayed.

San Marco Vallaressa

Giardinetti Reali, the Royal Gardens, were created by Napoleon to improve his view from the Procuratie Nuove.

Palazzo Treves Bonfili, a Classical building of the 17th century, is decorated with Neo-Classical frescoes, paintings and statuary.

The view from the Dogana, *taking in the Doge's Palace, the Campanile of San Marco and the Zecca, is one of the most memorable in Venice.*

Santa Maria della Salute, *a Baroque church of monumental proportions, is supported by over a million timber piles. Built to com-memorate the end of the 1630 plague, it was the work of Baldassare Longhena (see p135).*

The Punta della Dogana, *the former customs house, is topped by a weathervane figure of Fortune (see p135).*

SAN MARCO

Home of the political and judicial nerve centres of Venice, the *sestiere* of San Marco has been the heart of Venetian life since the early days of the Republic. The great showpiece of the Serenissima was the Piazza San Marco, conceived as a vista for the Doge's Palace and the Basilica, described by Napoleon as "the most elegant drawing room in Europe",

Adam and Eve on the corner of the Doge's Palace

was the only one deemed fit to be called a piazza – the others were merely *campi*, or fields.

The San Marco area has the bulk of luxury hotels, restaurants and shops. It is also home to several imposing churches, three theatres, including the famous Fenice, and a wealth of handsome *palazzi*. Many of these line the sweeping southern curve of the Grand Canal which borders the *sestiere*.

SIGHTS AT A GLANCE

Churches
Basilica San Marco
pp78–83 ❸
San Moisè ⓫
San Salvatore ⓲
Santa Maria Zobenigo ⓭
Santo Stefano ⓰
San Zulian ㉑

Museums and Galleries
Libreria Sansoviniana ❺
Museo Archeologico ❻
Museo Correr ❽
Museo Fortuny ⓱

Palaces
Doge's Palace pp84–9 ❹
Palazzo Contarini
del Bovolo ⓬

Historic Buildings and Monuments
Campanile ❶
Columns of San Marco
and San Teodoro ❼
San Giorgio Maggiore ㉒
Torre dell'Orologio ❷

Streets and Squares
Campo San Bartolomeo ⓳
Campo Santo Stefano ⓯
Mercerie ⓴

Bars
Harry's Bar ❾

Theatres
La Fenice ⓮
Ridotto ❿

KEY

■ Street-by-Street map
See pp74–5

■ Street-by-Street map
See pp90–91

🚤 Vaporetto boarding point

🚹 Traghetto crossing

0 metres   250
0 yards   250

SAN GIORGIO MAGGIORE

◁ **Central dome of the Basilica San Marco**

Street-by-Street: Piazza San Marco

Throughout its long history the Piazza San Marco has witnessed pageants, processions, political activities and countless Carnival festivities. Tourists flock here in their thousands, for the Piazza's eastern end is dominated by two of the city's most important historical sights – the Basilica and the Doge's Palace. In addition to these magnificent buildings there is plenty to entertain, with elegant cafés, open-air orchestras and smart boutiques beneath the arcades of the Procuratie.

Lion of St Mark

So close to the waters of the lagoon, the Piazza is one of the first points in the city to suffer at *acqua alta* (high tide). Tourists and Venetians alike can then be seen picking their way across the duckboards which are set up to crisscross the flooded square.

Gondolas
Traditionally gondolas have moored in the Bacino Orseolo, named after Doge Orseolo.

Quadri's café was the favourite haunt of Austrian troops during the Occupation (*see p48*).

Museo Correr
Giovanni Bellini's Pietà *(1455–60) is one of many Renaissance masterpieces hanging in the picture galleries of the Correr* **8**

The Ala Napoleonica is the most recent wing enclosing the square, built by Napoleon to create a new ballroom.

PROCURATIE VECCHIE

PIAZZA
SAN MARC

PROCURATIE NUOVE

| 0 metres | 75 |
| 0 yards | 75 |

Caffè Florian
(*see p250*) was the favourite haunt of 19th-century literary figures such as Byron, Dickens and Proust.

The Giardinetti Reali (royal gardens) were laid out in the early 19th century.

San Marco Vallaresso

STAR SIGHTS

★ Basilica San Marco

★ Doge's Palace

★ Campanile

For hotels and restaurants in this region see pp228–33 and pp242–7

Torre dell'Orologio
The Madonna on the clock tower is greeted each Epiphany and Ascension by clockwork figures of the Magi ❷

Piazzetta dei Leoncini
was named after the pair of porphyry lions which stand in the square.

LOCATOR MAP
See Street Finder, map 7

★ **Basilica San Marco**
The remarkable Basilica of St Mark is a glorious reflection of the city's Byzantine connection ❸

★ **Doge's Palace**
Once the Republic's seat of power and home to its rulers, the Doge's Palace, beside the Basilica, is a triumph of Gothic architecture ❹

★ **Campanile**
Today's tower replaced the one that collapsed in 1902. The top provides spectacular views of the city ❶

Museo Archeologico
The museum sculptures had a marked influence on Venetian Renaissance artists ❻

Columns of San Marco and San Teodoro
The columns marked the main entrance to Venice when the city could be reached only by sea ❼

San Marco Giardinetti

The Zecca, designed by Sansovino, was the city mint until 1870, and gave its name to the *zecchino* or Venetian ducat. It houses the Biblioteca Marciana.

Libreria Sansoviniana
The ornate vaulting of the magnificent library stairway is decorated with frescoes and gilded stucco ❺

Campanile ●

Piazza San Marco. **Map** 7 B2. *Tel 041 270 83 11.* San Marco. daily. Nov–Easter: 9:30am–3:45pm (to 4:45pm Sat & Sun); Easter–Oct: 9am–7pm (Jul–Sep: to 9pm).

From the top of St Mark's campanile, high above the Piazza, visitors can enjoy sublime views of the city, the lagoon and, visibility permitting, the peaks of the Alps. It was from this viewpoint

The spire, 98.5 m (323 ft) high, is topped with a golden weather-vane designed by Bartolomeo Bon.

The five bells in the tower each had their role during the Republic. The *marangona* tolled the start and end of the working day; the *malefico* warned of an execution; the *nona* rang at noon; the *mezza terza* summoned senators to the Doge's Palace; and the *trottiera* announced a session of the Great Council.

An internal lift, installed in 1962, provides visitors with access |to one of the most spectacular views across Venice.

The Loggetta was built in the 16th century by Jacopo Sansovino. Its Classical sculptures celebrate the glory of the Republic.

The allegorical reliefs from Verona depict Justice representing Venice, Jupiter as Crete and Venus as Cyprus. All were carefully rebuilt after the campanile's collapse in 1902.

that Galileo demonstrated his telescope to Doge Leonardo Donà in 1609. To do so, he would have climbed the internal ramp. Access today is via a lift for which there is usually a queue. Visitors at the top of the tower on the hour should note that the five bells ring quite loudly.

The first tower, completed in 1173, was built as a lighthouse to assist navigators in the lagoon. In the Middle Ages, it took on a less benevolent role as the support for a torture cage where offenders were imprisoned and in some cases left to die. The tower's present appearance dates from the early 16th century, when it was restored by Bartolomeo Bon after an earthquake.

The tower survived the vicissitudes of time until 14 July 1902 when its foundations gave way and it suddenly collapsed. The only casualties were the Loggetta at the foot of the tower and the custodian's cat. The following year, with the help of many donations, the foundation stone was laid for a campanile *"dov'era e com'era"* ("where it was and how it was"). The new tower was opened on 25 April (St Mark's Day) 1912. Due to small structural shifts, work has begun to re-inforce the foundations. There is no known end date for the work.

The highly ornamented clock face of the Torre dell'Orologio

Torre dell'Orologio ❷

Piazza San Marco. **Map** 7 B2. *Tel 041 4273 0892.* San Marco. 10 & 11am Mon–Wed, 2 & 3pm Thu–Sun for pre-booked tours in English.

The richly decorated Renaissance clock tower stands on the north side of the Piazza, over the archway leading to the Mercerie (*see p95*). It was built in the late 15th century, and the central section is thought to have been designed by Mauro Coducci. Displaying the phases of the moon and the zodiac, the gilt and blue enamel clock was originally designed with seafarers in mind. A story was spread by scandalmongers that once the clock was complete, the two inventors of the complex clock mechanism had their eyes gouged out to prevent them from ever creating a replica.

During Ascension Week and Epiphany, the clock draws large crowds who watch the figures of the Magi emerge from side doors to pay their respects to the Virgin and Child, whose figures are set above the clock. At the very top are two huge bronze figures, known as the *Mori*, or Moors, which strike the bell on the hour.

Basilica San Marco ❸

See pp78–83.

Doge's Palace ❹

See pp84–9.

Libreria Sansoviniana ❺

Piazzetta (entrance Ala Napoleonica).
Map 7 B3. *Tel 041 240 72 11
(Biblioteca Marciana).* 🚈 *San Marco.*
⭘ *10am–5pm daily.* ⬤ *public hols.*
🏛 ✔ 🚫

Praised by Andrea Palladio as the finest building since antiquity, the library was designed in the Classical style by the architect Jacopo Sansovino. During construction (1537–88) the vaulting collapsed: Sansovino was blamed and imprisoned. He was freed after appeals from eminent acquaintances, but had to reconstruct the building at his own expense.

At the top of the monumental stairway *(see p75)*, behind a booth, is a rare example of Jacopo de' Barbari's bird's-eye map of Venice dating to 1500.

The salon is sumptuously decorated and features two fine ceiling paintings by Paolo Veronese, *Arithmetic and Geometry* and *Music*.

Museo Archeologico ❻

Piazzetta (9am–7pm: entrance Ala Napoleonica). **Map** 7 B3.
Tel 041 522 59 78. 🚈 *San Marco.*
⭘ *10am–5pm daily.* ⬤ *1 Jan,
25 Dec.* 🏛 ✔ 🚫

Housed in rooms in both the Libreria Sansoviniana and the Procuratie Nuove, the museum provides a quiet retreat from the bustle of San Marco. The collection owes its existence to the generosity of Domenico Grimani, son of Doge Antonio Grimani, who bequeathed all of his Greek, Roman and earlier sculpture, together with his library, to the State in 1523.

Columns of San Marco and San Teodoro ❼

Piazzetta. **Map** 7 C3. 🚈 *San Marco.*

Along with all the bounty from Constantinople came the two huge granite columns which now tower above the Piazzetta. These were said to have been erected in 1172 by the engineer Nicolò Barattieri, architect of the very first Rialto Bridge. For his efforts he was granted the right to set up gambling tables between the columns. A more gruesome spectacle on the same spot was the execution of criminals, which took place here until the mid-18th century. Even today, superstitious Venetians will not be seen walking between the columns.

The western column is crowned by a marble statue of St Theodore, who was the patron saint of Venice before St Mark's relics were smuggled from Alexandria in AD 828. The statue is a modern copy – the original is kept for safety in the Doge's Palace *(see p88)*.

The second column is surmounted by a huge bronze of the Lion of St Mark. Its origin remains a mystery, though it is thought to be a Chinese chimera with wings added to make it look like a Venetian lion. In September 1990 the 3,000-kg (3-ton) beast went to the British Museum in London for extensive restoration, and was returned with great ceremony and skill to the top of the column.

Columns of San Marco and San Teodoro

Fragment from a monumental statue, in the Museo Archeologico

A Portrait of a Young Man in a Red Hat by Carpaccio (c.1490)

Museo Correr ❽

Procuratie Nuove (entrance Ala Napoleonica). **Map** 7 B2. *Tel 041 240 52 11.* 🚈 *San Marco.*
⭘ *10am–7pm daily (Nov–Mar: to 5pm).* ⬤ *1 Jan, 25 Dec.* 🏛 *allows access to Libreria Sansoviniana & Museo Archeologico.* 🚫 ⬛ 🛗

The wealthy Abbot Teodoro Correr's collection of works of art and documents forms the nucleus of the civic museum.

The first rooms form a suitably Neo-Classical backdrop for early statues by Antonio Canova (1757–1822). The rest of the floor covers the history of the Venetian Republic, with maps, coins, armour and a host of doge-related exhibits.

On the second floor, the Museo del Risorgimento is devoted to the history of the city, until Venice became part of unified Italy in 1866. Also here is the Quadreria, or picture gallery. The paintings are hung chronologically and the rooms have the bonus of explanations in English. The collection enables you to trace the evolution of Venetian painting, and to see the influence that Ferrarese, Paduan and Flemish artists had on the Venetian school. The most famous works in the gallery are the Carpaccios: *A Portrait of a Young Man in a Red Hat* (c.1490) and *Two Venetian Ladies* (c.1507). The latter is traditionally, but probably incorrectly, known as *The Courtesans* because of the ladies' décolleté dresses.

Basilica San Marco ❸

This awesome Basilica, built on a Greek cross plan and crowned with five huge domes, is the third church to stand on this site. The first, built to enshrine the body of St Mark in the 9th century, was destroyed by fire. The second was pulled down in the 11th century in order to make way for a more spectacular edifice designed by an unknown architect (1063–94), reflecting the escalating power of the Republic. The basilica continued to be remodelled over the following centuries, and in 1807 it succeeded San Pietro in the *sestiere* of Castello *(see p120)* as the cathedral of Venice; it had until then served as the doge's private chapel for State ceremonies.

The Pentecost Dome, showing the Descent of the Holy Ghost as a dove, was probably the first dome to be decorated with mosaics.

St Mark and Angels
The statues crowning the central arch are additions from the early 15th century.

★ Horses of St Mark
The four horses are replicas of the gilded bronze originals (see p80), now protected inside the Basilica.

★ Central Doorway Carvings
The central arch features 13th-century carvings of the Labours of the Month. The grape harvester represents September.

★ Façade Mosaics
A 17th-century mosaic shows the smuggling out of Alexandria of St Mark's body, reputedly under slices of pork to deter prying Muslims.

Ciborium
The fine alabaster columns of the altar canopy, or ciborium, are adorned with scenes from the New Testament.

The Ascension Dome features a magnificent 13th-century mosaic of Christ surrounded by angels, the 12 Apostles and the Virgin Mary.

VISITORS' CHECKLIST

Piazza San Marco. **Map** 7 B2. **Tel** 041 270 83 11. 🚤 San Marco. **Basilica, Museum, Treasury and Pala d'Oro** 🕐 9:45am–4:45pm Mon–Sat, 2–5pm Sun & public hols. 📷 for Treasury only. 📷 Museum, Treasury and Pala d'Oro only. 🔔 9 times a day. Sightseeing is limited during services. 🎧 in English twice a week in season. Ⓟ 📷 🚻 🛍 www.basilicasanmarco.it

St Mark's body, believed lost in the fire of AD 976, supposedly reappeared when the new church was consecrated in 1094. The remains are housed in the altar.

★ The Tetrarchs
This charming sculptured group in porphyry (4th-century Egyptian) is thought to represent Diocletian, Maximian, Valerian and Constance. Collectively they were the tetrarchs, appointed by Diocletian to help rule the Roman Empire.

Allegorical mosaics

St Mark's Treasury

The so-called Pilasters of Acre in fact came from a 6th-century church in Constantinople.

Baptistry

Baptistry Mosaics
Herod's Banquet (1343–54) is one of the mosaics in a cycle of scenes from the life of St John the Baptist.

STAR FEATURES

★ Façade Mosaics

★ Central Doorway Carvings

★ Horses of St Mark

★ The Tetrarchs

Inside the Basilica

Dark, mysterious and enriched with the spoils of
conquest, the Basilica is a unique blend of Eastern and
Western influences. This oriental extravaganza,
embellished over a period of six centuries with fabulous
mosaics, marble and carvings, made a fitting location
for the ceremonies of the Serene Republic. It was here
that the doge was presented to the city following his
election, that heads of State, popes, princes and ambassadors were received, and where sea captains came to
pray for protection before embarking on epic voyages.

Mascoli Chapel
*Formerly called the
"New Chapel", this is
named after an all-
male confraternity,
or* mascoli.

The Porta dei Fiori or
Gate of Flowers is
decorated with 13th-
century reliefs.

North Aisle
*The gallery leading off the museum
affords visitors a splendid overall
view of the mosaics.*

★ **Pentecost Dome**
*Showing the Apostles touched
by tongues of flame, the
Pentecost Dome was decorated
in the 12th century.*

The columns of
the inner façade
are thought to
be fragments of
the first basilica.

Main entrance

★ **Atrium Mosaics**
*In the glittering
Genesis Cupola the
Creation of the
World is described
in concentric
circles. Here,
God creates the
fish and birds.*

The baptistry is also
called Chiesa dei Putti
(church of the cherubs).

The Altar of the Virgin has a 10th- century icon of the Madonna of Nicopeia, which came with the spoils of war in 1204 (see p42).

The Chapel of St Peter has a 14th-century altar screen relief of St Peter worshipped by two Procurators.

★ **Pala d'Oro**
The magnificent altarpiece, created in the 10th century by medieval goldsmiths, is made up of 250 panels such as this one, each adorned with enamels and precious stones.

The sacristy door (always locked) has fine bronze panels by Sansovino, including portraits of himself with Titian and Aretino.

★ **Ascension Dome**
A mosaic of Christ in Glory decorates the enormous central dome. This masterpiece was created by 13th-century Venetian craftsmen, who were strongly influenced by the art and architecture of Byzantium.

The Altar of the Sacrament is surrounded by mosaics of the parables and miracles of Christ dating from the late 12th or early 13th century.

South aisle

★ **Treasury**
A repository for precious booty from Constantinople, the Treasury also houses ancient Italian works of art, such as this 12th- or 13th-century incense burner.

STAR FEATURES

★ Atrium Mosaics

★ Ascension and Pentecost Domes

★ Pala d'Oro

★ Treasury

Exploring the Basilica

The Basilica cannot comfortably be covered in one visit. The mosaics, the rich store of eastern bounty, the mysterious lighting and the sheer size of the place create a feeling of confusion for first-time visitors. Make several visits, ideally at different times of the day. The mosaics look especially splendid when the church is fully illuminated (11:30am–12:30pm Mon–Fri, 11:30am–4pm Sat, 2–4pm Sun). Visitors with organized tours are often led towards the Pala d'Oro and Treasury and miss out on other sections of the church. Avoid the crowds by visiting early in the morning or in the evening. If a mass is in progress, visitors are expected to be silent and will only be able to visit certain areas.

The Genesis Cupola of the atrium

Stories of Joseph and of Moses in the domes at the north end. The figures of saints on either side of the main doorway date from the 11th century and are among the earliest mosaics in the church. Just in front of the central doorway there is a lozenge of porphyry to mark the spot where the Emperor Frederick Barbarossa was obliged to make peace with Pope Alexander III in 1177 (see p41).

MUSEO MARCIANO

A precarious stairway from the atrium, marked *Loggia dei Cavalli*, takes you up to the church museum. The gallery gives a splendid view into the basilica, while from the exterior loggia visitors can survey the Piazza San Marco and take a closer look at the replica horses on the church façade. It was from this panoramic balcony that doges and dignitaries once looked down on ceremonies taking place in the square. The original gilded bronze horses, housed in a room at the far end of the museum, were stolen from the top of the Hippodrome (ancient racecourse) in Constantinople in 1204 but their origin, either Roman or Hellenistic, remains a mystery. In the same room is Paolo Veneziano's 14th-century *pala feriale*, painted with stories of St Mark, which once covered the Pala d'Oro. Also on show are medieval

MOSAICS

Clothing the domes, walls and floor of the basilica are over 4,000 sq m (40,000 sq ft) of gleaming golden mosaics. The earliest, dating from the 12th century, were the work of mosaicists from the east. Their techniques were adopted by Venetian craftsmen who gradually took over the decoration, combining Byzantine inspiration with western influences. During the 16th century, sketches and cartoons by Tintoretto, Titian, Veronese and other leading artists were reproduced in mosaic. The original iconographical scheme, depicting stories from the Testaments, has more or less been preserved by careful restoration.

Among the finest mosaics in the basilica are those decorating the 13th-century central Dome of the Ascension and the 12th-century Dome of the Pentecost over the nave.

The *pavimento*, or basilica floor, spreads out like an undulating Turkish carpet. Mosaics, made of marble, porphyry and glass are used to create complex and colourful geometric

patterns and beautiful scenes of beasts and birds. Some of these scenes are allegorical. The one in the left transept of two cocks carrying a fox on a stick was designed to symbolize cunning vanquished by vigilance.

ATRIUM (VESTIBULE)

The 13th-century mosaics decorating the cupolas, vaults and lunettes of the atrium are among the finest in the basilica. The scenes depict Old Testament stories, starting at the southern end with the Genesis Cupola (showing 26 detailed episodes of the Creation), to the

The Quadriga, the original gilded bronze horses in the museum

Noah and the Flood – atrium mosaics from the 13th century

illuminated manuscripts, fragments of ancient mosaics and antique tapestries.

SANCTUARY AND PALA D'ORO

Beyond the Chapel of St Clement, tickets are sold to view the most valuable treasure of San Marco: the Pala d'Oro. This jewel-spangled altarpiece situated behind the high altar consists of 250 enamel paintings on gold foil, enclosed within a gilded silver Gothic frame. Originally commissioned in Byzantium in AD 976, the altarpiece was embellished over the centuries. Following the fall of the Republic, Napoleon helped himself to some of the precious stones, but the screen still gleams with pearls, rubies, sapphires and amethysts.

Statue of St Mark on the iconostasis

The iconostasis, the screen dividing nave from chancel, is adorned with marble Gothic statues of the Virgin and Apostles, and was carved in 1394 by the Dalle Masegne brothers. Above the high altar the imposing green marble baldacchino is supported by finely carved alabaster columns featuring scenes from the New Testament.

BAPTISTRY AND CHAPELS

The Baptistry (closed to the public) was added in the 14th century by Doge Andrea Dandolo (1343–54) who is buried here. Under his direction the baptistry was decorated with outstanding mosaics depicting scenes from the lives of Christ and John the Baptist. Sansovino, who designed the font, is buried by the altar.

The adjoining Zen Chapel (currently closed to the public) originally formed part of the atrium. It became a funeral chapel for Cardinal Zen in 1504 in return for his bequest to the State.

In the left transept of the basilica the Chapel of St Isidore, normally accessible only for worship, was also built by Dandolo. Mosaics in the barrel vault ceiling tell the tale of the saint, whose body

was stolen from the island of Chios and transported to Venice in 1125. To its left the Mascoli Chapel, used in the early 17th century by the confraternity of Mascoli (men), is decorated with scenes from the life of the Virgin Mary. The altarpiece has statues depicting the Virgin and Child between St Mark and St John.

The third chapel in the left transept is home to the icon of the Madonna of Nicopeia. Looted in 1204, she was formerly carried into battle at the head of the Byzantine army.

The revered icon of the Nicopeia Madonna, once a war insignia

TREASURY

Although plundered after the fall of the Republic and much depleted by the fundraising sale of jewels in the early 19th century, the treasury nevertheless has a precious collection of Byzantine silver, gold and glasswork. Today, most of the treasures are housed in a room whose remarkably thick walls are believed to have been a 9th-century tower of the Doge's Palace. Exhibits include chalices, goblets, reliquaries, two intricate icons of the archangel Michael and an 11th-century silver-gilt reliquary made in the form of a five-domed basilica (see p81). The sanctuary, with over 100 reliquaries, is normally open to the public.

The archangel Michael, a Byzantine icon from the 11th century in the Treasury

Doge's Palace ❹

The Palazzo Ducale started life in the 9th century as a fortified castle, but this and several subsequent buildings were destroyed by a series of fires. The existing palace owes its external appearance to the building work of the 14th and early 15th centuries. The designers broke with tradition by perching the bulk of the pink Verona marble palace on lace-like Istrian stone arcades, with a portico supported by columns below. The result is a light and airy masterpiece of Gothic architecture.

Arco Foscari
The Adam and Eve figures on this triumphal arch in the courtyard are copies of the 15th-century originals by Antonio Rizzo.

★ Porta della Carta
This 15th-century Gothic gate was the principal entrance to the palace. From it, a vaulted passageway leads to the Arco Foscari and the internal courtyard.

Exit

STAR FEATURES

★ Giants' Staircase

★ Porta della Carta

The balcony on the west façade was added in 1536 to mirror the early 15th-century balcony looking on to the quay.

★ Giants' Staircase
This late 15th-century staircase by Antonio Rizzo was used for ceremonial purposes. It was on the landing at the top that the doges were crowned with the glittering zogia.

Torture Chamber
"The court of the room of the Cord" recalls the practice of interrogating suspects as they hung by their wrists.

VISITORS' CHECKLIST

Piazzetta. **Map** 7 C2. *Tel 041 271 59 11.* San Marco.
8:30am–6:30pm daily (Nov–Mar: to 5:30pm). **Last adm:** 90 mins before closing. **Secret Itineraries** (in English, 9:55am, 10:45am & 11:35am daily): book in advance at the palace or on the phone. 1 Jan, 25 Dec.
partial.
www.museicivicivenezionani.it

Sala dei Tre Capi
(Chamber of the Three Heads of the Council of Ten)

Sala della Bussola
(Compass Room)

Bridge of Sighs
The famous bridge once crossed by offenders on their way to the State interrogators.

Drunkenness of Noah
This early 15th-century sculpture, symbolic of the frailty of man, is set on the corner of the palace.

Ponte della Paglia
(see p113)

Main entrance

Adam and Eve
with the serpent are depicted in stone on the corner of the Piazzetta.

Sala del Maggior Consiglio
An entire wall of the Great Council Hall is taken up by Domenico and Jacopo Tintoretto's Paradise *(1588–92).*

Inside the Doge's Palace

From the early days of the Republic, the Doge's Palace was the seat of the government, the Palace of Justice and the home of the doge. For centuries this was the only building in Venice entitled to the name palazzo (the others were merely called Ca', short for Casa). The power of the Serenissima is ever present in the large and allegorical historical paintings which embellish the walls and ceilings of the splendid halls and chambers. These ornate rooms are testament to the glory of the Venetian Republic, and were designed to impress and overawe visiting ambassadors and dignitaries.

Intricate carved Gothic capital

STAR FEATURES

★ Collegiate Rooms

★ Sala del Maggior Consiglio

★ Prisons

Colonnade
Sunlight streams through the arches of the Loggia on the first floor of the palace.

Mars
The Giants' Staircase is named after Sansovino's monumental figures, statues of Mars and Neptune, sculpted in 1567.

Ground floor

Scala d'Oro
Sansovino's lavish staircase was built between 1554 and 1558. The arched ceiling is embellished with gilded stucco by Alessandro Vittoria.

Exit through Porta della Carta

KEY TO FLOORPLAN

- State Apartments
- Collegium and Senate Rooms
- Council of Ten and Armoury
- Great Council Rooms
- Prisons
- Non-exhibition space

Wellhead
The two 16th-century bronze wellheads in the courtyard are considered to be the finest in Venice.

★ Collegiate Rooms
Bacchus and Ariadne Crowned by Venus *is the finest of four mythological scenes by Tintoretto in the Anticollegio.*

Third floor

The **Sala del Consiglio dei Dieci** has a ceiling decorated with paintings by Veronese (1553–4).

Sala dello Scudo
The walls of this room are covered with maps of the world. In the centre are two huge 18th-century globes.

First floor

Second floor

★ Sala del Maggior Consiglio
The first 76 doges, with the exception of the traitor Marin Falier, are portrayed on a frieze round the upper walls of the room.

★ Prisons
These 16th-century cells were mainly used for petty offenders. Serious criminals were lodged in the dank pozzi *(wells).*

Entrance

THE SECRET ITINERARY

The fascinating, though poorly publicized, Secret Itinerary (Itinerari Segreti) tour *(see* Visitors' Checklist *p85)* takes visitors behind the scenes in the palace to the offices and Hall of the Chancellery, the State Inquisitors' room, the Torture Chamber and the prisons. It was from these cells that Casanova made his spectacular escape in 1755. Tours are available in Italian, English and French. Each is limited to 25 people and lasts for 75 minutes.

Casanova's cell door

Exploring the Doge's Palace

A tour of the palace takes visitors through a succession of richly decorated chambers and halls. The rooms are on four levels, and they all have name boards carrying an explanation of their function in Italian and English. The latest equipment available is an up-to-date infrared audioguide, which can be hired for a commentary on the whole palace or just the areas that are of particular interest.

Allow plenty of time for the visit, and try to take a break at the coffee shop. Located at water level, it affords evocative views of gondolas gliding past in the canal.

St Theodore in the palace courtyard

COURTYARD

The courtyard is reached via a vaulted passage from the Porta del Frumento. At the top of the Giants' Staircase, on the opposite side of the courtyard, new doges were crowned with the *zogia* or dogal cap.

SCALA D'ORO AND STATE APARTMENTS

The sumptuous Scala d'Oro (golden staircase), built between 1538 and 1559, was designed by Jacopo Sansovino. It takes its name, however, from the elaborate gilt stucco vault, which was added by Alessandro Vittoria (1554–8). The doge's private apartments on the second floor were built after the fire of 1483 and later looted on the orders of Napoleon. They are bare of furnishings, but the lavish ceilings and colossal carved chimneypieces in some of the rooms give an idea of the doges' lifestyle. The most ornate is the Sala degli Scarlatti, with a richly carved gilt ceiling, a fireplace (c.1501) designed by Antonio and Tullio Lombardo and a relief (1501–21) by Pietro Lombardo of Doge Leonardo Loredan at the feet of the Virgin.

The Sala dello Scudo, or map room, contains maps and charts. The picture gallery further on features works by Vittore Carpaccio and Giovanni Bellini, and some incongruous wooden demoniac panels by Hieronymus Bosch.

A bocca di leone used for denouncing tax evaders

SALA DELLE QUATTRO PORTE TO SALA DEL SENATO

The second flight of the Scala d'Oro leads to the third floor and its council chambers. The first room, the Sala delle Quattro Porte, was completely rebuilt after the 1574 fire, its ceiling designed by Andrea Palladio and frescoed by Tintoretto.

The next room, the Anticollegio, was the waiting room. The end walls are decorated with mythological scenes by Tintoretto: *Vulcan's Forge; Mercury and the Graces; Bacchus and Ariadne* and *Minerva Dismissing Mars*, all painted in 1578. Veronese's masterly *Rape of Europa* (1580), opposite the window, is one of the most eyecatching works in the palace.

Off the Anticollegio, the Sala del Collegio was the hall where the doge and his counsellors met to receive ambassadors and discuss matters of State. Embellishing the magnificent ceiling are 11 paintings by Veronese (c.1577), of which the most notable – in the centre, far end – is *Justice and Peace Offering Sword, Scales and Olive Branch to Venice*.

It was in the next room, the Sala del Senato, that the doge would sit with some 200 senators to discuss matters such as foreign affairs or nominations of ambassadors. The wall and ceiling paintings, by pupils of Tintoretto or the master himself, are further propaganda for the Republic.

SALA DEL CONSIGLIO DEI DIECI TO THE ARMERIA

The route returns through the Sala delle Quattro Porte to the Sala del Consiglio dei Dieci. This was the meeting room of the awesomely powerful Council of Ten, founded in

Veronese's *Dialectic* (c.1577), Sala del Collegio

1310 to investigate and prosecute crimes concerning the security of the State. Napoleon pilfered some of the Veroneses from the ceiling but two of the finest found their way back here in 1920: *Age and Youth* and *Juno Offering the Ducal Crown to Venice* (both 1553–54).

In the next room, the Sala della Bussola, offenders awaited their fate in front of the Council of Ten. The room's *bocca di leone* (lion's mouth), used to post secret denunciations, was just one of several within the palace. The wooden door here leads to the rooms of the Heads of the Ten, the State Inquisitors' Room and thence to the torture chamber and prisons. This is the route taken by those on the Secret Itinerary.

Age and Youth (1553–54) by Veronese

Others follow the flow to the Armoury – one of the finest collections in Europe, thanks in part to bequests by European monarchs.

SALA DEL MAGGIOR CONSIGLIO

Another staircase, the Scala dei Censori, leads down to the second floor, along the hallway and past the Sala del Guariento with fresco fragments of *The Coronation of the Virgin* by Guariento (1365–67). From the *liagò*, or veranda, where Antonio Rizzo's marble statues of Adam and Eve (1480s) are displayed, visitors pass into the magnificent Sala del Maggior Consiglio or Hall of the Great Council. A chamber of monumental proportions, it was here that the Great Council convened to vote on constitutional questions, to pass laws and elect the top officials of the Serene Republic. The hall was also used for State banquets. When Henry III of France paid a royal visit, 3,000 guests were entertained in this spectacular room.

By the mid-16th century the Great Council had around 2,000 members. Any Venetian of high birth over 25 was entitled to a seat – with the exception of those married to a commoner. From 1646, by which time the Turkish wars had depleted state coffers, nobility from the *terra firma* or those from merchant or professional classes with 100,000 ducats to spare could purchase their way in.

Tintoretto's huge, highly restored work called *Paradise* (1587–90) occupies the eastern wall. Measuring 7.45 by 24.65 m (25 by 81 ft) it is one of the largest paintings in the world. For a man in his late seventies, albeit assisted by his son, it is a remarkably vigorous composition.

The ceiling of the hall is decorated with panels glorifying the Republic. One of the finest is Veronese's *Apotheosis of Venice* (1583). A frieze along the walls illustrates 76 doges by Tintoretto's pupils. The portrait covered by a curtain is Marin Falier, beheaded for treason in 1355. The other 42 doges are portrayed in the Sala dello Scrutinio, where new doges were nominated.

PRISONS

View of the lagoon through a grille on the Bridge of Sighs

From the Sala del Maggior Consiglio a series of passageways and stairways leads to the Bridge of Sighs (*see p113*) which links the palace to what were known as the New Prisons, built between 1556 and 1595.

Situated at the top of the palace, just below the leaded roof, are the *piombi* cells (*piombo* means lead). These cells are hardly inviting but prisoners here were far more comfortable than the criminals who were left to fester in the *pozzi* – the dark dank dungeons at ground level. The windowless cells of these ancient prisons are still covered with the graffiti of the convicts. Visitors on the Secret Itinerary tour are shown Casanova's cell in the *piombi* and told of how he made his daring escape from the palace through a hole in the roof.

Visits end with the offices of the Avogaria, where the state prosecutors (*avogadori*) prepared the trials.

The splendid Sala del Maggior Consiglio, the hall of the Great Council

Street-by-Street: Around La Fenice

West of the huge expanse of the ever-crowded Piazza San Marco there is a labyrinth of alleys to explore. At the centre of this part of the *sestiere* is Campo San Fantin, flanked by the Renaissance church of San Fantin. Nearby is the Ateneo Veneto, formerly a *scuola* whose members had the unenviable role of escorting prisoners to the scaffold. The narrow streets around these sights have some wonderfully exotic little shops, while the Calle Larga XXII Marzo, further south, boasts big names in Italian fashion. The quarter in general has some excellent restaurants but, being San Marco, the prices in the majority of establishments are fairly steep.

Campo San Fantin has a late Renaissance church, San Fantin, with a particularly beautiful apse designed by Jacopo Sansovino.

★ La Fenice
The opera house gained its name (the phoenix) after a fire in 1836. Destroyed by fire again in 1996, it is now beautifully restored ⓮

The Rio delle Veste
leads past the rear of the theatre. This is the route taken by those fortunate enough to arrive for their night out by gondola.

KEY

– – – Suggested route

| 0 metres | 75 |
| 0 yards | 75 |

STAR SIGHTS

★ La Fenice

★ San Moisè

Santa Maria Zobenigo
The carvings feature the Barbaro family who paid for the church façade. Ground-level reliefs show towns where the family held high ranking posts ⓭

LOCATOR MAP
See Street Finder, map 7

The statue of Daniele Manin, *leader of the 1848 uprising, stands on Campo Manin gazing towards the house where he once lived.*

Palazzo Contarini del Bovolo
This palazzo is often difficult to find, but worth seeking out for its fairy-tale external stairway (c.1499) ⓬

Frezzeria, *in medieval times, was the street where citizens went to purchase their arrows (frecce). Its shops now sell exotic clothes.*

Calle Larga XXII Marzo *was named after 22 March 1848, the day of Manin's rebellion. Today the street is best known for its trendy designer boutiques.*

★ San Moisè
The exuberant Baroque façade of San Moisè (c.1668) was funded by a legacy from the patrician Vincenzo Fini, whose bust features above a side door ⓫

Harry's Bar ❾

Calle Vallaresso 1323. **Map** 7 B3.
🚤 San Marco. See also **Restaurants,
Cafés and Bars** pp250–51.

Celebrated for cocktails,
carpaccio and American
clientèle, Harry's Bar is famous
throughout Venice. Founded
in 1931 by the late Giuseppe
Cipriani, it was financed by a
Bostonian called Harry who
thought Venice had a dearth
of decent bars. They chose a
storeroom at the Grand Canal
end of the Calle Vallaresso as
their location,
conveniently
close to
the Piazza
San Marco.
Since then, the bar
has seen a steady
stream of American
visitors, among them
Ernest Hemingway
who used to come
here after shooting in the
lagoon. The bar became the
most popular venue in Venice,
patronized by royalty, film
stars and heads of state.

**Ernest Hemingway, a
regular at Harry's Bar**

These days there are far
more American tourists than
famous figures, often there
to sample the Bellini cocktail
that Cipriani invented *(see
p241)*. Aesthetically, the place
is unremarkable and there is
no terrace for meals alfresco.

Ridotto ❿

Calle del Ridotto, 1332 San Marco.
Map 7 B3. **Tel** 041 520 02 11. 🚤
San Marco. ⬜ to hotel guests and
on request. **www**.hotelmonaco.it

In an effort to control the
gambling mania that swept
Venice in the 1600s, the State
allowed Marco Dandolo to use
his palace as the first public
gaming house in Europe. In
1638 the Ridotto was opened,
with the proviso that players
came disguised in a mask. In
1774 the Great Council closed
the casino's doors on account
of the number of Venetians
ruined at its tables.

In 1947 the old Palazzo
Dandolo was converted into
a theatre. Now restored, it is
part of the Hotel Monaco and
Grand Canal *(see p228)*.

San Moisè ⓫

Campo San Moisè. **Map** 7 A3. *Tel*
041 296 06 30. 🚤 San Marco. ⬜
9:30am–12:30pm, 4–6:30pm daily.

One of the churches in
Venice that people love to
hate, San Moisè displays a
ponderous Baroque façade.
Completed in 1668, it is covered in grimy statues, swags
and busts. John Ruskin, in a
characteristic anti-Baroque
outrage, described it
as the clumsiest
church in Venice.
The interior has a
mixed collection of
paintings and
sculpture from
the 17th and
18th centuries.
In the nave is
the tombstone
of John Law, a
financier from
Scotland who
founded the Compagnie
d'Occident to develop the
Mississippi Valley. His shares
collapsed in 1770 in the notorious South Sea Bubble, and
he fled to Venice, surviving
on his winnings at the Ridotto.

**Façade of San Moisè, encrusted
with Baroque ornamentation**

Palazzo Contarini
del Bovolo ⓬

Corte Contarini del Bovolo, 4299 San
Marco. **Map** 7 A2. *Tel* 041 271 90
12. 🚤 Rialto or Sant'Angelo. ⬤ for
restoration until 2012. Call ahead for
up-to-date information. 📷 📷

Tucked away in a maze of
alleys (follow signs from
Campo Manin), this *palazzo*
is best known for its graceful

**The external stairway of the
Palazzo Contarini del Bovolo**

external stairway, which is
currently closed for renovation.
In Venetian dialect *bovolo*
means snail shell, appropriate
to the spiral shape of the
stairway. The Contarini, a
learned family who had the
15th-century palace built,
were known as "the philoso-
phers". There is also a collection of Byzantine well-heads.

Santa Maria
Zobenigo ⓭

Campo Santa Maria del Giglio. **Map**
6 F3. *Tel* 041 275 04 62. 🚤 Santa
Maria del Giglio. ⬜ 10am–5pm
Mon–Sat. ⬤ 1 Jan, 25 Dec. 📷 📷
📷 📷 **www**.chorusvenezia.org

Named after the Jubanico
family who are said to have
founded it in the 9th century,
this church is also referred to
as "del Giglio" ("of the lily").
The exuberant Baroque
façade was financed by the
affluent Barbaro family and
was used to glorify their naval
and diplomatic achievements.

Inside is a tiny museum of
church ornaments and paintings including *The Sacred
Family* attributed to Rubens
and two works by Tintoretto.

La Fenice ⓮

Campo San Fantin. **Map** 7 A3.
Box office *Tel* 041 24 24. 🚢 *San
Marco*. 🔲 **www**.teatrolafenice.it

Theatre houses were
enormously popular in the
18th century and La Fenice,
the city's oldest theatre, was
no exception. Built in 1792
in Classical style, it was one
of several privately owned
theatres showing plays and
operas to audiences from all
strata of society. In December
1836 a fire destroyed the
interior but a year later it
was resurrected, just like the
mythical bird, the phoenix
(fenice) which is said to have
arisen from its ashes.

Another fire in early 1996
again destroyed the theatre,
except for its façade. Now
beautifully rebuilt, La Fenice
shares the concert and opera
season with the Malibran
Theatre near Rialto.

Throughout the 19th century
the name of La Fenice was
linked with great Italian com-
posers. The many operatic
premières that took place here
include Verdi's *La Traviata*
(1853) and Rossini's *Tancredi*
(1813) and *Semiramide*
(1823). During the Austrian
Occupation *(see p48)* red,
white and green flowers, symbolizing the Italian flag, were
thrown on stage, to shouts of
"Viva Verdi" – the letters of
the composer's name standing
for Vittorio Emanuele Re
d'Italia. More recently, the
theatre saw premières of
Stravinsky's *The Rake's
Progress* (1951) and Britten's
Turn of the Screw (1954).

Shop in Campo Santo Stefano selling antiques and masks

Campo Santo Stefano ⓯

Map 6 F3. 🚢 *Accademia or
Sant'Angelo*.

Also known as Campo
Francesco Morosini after the
17th-century doge who once
lived here, this *campo* is one
of the most spacious in the
city. Bullfights were staged
until 1802, when a stand fell
and killed some of the spectators. It was also a venue for
balls and Carnival festivities.
Today it is a pleasantly informal square where children
play and visitors drink coffee
in open-air cafés.

The central statue is Nicolò
Tommaseo (1802–74), a
Dalmatian scholar who was
a central figure in the 1848
rebellion against the Austrians.

At the southern end of the
square the austere-looking
Palazzo Pisani, overlooking
the Campiello Pisani, has been
the Conservatory of Music
since the end of the 19th
century. Music wafts from
its open windows all through
the year. On the opposite
side of the square No. 2945,
Palazzo Loredan, is the home
of the Venetian Institute of
Sciences, Letters and Arts.

The ceiling of Santo Stefano, in the
form of a ship's keel

Santo Stefano ⓰

Campo Santo Stefano. **Map** 6 F2.
Tel 041 275 04 62. 🚢 *Accademia
or Sant'Angelo*. 🕙 10am–5pm
Mon–Sat. ⬤ 1 Jan, 25 Dec.
📷 Sacristy only. 🔲 📵 📷
www.chorusvenezia.org

Deconsecrated six times on
account of the violence that
took place within its walls,
Santo Stefano today is remarkably serene. Built in the 14th
century and radically altered
in the 15th, the church has a
notable carved portal by Bartolomeo Bon and a campanile
with a typical Venetian tilt. The
interior has a splendid ship's
keel ceiling, carved tie-beams
and tall pillars of Veronese
marble. The most notable
works of art, including some
paintings by Tintoretto, are
housed in the damp sacristy.

La Fenice, rebuilt after it was destroyed by fire in 1996

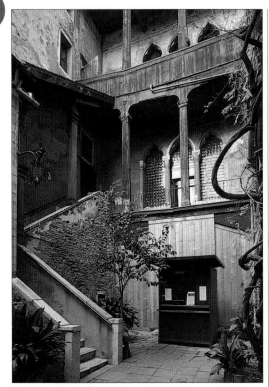

Courtyard of the Palazzo Pesaro, where Fortuny lived

Museo Fortuny ⑰

Palazzo Pesaro degli Orfei, Campo San Beneto, San Marco 3958. **Map** 6 F2. **Tel** 041 520 09 95. 🚏 Sant'Angelo. 🕐 10am–6pm Wed–Mon. 📷 🚫 www.museiciviciveneziani.it

Known principally for his fantastic pleated silk dresses, Fortuny was also a painter, sculptor, set designer, photographer and scientist. One of his inventions was the Fortuny Dome which is used in theatre performances to create the illusion of sky.

Mariano Fortuny y Madrazo, or Don Mariano as he liked to be called, was born in 1871 in Granada and moved to Venice in 1889. In the early 20th century he purchased the Palazzo Pesaro, a late Gothic *palazzo* that had originally been owned by the fabulously rich and influential Pesaro family. Fortuny spent the remainder of his life here and both the house and its contents were bequeathed to the city by his wife in 1956.

The large rooms and *portego* make a splendid and appropriate setting for the precious Fortuny fabrics. Woven with gold and silver threads, these were created by Fortuny's reintroduction of Renaissance techniques and use of ancient dyes. The collection also includes paintings by Fortuny (less impressive than the fabrics), decorative panels and a few of the finely pleated, clinging silk dresses regarded as a milestone in early 20th-century women's fashion.

San Salvatore ⑱

Campo San Salvatore. **Map** 7 B1. **Tel** 041 523 67 17. 🚏 Rialto. 🕐 9am–noon, 3–7pm Mon–Sat, 3–7pm Sun.

The interior of this church is an excellent example of Venetian Renaissance architecture. If the main door is closed visitors can enter by the side entrance, which is squeezed between shops along the Mercerie. The present church was designed by Giorgio Spavento in the early 16th century, and continued by Tullio Lombardo and Jacopo Sansovino. The pictorial highlight is Titian's *Annunciation* (1566) over the third altar on the right. Nearby, Sansovino's monument to Doge Francesco Venier (1556–61) is one of several Mannerist tombs in the church.

On the high altar is Titian's *Transfiguration of Christ* (1560). The end of the right transept is dominated by a vast monument to Caterina Cornaro, Queen of Cyprus *(see p43)*. Executed by the sculptor Bernardino Contino in 1580–84, the tomb shows the queen handing over her kingdom to the doge.

Campo San Bartolomeo ⑲

Map 7 B1. 🚏 Rialto.

Close to the Rialto, the square of San Bartolomeo bustles with life, particularly in the early evening when young Venetians rendezvous here. They meet at cafés, bars or by the statue of Carlo Goldoni (1707–93), Venice's prolific and most celebrated playwright. His statue, in a fitting spot for a writer who drew his inspiration from daily social intercourse, is by Antonio del Zotto (1883).

The beautiful Renaissance interior of the church of San Salvatore

St George and Dragon bas-relief on a corner of the Mercerie

Mercerie ②⓪

Map 7 B2. 🚊 San Marco or Rialto.

Divided into the Merceria dell'Orologio, Merceria di San Zulian and Merceria di San Salvatore, this is, and always has been, a principal shopping thoroughfare. Linking Piazza San Marco with the Rialto, it is made from a string of narrow, bustling alleys, lined by small shops and boutiques. The 17th-century English author John Evelyn described it as "the most delicious streete in the World for the sweetnesse of it … tapisstry'd as it were, with Cloth of Gold, rich Damasks & other silk". He wrote of perfumers, apothecary shops and nightingales in cages. Today all this has been replaced with fashions, footwear and glass.

At the southern end, the relief over the first archway on the left portrays the woman who in 1310 accidentally stopped a revolt. She dropped her pestle out of the window, killing the standard-bearer of a rebel army. They retreated, and the woman was given a guarantee that her rent would never be raised.

San Zulian ②①

Campo San Zulian. **Map** 7 B2.
Tel 041 523 53 83. 🚊 San Marco.
⬤ 8:30am–7pm daily. 🔺 in English: 11:30am daily.

On the busy Mercerie, the church of San Zulian (or Giuliano) provides a refuge from the crowded alleys. Its interior features gilded woodwork, 16th- and 17th-century paintings, and sculpture. The central panel of the frescoed ceiling portrays *The Apotheosis of St Julian*, painted in 1585 by Palma il Giovane. The 16th-century church façade was designed by Sansovino and paid for by the rich and immodest physician Tommaso Rangone. His bronze statue stands out against the white Istrian stone walls.

Bronze statue of Tommaso Rangone

San Giorgio Maggiore ②②

Map 8 D4. **Tel** 041 522 78 27. 🚊 San Giorgio. ⬤ 9:30am–12:30pm, 2:30–4:30pm (later in summer). **Campanile** ⬤ 9:30am–12:30pm, 2:30–4:30pm (later in summer). 🎫 **Foundation Tel** 041 524 01 19. ⬤ Sat & Sun; Mon–Fri by appt. 🎫 www.cini.it

Appearing like a stage set across the water from the Piazzetta, the little island of San Giorgio Maggiore has been captured on canvas countless times.

The church and monastery, built between 1559–80, are among Andrea Palladio's greatest architectural achievements. The church's temple front and the spacious, serene interior with its perfect proportions and cool beauty are typically Palladian in that they are modelled on the Classical style of ancient Rome. Within the church, the major works of art are the two late Tintorettos on the chancel walls:

The Last Supper and *Gathering of the Manna* (both 1594). In the Chapel of the Dead is his last work, *The Deposition* (1592–4), finished by his son Domenico.

The top of the tall campanile, reached by a lift, affords a superb panorama of the city and lagoon.

Centuries ago Benedictine monks occupied the original monastery, which was rebuilt in the 13th century following an earthquake. It later became a centre of learning and a residence for eminent foreign visitors. Following the Fall of the Republic in 1797 (*see p48*) the monastery was suppressed and its treasures plundered.

In 1829 the island became a free port, and in 1851 the headquarters of the artillery. By this time it had changed out of recognition. The complex regained its role as an active cultural centre when the monastery, embracing Palladio's cloisters, refectory and library, was purchased in 1951 by Count Vittorio Cini (*see p134*). Today it is a thriving centre of Venetian culture, with international events and exhibitions. There is also an evocative open-air theatre.

Cloisters designed by Palladio in the monastery of San Giorgio Maggiore

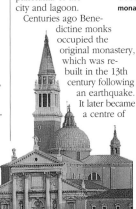

Palladio's church of San Giorgio Maggiore on the island of the same name

SAN POLO AND SANTA CROCE

The *sestieri* of San Polo and Santa Croce, bordered by the upper sweep of the Grand Canal, were both named after churches which stood within their boundaries. The first inhabitants are said to have settled on the cluster of small islands called *Rivus Altus* (high bank) or Rialto. When markets were established in the 11th century, the quarter became the commercial hub of Venice. San Polo is still one of the liveliest *sestieri* of the city, with its market stalls, small shops and

Shuttered window in Campo Sant'Aponal

local bars. The bustle of the market gives way to a maze of narrow alleys opening on to squares. Focal points are the spacious Campo San Polo, the Frari church and the neighbouring Scuola di San Rocco. Santa Croce for the most part is a *sestiere* of very narrow, tightly packed streets and squares where you will see the humbler side of Venetian life. Its grandest *palazzi* line the Grand Canal. Less alluring is the Piazzale Roma, the city's giant car park, lying to the west.

SIGHTS AT A GLANCE

Churches
San Cassiano ❹
San Giacomo dell'Orio ❹
San Giacomo di Rialto ❷
San Giovanni Evangelista ❸
San Nicolò da Tolentino ❷
San Pantalon ❶
San Polo ❻
San Rocco ❿
San Stae ❻
Santa Maria Gloriosa dei Frari pp102–3 ❽

Museums and Galleries
Ca' Pesaro ❽
Casa di Goldoni ❼
Fondaco dei Turchi (Natural History Museum) ❺
Palazzo Mocenigo ❼
Scuola Grande di San Rocco pp106–7 ❾

Streets and Squares
Campo San Polo ❺

Bridges
Rialto Bridge ❶

Markets
Rialto Markets ❸

KEY

▮ Street-by-Street map
See pp98–9

🚊 *Vaporetto* boarding point

🚶 *Traghetto* crossing

0 metres   250
0 yards   250

◁ **Ponte del Megio, in a quiet corner of Santa Croce**

Street-by-Street: San Polo

The Rialto bridge and markets make this a magnet for tourists. Traditionally the city's commercial quarter, it was here that bankers, brokers and merchants conducted their affairs. Streets are no longer lined with stalls selling spices and fine fabrics, but the food markets and pasta shops are a colourful sight. The old-fashioned standing-only bars called *bacari* are packed with locals. In contrast, Riva del Vin to the south, by the Grand Canal, is strictly tourist territory.

San Cassiano
Inside this church is a carved altar (1696) and a Crucifixion *by Tintoretto (1568)* ❹

Ponte Storto
is crooked, like many bridges in the city. It leads under a portico to Calle Stretta, a narrow alley that is only 1 m (3 ft) wide in places.

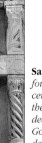

Sant'Aponal,
founded in the 11th century, rebuilt in the 15th, is now deconsecrated. Gothic reliefs decorate the façade.

Riva del Vin,
where wine was offloaded from boats, is one of the few accessible quaysides along the Grand Canal.

San Silvestro

STAR SIGHTS

★ Rialto Markets

★ Rialto Bridge

For hotels and restaurants in this region see pp228–33 and pp242–7

★ **Rialto Markets**
*The Rialto markets have been in
operation for centuries. The Pescheria
(above) sells fresh fish and seafood, and
the Erberia sells fruit and vegetables* ❸

LOCATOR MAP
See Street Finder, maps 2, 3, 7

**The statue of Gobbo
of the Rialto**, the
hunchback, was
sculpted in 1541
(see p100).

San Giacomo di Rialto
*Since its installation in 1410,
the clock on this church has
been a notoriously poor
time-keeper* ❷

KEY

− − − Suggested route

| 0 metres | 75 |
| 0 yards | 75 |

Calle della Madonna
looks distinctly
medieval with its
overhanging first
floors.

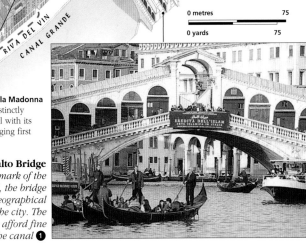

★ **Rialto Bridge**
*A beloved landmark of the
Grand Canal, the bridge
marks the geographical
centre of the city. The
balustrades afford fine
views of the canal* ❶

Rialto Bridge ❶

Ponte di Rialto. **Map** 7 A1. 🚤 *Rialto*.

The Rialto Bridge has been a busy part of the city for centuries. At any time of day, you will find crowds jostling on the bridge, browsing for souvenirs or taking a break to watch the constant swirl of activity on the Grand Canal from the bridge's balustrades.

Stone bridges were built in Venice as early as the 12th century, but it was not until 1588, after the collapse, decay or sabotage of earlier wooden structures, that a solid stone bridge was designed for the Rialto. One of the early wood crossings collapsed in 1444 under the weight of spectators at the wedding ceremony of the Marchese di Ferrara.

Vittore Carpaccio's painting *The Healing of the Madman* (1496, *see p133*) in the Accademia shows the fourth bridge – a rickety-looking structure with a drawbridge for the tall-masted galleys. By the 16th century this was in a sad state

Busy canalside restaurant near the Rialto Bridge

of decay and a competition was held for the design of a new bridge to be built in stone. Michelangelo, Andrea Palladio and Jacopo Sansovino were among the eminent contenders, but after months of deliberation it was the aptly named Antonio da Ponte who won the commission. The bridge was built between 1588 and 1591 and, until 1854, when the Accademia Bridge was constructed, this remained the only means of crossing the Grand Canal on foot.

San Giacomo di Rialto ❷

Campo San Giacomo, San Polo. **Map** 3 A5. **Tel** 041 522 47 45. 🚤 *Rialto, Rialto Mercato, San Silvestro*. ⏰ 9:30am–noon, 4–5pm Mon–Sat, 11am–noon Sun. ⛪ during mass.

The first church to stand on this site was allegedly founded in the 5th century, making it the oldest church in Venice. The present building dates from the 11th–12th centuries, with major restoration in 1601. The original Gothic portico and huge 24-hour clock are the most striking features.

The crouching stone figure on the far side of the square is the so-called Gobbo (hunchback) of the Rialto. In the 16th century this was a welcome sight for minor offenders who were forced to run the gauntlet from Piazza San Marco to this square at the Rialto.

Traghetto **ferrying passengers across to the Erberia**

Rialto Markets ❸

San Polo. **Map** 3 A5. 🚤 *Rialto*. **Erberia** *(fruit and vegetable market)* until 12:30pm Mon–Sat. **Pescheria** *(fish market)* until 12:30pm Tue–Sat.

Venetians have come to the Erberia to buy fresh produce for hundreds of years. Heavily laden barges arrive at dawn and offload their crates on to the quayside by the Grand Canal. Local produce includes red radicchio from Treviso, and succulent asparagus and baby artichokes from the islands of Sant'Erasmo and Vignole *(see p149)*. In the adjoining fish market are sole, sardines, skate, squid, crabs, clams and other species of seafood and fish. To see it all in full swing you must arrive early in the morning – by noon the vendors are starting to pack up.

RIALTO BRIDGE
Until the 19th century this was the only link between the two sides of the Grand Canal.

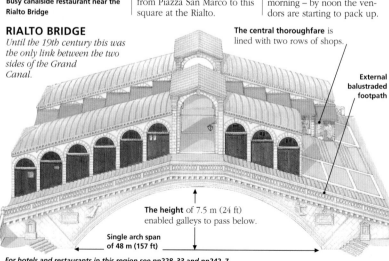

The central thoroughfare is lined with two rows of shops.

External balustraded footpath

The height of 7.5 m (24 ft) enabled galleys to pass below.

Single arch span of 48 m (157 ft)

San Cassiano ❹

Campo San Cassiano, San Polo.
Map 2 F5. *Tel 041 721 408.*
San Stae. 9am–noon, 5–7pm
Tue–Sat. during mass.

The Medieval Church of San
Cassiano is a bizarre mix of
architectural styles. Of the
original church, which was
restored in the 19th century,
only the campanile survives.
The highlight of the interior is
Jacopo Tintoretto's immensely
powerful *Crucifixion* (1568),
which is in the sacristy.

The campo in which the
church stands was notorious
for prostitutes in the 1500s.

Campo San Polo ❺

Map 6 F1. San Silvestro.

The spacious square of San
Polo has traditionally been
host to spectacular events. As
far back as the 15th century it
was the venue for festivities,
masquerades, ceremonies,
balls and bullbaiting.

The most dramatic event
was the assassination of
Lorenzino de' Medici in 1548.
He had taken refuge in Venice
after brutally killing his cousin
Alessandro, Duke of Florence.
Lorenzino was stabbed in the
square by two assassins who
were in the service of Cosimo
de' Medici, and both were
handsomely rewarded by
the Florentine duke.

On the eastern side of the
square is the beautiful Gothic
Palazzo Soranzo. This was
originally two palaces – the
one on the left is the older.
The building is still owned
by the Soranzo family.

Palazzo Corner Mocenigo,
which is situated in the
northwest corner (No. 2128),
was once the residence of
the eccentric English writer
Frederick Rolfe (1860–1913),
alias Baron Corvo. He
was thrown out of his
lodgings when his
English hostess read
his manuscript of *The
Desire and Pursuit
of the Whole* – a
cruel satirization
of English society
in Venice.

A detail of the Gothic façade of Palazzo Soranzo, Campo San Polo

Since 1979 the square has
enjoyed a revival of Carnival
festivities. This wide open
space is also a haven for
local youngsters, who ride
bikes, rollerskate or play
football. Such activities
would not have gone down
well in the 17th century –
a plaque on the apse of
the church, dated 1611,
forbids all games (or selling
merchandise) on pain of
prison, galley service or exile.

San Polo ❻

Campo San Polo. **Map** 6 F1.
Tel 041 275 04 62. San Silvestro.
10am–5pm Mon–Sat.
1 Jan, 25 Dec.
www.chorusvenezia.org

Founded in the 9th century,
rebuilt in the 15th and
revamped in the early 19th in
Neo-Classical style, the church
of San Polo lacks any sense of
homogeneity. Yet it is worth
visiting for individual features
such as the lovely Gothic
portal and the Romanesque
lions at the foot of the
14th-century campanile – one
holds a serpent between its
paws, the other a human head.

Inside, follow the signs for
the *Via Crucis del Tiepolo* –
fourteen canvases of the
Stations of the Cross

by Giandomenico Tiepolo.
The church also has paintings by Veronese, Palma
il Giovane (the Younger)
and a dark and dramatic
Last Supper by Tintoretto.

Carlo Goldoni 1707–93

Casa di Goldoni ❼

Palazzo Centani, Calle dei Nomboli,
San Polo 2794. **Map** 6 E1. *Tel 041
275 93 25.* San Tomà. 10am–
4pm Thu–Tue (to 5pm Apr–Oct).
public hols.
www.museiciviciveneziani.it

Carlo Goldoni, one of the
city's favourite sons, wrote
over 250 comedies, many
based on Commedia dell'Arte
figures. Goldoni was born in
the beautiful Gothic Palazzo
Centani (or Zantani) in 1707.
The house was left to the
city in 1931 and is now a
centre for theatrical studies
and has a collection
of theatrical memora-
bilia. The enchanting
courtyard has a 15th-
century open stairway
and a magnificent
wellhead, which
features carved lions
and a coat of arms
bearing a hedgehog.

A lion at the foot of the campanile, Church of San Polo

Santa Maria Gloriosa dei Frari ●

Known by all simply as the Frari (a corruption of *Frati*, meaning brothers), this huge, plain Gothic church dwarfs the eastern section of San Polo. The first church was built by Franciscan friars in 1250–1338, but was replaced by a larger building which was completed by the mid-15th century. The interior is striking for its sheer size and for the quality of its works of art. These include masterpieces by Titian and Giovanni Bellini *(see pp26–7)*, a statue by Donatello and a number of imposing monuments to famous Venetians.

The campanile
is 80 m (262 ft) high, the tallest in the city after that of San Marco.

Foscari Monument
Doge Foscari set a record by reigning for 34 years (1423–57).

★ **Assumption of the Virgin**
Titian's glowing and spectacular work (1518) inevitably draws the eye through the monk's choir towards the altar.

Rood Screen *(1475)*
Pietro Lombardo and Bartolomeo Bon carved this and decorated it with marble figures.

Madonna di Ca' Pesaro (1526) shows Titian's mastery of light and colour.

★ **Monks' Choir**
This consists of three-tiered stalls (1468), carved with bas-reliefs of saints and Venetian city scenes.

FLOORPLAN

Exploration of the huge interior can be daunting. The floorplan pinpoints 12 highlights that should not be missed.

KEY TO FLOORPLAN

1 Canova's tomb
2 Monument to Titian
3 Titian's *Madonna di Ca' Pesaro*
4 Choir stalls
5 Corner Chapel
6 Tomb of Monteverdi
7 Tomb of Doge Nicolò Tron
8 High altar with Titian's *Assumption of the Virgin*
9 Tomb of Doge Francesco Foscari
10 Donatello's *John the Baptist* (c.1450)
11 B Vivarini's altar painting (1474), Bernardo Chapel
12 Giovanni Bellini's *Madonna Enthroned with Saints* (1488)

VISITORS' CHECKLIST

Campo dei Frari. **Map** 6 D1. **Tel** 041 275 04 62. 🚊 San Tomà. 🕐 9am–6pm Mon–Sat, 1–6pm Sun & religious hols. 🔴 1 Jan, 25 Dec. 🎟️ except those attending mass. 📷 📱 ✝️ frequent. **www**.chorusvenezia.org

Monument to Titian *(1853)*
Canova's pupils, Luigi and Pietro Zandomeneghi, built this monument to Titian in place of the one conceived by Canova himself.

The former monastery, which houses the State Archives, has two cloisters, one in the style of Sansovino, another designed by Palladio.

Entrance

Canova's Tomb
Canova designed, but never actually made, a Neo-Classical marble pyramid like this as a monument for Titian. After Canova's death in 1822, his pupils used a similar design for their master's tomb.

STAR FEATURES

★ Monks' Choir

★ Assumption of the Virgin by Titian

Scuola Grande di San Rocco ❾

See pp106–7.

San Rocco ❿

Campo San Rocco, San Polo. **Map** 6 D1. **Tel** 041 523 48 64. 🚤 *San Tomà*. ⏱ *9:30am–5:30pm daily.*

Sharing the little square with the celebrated Scuola Grande di San Rocco is the church of the same name. Designed by Bartolomeo Bon in 1489 and largely rebuilt in 1725, the exterior is a mix of architectural styles. The façade was added in 1765–71.

Inside, the main interest lies in Tintoretto's paintings in the chancel, which depict scenes from the life of St Roch, patron saint of contagious diseases. Of these the most notable is *St Roch Curing the Plague Victims* (1549).

San Pantalon ⓫

Campo San Pantalon, Dorsoduro. **Map** 6 D2. **Tel** 041 523 58 93. 🚤 *San Tomà, Piazzale Roma.* ⏱ *10am–noon, 1–3pm Mon–Sat (9–10:30pm Thu).*

Fumiani's ceiling painting (1680–1704), San Pantalon

The overwhelming feature of this late 17th-century church is the painted ceiling, dark, awe-inspiring and remarkable for its illusionistic

effects. The ceiling comprises a total of 40 scenes (admirers claim this makes it the world's largest work of art on canvas), depicting the martyrdom and apotheosis of the physician St Pantalon. The artist, Gian Antonio Fumiani, took 24 years (1680–1704) to achieve this masterpiece, but then he allegedly fell to his death from the scaffolding.

Paolo Veronese's emotive painting *St Pantalon Healing a Boy* (second chapel on the right) was his final work of art (1587). To see Antonio Vivarini and Giovanni d'Alemagna's *Coronation of the Virgin* (1444) and *The Annunciation* (1350), attributed to Paolo Veneziano, ask the custodian for access to the Chapel of the Holy Nail (*Cappella del Sacro Chiodo*).

San Nicolò da Tolentino ⓬

Campo dei Tolentini, Santa Croce. **Map** 5 C1. **Tel** 041 522 21 60. 🚤 *Piazzale Roma.* ⏱ *8am–noon, 4–7pm daily.* 🚫 *during mass.*

Close to Piazzale Roma (*see p271*), San Nicolò da Tolentino is an imposing 17th-century church with a Classical portico. The interior, decorated with 17th-century paintings, is the resting place of Francesco Morosini (d.1678), the Venetian patriarch.

A cannonball embedded in the façade is a memento of an Austrian bombardment during the siege of 1849.

San Giovanni Evangelista ⓭

Campiello de la Scuola, San Polo. **Map** 6 D1. **Tel** 041 71 82 34. 🚤 *San Tomà.* ⏱ *by appointment; church is open for temporary art exhibitions.*

A confraternity of flagellents founded the Scuola of St John the Evangelist in 1261. The complex, just north of the Frari (*see pp102–3*), has a church, *scuola* and courtyard. Separating the square from the street is Pietro Lombardo's elegant white and grey screen and portal (1480), and in the

Lombardo's marble screen and portal, San Giovanni Evangelista

arch crowning the portal there is a carved eagle, which is the symbol representing St John the Evangelist.

The main hall of the Scuola is reached via a splendid 15th-century double stairway by Mauro Coducci (1498). Large, dark canvases decorate the ceiling and walls of the 18th-century hall. The Scuola's greatest art treasure, the cycle of paintings depicting *The Stories of the Cross*, is now on display in the Accademia gallery (*see p133*). It formerly embellished the oratory (off the main hall) where the Reliquary of the True Cross is still carefully preserved.

San Giacomo dell'Orio ⓮

Campo San Giacomo dell'Orio, Santa Croce. **Map** 2 E5. **Tel** 041 275 04 62. 🚤 *Riva di Biasio or San Stae.* ⏱ *10am–5pm Mon–Sat.* 🚫 *1 Jan, 25 Dec.* 🌐 📷 🚫

This church is a focal point of a quiet quarter of Santa Croce. The name "dell'Orio" (locally dall'Orio) may derive from a laurel tree (*alloro*) that once stood near the church.

Founded in the 9th century, rebuilt in 1225 and repeatedly modified, the church is a mix of architectural styles. The campanile, basilica ground plan and Byzantine columns survive from the 13th century. The ship's keel roof and the columns are from the Gothic period, and the apses are Renaissance. The sacristy ceiling was decorated by Veronese and there are some interesting altar paintings.

Fondaco dei Turchi ⑮

Canal Grande, Santa Croce 1730.
Map 2 E4. **Tel** *041 275 02 06.*
🚢 *San Stae.* ⬜ *9am–5pm Wed,*
10am–6pm Sat & Sun. 📷

The building that now contains Venice's natural history museum has a chequered history. In the 13th century it was one of the largest *palazzi* on the Grand Canal. In 1381 it was bought by the state for the Dukes of Ferrara and its lavishly decorated rooms were used for banquets and state functions. In 1621 the Turks set up a warehouse *(fondaco)*, and the spacious portico was used for loading merchandise. As commerce with the Orient declined further, the structure fell into disrepair until, roused by Ruskin's passionate interest, the Austrians began restoration work in the 1850s.

Since 1924 the Fondaco has housed the natural history museum (Museo di Storia Naturale). There is a collection of stuffed animals, crustacea and dinosaur fossils and a section on lagoon life. Prize exhibits include a skeleton of an *Ouranosaurus nigeriensis,* 7 m (23 ft) long and 3.6 m (12 ft) tall, and a fossil of a *Sarcosuchus imperator* – an ancestor of the crocodile.

Ouranosaurus
skeleton in
the Fondaco
dei Turchi

San Stae ⑯

Campo San Stae, Santa Croce.
Map 2 F4. **Tel** *041 275 04 62.*
🚢 *San Stae.* ⬜ *10am–5pm Mon–*
Sat. ⬤ *1 Jan, 25 Dec.* 📷 🎧 📷

Restored in 1977–8 by the Pro Venezia Foundation, San Stae (or Sant'Eustachio) has a spick-and-span sculpted

façade. It was built in 1709 by Domenico Rossi. Works by Piazzetta, Tiepolo and other 18th-century artists decorate the chancel. Near the second altar on the left is the bust of Antonio Foscarini, executed for treason in 1622 but pardoned the following year.

One of the finely furnished rooms of Palazzo Mocenigo

Palazzo Mocenigo ⑰

Salizzada San Stae, Santa Croce
1992. **Map** 2 F5. **Tel** *041 72 17 98.*
🚢 *San Stae.* ⬜ *10am–5pm Tue–Sun*
(Nov–Mar: to 4pm). ⬤ *1 Jan, 1 May,*
25 Dec. 📷 📷 📷

One of the oldest Venetian families, the Mocenigos produced seven doges. There were various branches of the family, one of which resided in this handsome 17th-century mansion. Count Alvise Nicolò Mocenigo, the last of this particular branch, died in 1954, bequeathing the palace to the Comune di Venezia (city authorities). The entrance façade is unremarkable, but the interior is elegantly furnished and gives you a rare opportunity of seeing inside a *palazzo* preserved more or less as it was in the 18th century. The frescoed ceilings and other works of art are celebrations of the family's achievements. The illustrious Mocenigos are portrayed in a frieze around the portego on the first floor.

The Museo del Tessuto e del Costume inside the house contains antique fabrics and exquisitely made costumes.

Ca' Pesaro ⑱

Canal Grande, Santa Croce 2076.
Map 2 F5. 🚢 *San Stae.* **Galleria**
d'Arte Moderna & Museo
Orientale Tel *041 72 11 27.*
⬜ *10am–6pm Tue–Sun (Nov–Mar:*
to 5pm); ticket office closes one hour
earlier. ⬤ *1 Jan, 1 May, 25 Dec.* 📷
📷 📷 📷 📷 combined ticket.

It took 58 years to complete this magnificent Baroque palace. Built for the Pesaro family, it was the masterpiece of Baldassare Longhena, who worked on it until his death in 1682. Antonio Gaspari then took over Longhena's design, eventually completing the structure in 1710.

In the 19th century the Duchess of Bevilacqua La Masa bequeathed the palace to the city for exhibiting the works of unestablished Venetian artists. The Galleria d'Arte Moderna was founded in 1897. Today this features a permanent exhibition of work by artists such as Bonnard, Matisse, Miró, Klee, Klimt and Kandinsky, in addition to works by Italian artists of the 19th and 20th centuries.

The Museo Orientale has an idiosyncratic collection of Chinese and Japanese artifacts collected by the Count of Bardi during his 19th-century travels.

Gustav Klimt's *Salome*, Gallery of Modern Art, Ca' Pesaro

Scuola Grande di San Rocco 🄾

Founded in honour of St Roch (San Rocco), the Scuola was set up as a charitable institution for the sick. Construction began in 1515 under Bartolomeo Bon and was completed in 1549 by Scarpagnino, financed largely by donations from Venetians who believed that St Roch, the patron saint of contagious diseases, would save them from the plague. In 1564 Tintoretto *(see p140)* was commissioned to decorate the walls and ceilings of the Scuola. His remarkable cycle of paintings starts in the Sala dell'Albergo *(see Gallery Guide)*.

Pianta's caricature of Tintoretto

Restored main entrance to the Scuola di San Rocco

SALA DELL'ALBERGO

THE CRUCIFIXION
In this panorama of Calvary, Tintoretto reached a pitch of religious feeling never hitherto achieved in Venetian art.

A self-portrait was often a feature of Tintoretto's paintings.

The subsidiary figures are full of life but do not lessen the central drama.

Figure of Christ
The crucified figure of the Redeemer is raised and leaning, accentuating His divinity and saving grace.

A competition was held in 1564 to select an artist to paint the central ceiling panel of the Sala dell'Albergo in the Scuola. To the fury of his rivals, Tintoretto pre-empted his fellow competitors by installing his painting *in situ* prior to judging. He won the commission and was later made a member of the Scuola. Over the next 23 years, Tintoretto decorated the entire building.
   The series of paintings, completed in 1587, reveals Tintoretto's revolutionary use of light, mastery of foreshortening and visionary use of colour. The winning painting, *St Roch in Glory* ①, can be seen on the ceiling

of the Sala dell'Albergo. The most moving work in the cycle is the *Crucifixion* (1565) ②. Henry James wrote:"Surely no single picture contains more of human life; there is everything in it, including the most exquisite beauty." Of the paintings on the entrance wall, portraying the Passion of Christ, the most notable is *Christ Before Pilate* (1566–7) ③.

Sala dell'Albergo

UPPER HALL

Scarpagnino's great staircase (1544–6), decorated with two vast paintings commemorating the plague of 1630, leads to the Upper Hall. The biblical subjects on the walls and ceiling were painted in 1575–81. The ceiling paintings (viewed most comfortably with a hired mirror) portray scenes from the Old Testament. The three large central square paintings represent: *Moses Striking Water from the Rock* ④, *The Miracle of the Bronze Serpent* ⑤ and *The Gathering of the Manna* ⑥, all alluding to the Scuola's charitable aims in alleviating thirst, sickness and hunger respectively. All three paintings are crowded compositions with much violent movement. The vast wall paintings in the hall feature episodes from the

New Testament. The most striking paintings are *The Temptation of Christ* ⑦, which shows a handsome young Satan offering Christ two loaves of bread, and *Adoration of the Shepherds* ⑧. Like *The Temptation of Christ*, the *Adoration* is composed in two halves, with a female figure, shepherds and ox below, and the Holy Family and onlookers above.

The beautiful carvings below the paintings were added in the 17th century by Francesco Pianta. The allegorical figures include (near the altar) a caricature of Tintoretto with his palette and brushes, which is meant to represent Painting. Near the entrance to the Sala dell'Albergo you can see Titian's *Annunciation*. The easel painting *Christ Carrying the Cross* is attributed to Giorgione, though many believe it to be a Titian.

GROUND FLOOR HALL

The Flight into Egypt (1582–7) (detail)

This final cycle, executed in 1583–7, consists of eight paintings illustrating the life of Mary. The series starts with an *Annunciation*, and ends with an *Assumption*, which was restored some years ago. The tranquil scenes of *St Mary of Egypt* ⑨, *St Mary Magdalene* ⑩ and *The Flight into Egypt* ⑪, painted when Tintoretto was in his late sixties, are remarkable for their serenity. This is portrayed most lucidly by the Virgin's isolated spiritual contemplation in the *St Mary of Egypt*. In all three paintings, the landscapes, rendered with rapid strokes, play a major role.

The Temptation of Christ, 1578–81 (detail)

GALLERY GUIDE

The paintings, which unfortunately are not well lit, have no labels, but a useful plan of the Scuola is available (in several languages) free of charge at the entrance.
To see the paintings in chronological order, start in the Sala dell'Albergo (off the Upper Hall), followed by the Upper Hall and finally the Ground Floor Hall.

Upper Hall   **Ground Floor Hall**

Main entrance

KEY

☐ Wall paintings

☐ Ceiling paintings

CASTELLO

The largest *sestiere* of the city, Castello stretches from San Marco and Cannaregio in the west to the modern blocks of Sant'Elena in the east. The area takes its name from the 8th-century fortress that once stood on what is now San Pietro, the island which for centuries was the religious focus of the city. The church here was the episcopal see from the 9th century and the city's cathedral from 1451

Water stoup, Santa Maria Formosa

to 1807. The industrial hub of Castello was the Arsenale, where the great shipyards produced Venice's indomitable fleet of warships. Castello's most popular and solidly commercial area is the Riva degli Schiavoni promenade. Behind the waterfront it is comparatively quiet, characterized by narrow alleys, elegantly faded *palazzi* and fine churches, including the great Santi Giovanni e Paolo *(see pp116–17)*.

SIGHTS AT A GLANCE

Churches
La Pietà ❸
San Francesco della Vigna ⓮
San Giorgio dei Greci ❷
San Giovanni in Bragora ⓱
San Lorenzo ⓯
Santi Giovanni e Paolo pp116–17 ⓬
San Zaccaria ❶

Historic Buildings and Monuments
Arsenale ⓳
Hotel Danieli ❹
Ospedaletto ⓭
Statue of Colleoni ❿

Streets, Bridges and Squares
Campo Santa Maria Formosa ❾
Ponte della Paglia and Bridge of Sighs ❻
Riva degli Schiavoni ❺

Walk
Exploring Eastern Castello ⓴

Museums, Galleries and Scuole
Fondazione Querini Stampalia ❽
Museo Diocesano d'Arte Sacra ❼
Museo Storico Navale ⓲
Scuola di San Giorgio degli Schiavoni ⓰
Scuola Grande di San Marco ⓫

KEY

▨ Street-by-Street map
   See pp110–11

🚏 *Vaporetto* boarding point

0 metres   250
0 yards   250

◁ **Bas relief on Rio Terrà Garibaldi, eastern Castello**

Street-by-Street: Castello

13th-century Madonna in the Museo Diocesano

A stroll along the Riva degli Schiavoni is an integral part of a visit to Venice. Glorious views of San Giorgio Maggiore compensate for the commercialized aspects of the quayside: souvenir stalls, excursion touts and an overabundance of tourists. Associations with literary figures are legion. Petrarch lived at No. 4145, Henry James was offered "dirty" lodgings at No. 4161, and Ruskin stayed at the Hotel Danieli. Inland, the quiet, unassuming streets and squares of Castello provide a contrast to the bustling waterfront.

★ **Museo Diocesano**
The cloisters of the ancient Benedictine monastery of Sant'Apollonia herald the museum ⑦

Palazzo Trevisan-Cappello, used as a showroom for Murano glass, was the home of Bianca Cappello, wife of Francesco de' Medici.

Ponte della Paglia and Bridge of Sighs
Crowds throng the Istrian stone Ponte della Paglia – the "straw bridge" – for the best views of the neighbouring Bridge of Sighs, the covered bridge that links the Doge's Palace to the old prisons ⑥

Riva degli Schiavoni
This paved quayside was established over 600 years ago, and widened in 1782 ⑤

San Zaccaria Paglia

San Zaccaria Danieli

Hotel Danieli
Joseph da Niel, after whom this hotel was named, turned the Palazzo Dandolo into a haunt for 19th-century writers and artists ④

STAR SIGHTS

★ Museo Diocesano

★ San Zaccaria

★ La Pietà

Palazzo Priuli,
*overlooking the quiet
Fondamenta Osmarin, is a
fine Venetian Gothic palace.
The corner window is
particularly beautiful, but the
early 16th-century façade
frescoes have long since
disappeared.*

LOCATOR MAP
See Street Finder, maps 7, 8

San Giorgio dei Greci
*Subsidence is the cause of the
city's tilting bell-towers: San
Giorgio dei Greci's looks
particularly perilous* ❷

★ San Zaccaria
*Coducci added Renaissance
details such as this panel to
the Gothic façade* ❶

KEY

— — — Suggested route

0 metres	75
0 yards	75

Pensione Wildner
is where Henry
James completed
Portrait of a Lady
(1881).

**The Statue of
Vittorio
Emanuele II,**
*the first king
of a united Italy, was
sculpted by Ettore
Ferrari in 1887.*

★ La Pietà
*In Vivaldi's day, the church became
famous for the superb quality of its
musical performances* ❸

San Zaccaria ❶

Campo San Zaccaria. **Map** 8 D2.
Tel 041 522 12 57. 🚤 *San Zaccaria.*
🕐 *10am–noon, 4–6pm Mon–Sat,
4–6pm Sun & public hols.* 🎨 *Chapels
& Crypt.* 📷

Set in a quiet square a stone's
throw from the Riva degli
Schiavoni, this church blends
Flamboyant Gothic and
Classical Renaissance styles.
Founded in the 9th century,
San Zaccaria was completely
rebuilt between 1444 and
1515. Antonio Gambello
began the façade in Gothic
style and, when Gambello
died in 1481, Mauro Coducci
completed the upper section,
adding all the Classical detail.
    The adjoining Benedictine
convent, which had close
links with the church, became
quite notorious for the riotous
behaviour of its nuns. The
majority were from families
of Venetian nobility, many of
them sent to the convent to
avoid the expense of a dowry.
    Every Easter the doge came
with his entourage to San
Zaccaria – a custom which
originated as an expression
of gratitude to the nuns, who
had relinquished part of their
garden so that Piazza San
Marco could be enlarged.
    The artistic highlight of the
interior (illuminate with coins
in the meter) is Giovanni
Bellini's sumptuously coloured
and superbly serene *Madonna
and Child with Saints* (1505)
in the north aisle.
    On the right of the church
is a door to the Chapel of St
Athanasius which leads to the
Chapel of San Tarasio. The
chapel is decorated with vault
frescoes (1442) by Andrea del
Castagno of Florence, and

Gothic polyptychs painted
in 1443–4 by Antonio Vivarini
and Giovanni d'Alemagna. The
relics of eight doges lie buried
in the waterlogged crypt.

**Distant view of San Giorgio dei
Greci's tilting campanile**

San Giorgio dei Greci ❷

Map 8 D2. *Tel* 041 523 95 69.
🚤 *San Zaccaria.* 🕐 *9am–12:30pm,
2:30–5pm Mon & Wed–Sat,
9am–1pm Sun (for mass only).*
Museo dell'Icone *Tel* 041 522 65
81. 🕐 *9am–5pm daily.* 🎨 📷

The most remarkable feature
of this 16th-century Greek
church is the listing
campanile, which looks as if
it is about to topple into the
Rio dei Greci. Inside is the
matroneo – the gallery where,
in keeping with Greek Orthodox custom, the women sat
apart from the men. Note also
the iconostasis separating the
sanctuary from the nave. The
nearby Scuola di San Nicolò
dei Greci, redesigned in 1678,
is now the museum of icons
of the Hellenic Institute.

La Pietà ❸

Riva degli Schiavoni. **Map** 8 D2.
Tel 041 522 21 71. 🚤 *San Zaccaria.*
🕐 *10am–5pm Thu–Sun.*
www.pietavenezia.org

The church of La Pietà (or
Santa Maria della Visitazione)
dates from the 15th century.
It was rebuilt in 1745–1760
by Giorgio Massari, and the
Classical façade was added in
1906. The church has a cool,
elegant interior, with an oval
plan. The resplendent ceiling
fresco, *Triumph of Faith*
(1755), was painted by
Giambattista Tiepolo.
    The Pietà started its life as a
foundling home for orphans.
It proved so popular that a
warning plaque was set up
(still to be seen on the side
wall), threatening damnation
to parents who tried to pass
off their children as orphans.
    From 1703 until 1740
Antonio Vivaldi directed the
musical groups and wrote
numerous oratorios, cantatas
and vocal pieces for the Pietà
choir, and the church became
famous for its performances.
    The church is now a popular
venue for concerts, with a
strong emphasis on the music
of Vivaldi. These are held
throughout the year, usually
on Mondays and Thursdays.

**Bas relief on La Pietà's early
20th-century façade**

Hotel Danieli ❹

Riva degli Schiavoni 4196.
Map 7 C2. 🚤 *San Zaccaria.*
See also **Where to Stay** *p231.*

One of the most celebrated
hotels in Europe, the
Danieli's deep pink façade is
a landmark on the Riva degli
Schiavoni. Built in the 14th
century, it became famous as
the venue for the first opera
performed in Venice, Monteverdi's *Proserpina Rapita*

Detail from *The Nun's Parlour at San Zaccaria* by Francesco Guardi

(1630). The palace became a hotel in 1822 and soon gained popularity with the literary and artistic set. Its famous guests included Balzac, Proust, Dickens, Cocteau, Ruskin, Debussy and Wagner. In the 1830s Room 10 witnessed an episode in the love affair between the French poet and dramatist Alfred de Musset, and novelist George Sand: when de Musset fell ill after a surfeit of orgies, Sand ran off with her Venetian doctor.

Riva degli Schiavoni **5**

Map 8 D2. 🚤 *San Zaccaria.*

The sweeping promenade that forms the southern quayside of Castello was named after the traders from Dalmatia (Schiavonia) who used to moor their boats and barges here. For those who arrive in Venice by water, this long curving quayside is a spectacular introduction to the charms of the city.

At its western end, close to Piazza San Marco, the broad promenade teems during the day with tourists thronging around the souvenir stalls and people hurrying to and from the *vaporetto* stops. Nothing can detract, however, from the glorious views across the lagoon to the island of San Giorgio Maggiore *(see p95).*

The Riva degli Schiavoni has always been busy with boats. Canaletto's drawings in the 1740s and 1750s show the Riva bustling with gondolas, sailing boats and barges. The gondolas are still here, but it is also chock-a-block with water taxis, *vaporetti*, excursion boats and tugs. Naval ships and ocean liners can also often be seen.

The modern annexe of the Hotel Danieli caused a great furore when it was built in 1948. Intruding on a waterfront graced by fine Venetian palaces and mansions, its stark outline is still something of an eyesore. The annexe marks the spot where Doge Vitale Michiel II was

Riva degli Schiavoni – the city's most famous promenade

stabbed to death in 1172. Three centuries earlier, in 864, Doge Pietro Tradonico had suffered the same fate in nearby Campo San Zaccaria.

Ponte della Paglia and Bridge of Sighs **6**

Map 7 C2. 🚤 *San Zaccaria.*

The name of the Ponte della Paglia may derive from the boats that once moored here to off-load their cargoes of straw *(paglia)*. Originally built in 1360, the existing structure dates from 1847.

According to legend, the Bridge of Sighs, built in 1600 to link the Doge's Palace with the New Prisons, takes its name from the lamentations of the prisoners as they made their way over to the offices of the feared State Inquisitors. Access to the bridge is available to the public via the Doge's Palace *(see p87).*

Museo Diocesano d'Arte Sacra **7**

Sant'Apollonia, Ponte della Canonica, Castello 4312. **Map** 7 C2. **Tel** 041 522 91 66. 🚤 *San Zaccaria.* ⏱ *10am–5pm Thu–Tue.* ⬤ *public hols.* 🔲 *includes entry to cloisters.*

One of the architectural gems of Venice, the cloister of Sant'Apollonia is the only Romanesque building in the city. Only a few steps from St Mark's, the cloister provides a quiet retreat from the hubbub of the Piazza.

The monastery was once the home of Benedictine monks, but its non-ecclesiastical uses have been manifold. In 1976 its cloisters became the home of the diocesan museum of sacred art, founded in order to provide a haven for works of art from closed or deconsecrated churches. The collection includes paintings, statues, crucifixes and many pieces of valuable silver. The museum has two workshops, staffed by volunteers who restore the paintings and statues. The collection is ever-changing, but among the major permanent exhibits are works by Luca Giordano (1634–1705), which came from the Church of Sant'Aponal, and a 16th-century wood and crystal tabernacle.

Ponte della Paglia behind the Bridge of Sighs

Fondazione Querini Stampalia ❽

Campo Santa Maria Formosa, 5252 Castello. **Map** 7 C1. *Tel* 041 271 14 11. 🚤 San Zaccaria. **Palace** ⬜ 10am–7pm Tue–Sun (to 10pm Fri & Sat). 🔲 🖼 📷 💈 **Library** ⬜ 10am–11pm Tue–Sat, 10am–7pm Sun. **www**.querinistampalia.it

The large Palazzo Querini Stampalia was commissioned in the 16th century by the descendants of the old Venetian Querini family. Great art lovers, they filled the palace with fine paintings.

In 1868 the last member of the dynasty bequeathed the palace and the family collection of art to the foundation that bears his name. The paintings include works by Giovanni Bellini, Giambattista Tiepolo, and some vignettes by Pietro and Alessandro Longhi. The library on the first floor, which is open to the public, contains over 200,000 books.

Campo Santa Maria Formosa ❾

Map 7 C1. 🚤 Rialto, Fondamente Nuove. **Church** *Tel* 041 275 04 62. ⬜ 10am–5pm Mon–Sat. 🚫 1 Jan, 25 Dec. 🔲 🖼 🚫 **www**.chorusvenezia.org

Large, rambling and flanked by handsome palaces, this market square is one of the most characteristic *campi* of Venice. On the southern side is the church of Santa Maria Formosa, distinctive for its swelling apses. Built on ancient foundations, the church was designed by Mauro Coducci in 1492 but took over a century to assume its current form. Unusually, it has two main façades – one overlooking the *campo*, the other the canal. The campanile was added in 1688. Its most notable feature is the truly grotesque stone face that decorates its foot.

Inside, Palma il Vecchio's polyptych *St Barbara and Saints* (c.1523) ranks among the great Venetian master-pieces and looks particularly splendid since its restoration

by the American Save Venice organization. Palma's por-trayal of the handsome and dignified figure of St Barbara glorifies Venice's ideal female beauty. She is surrounded by saints, with a central lunette of the *pietà* above. St Barbara was the patron saint of soldiers: in wartime they prayed to her for protection, in victory they came for thanksgiving.

Statue of Colleoni ❿

Campo Santi Giovanni e Paolo. **Map** 3 C5. 🚤 Ospedale Civile.

Bartolomeo Colleoni, the famous *condottiere* or commander of mercenaries, left his fortune to the Republic on condition that his statue was placed in front of San Marco. A prominent statue in the Piazza would have broken with precedent, so the Senate cunningly had Colleoni raised before the Scuola di San Marco instead of the basilica. A touch-stone of early Renaissance sculpture, the equestrian statue of the proud warrior (1481–8) is by the Florentine Andrea

Palma il Vecchio's *St Barbara* **in Santa Maria Formosa**

Statue of Bartolomeo Colleoni

Verrocchio and, after his death, was cast in bronze by Alessandro Leopardi. The statue has a strong sense of power and movement which arguably ranks it alongside works of Donatello.

Scuola Grande di San Marco ⓫

Campo Santi Giovanni e Paolo. **Map** 3 C5. 🚤 Ospedale Civile. **Library** *Tel* 041 529 43 23. ⬜ 8:30am–2pm Mon–Fri (ring bell). 🚫 public hols, one week in mid-Aug, 24 Dec–1 Jan. **Church** *Tel* 041 522 56 62. ⬜ 8am–noon Mon–Sat, 9–10am Sun.

Few hospitals can boast as rich and unusual a façade as that of Venice's Ospedale Civile. It was built originally as one of the six great confra-ternities of the city (*see p127*). Their first headquarters were destroyed by fire in 1485, but the Scuola was rebuilt at the end of the 15th century.

The delightful asymmetrical façade, with its arcades, marble panels and *trompe l'oeil* effects, was the work of Pietro Lom-bardo working in conjunction with Giovanni Buora. The upper order was finished by Mauro Coducci in 1495. The interior was revamped in the 19th century and, since then, most of the artistic master-pieces have been dispersed.

The library has a fine carved 16th-century ceiling, and the hospital chapel, the Church of San Lazzaro dei Mendicanti, contains an early Tintoretto and a work by Veronese.

Santi Giovanni e Paolo ⓬

See pp116–17.

Ospedaletto ⓭

Calle Barbaria delle Tole, 6691 Castello. **Map** 4 D5. **Tel** *041 532 29 20.* Ospedale Civile. on request (€60 for guided tour).

Beyond the south flank of Santi Giovanni e Paolo *(see pp116–17)* is the façade of the Ospedaletto or, more correctly, Santa Maria dei Derelitti. The Ospedaletto was set up by the Republic in 1527 as a charitable institution to care for the sick and aged, and to educate orphans and abandoned girls. Such an education consisted largely of the study of music. The girls became leading figures in choirs and orchestras, with concerts bringing in funds for the construction in 1776 of a *sala della musica,* which became the main performance venue. This elegant room features frescoes by Jacopo Guarana.

The church, which formed part of the Ospedaletto, was built by Andrea Palladio in 1575. Its façade was added in 1674 by Baldassare Longhena. The huge, hideous heads on the façade have been described as anti-Classical abominations, likened to diseased figures and swollen fruit. The interior of the church is decorated with

The decorative façade of the Scuola Grande di San Marco

less provocative works of art and notable paintings from the 18th century, including *The Sacrifice of Isaac* (1720) by Giambattista Tiepolo.

San Francesco della Vigna ⓮

Campo della Confraternità. **Map** 8 E1. **Tel** *041 520 61 02.* Celestia. *8am–12:30pm, 3–7pm daily.*

The name "della Vigna" derives from a vineyard that was bequeathed to the Franciscans in 1253. The church which the order built here in the 13th century was rebuilt under Jacopo Sansovino in 1534, with a façade added in 1562–72 by Palladio.

The interior has a rich collection of works of art, including sculpture by Alessandro Vittoria, Paolo Veronese's *The Holy Family with Saints* (1562) and Antonio da Negroponte's *Virgin and Child* (c.1450). The *Madonna and Child with Saints* (1507) by Giovanni Bellini hangs near the cloister.

San Lorenzo ⓯

Campo San Lorenzo. **Map** 8 D1. San Zaccaria. for restoration.

Deconsecrated and closed for restoration, the church of San Lorenzo's only claim to fame is as the alleged burial place of Marco Polo *(see p143)*. Unfortunately there is nothing to show for it because his sarcophagus disappeared during rebuilding in 1592. A collection of paintings was dispersed, and for many years the church was abandoned.

In 1987 restorers discovered the foundations of two earlier churches, dating from AD 850 and the late 12th century. The foundations of the present medieval structure, as well as substantial remains of the marble floor, have been damaged by water seeping in from the adjacent canal. Restoration work funded by the British Venice in Peril Fund has long been at a standstill.

Marco Polo

Fresco by Guarana in the *sala della musica* **of the Ospedaletto**

Santi Giovanni e Paolo ⑫

Figure in left transept

More familiarly known as San Zanipolo, Santi Giovanni e Paolo vies with the Frari *(see pp102–3)* as the city's greatest Gothic church. It was built in the late 13th to early 14th centuries by the Dominican friars, and is striking for its huge dimensions and architectural austerity. Known as the Pantheon of Venice, it houses monuments to no less than 25 doges. Many of these are outstanding works, executed by the Lombardi family and other leading sculptors of the day.

★ Cappella del Rosario
The Adoration of the Shepherds *is one of many works by Paolo Veronese which decorate the Rosary Chapel.*

The sacristy has paintings that celebrate the Dominican Order.

★ Tomb of Nicolò Marcello
This magnificent Renaissance monument to Doge Nicolò Marcello (d.1474) was sculpted by Pietro Lombardo.

The doorway, which is decorated with Byzantine reliefs, is one of the earliest Renaissance architectural features in Venice. The portico carvings are attributed to Bartolomeo Bon.

The marble columns were taken from a former church on the island of Torcello.

★ Tomb of Pietro Mocenigo
Pietro Lombardo's great masterpiece (1481) commemorates the doge's military pursuits when he was Grand Captain of the Venetian forces. This west side wall is largely devoted to Mocenigo monuments.

STAR SIGHTS

★ Doges' Tombs

★ Cappella del Rosario

★ Cappella di San Domenico

The bronze statue is a monument to Doge Sebastiano Venier, who was Commander of the Fleet at Lepanto.

The Baroque high altar is attributed to Baldassare Longhena.

The panel by Vivarini shows *Christ Bearing the Cross* (1474).

St Catherine of Siena's foot is buried here in a precious reliquary; her relics are scattered in churches throughout Italy.

★ **Tomb of Andrea Vendramin**
The nude figures of Lombardo's masterpiece (1476–8) were considered unsuitable and replaced by St Catherine and St Mary Magdalene (side statues).

The Nave
The vast interior is cross-vaulted, held by wooden tie-beams and supported by ten huge columns of Istrian stone blocks.

★ **Cappella di San Domenico**
Piazzetta's Glory of St Dominic for this chapel – his only ceiling painting – displays a mastery of colour, perspective and foreshortening. The artist had a profound influence on the young Tiepolo.

St George slaying the Dragon by Carpaccio, in the Scuola di San Giorgio degli Schiavoni

Scuola di San Giorgio degli Schiavoni ⑯

Calle Furlani, Castello 3959A.
Map 8 E1. *Tel 041 522 88 28.*
🚤 *San Zaccaria.* ⏰ *2:45–6pm Mon,
9am–1pm, 2:45–6pm Tue–Sun.* 📷
public hols & special events. 📷 📷

Within this surprisingly simple
Scuola are some of the finest
paintings of Vittore Carpaccio,
which were commissioned by
the Schiavoni community in
Venice during the 15th century.

From the earliest days of
the Republic, Venice forged
trade links with the coastal
region of Schiavonia
(Dalmatia) across the Adriatic.
By 1420 permanent Venetian
rule was established there,
and many of the Schiavoni
came to live in Venice. By
the mid-15th century the
Slav colony in the city had
grown considerably and the
State gave permission for
them to found their own
confraternity *(see p127).*

The Scuola was established
in 1451. It is a delightful spot
to admire Carpaccio's exceptional works of art, and has
changed very little since the
rebuilding of the Scuola in
1551. The exquisite frieze,
executed between 1502
and 1508, shows
scenes from the lives
of favourite saints: St
George, St Tryphon
and St Jerome. Each
episode of the narrative
cycle is remarkable for its
vivid colouring, minutely
observed detail and historic
record of Venetian life.
Outstanding among them

are *St George Slaying the
Dragon, St Jerome Leading the
Tamed Lion to the Monastery,*
and *The Vision of St Jerome.*

San Giovanni in Bragora ⑰

Campo Bandiera e Moro. **Map** 8 E2.
Tel 041 520 59 06. 🚤 *Arsenale.*
⏰ *9–11am, 3:30–5:30pm Mon–Sat.*

The foundations of this
simple church date back to
ancient times but the existing
building is essentially Gothic
(1475–9). The intimate
interior has major works of
art which demonstrate the
transition from Gothic to early
Renaissance. Bartolomeo
Vivarini's altarpiece, *Madonna
and Child with Saints* (1478)
is unmistakably Gothic.
Contrasting with this is Cima
da Conegliano's *Baptism of
Christ* (1492–5) on the main
altar. This large-scale narrative
scene, in a realistic landscape,
set a precedent for later
Renaissance painters.

Museo Storico Navale ⑱

Campo San Biagio, Arsenale, Castello
2148. **Map** 8 F3. *Tel 041 244 13 99.*
🚤 *Arsenale.* ⏰ *8:45am–1:30pm
Mon–Fri (to 1pm Sat).* 📷 *public hols.*
📷 www.marina.difesa.it/venezia

It was the Austrians who, in
1815, first had the idea of
assembling the remnants of
the Venetian navy and creating
a historical naval museum.
They began with a series of
models of vessels that had
been produced in the 17th
century by the Arsenale, and
to these added all the naval
paraphernalia they could
obtain. The exhibits include
friezes preserved from famous
galleys of the past, a variety
of maritime firearms and a
replica of the Doge's cermo-
nial barge, the *Bucintoro.*

The collection has been
housed in an ex-warehouse
on the waterfront since 1958,
and now traces Venetian and
Italian naval history to the
present day.

The first exhibits you see on
entering are the World War II
human torpedoes or "pigs".
Torpedoes such as these
helped sink HMS *Valiant* and
HMS *Queen Elizabeth*: they
were guided to their target
by naval divers who jumped
off just before impact.

The rest of the museum is
divided into the Venetian navy,
the Italian navy from 1860 to
today, Adriatic vessels and the
Swedish room. The museum
is well laid out and has informative explanations in English.

Model of the *Bucintoro* in the Museo Storico Navale

Arsenale ⑲

Map 8 F1. 🚤 *Arsenale.*
Limited public access.

Heart of the city's maritime-power, the Arsenale was founded in the 12th century and enlarged in the 14th to 16th centuries to become the greatest naval shipyard in the world. The word "arsenal" derives from the Arabic *darsina'a,* house of industry – which indeed it was.

At its height in the 16th century, a workforce of 16,000, the *arsenalotti,* was employed to construct, equip and repair the great Venetian galleys *(see pp44–5).* One of the first production lines in Europe, it was like a city within a city, with its own workshops, warehouses, factories, foundries and docks.

Entrance to the Arsenale, guarded by 16th-century towers

THE ASSEMBLY-LINE SYSTEM

The *arsenalotti,* master ship-builders of the 16th century

During the Arsenale's heyday, a Venetian galley could be constructed and fully equipped with remarkable speed and efficiency. From the early 16th century the hulls, which were built in the New Arsenal, were towed past a series of buildings in the Old Arsenal to be equipped in turn with rigging, ammunition and food supplies. By 1570, when Venice was faced with the Turkish threat to take Cyprus, the Arsenale was so fast it was capable of turning out an entire galley in 24 hours. Henry III of France witnessed the system's efficiency in 1574 when the *arsenalotti* completed a galley in the time it took for him to partake in a state feast.

Surrounded by crenellated walls, the site today is largely abandoned. The huge gateway and vast site are the only evidence of its former splendour. The gateway, in the form of a triumphal arch, was built in 1460 by Antonio Gambello and is often cited as Venice's first Renaissance construction.

The two lions guarding the entrance were pillaged from Piraeus (near Athens) by Admiral Francesco Morosini in 1687. A third lion, bald and sitting upright, bears runic inscriptions on his haunches, thought to have been carved by Scandinavian mercenaries who in 1040 fought for the Byzantine emperor against some Greek rebels.

By the 17th century, when the seeds of Venetian decline were well and truly sown, the number of *arsenalotti* plummeted to 1,000. Following the Fall of the Republic in 1797,

Napoleon destroyed the docks and stripped the *Bucintoro* (the Doge's ceremonial ship) of its precious ornament. Cannons and bronzes were melted down to contribute to victory monuments celebrating the French Revolution.

Today the area is under military administration and for the most part closed to the public. The bridge by the arched gateway affords partial views of the shipyard, or try taking a scenic trip on a *vaporetto* (either route 41 or 42), which follows the perimeter of the Arsenal.

Some parts of the Arsenale, such as the Corderie, the old rope factory, are now being used as performance spaces or exhibition centres, mostly for the Biennale *(see p260).* A research consortium developing marine and coastal technologies also operates from the Arsenale.

Lagoon entrance

Arsenale Novissimo, 15th–16th century

Old sail factory

Arsenale Vecchio, 12th–13th century

Arsenale Nove, 14th century

Corderia

Late 18th-century engraving of the Arsenale

Exploring Eastern Castello ⑳

This peaceful stroll takes you from the animated Castello quayside to the quieter eastern limits of the city. The focal point of the tour is the solitary island of San Pietro di Castello, site of the former cathedral of Venice. From here you head south to the island of Sant'Elena with its historic church and Venice's football stadium, and return via the public gardens along the scenic waterfront.

The calm and leafy Giardini Pubblici ⑯

A tribute to the women fallen in World War II ⑱

Via Garibaldi

This broad, busy street ① was created by Napoleon in 1808 by filling in a canal. The first house on the right ② was the home of John Cabot and his son Sebastian, the Italian navigators who in 1497 found what they thought to be the coast of China (but in reality was the Labrador coast of Newfoundland). Near the end of the street, through a gate on the right, a bronze monument of Garibaldi ③ by Augusto Benvenuti (1885) marks the northern end of the Viale Garibaldi, which leads to the public gardens.

Returning to Via Garibaldi, take the left-hand embankment at the end of the street, pausing on the bridge ④ for distant views of the Arsenale

(see p119). Then take the first on the left, marked Calle San Gioachin, cross a small bridge and turn left at the "crossroads". Once you are past Campo Ruga ⑤, take the second turning on the right and cross the bridge over the broad Canale di San Pietro.

The island of San Pietro di Castello

The old church of San Pietro di Castello ⑥ and its free-standing, tilting campanile ⑦ overlook a grassy square. The island, once occupied by a fortress (castello), was one of Venice's earliest settlements. The church, which was probably founded in the 7th century, became the cathedral of Venice and remained so until 1807 when San Marco took its place (see p80). The existing church, built to a

Palladian design in the mid-16th century, has several notable features. These include the Lando Chapel, the Vendramin Chapel and the marble throne from an Arabic tombstone, originally said to have been the Seat of St Peter.

In the south of the square, Mauro Coducci's elegant stone campanile was built in 1482–8, and the cupola was added in 1670. Beside the church, the Palazzo Patriarcale (Bishop's

KEY

··· Walk route

✲ View point

▭ Vaporetto boarding point

The busy Via Garibaldi, with John Cabot's house on the far right ②

For hotels and restaurants in this region see pp228–33 and pp242–7

Palace) ⑧ was turned into barracks by Napoleon. The old cloisters are overgrown and strung with washing and fishing nets.

From the Bishop's Palace take the Calle drio il Campanile south from the square and turn left when you come to the canal. The first turning right takes you across the Ponte di Quintavalle ⑨, a wooden bridge with good views of brightly coloured boats anchored on either side of the waterway.

The island of San Pietro, with its curious leaning campanile ⑦

San Pietro to Sant'Elena

Campanile,
San Pietro

The large and semi-derelict building at the foot of the bridge is the ex-church and monastery of Sant'Anna ⑩. Take the first left off the *fondamenta*, cross Campiello Correr and then take Calle GB Tiepolo and cross the Secco Marina. Continue straight ahead and over the bridge for the Church of San Giuseppe ⑪. On the rare occasions it is open you can see Vincenzo Scamozzi's monument to Doge Marino Grimani

(1595–1605). Cross the square beyond the church and zigzag left, right and left again for Paludo San Antonio, an uninspiring modern street that has been reclaimed from marshland *(palude)*. At the far end cross the bridge over the Rio dei Giardini ⑫ and take the street ahead. A right turn along Viale 4 Novembre brings you down to the spacious gardens of Parco delle Rimembranze ⑬. At the southern end of the park, cut left at Calle Buccari ⑭, then right for the bridge over Rio di Sant'Elena. In front, the Church of Sant'Elena ⑮ is a pretty Gothic church founded in the 13th century. Retrace your steps over the bridge and turn left, following the waterfront back through the park.

Detail from Gothic façade of Sant'Elena ⑮

Giardini Pubblici and the Biennale Pavilions

At the far side of the park, the bridge across the Rio dei Giardini brings you to the public gardens and to the Biennale gate entrance ⑯. If it happens to be summer in an odd-numbered year, the gardens will be open with the Biennale pavilions ⑰ at which 40 to 50 nations exhibit many examples of contemporary art *(see p260)*.

Riva dei Partigiani

Outside the public gardens on Riva dei Partigiani is a large bronze statue. Lying on the steps of the embankment, the monument can only be seen at low tide. Known as La Donna Partigiana, this is a memorial to all the women who were killed fighting in World War II ⑱.

TIPS FOR WALKERS

Starting point: *The western end of Via Garibaldi.*

Length: *Just under 5 km (3 miles).*

Getting there: *Vaporetto No. 1, 41 or 42 to Arsenale.*

Stopping-off points: *There are a handful of simple cafés and trattorias along the route, most of them on Via Garibaldi. The waterside Caffè Paradiso at the entrance to the Giardini Pubblici has excellent views. For good seafood, try the Hostaria Da Franz (see p241) along Fondamenta San Giuseppe (No. 754). The green shady parks are a welcome retreat from the bustle of the city.*

0 metres   200
0 yards   200

SIGHTS AT A GLANCE

Churches

Museums and Galleries

Historic Buildings

Streets, Bridges and Squares

FONDAMEN
PROCU
FONDAMEN
Rio de
FMTA DELL'AZZERE
⑦
Rio di San Nicolò
FMTA BARBARIGO
FON
FMTA DI PESCHERIA
l Rd. Am
CORTE
LARDONA
⑧
CAMPO
ANGELO RAFFAE
SAL SAN BASE
BANCHINA DI SAN BASEG
Ba

KEY

■ Street-by-Street map
See pp124–5

🚤 *Vaporetto* boarding point

🚣 *Traghetto* crossing

◁ **View across the Grand Canal to Santa Maria della Salute**

DORSODURO

Dorsoduro is named after the solid subsoil on which this area has been built up (the name means "hard backbone"). The western part, the island of Mendigola, was colonized centuries before the Rialto was established in AD 828 as the permanent seat of Venice. The settlement then spread eastwards, covering another six islands.

Squero di San Trovaso, the gondola boatyard

East of the Accademia, the Dorsoduro is a quiet and pretty neighbourhood with shaded squares, quiet canals and picturesque residences belonging to wealthy Venetians and foreigners. In the early 1900s the area was favoured by British expatriates who used to attend the Anglican church of St George in Campo San Vio. Among the area's attractions are the wide-embracing lagoon views,

both from the eastern tip near the Salute and from the Zattere across to the island of Giudecca. West of the Accademia, the *sestiere* is more vibrant, with the busy Campo Santa Margherita as its attractive focal point. Further west, the shabbier area around the beautiful church of San Nicolò dei Mendicoli was originally the home of fishermen and sailors. The Dorsoduro plays host to several major collections of art, notably the Accademia Gallery and the Peggy Guggenheim Collection of 20th-century art. The churches are also rich repositories of paintings and sculpture: San Sebastiano has fine paintings by Paolo Veronese; the Scuola Grande dei Carmini and the church of the Gesuati have ceilings painted by Giambattista Tiepolo.

Michele Giambono's
St Michael (c.1450)
in the Accademia

0 metres   250

0 yards   250

Street-by-Street: Dorsoduro

Between the imposing palaces on the Grand Canal and the Campo Santa Margherita lies an almost silent neighbourhood of small squares and narrow alleys. The delightful Rio San Barnaba is best appreciated from the Ponte dei Pugni, near the barge selling fruit and vegetables. The Rio Terrà, though architecturally uninspiring, has a fascinating mask shop and some cafés that are lively at night-time. All roads seem to lead to Campo Santa Margherita, the heart of Dorsoduro. The square bustles with activity, particularly in the morning when the market stalls are functioning.

Reliefs on a house at Ponte Trovaso

★ Scuola Grande dei Carmini
Tiepolo painted nine ceiling panels for the Scuola in 1739–44. The central panel features the Virgin and St Simeon Stock **5**

Palazzo Zenobio has
been an Armenian college since 1850. Occasionally visitors can see the sumptuous 18th-century ballroom.

Santa Maria dei Carmini
The church's oldest feature is the Gothic side porch with fragments of decorative Byzantine reliefs **6**

KEY

– – – Suggested route

0 metres   50
0 yards   50

STAR SIGHTS

★ Scuola Grande dei Carmini

★ Ca' Rezzonico

★ San Barnaba

Fondamenta Gherardini
runs beside the Rio San Barnaba, one of the prettiest canals in the sestiere.

Campo Santa Margherita
Open-air cafés are an integral part of the square. Causin sells particularly delicious Italian ice cream ❹

SAN POLO AND SANTA CROCE

SAN MARCO

DORSODURO

Palazzo Giustinian
is the 15th-century palace where Richard Wagner stayed while he was writing the second act of Tristan and Isolde in 1858.

Ca' Foscari, with its splendid setting, was chosen as the lodging place for Henry III of France in 1574.

CANAL GRANDE

Palazzo Nani is one of the fine palaces that lie on the great curve called the Volta del Canal.

Ca' Rezzonico

CALLE BERNADO

CAMPO SAN BARNABA

CALLE DEL TRAGHETTO

Ponte dei Pugni
Vicious fistfights used to take place on the top of this bridge ❷

★ **San Barnaba**
A floating barge crammed with crates of fruit and vegetables lends a colourful note to the area ❶

★ **Ca' Rezzonico**
The grand stairway has two putti, symbolizing winter and autumn ❸

Campo San Barnaba ❶

Map 6 D3. 🚤 *Ca' Rezzonico.*

The Parish of San Barnaba, with its canalside square at the centre, was known in the 18th century as the home of impoverished Venetian patricians. They were attracted by the cheap rents, and while some relied on state support or begging, others worked in the State gambling house.

Today the square and canal, with its vegetable barge, are quietly appealing. The church (Tel: 041 296 06 30, open am Mon–Sat) is fairly unremarkable, apart from a Tiepolesque ceiling and a *Holy Family* attributed to Paolo Veronese.

Ponte dei Pugni ❷

Fondamenta Gherardini. **Map** 6 D3. 🚤 *Ca' Rezzonico.*

Venice has several Ponti dei Pugni ("bridges of fists"), but this is the most famous. Spanning the peaceful Rio San Barnaba, the small bridge is distinguished by two pairs of footprints set in white stone on top of the bridge. These mark the starting positions for the fights which traditionally took place between rival factions. Formerly there were no balustrades and contenders hurled each other straight into the water. The battles became so bloodthirsty that they were banned in 1705.

Boats and barges moored along the Rio San Barnaba

Tiepolo's *New World* fresco, part of a series in Ca' Rezzonico

Ca' Rezzonico ❸

Fondamenta Rezzonico 3136. **Map** 6 E3. *Tel* 041 241 01 00. 🚤 *Ca' Rezzonico.* ⬜ 10am–6pm Wed–Mon (Nov–Mar: to 5pm). ● 1 Jan, 1 May, 25 Dec. 🎦 🚫 🔲 📷 🛗 🔲 **www.**museiciviciveneziani.it

This richly furnished Baroque palace is one of the most splendid in Venice. It is also one of the few palaces in the city, which opens its doors to the public. Since 1934 it has housed the museum of 18th-century Venice, its rooms furnished with frescoes, paintings and period pieces taken from other local palaces or museums.

The building was begun by Baldassare Longhena (architect of La Salute, *see p135*) in 1667, but the funds of the Bon family, who commissioned it, ran dry before the second floor was started. In 1712, long after Longhena's death, the unfinished palace was bought by the Rezzonicos, a family of merchants-turned-bankers from Genoa. A large portion of the Rezzonico fortune was spent on the purchase, construction and decoration of the palace. By 1758 it was in a fit state for the Rezzonicos to throw the first of the huge banquets and celebratory parties for which they later became renowned.

In 1888 the palace was bought by the poet Robert

Allegory of Strength, Andrea Brustolon

Browning and his son, Pen, who was married to an American heiress. Browning spoke of the "gaiety and comfort of the enormous rooms" but had little time to enjoy them. In 1889 he died of bronchitis.

The outstanding attraction in the palace today is Giorgio Massari's ballroom, which occupies the entire breadth of the building. It has been beautifully restored and is embellished with gilded chandeliers, carved furniture by Andrea Brustolon and a ceiling with *trompe l'oeil* frescoes. Three rooms between the ballroom and Grand Canal side of the palace have ceilings with frescoes by Giambattista Tiepolo including, in the Sala della Allegoria Nuziale, his lively *Nuptial Allegory* (1758).

Eighteenth-century paintings occupy the *piano nobile* (second floor). A whole room is devoted to Pietro Longhi's portrayals of everyday Venetian life. Other paintings worthy of note are Francesco Guardi's *Ridotto* (1748) and *Nuns' Parlour* (1768), and one of the few Canalettos in Venice, his *View of the Rio dei Mendicanti* (1725). Giandomenico Tiepolo's fascinating series of frescoes painted for his villa at Zianigo (1770–1800) are also to be found here. On the floor above is a reconstructed 18th-century apothecary's shop and a puppet theatre.

Campo Santa Margherita ❹

Map 6 D2. 🚤 *Ca' Rezzonico.*

The sprawling square of Santa Margherita, lined with houses from the 14th and 15th centuries, is the lively hub of western Dorsoduro. Market stalls, off-beat shops and cafés attract many young people. The fish stalls sell live eels and lobster, the *erborista* alternative medicine, and the bakers some of the tastiest loaves in Venice.

The former church of Santa Margherita, now an auditorium owned by the university, lies to the north of the square. Visitors can see sculptural fragments from the original 18th-century church, including gargoyles, on the truncated campanile and adjacent house. The Scuola dei Varotari (Scuola of the tanners), the isolated

A 15th-century carving of Santa Margherita and the dragon

building in the centre of the square, has a faded relief of the Madonna della Misericordia protecting the tanners.

Scuola Grande dei Carmini ❺

Campo Carmini. **Map** 5 C2.
Tel 041 528 94 20. 🚤 *Ca' Rezzonico.* ⬜ *11am–4pm daily.* ⬛ *1 Jan, 25 Dec.* 🎟 🚫
www.scuolagrandecarmini.it

The headquarters of the Carmelite confraternity was built beside their church in 1663. In the 1740s Giambattista Tiepolo was commissioned to decorate the ceiling of the *salone* (hall) on the upper floor. The nine ceiling paintings that he produced so impressed the Carmelites that Tiepolo was promptly made an honorary member of the brotherhood.

The ceiling used to show *St Simeon Stock Receiving the Scapular of the Carmelite Order from the Virgin* but, unfortunately, in 2000 the painting crashed to the floor, its support having been eaten by woodworm. The work is currently being restored in Bologna. The Carmelites honoured St Simeon Stock because he re-established the order in Europe after its expulsion from the Holy Land in the 13th century.

Santa Maria dei Carmini ❻

Campo Carmini. **Map** 5 C3.
Tel 041 296 06 30. 🚤 *Ca' Rezzonico or San Basilio.*
⬜ *2:30–5pm Mon–Sat.*

Known also as Santa Maria del Carmelo, this church was built in the 14th century but has since undergone extensive alterations.

Santa Maria dei Carmini

The most prominent external feature is the lofty campanile, whose perilous tilt was skilfully rectified in 1688. The impressive interior is large, sombre and richly decorated. The arches of the nave are adorned with gilded wooden statues, and a series of paintings illustrating the history of the Carmelite Order.

There are two interesting paintings in the church's side altars. Cima da Conegliano's *Adoration of the Shepherds* (c.1509) is in the second altar on the right (coins in the light meter are essential). In the second altar on the left is Lorenzo Lotto's *St Nicholas of Bari with Saints Lucy and John the Baptist* (c.1529). This painting demonstrates the artist's religious devotion, personal sensitivity and his love of nature. On the right-hand side of this highly detailed, almost Dutch-style landscape, there is a tiny depiction of St George killing the dragon.

SCUOLE

The *scuole* were peculiarly Venetian institutions. Founded mainly in the 13th century, they were lay confraternities existing for the charitable benefit of the neediest groups of society, the professions or resident ethnic minorities (such as the Scuola dei Schiavoni, *see p118*). Some became extremely rich, spending large sums on buildings and paintings, often to the disadvantage of their declared beneficiaries.

Upper Hall of the Scuola Grande dei Carmini

Nave of San Nicolò dei Mendicoli, one of the oldest churches in Venice

San Nicolò dei Mendicoli ❼

Campo San Nicolò. **Map** 5 A3.
Tel 041 275 03 82. 🚤 San Basilio.
🕐 10am–noon, 3–5:30pm Mon–Sat.

Contrasting with the remote and rundown area that surrounds it, this church remains one of the most charming and delightful in Venice. Originally constructed in the 12th century, it has been rebuilt extensively over the centuries; the little porch on the north flank dates from the 15th century.

Thanks to the Venice in Peril Fund, in the 1970s the church underwent one of the most comprehensive restoration programmes since the floods of 1966 (*see p50*). The floor, which was 30 cm (1 ft) below the level of the canals, was rebuilt and raised slightly to prevent further damage, the roofs and lower walls were reconstructed, and paintings and statues restored. The interior is richly embellished, particularly the nave with its 16th-century gilded wood statues. On the upper walls is a series of paintings of the life of Christ by Alvise dal Friso and other pupils of Veronese.

Angelo Raffaele ❽

Campo Angelo Raffaele. **Map** 5 B3.
Tel 041 522 85 48. 🚤 San Basilio.
🕐 9am–noon, 3–5:30pm Mon–Sat,
varies on Sun & public hols.

The main attraction of this 17th-century church is the series of panel paintings on the organ balustrade. These were executed in 1749 by Antonio Guardi, brother of the more famous Francesco. They tell the tale of Tobias, the blind prophet cured by the archangel Raphael, after whom the church is named.

San Sebastiano ❾

Campo San Sebastiano. **Map** 5 C3.
Tel 041 275 04 62. 🚤 San Basilio.
🕐 10am–5pm Mon–Sat.
🔴 1 Jan, 25 Dec. 🎫 🚫 🎧
www.chorusvenezia.org

This 16th-century church has one of the most colourful and homogeneous interiors of Venice. This is thanks to the artist Veronese who, from 1555 to 1560 and again in the 1570s, was commissioned to decorate the sacristy ceiling, the nave ceiling, the frieze, the east end of the choir, the high altar, the doors of the organ panels and the chancel – in that order. The paintings, which are typical of Veronese, are rich and radiant, with sumptuous costumes and colours. Among the finest of his works are the three ceiling paintings that tell the story of Esther, Queen of Xerxes I of Persia, who brought about the deliverance of the Jewish people. Appropriately, the artist is buried in San Sebastiano, alongside the organ.

Zattere ❿

Map 5 C4. 🚤 Zattere or San Basilio.

Stretching along the southern part of the *sestiere*, the Zattere is the long quayside looking across to the island of Giudecca. The name derives from the rafts (*zattere*) made of and carrying timber from the Republic's forests. After skilful navigation along the River

San Sebastiano, viewed from the bridge of the same name

Café tables laid out along the Zattere

Piave, the rafts were dismantled on arrival in Venice. On a sunny day it is a pleasure to sit at a waterside café here, looking across to the Church of the Redentore (see p154) or watching the waterbuses as they cross back and forth between the shores.

Squero di San Trovaso ⓫

Rio San Trovaso. **Map** 6 D4. Zattere. **No public access.**

This is one of the few surviving gondola workshops in Venice (see pp28–9), and the most picturesque. Its Tyrolean look dates from the days when craftsmen came down from the Cadore area of the Dolomites (see p215).

It is not open to the public, but from the far side of the Rio San Trovaso it is possible to watch the upturned gondolas being given their scraping and tarring treatment. Nowadays, only around ten boats are made each year, but there is still plenty to see.

San Trovaso ⓬

Campo San Trovaso. **Map** 6 D4. **Tel** 041 522 21 33. Zattere or Accademia. 8–11am, 2:30– 5:30pm Mon–Sat, 8–9:30am Sun.

The church of Santi Gervasio e Protasio, which in the eccentric Venetian dialect is slurred to San Trovaso, was built in 1590. Unusually it has two identical façades, one overlooking a canal, the other a quiet square. The church stood on neutral ground between the parishes of the rival factions of the Castellani and Nicolotti families, and tradition has it that this necessitated a separate entrance for each party.

The interior houses some late paintings by Jacopo Tintoretto, and there are two notable works of art worth seeking out. Michele Giambono's 15th-century Gothic painting, *St Chrysogonus on Horseback*, is situated in the chapel on the right of the chancel, and exquisite marble reliefs of angels with instruments decorate the altar of the Clary chapel opposite.

Santa Maria della Visitazione ⓭

Fondamenta delle Zattere. **Map** 6 E4. **Tel** 041 522 40 77. Zattere. for restoration. Due to re-open in 2012/13.

Situated beside the Gesuati, this Renaissance church was built between 1494 and 1524 by the Order of the Gesuati. Inside the church is a fine wooden ceiling painted by 16th-century Umbrian and Tuscan artists.

The exterior *bocca di leone* to the right of the façade is one of several "lion's mouth" denunciation boxes surviving from the rule of the Council of Ten (see p42); this one was used to complain about the state of the streets.

Gesuati ⓮

Fondamenta delle Zattere. **Map** 6 E4. **Tel** 041 275 04 62. Zattere. 10am–5pm Mon–Sat. **www**.chorusvenezia.org

Not to be confused with the Gesuiti (see p142), this church was built by the Dominicans, who took possession of the site in the 17th century, when the Gesuati Order was suppressed. Work began in 1726 and the stately façade reflects that of Palladio's Redentore church across the Giudecca. It is the most conspicuous landmark of the long Zattere quayside. The interior of the church is richly decorated.

Gesuati façade statue

Tiepolo's frescoed ceiling, *The Life of St Dominic* (1737– 39) demonstrates the artist's mastery of light and colour. Equally impressive (and far easier to see) is his *Virgin with Saints* (1740), situated in the first chapel on the right. The church also boasts two altar paintings by Sebastiano Ricci and Giambattista Piazzetta.

Squero di San Trovaso, where gondolas are given a facelift

Accademia ⑮

The largest collection of Venetian art in existence, the Gallerie dell'Accademia, is housed in three former religious buildings. The basis of the collection was the Accademia di Belle Arti, founded in 1750 by the painter Giovanni Battista Piazzetta. In 1807 Napoleon moved the academy to these premises, and the collection was greatly enlarged by works of art from churches and monasteries he suppressed.

Exterior detail of the Accademia

Ceiling Sketch
Tiepolo's The Translation of the Holy House to Loreto (c.1742) was a sketch for the ceiling of the Scalzi church (see p145).

The Apothecary's Shop
Pietro Longhi is best known for his witty, gently satirical depictions of domestic patrician life in Venice. This detail comes from a painting dated c.1752.

KEY TO FLOORPLAN

- ☐ Byzantine and International Gothic
- ☐ Early Renaissance
- ☐ High Renaissance
- ☐ Baroque, genre and landscapes
- ☐ Ceremonial paintings
- ☐ Temporary exhibitions
- ☐ Non-exhibition space

★ **Cycle of St Ursula** *(1495–1500) (detail)*
The Arrival of the English Ambassadors *is one of Vittore Carpaccio's eight paintings chronicling the tragic story of St Ursula.*

Sala dell'Albergo

The former Church of Santa Maria della Carità was rebuilt by Bartolomeo Bon in the mid-15th century.   **Entrance**

The inner courtyard was designed by Andrea Palladio.

VISITORS' CHECKLIST

Campo della Carità. **Map** 6 E3. **Tel** 041 520 03 45. 🚤 Accademia. ⏱ 8:15am–7pm daily (to 2pm Mon). **Last adm** 45 mins before closing. 🔴 1 Jan, 1 May, 25 Dec. 📷 🚫 📷 ✓ **Quadreria** ⏱ Fri am (booking essential). ✓ 🏪

The Stealing of St Mark

Jacopo Tintoretto's painting of 1562 shows the Christians of Alexandria abducting the body of St Mark, which was about to be burnt by the pagans.

★ The Tempest (c.1507)

In his enigmatic landscape, Giorgione was probably indulging his imagination rather than portraying a specific subject.

★ Coronation of the Virgin

Paolo Veneziano's polyptych (1325) has a central image of the Virgin surrounded by a panoply of religious scenes. This detail shows episodes from the Life of St Francis.

STAR SIGHTS

- ★ Cycle of St Ursula by Carpaccio
- ★ The Tempest by Giorgione
- ★ Coronation of the Virgin by Veneziano

GALLERY GUIDE

The current programme of restoration work is ongoing; be prepared for absent paintings or whole sections closed off. It is sensible to phone ahead for more details. The paintings are dependent on natural light, so to see them at their best try to visit on a bright morning. Upstairs, a second gallery called Quadreria contains works by artists such as Bellini and Tintoretto. Guided visits are free of charge, but it is essential to book in advance.

Exploring the Accademia's Collection

Spanning five centuries, the fascinating collection of
paintings in the Accademia provides a complete
spectrum of the Venetian school, from the medieval
Byzantine period through the Renaissance to the
Baroque and Rococo *(see pp26– 7)*. The order is more
or less chronological, with the exception of the final
rooms, which take visitors back to the Renaissance.

Portrait of a Gentleman (c.1525) by
Lorenzo Lotto (detail)

BYZANTINE AND INTERNATIONAL GOTHIC

Room 1 shows the influence
of Byzantine art on the early
Venetian painters. Paolo Veneziano, the true founder of
the Venetian school, displays
a blend of both western and
eastern influences in his
sumptuous *Coronation of
the Virgin* (1325). The
linear rhythms are quite
unmistakably Gothic, yet
the overall effect and the
glowing gold background
are distinctly Byzantine.

In the same room,
*Coronation of the
Virgin* (1448) by
Michele Giam-
bono shows the
influence of
International
Gothic style,
which was
brought to
Venice by Gentile da Fabriano
and Pisanello. This particular
style was characterized by
delicate naturalistic detail, as
typified by the birds and
animals in the foreground of
Giambono's painting.

Coronation of the Virgin (c.1448)
by Michele Giambono

Florence and Rome. The Bellini
family – Jacopo, the father,
and his two sons Gentile and
Giovanni – played a dominant
role in the early Venetian
Renaissance.

Central to Venetian art in
the 15th century was the *Sacra
Conversazione*, where the
Madonna is portrayed in a
unified composition with saints.
Giovanni Bellini's altar-
piece for San Giobbe
(c.1487) in Room 2 is
one of the finest
examples. Giovanni,
the younger Bellini,
was profoundly
influenced by the
controlled
rational style
and mastery of
perspective in
the works of his
brother-in-law,
Andrea Man-
tegna, whose
work *St George*
(c.1460) is in Room 4. To
Mantegna's rationality and
harsh realism Giovanni added
humanity. This is seen in his
Madonna paintings (Rooms 4
and 5), which are masterpieces
of warmth and harmony. Outstanding examples are *The
Virgin and Child between St
Catherine and St Mary Magdalene* (c.1490) in Room 4;
Madonna of the Little Trees
(c.1487) and *Virgin and Child
with John the Baptist and a
Saint* (c.1505) in Room 5.
The inventive young artist

EARLY RENAISSANCE

The Renaissance came late to
Venice, but by the second
quarter of the 15th century it
had transformed the city into
an art centre rivalling those of

Giorgione was influenced by
Bellini, but went way beyond
his master in his development
of the landscape to create
mood. In the famous, atmospheric *Tempest* (c.1507) in
Room 5, this treatment of the
landscape and the use of the
figures to intensify that mood
was an innovation adopted in
Venetian painting of the 16th
century and beyond.

Out on a limb from the
main 16th-century Venetian
tradition was the enigmatic
Lorenzo Lotto, best known for
portraits conveying moods of
psychological unrest. His
melancholic *Portrait of a
Gentleman* (c.1525) in Room
7 is a superb example. More
in the Venetian tradition, Palma
il Vecchio's sumptuously
coloured *Sacra Conversazione*
in Room 8, painted around
the same time, shows the
unmistakable influence of the
early work of Titian.

HIGH RENAISSANCE

Occupying an entire wall of
Room 10, the monumental
Feast in the House of Levi
by Paolo Veronese (1573)
was originally commissioned

Paolo Veronese's *Feast in the House of Levi* (detail)

as *The Last Supper*. However, the hedonistic detail in the painting, such as the drunkard and the dwarfs, was not well received and Veronese found himself before the Inquisition. Ordered to eliminate the profane content of the picture, he simply changed the title.

Jacopo Tintoretto made his reputation with *The Miracle of the Slave* (1548), which is also in Room 10. The painting shows his mastery of the dramatic effects of light and movement. This was the first of a series of works painted for the Scuola Grande di San Marco *(see p114)*. In the next room, Veronese's use of rich colour is best admired in the *Mystical Marriage of St Catherine* (c.1575).

Healing of the Madman (c.1496) by Vittore Carpaccio

BAROQUE, GENRE AND LANDSCAPES

The Rape of Europa (1740–50) by Francesco Zuccarelli (detail)

Venice suffered from a lack of native Baroque painters, but a few non-Venetians kept the Venetian school alive in the 17th century. The most notable among these was the Genoese Bernardo Strozzi (1581–1644). The artist was a great admirer of the work of Veronese, as can be seen in his *Feast at the House of Simon* (1629) in Room 11. Also represented in this room is Giambattista Tiepolo, the greatest Venetian painter of the 18th century.

The long corridor (12) and the rooms which lead from it are largely devoted to light-hearted landscape and genre paintings from the 18th century. Among them are pastoral scenes by Francesco Zuccarelli, works by Marco Ricci, scenes of Venetian society by Pietro Longhi and a view of Venice by Canaletto (1763). This was the painter's entry for admission to the Accademia, and is a fine example of his sense of perspective.

CEREMONIAL PAINTINGS

Rooms 20 and 21 return to the Renaissance, featuring two great cycles of paintings from the late 16th century. The detail in these large-scale anecdotal canvases provides a fascinating glimpse of the life, customs and appearance of Venice at the time. Room 20 houses *The Stories of the Cross* by Venice's leading artists, commissioned by the Scuola di San Giovanni Evangelista *(see p104)*. Each one depicts an episode of the relic of the Holy Cross, which the kingdom of Cyprus donated to the Scuola. In *The Procession in St Mark's Square* (1496) by Gentile Bellini, it is possible to compare the square with how it looks today.

Another, Vittore Carpaccio's *Healing of the Madman* (1496), shows the Rialto bridge which collapsed in 1524.

The second series, minutely detailed *Scenes from the Legend of St Ursula* (1490s) by Carpaccio in Room 21, provides a brilliant kaleidoscope of life. Mixing reality and imagination, Carpaccio relates the episodes from the life of St Ursula using settings and costumes of 15th-century Venice.

SALA DELL'ALBERGO

When the Scuola della Carità became the site of the Academy of Art in the early 19th century, the Scuola's *albergo* (where students lodged) retained its original panelling and 15th-century ceiling. The huge *Presentation of the Virgin* (1538) is one of the surprisingly few Titians in the gallery, and was painted for this very room. The walls are also adorned with a grandiose triptych (1446) by Antonio Vivarini and Giovanni d'Alemagna.

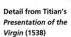
Detail from Titian's Presentation of the Virgin (1538)

Cini Collection ⓰

Palazzo Cini, San Vio 864. **Map** 6 E4.
Tel 041 521 07 55. 🚤 Accademia.
⏰ 10am–1pm, 2–7pm Tue–Sun. 🚫
Aug, Dec–Mar. 🎦 ♿ **www**.cini.it

The Palazzo Cini belonged
to Count Vittorio Cini
(1884–1977), a collector and
patron of the arts. Between
1951 and 1956 he restored
San Giorgio Maggiore (see
p95) and created the Cini
Foundation as a memorial
to his son, who was killed
in an air crash in 1949.

The collection displayed here
includes china, ivories, books,
illuminated manuscripts,
miniatures, porcelain and
furniture, but the outstanding
works of art are the Tuscan
Renaissance paintings that
Cini collected. These include
works by or attributed to
Botticelli, Piero di Cosimo,
Piero della Francesca, Filippo
Lippi and Pontormo.

The Cini Collection has
been open to the public since
1984, but unfortunately, it is
only open for 7 months of
the year.

Madonna col Bambino (c.1437) by
Filippo Lippi, the Cini Collection

Peggy Guggenheim Collection ⓱

Palazzo Venier dei Leoni, Dorsoduro
701. **Map** 6 F4. **Tel** 041 240 54 11.
🚤 Accademia. ⏰ 10am–6pm
Wed–Mon. 🚫 25 Dec. 🏛 🛈
📷 🎦 🛒 🚫 ♿ partial.
www.guggenheim-venice.it

Intended as a four-storey
palace, the 18th-century
Palazzo Venier dei Leoni in fact
never rose beyond the ground
floor – hence its nickname, *Il
Palazzo Nonfinito* (The Unfinished Palace). In 1949 the
building was bought as a home
by the American millionairess
Peggy Guggenheim (1898–
1979), a collector, dealer and
patron of the arts. A perspi-
cacious and high-spirited
woman, she befriended
and furthered the careers of
many innovative abstract and
surrealist artists. One was her
second husband, Max Ernst.

The collection consists of
200 paintings and sculptures,
representing almost every
modern art movement. The

Interno Olandese II (c.1928) by
Joan Miró

dining room has notable
Cubist works of art including
The Poet by Pablo Picasso.
An entire room is devoted to
Jackson Pollock, who was a
Guggenheim discovery. Other
artists represented are Miró, de
Chirico, Magritte, Kandinsky,
Mondrian and Malevich.

Sculpture is laid out in the
house and garden. One of
the most elegant works is
Constantin Brancusi's *Maiastra*
(1912). The most provocative
piece is Marino Marini's *Angelo*

della Città (Angel of the City,
1948), a prominently displayed
man sitting on a horse, erect
in all respects. Embarrassed
onlookers avert their gaze
to enjoy views of the
Grand Canal.

The Guggenheim is
one of Venice's most
visited sights. The
light-filled rooms
and the modern
canvases provide a
striking contrast to
the Renaissance
paintings which are
the main attraction
in Venetian churches
and museums. The
interns here are
usually arts gradu-
ates from English-
speaking countries,
which is a great help
to many tourists.

In 2009, a
contemporary art
gallery opened in
the Punta della Dogana. The
Guggenheim had planned to
acquire the site; however, the
French businessman Francois
Pinault was granted the lease.

Maiastra
**by Constantin
Brancusi**

Façade of the Palazzo Venier dei Leoni, the home of the Peggy Guggenheim Collection of modern art

For hotels and restaurants in this region see pp228–33 and pp242–7

Campiello Barbaro ⑱

Map 6 F4. 🚤 *Salute.*

An enchanting little square, Campiello Barbaro is shaded by trees and flanked on one side by the wisteria-clad walls of Ca' Dario. Throughout the history of this Grand Canal palace, its owners have been plagued by accidents, suicides and bankruptcy, from Giovanni Dario, who commissioned the building in 1479, to the industrialist Raul Gardini, who shot himself in 1993.

The ill-fated Ca' Dario, which backs on to Campiello Barbaro

Santa Maria della Salute ⑲

Campo della Salute. **Map** 7 A4.
Tel 041 274 39 11. 🚤 *Salute.*
◯ 9am–noon, 3–5:30pm daily.
◉ Sun am. 🖼 for Sacristy. 📷

This great Baroque Church standing at the entrance of the Grand Canal is one of the most imposing architectural landmarks of Venice. Henry James likened it to "some great lady on the threshold of her salon ... with her domes and scrolls, her scalloped buttresses and statues forming a pompous crown and her wide steps disposed on the ground like the train of a robe". The church was built in thanksgiving for the deliverance of the city from the plague of 1630, hence the name *Salute*, meaning health and salvation. Every 21 November, in celebration *(see p35)*, worshippers approach across a bridge of boats which span the mouth of the Grand Canal. Baldassare Longhena started the church in 1630. It was completed in 1687, 5 years after his death.

The interior consists of a large octagonal space below the cupola and six chapels radiating from the ambulatory. The altar's sculptural group by Giusto Le Corte represents the Virgin and Child protecting Venice from the plague. Some of the best works, such as Titian's ceiling paintings of *Cain and Abel, The Sacrifice of Abraham and Isaac and David and Goliath* (1540–49), are beyond the altar, where visitors are not allowed. In the sacristy is Titian's early altarpiece of *St Mark Enthroned with Saints Cosmos, Damian,*

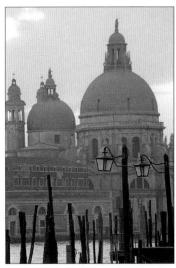

The Baroque church of Santa Maria della Salute viewed from across the Grand Canal

Roch and Sebastian (1511–12), while on the wall opposite the entrance is *The Wedding at Cana* (1551), a major work by Tintoretto.

Punta della Dogana ⑳

Campo della Salute. **Map** 7 A4.
Tel 199 139 139; 044 523 03 13.
🚤 *Salute.* ◯ 10am–7pm Wed–Mon.
◉ 1 Jan, 25 Dec. 🖼 📷

The building housing the sea customs post was originally built in the 15th century to inspect the cargo of ships that intended to enter Venice. The customs house visitors see today was constructed in the late 17th century and replaced a tower that originally guarded the entrance to the Grand Canal. On the corner tower of the house, two bronze Atlases support a striking golden ball with a weathervane figure of Fortuna on the top.

After standing empty for many years, the building was bought by French billionaire Henri François Pinault, who hired the Japanese architect Tadao Ando to revamp the interior. Punta della Dogana opened to the public in 2009, with an exhibition of Pinault's contemporary art collection.

Interior of the Salute showing the octagonal core of the church

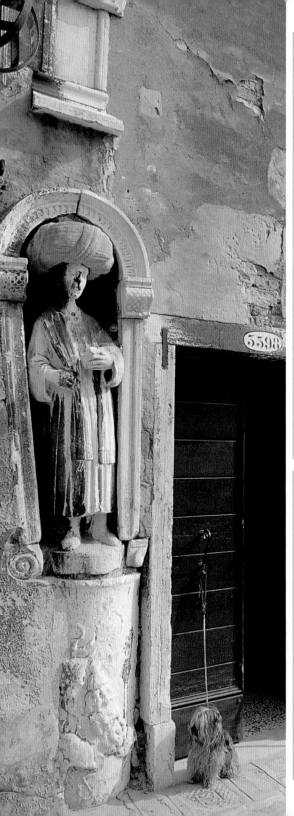

0 metres   250
0 yards   250

◁ The façade of
Tintoretto's house in
Fondamenta dei Mori

CANNAREGIO

The city's most northerly *sestiere,* Cannaregio, stretches in a large arc from the 20th-century railway station in the west to one of the oldest quarters of Venice in the east. The northern quays look out towards the islands in the lagoon, while to the south the *sestiere* is bounded by the upper sweep of the Grand Canal.

The name of the quarter derives either from the Italian *canne,* meaning canes or reeds, which grew here centuries ago, or perhaps from "Canal Regio" or Royal Canal – the former name of what is now the Canale di Cannaregio. This waterway was the main entry to Venice before the advent of the rail link with the mainland. Over a third

Hanukah lamp in the Ghetto

of the city's population lives in Cannaregio. For the most part it is an unspoilt area, divided by wide canals, crisscrossed by alleys and characterized by small stores, simple bars and the artisans' workshops. One of the prettiest and most remote quarters is in the north, near the church of Madonna dell'Orto and around Campo dei Mori.

Tourism is concentrated along two main thoroughfares: the Lista di Spagna and the wide Strada Nova, both on the well-worn route from the station to the Rialto. Just off this route lies the world's oldest ghetto. Though the Jewish community now lives all over the city, this is historically the most fascinating quarter of Cannaregio.

KEY

- Street-by-Street map
  See pp138–9
- **FS** Railway station
- Vaporetto boarding point
- Traghetto crossing

Street-by-Street: Cannaregio

Surprisingly few tourists find their way to this unspoilt quarter of northern Cannaregio. This is the more humble, peaceful side of Venice, where clean washing is strung over the water-ways and the streets are flanked by the softly crumbling façades of shuttered houses. Along the wide *fondamente*, the little shops and stores stock basic groceries and the bars are always crowded with local Venetians.

Channel marker in the lagoon

The quarter's cultural high-light is the lovely Gothic church of Madonna dell'Orto, Tintoretto's parish church.

To Madonna dell'Orto 🚉

CPO PIAVE

C LARGA PIAVE

FONDAMENTA MADONNA DELL

RIO MADONNA DELL'ORTO

FONDAMENTA DELLA SELLA

FONDAMENTA DEI MORI

Fondamenta della Sensa
This peaceful backwater, with its typically Venetian peeling façades, is undisturbed by tourism ❸

★ **Campo dei Mori**
This square is named after the stone statues of three Moors (Mori) which are carved on its walls ❷

★ **Madonna dell'Orto**
One of the finest Gothic churches in Venice, Madonna dell'Orto has a richly decorated façade and a wealth of works by Tintoretto ❶

Tintoretto *lived with his family in this house, No. 3399 Fondamenta dei Mori, from 1574 until his death in 1594.*

To Ca' d'Oro 🚉

KEY

– – – Suggested route

STAR SIGHTS

★ Madonna dell'Orto

★ Campo dei Mori

San Marziale
Ceiling paintings by Sebastiano Ricci (1700–25) and a bizarre Baroque altar adorn this Baroque church ❹

Fondamenta Gasparo Contarini *is named after the cardinal, diplomat and scholar who lived at Palazzo Contarini dal Zaffo (see p68) in the 16th century.*

(see p68)

LOCATOR MAP
See Street Finder, maps 2, 3

Venetian oarsmen *usually practise their technique on the lagoon, but they can also be seen on Cannaregio's quieter canals.*

La Sacca della Misericordia is a large man-made basin opening out into the lagoon, with views of the islands of San Michele and Murano.

Campo dell'Abbazia, *a peaceful open square with decorative herring-bone floor tiles, is over-looked by the Scuola Vecchia della Misericordia and a deconsecrated church.*

Fondamenta della Misericordia, *named after the nearby* scuola, *was built in the Middle Ages.*

0 metres   50
0 yards   50

The campanile of Madonna dell'Orto, crowned by an onion-shaped cupola

Madonna dell'Orto ❶

Campo Madonna dell'Orto. **Map** 2 F2. **Tel** 041 275 04 62. ⬛ *Madonna dell'Orto.* ⬜ 10am–5pm Mon–Sat. 🎫 📷 📵 www.chorusvenezia.org

This lovely Gothic church is frequently referred to as the English Church in Venice, for it was British funds that helped restore the building after the 1966 floods *(see p50)*. The original church, founded in the mid-14th century, was dedicated to St Christopher, patron saint of travellers, to protect the boatmen who ferried passengers to the islands in the northern lagoon. The dedication was changed and the church reconstructed in the early 15th century following the discovery, in a nearby vegetable garden *(orto)*, of a statue of the Virgin Mary said to have miraculous powers. However, a 15th-century statue of St Christopher still stands above the portal.

The interior, faced almost entirely in brick, is large, light and uncluttered. The greatest treasures are the works of art by Tintoretto, who was a parishioner of the church. His tomb, which is marked with a plaque, lies in the chapel to the right of the chancel. The most dramatic of his works are the towering paintings in the chancel (1562–4). On the right wall is *The Last Judgment*, whose turbulent content caused John Ruskin's wife Effie to flee the church. In the painting *The Adoration of the Golden Calf* on the left wall, the figure carrying the calf, fourth from the left, is said to depict Tintoretto himself.

Inside the chapel of San Mauro visitors can see the radically restored statue of the Madonna which inspired the reconstruction of the church.

To the right of the entrance is Cima da Conegliano's magnificent painting, *St John the Baptist and Other Saints* (c.1493). The vacant space opposite belongs to Giovanni Bellini's *Madonna with Child* (c.1478), which was stolen for the third time in 1993.

Campo dei Mori ❷

Map 2 F3. ⬛ *Madonna dell'Orto.*

According to popular tradition, the "Mori" were the three Mastelli brothers who came from the Morea (the Peloponnese). The brothers, who were silk merchants by trade, took refuge in Venice in 1112 and built the Palazzo Mastelli, visible from Fondamenta Gasparo Contarini and recognizable by its camel bas relief. The brothers' stone figures are embedded in the wall of the *campo* on its eastern side. The corner figure with the makeshift rusty metal nose (added in the 19th century) is "Signor Antonio Rioba" who, like the Roman Pasquino, was the focus of malicious fun and satire. A fourth oriental merchant with a large turban faces the Rio della Sensa on the façade of Tintoretto's house *(see p138)*.

One of the stone Moors which gave the Campo dei Mori its name

TINTORETTO (1518–94)

Jacopo Robusti, nicknamed Tintoretto because of his father's occupation as silk dyer, was born, lived and died in Cannaregio. He left Venice only once in his life. A devout Christian, volatile and unworldly, his was a highly individual and theatrical style, conveyed by vivid exaggeration of light and movement, bold foreshortening and fiery, fluid brushstrokes. His remarkably prolific output has never been ascertained, but scores of his works survive, many still in the places for which they were painted. Examples of his canvases can be seen in the church of Madonna dell'Orto, the Accademia *(see pp130–33)*, and the Doge's Palace *(see pp84–9)*. His crowning achievement, however, was the great series of works for the Scuola Grande di San Rocco *(see pp106–7)*.

The peaceful and atmospheric Fondamenta della Sensa

Fondamenta della Sensa ❸

Map 2 E2. 🚤 Madonna dell'Orto.

When the marshy lands of Cannaregio were drained in the Middle Ages, three long, straight canals were created, running parallel to each other. The middle of these is the Rio della Sensa, which stretches from the Sacca di Sant'Alvise at its western end to the Canale della Misericordia in the east. The Fondamenta cuts through a quiet quarter of Cannaregio, where daily life goes on undisturbed by tourism. With its small grocery shops, and simple local bars and *trattorias*, the neighbourhood feels far removed from San Marco.

This is one of the poorer areas of the city, though it is interspersed with fine (but neglected) palaces that once belonged to wealthy Venetians. Abbot Onorio Arrigoni lived at No. 3336 with his collection of antiques, and Palazzo Michiel (No. 3218) is an early Renaissance palace which became the French embassy.

San Marziale ❹

Campo San Marziale. **Map** 2 F3. **Tel** 041 71 99 33. 🚤 San Marcuola. ◯ by appointment only.

A Baroque church on medieval foundations, San Marziale was rebuilt between 1693 and 1721. The church is mainly visited for the ceiling frescoes by Sebastiano Ricci, a painter of the decorative Rococo style. Executed between 1700 and 1705, relatively early in Ricci's career, these bold, foreshort-ened frescoes already combine the Venetian tradition with flamboyant Rococo flourishes. Sadly though, the vivid colours for which Ricci was known have been sullied by decades of grime. The central painting shows *The Glory of Saint Martial*, while the side paintings relate to the image of the Virgin.

Fondamente Nuove ❺

Map 3 B3. 🚤 Fondamente Nuove.

The Fondamente Nuove or "New Quays" are actually over 400 years old. This chain

Altar of San Marziale showing a carving of the Virgin and Child

of waterside streets borders the northern lagoon for one kilometre (over half a mile), from the solitary Sacca della Misericordia to the Rio di Santa Giustina in Castello on the eastern side.

Before the construction of the quays in the 1580s, this was a desirable residential area where the air was said to be healthy and the houses had gardens sloping down to the lagoon.

One of the residents was Titian, who lived from 1531 to his death in 1576 in a now demolished house at Calle Larga dei Botteri No. 5182–3 (a plaque marks the site).

Today the quaysides are aesthetically uninspiring but they do provide splendid views of the northern lagoon and, on a clear day, the peaks of the Dolomites. The island most visible from the quays is San Michele in Isola (*see p151*), its dark, stately cypress trees rising high above the cemetery walls.

Oratorio dei Crociferi ❻

Campo dei Gesuiti, 4905 Cannaregio. **Map** 3 B3. **Tel** 041 532 29 20. 🚤 Fondamente Nuove. ◯ Apr–Jun & Sep–Oct: 3–6pm Fri–Sat; Jul–Aug: 4–7pm Fri–Sat. 🖼 ⚑

Founded in the 13th century as a hospital for returning Crusaders, the Oratorio dei Crociferi (built for the order of the Bearers of the Cross) was turned into a charitable institution for old people in the 15th century.

Between 1583 and 1591 the artist Palma il Giovane, com-missioned by the Crociferi, decorated the chapel with a glowing cycle of paintings, depicting the crucial events in the history of this religious order. The paintings suffered terrible damage in the floods of 1966 (*see p50*), but were successfully restored and the chapel reopened in 1984.

The inscriptions on the walls of some of the surrounding houses in the square are those of art and craft guilds, such as silk weavers and tailors, whose works formerly occu-pied the buildings.

The sumptuous ceiling frescoes of the Gesuiti church

Gesuiti ❼

Campo dei Gesuiti. **Map** 3 B4.
Tel 041 528 65 79. 🚤 Fondamente Nuove. ◯ 10am–noon, 4–6pm daily.

The Jesuits' close links with the papacy provoked Venetian hostility during the 17th century, and for 50 years they were refused entry to the city. However, in 1714 they were given permission to build this church in the north of Venice, on the site of a 12th-century church which had belonged to the Order of the Crociferi. Consecrated as Santa Maria Assunta, the church is always referred to simply as the Gesuiti; thus it is often confused with the Gesuati in Dorsoduro (*see p129*).

Domenico Rossi's imposing Baroque exterior gives only a hint of the opulence of the interior. The proliferation of green and white marble, carved in parts like great folds of fabric, gives the impression that the church is clothed in damask.

Titian's *Martyrdom of St Lawrence* (c.1555), above the first altar on the left, has been described by the art historian Hugh Honour as "the first successful nocturne in the history of art".

Santa Maria dei Miracoli ❽

Campo dei Miracoli. **Map** 3 B5. **Tel** 041 275 04 62. 🚤 Fondamente Nuove or Rialto. ◯ 10am–5pm Mon–Sat. 🎫 🚫 ✏ www.chorusvenezia.org

An exquisite masterpiece of the early Renaissance, the Miracoli is the favourite church of many Venetians and the one where they like to get married. Tucked away in a maze of alleys and waterways in eastern Cannaregio, it is small and somewhat elusive, but well worth the effort needed to find it.

Often likened to a jewel box, the façade is decorated with various shades of marble, with fine bas-reliefs and sculpture. It was built in 1481–9 by the architect Pietro Lombardo and his sons to enshrine *The Virgin and Child* (1408), a painting believed to have miraculous powers. The picture, by Nicolò di Pietro,

Decorative column, interior of **Santa Maria dei Miracoli**

can still be seen above the altar. The interior of the church, which ideally should be visited when pale shafts of sunlight are streaming in through the windows, is embellished by pink, white and grey marble and crowned by a barrel-vaulted ceiling (1528) which has 50 portraits of saints and prophets. The balustrade, between the nave and the chancel, is decorated by Tullio Lombardo's carved figures of St Francis, Archangel Gabriel, the Virgin and St Clare. The screen around the high altar and the medallions of the Evangelists in the cupola spandrels are also by Lombardo.

Above the main door, the choir gallery was used by the nuns from the neighbouring convent, who entered the church through an overhead gallery. The Miracoli was the subject of a major restoration programme, which was funded by the American Save Venice organization.

SANTA MARIA DEI MIRACOLI
The façade is a harmonious tapestry of decorated panels and multicoloured polished stone.

The semi-circular crowning lunette emphasizes the church's jewel-box appearance.

A false loggia is formed of Ionic arches, inset with windows. The marble used was reportedly left over from the building of San Marco.

The marble panels are fixed to the bricks by metal hooks. This method, which prevents the build-up of damp and salt water behind the panels, dates from the Renaissance.

San Giovanni Grisostomo, the last work of Mauro Coducci

San Giovanni Grisostomo ❾

Campo S Giovanni Grisostomo.
Map 3 B5. **Tel** 041 523 52 93.
🚤 Rialto. ⏲ 8:15am–12:15pm,
3–7:30pm daily. No entry during mass.

This pretty terracotta-coloured church is found near the Rialto. Built between 1479 and 1504, the church was the last work of Mauro Coducci.

The interior, built on a Greek-cross plan, is dark and intimate. Notable works of art include Giovanni Bellini's *St Jerome with Saints Christopher and Augustine* (1513), above the first altar on the right. Influenced by Giorgione, this was probably Bellini's last painting. Another artist inspired by Giorgione was Sebastiano del Piombo, whose *St John Chrysostom and Six Saints* (1509–11) hangs above the high altar. Some believe that the figures of St John the Baptist and St Liberal were painted by Giorgione himself.

Santi Apostoli ❿

Campo Santi Apostoli. **Map** 3 B5.
Tel 041 523 82 97. 🚤 Ca' d'Oro. ⏲
10am–noon, 3–7pm daily (may vary).

The Campo Santi Apostoli is a busy crossroads for pedestrians en route to the Rialto or the railway station. Its church is unremarkable architecturally and little

MARCO POLO

Born around 1254 in the quarter of Cannaregio near the Rialto, Marco Polo left Venice at the age of 18 for his four-year voyage to the court of the Emperor Kublai Khan. He impressed the Mongol emperor and stayed for some 20 years, working as a travelling diplomat.

Returning to Venice in 1295, he brought with him a fortune in jewels and a host of spellbinding stories about the Khan's court.

As a prisoner of war in Genoa in 1298 he compiled an account of his travels, with the cooperation of an inmate. Translated into French, this was to become *Le Livre des merveilles.* Despite the fact that many Italians disbelieved his wondrous tales of the east, the book was an instant success.

His nickname became Marco Il Milione (of the million lies); hence the name of the two little courtyards where the Polo family lived: Corte Prima del Milion and Corte Seconda del Milion.

Marco Polo leaving on his travels, from a manuscript c.1338

remains of the 16th-century building. A notable exception, however, is the enchanting late 15th-century Renaissance Corner Chapel on the right of the nave, believed to have been designed by Mauro Coducci. The chapel contains *The Communion of St Lucy* by Giambattista Tiepolo (1748), the tomb of Marco Corner, probably by Tullio Lombardo (1511), and an inscription to Corner's daughter, Caterina Cornaro, Queen of Cyprus, who was buried here before she was moved to the Church of San Salvatore *(see p94).*

Tomb of Doge Marco Corner in Santi Apostoli (Corner Chapel)

Ca' d'Oro ⓫

See p144.

Palazzo Labia ⓬

Fondamenta Labia (entrance on Campo S Geremia). **Map** 2 D4.
Tel 041 781 111. 🚤 Ponte Guglie.
⚙ renovation in progress; call ahead.

The Labias were a wealthy family of merchants from Catalonia who bought their way into the Venetian patriciate in 1646. Towards the end of the century they built their prestigious palace on the wide Cannaregio Canal, close to its junction with the Grand Canal. In 1745–50 the ballroom was frescoed by Giambattista Tiepolo. The wonderfully painted scenes are taken from the life of Cleopatra but the setting is Venice, and the queen's attire is that of a 16th-century noble lady.

Passed from one owner to another the palace gradually lost all trace of its former grandeur and variously served as a religious foundation, a school and a doss-house. Between 1964 and 1992 it was owned by the Italian broadcasting network, RAI, who undertook its restoration.

The frescoes can be seen free of charge, but only by making an appointment.

Ca' d'Oro ⓫

One of the great showpieces of the Grand Canal, the Ca' d'Oro (or House of Gold) is the finest example of Venetian Gothic architecture in the city. The façade, with its finely carved ogee windows, oriental pinnacles and exotic marble tracery, has an unmistakable flavour of the east. But this once gloriously embellished *palazzo* suffered many changes of fortune and there is now little inside to remind visitors that this was once a 15th-century palace. Since 1984 it has been home to the Giorgio Franchetti Collection.

HISTORY

In 1420 the wealthy patrician, Marino Contarini, commissioned the building of what he was determined would be the most magnificent palace in the city. The decoration and the intricate carving were executed by a team of Venetian and Lombard craftsmen, and he had the façade adorned in ultramarine, gold leaf and vermilion.

Tullio Lombardo's Double Portrait

In the course of the 16th century the house was remodelled by a succession of owners, and by the early 18th century was semi-derelict. In 1846 the Russian Prince Troubetzkoy bought it for the famous ballerina Maria Taglioni. Under her direction, the Ca' d'Oro suffered barbaric restoration. The open staircase was ripped out, the wellhead by Bartolomeo Bon (1427–8) was sold and much of the stonework removed. It was finally rescued by Baron Franchetti, a patron of the arts, who restored it to its former glory and bequeathed it to the state in 1915. A restoration programme for the façade, first put into action in the 1970s, is now finally completed, revealing the building's exotic design. The pretty paved courtyard contains Bon's beautifully carved wellhead. This was one of the pieces retrieved by Franchetti.

FIRST FLOOR

Pride of place is given to Andrea Mantegna's *St Sebastian* (1506), the artist's last painting and Franchetti's favourite work of art. The *portego* (gallery) opening on to the Grand Canal is a showroom of sculpture. Among the finest pieces are bronze reliefs by the Paduan sculptor, Il Riccio (1470–1532), Tullio Lombardo's marble *Double Portrait* (c.1493) and Sansovino's lunette of the Virgin and Child (c.1530). Rooms to the right of the *portego* have some fine Renaissance bronzes and, among the paintings, an *Annunciation* and *Death of the Virgin* (both c.1504) by Vittore Carpaccio and assistants. A room to the left of the *portego* is devoted to non-Venetian painting, and includes Luca Signorelli's *Flagellation* (c.1480).

SECOND FLOOR

The upper floor houses paintings by Venetian masters, including a *Venus* by Titian, two Venetian views by Guardi, and fresco fragments by Titian. Other exhibits include tapestries and ceramics. Explanatory cards in each room aid visitors.

VISITORS' CHECKLIST

Canal Grande (Calle Ca' d'Oro).
Map 3 A4. **Tel** 041 520 03 45.
Ca' d'Oro. 8:15am–7:15pm daily (to 2pm Mon). 1 Jan, 1 May, 25 Dec.

The *Annunciation* (1504) by Vittore Carpaccio and assistants

Scalzi 🅱

Fondamenta Scalzi. **Map** 1 C4.
Tel 041 71 51 15. 🚉 *Ferrovia.*
⏱ *7am–noon, 3:30–7pm daily.*

Beside the modern railway
station *(see p58)* stands
the church of Santa Maria
di Nazareth, known as the
Scalzi. The *scalzi* were
"barefooted" Carmelite friars
who came to Venice during
the 1670s and commissioned
their church to be built on
the Grand Canal. Designed
by Baldassare Longhena,
the huge Baroque interior
is an over-elaboration of
marble, gilded woodwork
and sculptures. The ceiling

painting, *The Council of
Ephesus* by Ettore Tito (1934),
replaced Giambattista Tiepolo's
fresco of *The Translation of the
Holy House to Loreto* (1743–5),
which was destroyed by the
Austrian bombardment of
24 October 1915.

San Giobbe 🅲

Campo San Giobbe. **Map** 1 C3. *Tel*
041 275 04 62. 🚉 *Ponte dei 3 Archi.*
⏱ *10am–1:15pm Mon–Sat.* 🚫

The church of San Giobbe
stands in a remote *campo*
full of cats. The early Gothic
structure of the church was
modified in the 1470s by

Pietro Lombardo who added
Renaissance elements to the
design, such as the saints over
the portal. The Martini chapel,
second on the left, is
decorated with Della
Robbia-style glazed
terracotta. The altar-
pieces by Giovanni
Bellini and Vittore
Carpaccio were
removed when
Napoleon
suppressed the
monastery of San
Giobbe, and are now
in the Accademia
Gallery *(pp130–33).*

**Saint by Lombardo,
San Giobbe portal**

The Ghetto 🅳

Map 2 E3. *Tel* 041 71 53 59.
🚉 *Ponte Guglie.* **Museo Ebraico**
Campo del Ghetto Nuovo. 🚉 *Ponte
Guglie.* ⏱ *10am–7pm (Oct–May:
to 6pm) Sun–Fri.* ⏺ *1 Jan, 1 May,
25 Dec, Jewish hols.* 📷 🔲 🔲
www.museoebraico.it

In 1516 the Council of Ten
(see p42) decreed that all
Jews in Venice be confined to
an islet of Cannaregio. The
quarter was cut off by wide
canals and the two watergates
were manned by Christian
guards. The area was named
the Ghetto after a foundry –
geto in Venetian – that
formerly occupied the site.
The name was subsequently
given to Jewish enclaves
throughout the world. By day
Jews were allowed out of the
Ghetto, but at all times they
were made to wear identify-
ing badges and caps. The
only trades they could pursue
were in textiles, money-
lending and medicine.

**Campo del Ghetto Nuovo, the
oldest part of the Ghetto**

The wrought-iron bridge leading northwards out of the Ghetto

The rising number of Jews
forced the Ghetto to expand.
Buildings rose vertically and
spread into the Ghetto Vecchio
(1541) and the neighbouring
Ghetto Novissimo
(1633). By the
mid-17th century
the Jewish popula-
tion numbered
over 5,000.

In 1797 Napoleon
pulled down the
gates, but under
the Austrians the
Jews were again forced into
confinement. It was not until
1866 that they were granted
their freedom.

Of the 500 Jews now in
Venice, only 33 live in the
Ghetto. However, the quarter
has not lost its ethnic character.
There are kosher food shops,
a Jewish baker, a Jewish
library, and two synagogues
where religious ceremonies

**Flowers in front of the
Holocaust Memorial**

still take place. There are also
several shops on the large
Campo del Ghetto Nuovo,
which sell items such as glass
rabbis and Hanukah lamps.

Museo Ebraico
The small Jewish
Museum in the
Ghetto Nuovo
houses a collection
of artifacts from
the 17th–19th
centuries. A guided
tour of the quarter's
synagogues leaves from the
museum daily except Saturday, every hour from 10:30am
to 5:30pm (4:30pm in winter).
Led by English-speaking
guides, the tours give a fascinating glimpse into the past
life of the Ghetto. A short history of the quarter is followed
by a visit to the lavishly
decorated German, Spanish
and Levantine synagogues.

THE LAGOON ISLANDS

Shrouded in myth and super-stition, the lagoon was once the preserve of fishermen and hunters. But marauders in the 5th and 6th centuries AD drove mainland dwellers to the safety of the marshy lagoon *(see p40)*. Here, they conquered their watery environment, which was protected from the open sea by thin sandbanks *(lidi)*, created from silt washed down by the rivers of the Po delta. In the 13th century the first *murazzi* were built – sea walls of angular stone which safeguard the *lidi* from erosion. Experiments with tidal barriers continue in an effort to combat the ever-present threat of flooding *(see p51)*.

The thriving communities that once lived and traded here are long gone. Many of the islands, formerly used as sites for monasteries, hospitals or powder factories, are now abandoned, but a handful of them are undergoing development – one as an international university, another as an exclusive resort.

Image of the Madonna, Torcello

SIGHTS AT A GLANCE

Burano ❷
Giudecca ❻
Lazzaretto Nuovo ⓬
Lido ❿
Murano ❹
Poveglia ⓭
San Clemente ⓫

San Francesco del Deserto ❸
San Lazzaro degli Armeni ❾
San Michele ❺
San Servolo ❼
Santa Maria della Grazia ❽
Torcello pp152–3 ❶

Treviso
Belluno
Canale Bazzera
S14
S Dona
Portogruaro
S146
S14
Canale Osellino
Marco Polo
Mestre
Veneta
S11
Laguna
FS
VENEZIA
Giacomo Nicelli
Lido di Jesolo
MARE ADRIATICO

KEY

✈ Airfield

FS Railway station

| 0 kilometres | 5 |
| 0 miles | 3 |

◁ **Colourful houses in Burano**

Exploring the Lagoon

A trip to the Lagoon Islands makes a welcome break from the densely packed streets of the city. Murano, celebrated for its glass, can be reached in a matter of minutes. Further north, Burano, the "lace island", and ancient Torcello are well worth the longer ride. The Lido, with its sandy beaches, is an easy journey from San Marco. Some of the lesser known islands are worth exploring too, but access can sometimes be difficult.

Murano
Some of Murano's canalside porticoes survive from medieval days ❹

Murano and San Michele
are clearly visible from the northern quaysides of Venice.

San Michele
World-famous writers and artists are buried alongside Venetians on this island ❺

VENEZIA

San Giorgio in Alga had its monastery partially destroyed by fire in 1717. It was demolished in the 19th century.

SANTA MARIA DELLA GRAZIA ❽

SAN CLEMENTE ⓫

Giudecca
Palladio's great church of the Redentore, on the waterfront, is the island's cultural highlight ❻

Sant'Angelo della Polvere, recognizable by its towers, was formerly a powder factory.

SAN SPIRITO

Sacca Sessola, an artificial island, was the site of a hospital until 1980.

POVEGLIA ⓭

Lido
Behind the crowded beaches and grand hotels, the Lido has some pleasantly peaceful waterways ❿

Torcello
The island's cathedral, founded in AD 639, is the oldest building in the lagoon ❶

Sant'Ariano is a former ossuary island where the bones of Venetians were taken.

Burano
Gaily painted, shuttered houses are a distinctive feature of the island's streets and quaysides ❷

MAZZORBO

Le Vignole has market gardens and an ancient fort.

MADONNA DEL MONTE

SAN GIACOMO IN PALUDE

❸ *SAN FRANCESCO DEL DESERTO*

TREPORTI

❿ *LAZZARETTO NUOVO*

PUNTA SABBIONI

Sant' Erasmo, once a Roman pleasure ground, is now a vegetable garden.

PORTO DI LIDO

SAN NICOLO

LIDO

GOLFO DI VENEZIA

San Servolo
This is now a centre for artisans learning restoration techniques, such as stucco and plasterwork ❼

GETTING AROUND
The main islands of the northern lagoon are well served by the *vaporetti* (see pp282–3) and the Laguna Nord boat route from Fondamente Nuove. A few of the smaller islands have a limited public service; others can only be reached by water taxi.

Lazzaretto Vecchio
is a tiny island with a varied past. It can be seen in the distance from the boat that runs from San Marco to the Lido.

San Lazzaro degli Armeni
Visits to this green and pretty monastery island take in the church, library, museum and printing press ❾

KEY

▨ Major road

▨ Minor road

0 kilometres — 2

0 miles — 1

Torcello ❶

See pp152–3.

A stall selling lace and linen in Burano's main street

Burano ❷

🚢 *LN, either from Fondamente Nuove, approx. 40–50 minutes, or from San Zaccaria via the Lido and Punta Sabbioni, approx. 1½ hours.*

Burano is the most colourful of the lagoon islands. Lying in a lonely expanse of the northern lagoon, it is distinguished from a distance by the tall, dramatically tilted tower of its church. In contrast to the desolate Torcello, the island is densely populated, its waterways lined by brightly painted houses.

A tour of the island's sights will take an hour or so. The street from the ferry stop takes visitors to the main thoroughfare, Via Baldassare Galuppi, named after the Burano-born composer (1706–85). The

street is lined with lace and linen stalls and open-air trattorias serving fresh fish.

🏛 Museo del Merletto

Piazza Baldassare Galuppi. **Tel** 041 730 034. ⭘ see website for up-to-date information. ⭘ 1 Jan, 1 May, 25 Dec. 🖳 www.museiciviciveneziani.it

The Buranese are fishermen and lacemakers by trade. Visitors can still see the men scraping their boats or mending nets, but lacemakers are rare. In the 16th century the local lace was the most sought after in Europe. It was so delicate it became known as *punto in aria* ("points in the air"). Foreign competition, coupled with the Republic's decline, led to a slump in the 18th century in Burano's industry. However, the need for an alternative source of income led to a revival of the skill in 1872 and the founding of a lacemaking school, the Scuola dei Merletti.

Today, authentic Burano lace is hard to find. Genuine pieces take weeks of painstaking labour, and are expensive. Original pieces can be seen at the informative Museo del Merletto. Displays of household linens and clothing feature fine antique lace, much of it created at the school.

Mazzorbo

Linked to Burano by a footbridge, Mazzorbo is an island of orchards and gardens. Ferries en route to Burano and Torcello pass through its canal. The only surviving church is the Romanesque-Gothic Santa Caterina.

San Francesco del Deserto ❸

Access via water taxi from the landing stage in Burano. *Visits to the island: usually 9–11am, 3–5pm Tue–Sun, but call ahead for up-to-date information.* **Monastery Tel** 041 528 68 63. *Donations welcome.*

This little oasis of greenery, inhabited by nine friars, lies just south of Burano. There is no *vaporetto* service and to get there you must bargain with the boatmen on Burano's quayside, who will ferry you across and await your return.

The multilingual friars who live on the island give tours of the old church and the lovely gardens, which have a tree said to have sprouted from the staff of St Francis of Assisi.

A Buranese fisherman about to haul in the day's catch

Murano ❹

🚢 *No. 41, 42 or LN from Fondamente Nuove; DM from Piazzale Roma.*

Like the city of Venice, Murano comprises a cluster of small islands, connected by bridges. It has been the centre of the glassmaking industry since 1291, when the furnaces and glass craftsmen were moved here from the city, prompted by the risk of fire to the buildings and the disagreeable effects of smoke.

Historically Murano owes its prosperity entirely to glass. From the late 13th century, when the population numbered over 30,000, Murano enjoyed self-government, minted its own coins and had its own Golden Book *(see p42)* listing members of the aristocracy. In the 15th and 16th centuries it was the principal glass-producing centre in Europe. Murano's glass artisans were granted unprecedented privileges, but for those who

Brightly painted street in Burano

left the island to found businesses elsewhere there were severe penalties – even death.

Although a few of Murano's *palazzi* bear testimony to its former splendour, and its basilica still survives, most tourists visit for glass alone. Some are enticed by offers of free trips from factory touts in San Marco, others go by excursion launch or independently on the public *vaporetti*.

Some of the factories are now derelict, but glass is still produced in vast quantities. Among the plethora of kitsch (including imports from the Far East) are some wonderful pieces, and it pays to seek out the top glass factories *(see p253)*. Many furnaces, however, close at the weekend.

🏛 Museo Vetrario

Palazzo Giustinian, Fondamenta Giustinian. *Tel* 041 739 586. ⬜ 10am–6pm daily (Nov–Mar: to 5pm). 🔴 1 Jan, 1 May, 25 Dec. 🎫 🚻

The Museo Vetrario (glass museum) in the huge Palazzo Giustinian houses a splendid collection of antique pieces. The prize exhibit of the collection is the Barovier wedding cup (1470–80), with enamelwork decoration by Angelo Barovier. There is also a section devoted to modern glass, with some splendid items on view.

🔒 Basilica dei Santi Maria e Donato

Fondamenta Giustinian. *Tel* 041 739 056. ⬜ 9am–noon, 3:30–7pm daily (Nov–Mar: to 6pm). 🔴 Sun am.

The colonnaded exterior of Murano's Basilica dei Santi Maria e Donato

The island's architectural highlight is the Basilica dei Santi Maria e Donato, whose magnificent colonnaded apse is reflected in the waters of the San Donato canal. Despite some heavy-handed restoration undertaken in the 19th century, this 12th-century church still retains much of its original beauty. Visitors should note the Veneto-Byzantine columns and Gothic ship's keel roof. An enchantingly evocative mosaic portrait of the Madonna, seen standing alone against a gold background, decorates the apse.

The church's floor, or *pavimento*, dating from 1140, is equally beautiful. With its medieval mosaics of geometric figures, exotic birds, mythical creatures and inexplicable symbols, it incorporates fragments of ancient glass from the island's foundries into its imagery.

Diaghilev's tombstone

GLASS BLOWING

A main attraction of a trip to Murano is a demonstration of the glass-blowing technique. Visitors can watch while a glass blower takes a blob of molten paste on the end of an iron rod and, by twisting, turning and blowing, miraculously transforms it into a vase, bird, lion, wine goblet or similar work of art. The display is followed by a tour of the showroom and a certain amount of pressure from the salespeople. There is no obligation to buy, however.

Glass blower at work in Murano

San Michele ❺

📷 No. 41 or 42 from Fondamente Nuove.

Studded with dark cypresses and enclosed within high terracotta walls, the cemetery island of San Michele lies just across the water from Venice's Fondamente Nuove. The bodies of Venetians were traditionally buried in church graveyards in Venice, but for reasons of hygiene and space, San Michele and its neighbour were designated cemeteries in the 19th century.

The church of San Michele in Isola stands by the landing stage. Designed by Mauro Coducci (c.1469), it was the first church in Venice to be faced in white Istrian stone. The cemetery itself rambles over most of the island. With its carved tombstones and chapels it has a curious fascination. Some graves have suffered neglect, but most are well-tended and enlivened by a riot of flowers. The most famous graves are those of foreigners: Ezra Pound (1885–1972), in the *Evangelisti* (Protestant) section, and Sergei Diaghilev (1872–1929) and Igor Stravinsky (1882–1971) in the *Greci* or Orthodox section. These bodies have been allowed to rest in peace. Most others are dug up after about ten years to make way for new arrivals, and the bones taken to the ossuary island of Sant'Ariano. Today, however, because of increasing lack of space on San Michele, most bodies are buried on the mainland.

Torcello ●

Established between the 5th and 6th centuries, Torcello grew into a thriving colony *(see p40)*, with palaces, churches and a population said to have reached 20,000. But with the rise of Venice the island went into decline. Today, the population is just 60 and all that remains of this once vigorous island is the Byzantine cathedral, the church of Santa Fosca and the memory of its former glory.

★ **Apse Mosaic**
The 13th-century Madonna, set against a gold background, is one of the most moving mosaics in Venice.

★ **Domesday Mosaics**
The huge and highly decorative mosaic of the Last Judgment covers the entire west wall.

Pulpit
The present basilica dates from 1008, but includes many earlier features. The marble pulpit is made of fragments from the first, 7th-century church.

The Roman sarcophagus
below the altar is said to contain the relics of St Heliodorus.

★ **Iconostasis**
The exquisite Byzantine marble panels of the rood screen are carved with peacocks, lions and flowers. This detailed relief shows two peacocks drinking from the fountain of life.

Nave Columns
The finely carved capitals on the marble nave columns date from the 11th century.

VISITORS' CHECKLIST

🚤 No. 12 from Fondamente Nuove. **Basilica di Santa Maria dell' Assunta Tel** 041 296 06 30. ⬜ Mar–Oct: 10:30am–6pm daily; Nov–Feb: 10am–5pm daily. 🎫 🔲 **Campanile** ⬜ Apr–Oct: 10:30am–5:30pm daily; Nov–Mar 10am–5pm daily. 🎫 **Santa Fosca** ⬜ mass. **Museo Tel** 041 73 07 61. ⬜ Mar–Oct:10:30am–5:30pm Tue–Sun; Nov–Feb: 10am–5pm Tue–Sun. ⬤ public hols. 🎫

Torcello's Last Canals
Silted canals and malaria hastened Torcello's decline. One of the remaining waterways runs from the vaporetto stop to the basilica.

Santa Fosca
Built in the 11th and 12th centuries on a Greek-cross plan, the church has a lovely portico and a serene Byzantine interior.

The central dome
and cross sections are supported by columns of Greek marble with fine Corinthian capitals.

Attila's Throne
It was said that the 5th-century king of the Huns used this marble seat as his throne.

To *vaporetto* boarding point →

Museo dell' Estuario
Old church treasures and archaeological fragments are housed here.

STAR FEATURES

★ Iconostasis

★ Domesday Mosaics

★ Apse Mosaic

Boats moored along the Ponte Lungo on the Giudecca

Giudecca ❻

No. 2, 41 or 42.

In the days of the Republic, the island of Giudecca was a pleasure ground of palaces and gardens. Today it is very much a suburb of the city, its dark, narrow alleys flanked by apartments, its squares overgrown and its *palazzi* neglected. Many of its old factories have been converted into modern housing. However, the long, wide quayside skirting the city side of the island makes a very pleasant promenade and provides stunning views of Venice across the water. The island was originally named Spinalunga (long spine) on account of its shape. The name Giudecca, once thought to have referred to the Jews, or *giudei*, who lived here in the 13th century, is more likely to have originated from the word *giudicati* meaning "the judged". This referred to troublesome aristocrats who, as early as the 9th century, were banished to the island.

The Hotel Cipriani (see p233), among the most luxurious places to stay in Venice, is quietly and discreetly located at the tip of the island. In contrast, at the western end of the island looms the massive Neo-Gothic ruin of the Mulino Stucky. It was built in 1895 as a flour mill by the Swiss entrepreneur Giovanni Stucky, an unpopular employer who was murdered by one of his workers in 1910. The mill ceased functioning in 1954. Following extensive renovations, it reopened in 2007 as a luxury hotel with a rooftop pool.

🔒 Il Redentore

Campo Redentore. **Tel** 041 275 04 62. Redentore. 10am–5pm Mon–Sat. 1 Jan, 25 Dec. www.chorusvenezia.org

Giudecca's principal monument is Palladio's church of Il Redentore (the Redeemer). It was built in 1577–92 in thanksgiving for the end of the 1576 plague, which wiped out a third of the city's population. Every year since its creation, the doge and his entourage would visit the church, crossing from the Zattere on a bridge of boats. The Feast of the Redeemer is still celebrated on the third weekend in July *(see p34)*.

The church of Il Redentore, styled on the architecture of ancient Rome, is a masterpiece of harmony and proportion. The Classical interior presents a marked contrast to the ornate and elaborate style of most Venetian churches. The main paintings, by Paolo Veronese and Alvise Vivarini are in the sacristy to the right of the choir. The most rewarding views of the Redentore are from Venice across the water. For special festivities the church is often floodlit after dark, which makes a spectacular sight.

🔒 Le Zitelle

Fondamenta delle Zitelle. **Tel** 041 521 74 11. Zitelle. Apr–Oct: 3:30–6:30pm Fri & Sat.

Palladio's church is now the site of Venice's most up-to-date congress centre. The building adjoining the church used to be a hostel for spinsters (*zitelle*), who occupied themselves by making fine lace.

An artisan at work at the San Servolo training centre

San Servolo ❼

No. 20 from San Zaccaria. **Venice International University Tel** 041 276 50 01. www. sanservolo.provincia.venezia.it

Half-way between San Marco and the Lido is the island of San Servolo. Now a centre for teaching crafts and home to the Venice International University, it started life as one of the original monastery islands of Venice. Benedictine monks established a monastery here in the 8th century, and later added a hospital.

In 1725 the island became a lunatic asylum and a new hospital was built to house the patients. The Council of Ten *(see p42)* declared that this was to be strictly a shelter for "maniacs of noble family or comfortable circumstances". Poor maniacs were imprisoned or left to their own devices. In 1797 Napoleon scrubbed this discriminatory decree and the asylum became free to all.

Palladio's Redentore church, Giudecca

In 1980 this spartan island was taken over by The Venice European Centre for the Trades and Professions of Conservation, and in 1996, Venice International University opened its doors here. The historic buildings and the large park in which they are set have been extensively restored.

Santa Maria della Grazia ❽

No public access.

Originally called La Cavana or Cavanell, the island lies a short distance from San Giorgio Maggiore *(see p95)*. Formerly a shelter for pilgrims journeying to the Holy Land, it became a monastery island in the 15th century. Its name was changed when a church was constructed to enshrine a miraculous image of the Virgin, brought from Constantinople. The religious buildings, including a Gothic church with some fine paintings, were secularized under Napoleon. The island became a military zone under his rule, but the buildings were destroyed in the 1848 revolutionary uprising *(see p48)*.

Until the end of the 20th century, the island was occupied by a hospital for infectious diseases; after this department moved to the main hospital in Venice, the island was sold.

San Lazzaro degli Armeni ❾

Tel 041 526 01 04. 🚌 No. 20. ⏰ for one visit daily. Boat leaves San Zaccaria at 2:45pm (Nov–Apr: 3:10pm). 📷 📹

Lying just off the Lido *(see p156)*, San Lazzaro degli Armeni is a small monastery island, recognizable by the onion-shaped cupola of its white campanile. The buildings are surrounded by gardens and groves of cypress trees. Since the 18th century it has been an Armenian monastery and centre of learning.

Early history

This small island served as an asylum in the 12th century and later became a hospital island for lepers, named after their patron saint, Lazarus. The lepers were then transferred to the Ospedale di San Lazzaro dei Mendicanti at Santi Giovanni e Paolo *(see pp116–17)*. In 1717 an Armenian monk, Manug di Pietro, known as Mechitar ("the consoler"), was forced to flee his homeland, the Morea, when the Turks invaded. Venetian rulers gave him the island of San Lazzaro in the southern lagoon as a place of shelter. Here, he established a religious order. The Armenians rebuilt the island, setting up a monastery, church, library, study rooms, gardens and

Illuminated manuscript, San Lazzaro degli Armeni

Prince Nehmekhet's sarcophagus (c.1000 BC), San Lazzaro

orchards. The island became a place of study where monks taught (and still teach) young Armenians their culture.

The island today

Today, multilingual monks give visitors guided tours of the church, the art collection, the library and the museum, which houses Armenian, Greek, Indian and Egyptian artifacts. One of the most famous is an Egyptian sarcophagus complete with mummy, which is one of the best-preserved in the world. The most impressive exhibit is the printing hall where, over 200 years ago, a press produced works in 36 languages. A polyglot press is still in use, producing postcards, maps and prints for visitors.

Lord Byron

In 1816 the poet Byron would often row from Venice to absorb Armenian culture. Full of admiration for the monks, he wrote that the monastery "appears to unite all the advantages of the monastic institution without any of its vices … the virtues of the brethren … are well fitted to strike a man of the world with the conviction that 'there is another and a better', even in this life." The room where he studied, with mementoes, has been carefully preserved.

The garden and cloisters of San Lazzaro degli Armeni

The Lido, away from the crowds and glare of the beaches

Lido ⑩

🚤 No's 1, 51, 52, 61, 62, 82 (summer) and LN to Santa Maria Elisabetta; No. 17 from Tronchetto to San Nicolò.

The Lido is a slender sand-bank 12 km (8 miles) long, which forms a natural barrier between Venice and the open sea. It is both a residential suburb of the city and – more importantly for tourists – the city's seaside resort. The only island in the lagoon with roads, it is linked to the Tronchetto island car park by car ferry. From Venice, the Lido is served by regular

The elegant bar of the Hôtel des Bains on the Lido

vaporetti. The fastest of these (Motonave LN) takes little more than ten minutes to reach its destination.

The Lido's main season runs from June to September, the most crowded months being July and August. In winter most hotels are closed.

The world's first lido

In the 19th century, before the Lido was developed, the island was a favourite haunt of Shelley, Byron and other literary figures. Byron swam from the Lido to Santa Chiara via the Grand Canal in under 4 hours.

Bathing establishments were gradually opened and by the turn of the century the Lido had become one of Europe's most fashionable seaside resorts, frequented by royalty, film stars and leading lights of the literati. They stayed in the grand hotels, swam in the sea or sat in deckchairs on the sands by the striped *cabanas*. Life in the Lido's heyday was brilliantly evoked in Thomas Mann's book *Death in Venice* (1912). The Hôtel des Bains, where the melancholic Von

Aschenbach stays, features in the novel and in Visconti's 1970 film. It is still a promi-nent landmark, though no longer a hotel.

The Lido is no longer the prestigious resort it was in the 1930s. Beaches are crowded, the streets busy and the fer-ries packed with daytrippers. Nevertheless the sands, sea and sporting facilities provide a welcome break from city culture. The backwaters provide a green respite from the heat of Venice.

Exploring the island

The Lido can be covered by bus but a popular form of transport is the bicycle. Visitors can hire one from the shop almost opposite the *vaporetto* stop at Santa Maria Elisabetta.

The east side of the island is fringed by sandy beaches. For passengers arriving by ferry at the main landing stage, these beaches are reached by bus, taxi or on foot along the Gran Viale Santa Maria Elisabetta. This is the main shopping street of the Lido. At the end of the Gran Viale turn left for the beaches of San Nicolò or right along the Lungomare G Marconi, which boasts the grandest hotels and the best beaches. The hotels control the beaches in this area, and levy exorbitant charges (except to hotel residents) for the use of their beach facilities.

The long straight road parallel to the beach leads southwest to the village of

Cabanas on the Lido beaches, hired out to holidaying Venetians

Malamocco. There are some pleasant fish restaurants here, but there is little evidence that this was once the 8th-century seat of the lagoon's government.

Alberoni, at the southern end of the Lido, is the site of a golf course, a public beach and the landing stage for the ferry across to Pellestrina.

San Nicolò

The Lido's only quarter of cultural interest is San Nicolò in the north.

Across the Porto di Lido, it is possible to see the fortress of Sant'Andrea on the island of Le Vignole, built by Michele Sanmicheli between 1435 and 1449 to guard the main entrance of the lagoon.

It was to the Porto di Lido that the doge was rowed annually to cast a ring into the sea in symbolic marriage each spring *(see p33)*. After the ceremony he would visit the nearby church and monastery of San Nicolò, which was founded in 1044 and rebuilt in the 16th century.

The nearby Jewish cemetery, open to the public, dates from 1386. The rest of this northern area is given over to an airfield. The aeroclub located there can organize private flying lessons.

Jewish Cemetery
Tel 041 71 53 59. 🚌 📷 *call in advance for a guided visit.*

San Clemente ⓫

San Clemente Palace Hotel
Tel 041 244 50 01. **www. sanclementepalacevenice.com**

From a refuge for pilgrims en route to the Holy Land, the island of San Clemente became the site of a monastery. During the Republic, doges frequently met distinguished visitors here, but from 1630, when it was hit by the plague, it served as a military depot. In the 19th century the island was turned into a lunatic asylum; most of the buildings date from that time. The beautifully restored San Clemente Palace Hotel can be reached by launch from Piazza San Marco.

INTERNATIONAL FILM FESTIVAL

Film fans flock to the Lido every year in late summer for the International Film Festival. The event was inaugurated in 1932 under the auspices of the Biennale *(see p256)* and was so successful that the Palazzo del Cinema was built four years later. During its history the festival has attracted big names in the film world; it has also been plagued by bureaucracy and political in-fighting. There are signs however that the event is making a comeback and the famous names are now returning to the Lido.

The event takes place over 2 weeks in late August/early September. Films are shown day and night in numerous venues including the Palazzo del Cinema (tickets are sold outside). You can normally spot the stars (along with the paparazzi) for the price of a drink on the terrace of the Excelsior Hotel. See also page 259.

Poster advertising the first Lido International Film Festival, 1932

Lazzaretto Nuovo ⓬

Tel 041 244 40 11. 🚌 *No. 13.* ⏰ *Apr–Oct: 9:45am & 4pm Sat & Sun.* 📷 📷 *donation.*

A mere stone's throw from Sant'Erasmo, in the northern lagoon, Lazzaretto Nuovo is one of the few uninhabited visitable islands. Archaeologists continue to unearth medieval structures dating back to the late 15th century, when the island was used as a quarantine station for crews of ships hailing from distant lands where the plague was rife. Cargoes would be fumigated with rosemary and juniper. During the terrible pestilence that afflicted Venice in 1576, the island housed 10,000 victims.

Poveglia ⓭

No public access.

Formerly called Popilia on account of all its poplar trees, the island was once a thriving community with its own government. After the 1380 war with Genoa, it fell into decline, and over the centuries became a refuge for plague victims, an isolation hospital and a home for the aged. Today the land is used for growing crops and vines.

San Clemente in the southern lagoon, seen through the evening mist

The picturesque lakeside setting of Alleghe in the Dolomites ▷

THE VENETO
AREA BY AREA

The Veneto at a Glance

The Veneto's sheer variety makes it one of Italy's most fascinating regions to explore. The cities of Verona, Padua and Vicenza are all noted for outstanding architecture, churches and museums. Villas in the rural hinterland are gorgeously frescoed with scenes from ancient mythology. The lagoon has busy fishing ports and beach resorts, while Lake Garda, with its glorious mountain scenery, historic castles and water sports, makes a perfect holiday play-ground. Northwards lie the majestic Dolomites, Italy's premier region for skiing, which attract visitors in the summer, too, with their alpine beauty and excellent hiking facilities.

Monti Lessini
Scores of scenic villages, such as Giazza (see p191), nestle in the vineyard-clad valleys of the Lessini mountains.

Verona
An ancient Roman stronghold, famous as the home of the lovers Romeo and Juliet, Verona today is a city of opera, theatre and art (see pp192–203).

VERONA AND LAKE GARDA
Pages 186–209

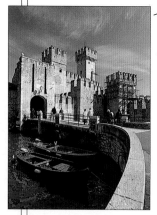

Lake Garda
Most beautiful of all the Italian lakes, Garda is surrounded by Scaligeri castles such as the magnificent Sirmione (see p204).

Vicenza
Dominated by the architecture of Palladio, Vicenza (see pp168–73) is the model Renaissance city.

Dolomites
Erosion has sculpted the limestone peaks of the Dolomites into bizarre columns and spires, with alpine villages hidden in steep valleys (see p216).

Villa Barbaro
Veronese's lavish frescoes are the perfect complement to one of Palladio's grandest rural villas, surrounded by statue-filled formal gardens, grottoes and pools (see p24).

THE DOLOMITES
Pages 210–219

| 0 kilometres | 30 |
| 0 miles | 15 |

THE VENETO PLAIN
Pages 162–185

Portogruaro
Roman and early Christian finds fill the museums of this ancient town (see p175).

Padua
The domes and minaret-like spires of St Anthony's basilica (see p182) lend an Eastern air to this historic university town.

Chioggia
Flocks of wading birds frequent the wild marshland around Chioggia (see p185), the Venetian lagoon's principal fishing port.

THE VENETO PLAIN

*T*he great arc of land that forms the Veneto Plain is one of tremendous contrast, and has much to offer the visitor. Its ancient cities are rich in history and their magnificent architecture is world-renowned. The source of the region's wealth is manifest in the industrial landscapes around the towns, but these are never far from beautiful countryside, which includes the green Euganean Hills, calm lagoons and the undulating foothills of the Dolomites.

The area known as the Veneto Plain sweeps round from the Po river delta in the southwest to the mountains that form the border between Italy and Slovenia. The whole region is crossed by a series of rivers, canals and waterways, all of which converge in the Adriatic sea.

The river-borne silt deposits that created the Venetian Lagoon cover the region, making the land fertile. The Romans established their frontier posts here, and these survive today as the great cities of Vicenza, Padua and Treviso. Their strategic position at the hub of the empire's road network enabled them to prosper under Roman rule, as they continued to do under the benign rule of the Venetian empire more than 1,000 years later.

Wealth from agriculture, commerce and the spoils of war paid for the beautification of these cities through the construction of Renaissance palaces and public buildings, many of them designed by the region's great architect, Andrea Palladio. His villas can be seen all over the Veneto, symbols of the idyllic and leisured existence once enjoyed by the region's aristocrats.

The symbols of modern prosperity – factories and scarred landscapes – are encountered frequently, especially around the town of Mestre. Yet there are areas of extraordinary beauty as well. Petrarch *(see p184)*, the great medieval romantic poet, so loved the area that he made his home among the gently wooded Euganean Hills.

Fishing from a breakwater in the lagoon at Chioggia

◁ **Classical figure in the nymphaeum of the Villa Barbaro near Asolo**

Exploring the Veneto Plain

The landscape of the Veneto Plain is as flat as a board, but it is far from dull. Villagers in the small communities dotted throughout the region used to compete to build the tallest church tower, and these seemingly needle-thin landmarks soaring skywards draw the traveller on. Great stone castles, dating from the 14th century, rise on almost every promontory, each with a backdrop on clear days of the distant Alps.

SEE ALSO

• *Where to Stay* pp233–4
• *Where to Eat* pp247–8

SIGHTS AT A GLANCE

The castellated walls of Montagnana, dating from medieval times

GETTING AROUND
An extensive rail network and good bus
services make this region easy to explore by
public transport. Roads are heavily used, so
avoid cities and *autostrade* during rush hours.

Palladio's Villa Rotonda near the town
of Vicenza

Follina

Vittorio Veneto

VALDOBBIADENE

10 CONEGLIANO

Vidór

Susegana

S13

A28

Ciano

Tezze

Spresiano

Oderzo

Motta di
Livanta

Annone
Véneto

11 PORTOGRUARO

Montebelluna

S248

S13

Candelú

Fossalta
Maggiore

Santo Stino
di Livenza

S14

Lugugnana

Udine,
Trieste

Vascón

Ponte
di Piave

S53

Paese

S348

S53

Quinto
di Treviso

9 TREVISO

Sile

Casale
sul Sile

San Donà
di Piave

San Giorgio
di Livenza

Bibione

Scorzè

Mogliano
Veneto

A27

Caposile

Eraclea

12 CAORLE

Noale

Martellago

S14

Eraclea Mare

Mirano

Spinea

13 MESTRE

Jésolo

Cortellazzo

Oriago

S11

Punta
Sabbioni

Lido
di Jésolo

olo

Fusina

Venézia
(Venice)

Lido

Cavallino

S309

Corte

ove
acco

Pellestrina

Pontelongo

CHIOGGIA

20

Treponti

S309

S. Anna

zere

Ádige

Rosolina

S516

Adria

19

Porto Viro

OLÉSINE

Taglia di Po

S309

La Pila

Ariano
I Polesine

Rivá

Porto
Tolle

Scardovari

Cassella

0 kilometres   20

0 miles   10

The colourful quayside market in the town of Chioggia, the
lagoon's principal fishing port

KEY

▬▬▬	Motorway
= =	Motorway under construction
▬▬	Major road
▬▬	Secondary road
▬▬	Minor road
▬▬	Scenic route
▬▬	Main railway
▬▬	Minor railway
▬▬	Regional border

Vicenza ❶

See pp168–73.

Thiene ❷

🏠 20,000. 🚌 ℹ️ *Piazza Ferrarin 20 (0445 36 95 44).* 🕑 *Mon am.*

Thiene is one of the area's many textile towns, manufacturing jeans and sweatshirts for sale all over Europe. Two villas nearby are worth a visit. The heavily fortified towers and battlemented walls of the **Castello Porto-Colleoni** are offset by pretty Gothic windows. At the time it was built, it stood in open countryside, and the defences were a precaution against bandits and raiders. Inside, 16th-century frescoes by Giambattista Zelotti add a lighter note and many portraits of horses remind the visitor that the villa's owners, the Colleoni family, were employed by the Venetian cavalry.

Zelotti also frescoed the **Villa Godi Malinverni**, the first villa designed by Palladio *(see pp24–5)*. The garden is charming and the frescoes are magnificent. Inside are works by Italian Impressionists and a lovely portrait by Pietro Annigoni (1910–88) called *La Strega* (the Sorceress).

🏛️ **Castello Porto-Colleoni**
Corso Garibaldi 12. **Tel** *0445 36 60 15.* 🕑 *mid-Mar–mid-Nov: Sun pm & public hols; Groups by appt.* 📷 🎥

🏛️ **Villa Godi Malinverni**
Via Palladio 44. **Tel** *0445 86 05 61.* 🕑 *Mar–Nov: Tue, Sat & Sun afternoons; other times, phone ahead.* 📷

The human chess game in the town square of Marostica

Marostica ❸

🏠 12,500. 🚌 ℹ️ *Piazza Castello 1 (0424 721 27).* 🕑 *Tue.*

Marostica is an almost perfect medieval fortified town, with town walls built in 1370 by the Scaligeri *(see p207)*. The rampart walk from the **Castello Inferiore** (lower castle) to the **Castello Superiore** (upper castle) has fine views.

The lower castle exhibits costumes worn by participants in the town's human chess tournament, the *Partita a Scacchi*, held every other September *(see p35)*. Up to 650 people participate in this colourful re-enactment of a game first played here in 1454.

🏛️ **Castello Inferiore**
Piazza Castello 1. **Tel** *0424 47 21 27.* 🕑 *9am–12:30pm, 3–6:30pm daily.* 📷 **www**.marosticascacchi.it

Bassano del Grappa ❹

🏠 38,770. 🚉 🚌 ℹ️ *Largo Corona d'Italia 35 (0424 52 43 51).* 🕑 *Thu & Sat am.*

This peaceful town is synonymous with Italy's favourite after-dinner drink. Although grappa is produced here, it is not named after the town, but after the Italian term for the lees *(graspa)* used to distil the liquor. Information on this and on the role played by Bassano during both world wars is given at the **Museo degli Alpini**, across the Ponte degli Alpini bridge. Designed in 1569 by Palladio, the current bridge dates from 1948: its timber allows it to flex when hit by spring meltwaters.

Bassano is also famous for the majolica wares *(see p256)* at **Palazzo Sturm**. The locally-born artist Jacopo Bassano (1510–92) and sculptor Canova (1757–1822) are celebrated in the **Museo Civico**.

🏛️ **Museo degli Alpini**
Via Angarano 2. **Tel** *0424 50 36 62.* 🕑 *9am–8pm Tue–Sun.* ● *10 days in Jan.*

🏛️ **Palazzo Sturm**
Via Schiavonetti 40. **Tel** *0424 52 49 33.* 🕑 *9am–1pm, 3–6pm Tue–Sun.* 📷

🏛️ **Museo Civico**
Piazza Garibaldi. **Tel** *0424 52 33 36.* 🕑 *9am–6:30pm Tue–Sat, 3:30–6:30pm Sun.* ● *public hols.* 📷

The Ponte degli Alpini at Bassano del Grappa

Cittadella ❺

🏛 18,000. **FS** 🚌 **ℹ** Porte
Bassanesi 2 (0499 40 44 85).
🛒 Mon am.

This attractive town is the
twin of Castelfranco. Each
was fortified and Cittadella
still preserves its 13th-century
moated walls. These are
interrupted by 4 gates and by
16 towers. The Torre di Malta
near the southern gate was
used as a torture chamber by
Ezzelino de Romano,
who ruled in the mid-13th
century. Far more pleasant
to contemplate is the *Supper
at Emmaus* in the **Duomo**,
a masterpiece by local
Renaissance
artist, Bassano.

**Fresco from the Villa Emo at
Fanzolo, near Castelfranco**

Castelfranco ❻

🏛 30,000. **FS** 🚌 **ℹ** Via
Francesco Maria Preti 66 (0423
49 50 00). 🛒 Tue & Fri am.

Fortified in 1199 by rulers
of Treviso, the historic core
of this town lies within the
well-preserved walls. **Casa di
Giorgione**, claimed to be the
birthplace of artist Giorgione
(1478–1511), houses a museum
devoted to his life. He created
such moody and mysterious
works as *The Tempest (see
p131)*. His *Virgin and Child
with Saints Liberal and Francis*
(1504) is displayed in the
Duomo. It was commissioned
by Tuzio Costanza to stand
above the tomb of his son,
Matteo, killed in battle in 1504.
    At Fanzolo, 8 km (5 miles)
northeast of Castelfranco, is
the **Villa Emo**, designed in
1564 by Palladio. Here,

The pretty town of Asolo in the foothills of the Dolomites

Zelotti's sumptuous frescoes
reveal the love lives of the
Greek deities.

🏛 Casa di Giorgione
Piazzetta del Duomo. **Tel** 0423 72
50 22. ⬭ 9am–noon, 3–6pm
Tue–Sun. ⬤ public hols. 🎟

🏛 Villa Emo
Fanzolo di Vedelago. **Tel** 0423 47
63 34. **FS** Fanzolo. 🚌 5. ⬭ Apr–
Oct: 3–6:30pm Mon–Sat, 10:30am–
12:30pm, 3–6:30pm Sun & pub hols;
Nov–Mar: 2–4pm daily (to 4:30pm
Sat, Sun & pub hols). ⬤ 25 & 26
Dec. 🎟 🌐 www.villaemo.org

Asolo ❼

🏛 2,000. 🚌 **ℹ** Piazza Garibaldi 73
(0423 52 90 46). 🛒 Sat.
www.asolo.it

Asolo is beautifully situated
among the cypress-clad foothills of the Dolomites. Queen
Caterina Cornaro (1454–1510)
once ruled this tiny walled
town *(see p43)*, and the poet
Cardinal Pietro Bembo coined
the verb *asolare* to describe
the bittersweet life of enforced
idleness she endured. Others
who have fallen in love with
these narrow streets include
poet Robert Browning, who
named a volume of poems
Asolando (1889) after the
town, and travel writer
Freya Stark, who lived here
until her death in 1993.
    Just 10 km (6 miles) east
of Asolo is the **Villa Barbaro**
at Masèr *(see pp24–5)*, while
10 km (6 miles) north is the
village of Passagno, birthplace
of Antonio Canova. Canova's
remains lie inside the huge
temple-like church which he
designed himself. Nearby is
the family home, the **Casa di
Canova**. The Gypsoteca here
houses the plaster casts and
clay models for many of
Canova's sculptures.

🏛 Villa Barbaro
Masèr. **Tel** 0423 92 30 04. ⬭ Mar–
Oct: 3–6pm Tue, Sat, Sun & public
hols; Nov–Feb: 2:30–5pm Sat, Sun
& public hols. ⬤ 24 Dec–6 Jan,
Easter. 🎟 🌐 www.villamaser.it

🏛 Casa di Canova
Piazza Canova. **Tel** 0423 54 43 23.
⬭ Tue–Sun. ⬤ 1 Jan, Easter,
25 Dec. 🎟

Valdobbiadene ❽

🏛 10,700. 🚌 **ℹ** Via Piva 53
(0423 97 69 75). 🛒 Mon.

Valdobbiadene, surrounded
by vine-covered hills, is a
centre for the sparkling white
wine called Cartizze, a type
of Prosecco. To the east, the
Strada del Vino Bianco (white
wine route) stretches 34 km
(21 miles) to the town of
Conegliano *(see p175)*,
passing vineyards offering
wine to try and to buy.

Environs
About 10 km (8 miles)
northeast of Valdobbiadene
is the small town of Follina,
which is renowned for its
wonderfully well-preserved
Romanesque abbey.

Vines near Valdobbiadene

Street-by-Street: Vicenza ●

Vicenza is known as the city of Andrea Palladio (1508–80), arguably the most influential architect of his time. Although Palladio was born in Padua, Vicenza was his adoptive home and, walking around the city, one can see the evolution of his distinctive style. In the centre is the monumental basilica he adapted to serve as the town hall, while all around are the palaces he built for Vicenza's wealthy citizens.

Detail on No. 21 Contrà Porti

Loggia del Capitaniato
This covered arcade was designed by Palladio in 1571.

Contrà Porti has some of the most elegant *palazzi* in Vicenza.

Palazzo Valmarana
Palladio's impressive building of 1566 was originally intended to be three times larger. It was not completed until 1680, 100 years after the architect's death.

Duomo
Vicenza's cathedral was rebuilt after bomb damage during World War II left only the façade and choir intact.

KEY

- - - Suggested route

STAR SIGHTS

★ Piazza dei Signori

★ Casa Pigafetta

0 metres   150
0 yards   150

VISITORS' CHECKLIST

116,000. **FS** Piazza
Stazione. Piazza Matteotti 12
(0444 32 08 54). Tue & Thu.
Concert season (May–Jun);
Classical music in villas (end
Jun–early Jul); Theatre season
(Sep–Oct). **www**.vicenzae.org

★ Piazza dei Signori
Encircled by grand 15th-century buildings including the city's green-roofed basilica and slender brick tower, the piazza is a lively spot, with a colourful market and cafés.

The Torre di Piazza is 82 m (269 ft) high. Begun in the 12th century, its height was increased in 1311 and 1444.

The 15th-century basilica has a magnificent loggia built by Palladio in 1549.

Andrea Palladio
This memorial to Vicenza's most famous citizen is often surrounded by market stalls.

The Quartiere delle Barche contains numerous attractive palaces built in the 14th-century Venetian Gothic style.

Piazza delle Erbe, the city's market square, is overlooked by a 13th-century torture chamber, the Torre del Tormento.

★ Casa Pigafetta
This striking house was the birthplace of Antonio Pigafetta, who in 1519 set sail round the world with Magellan.

Ponte San Michele
This elegant stone bridge, built in 1620, provides lovely views of the surrounding town.

Exploring Vicenza

Vicenza, the great palladian city, is celebrated all over the world for its architecture. It is also one of the wealthiest cities in the Veneto, with much to offer, from Roman and Renaissance art (a combined museum ticket is available) to elegant shops selling fine goods.

Statues gazing down from their pillars in the Piazza dei Signori

🏛 Piazza dei Signori

At the heart of Vicenza, this square is dominated by the startling bulk of the Palazzo della Ragione, often referred to as the "basilica". Open to the public, its green, copper-clad roof is shaped like an upturned boat with a balustrade bristling with the statues of Greek and Roman gods. The colonnades were designed by Palladio in 1549 to support the city's 15th-century town hall, which had begun to subside. This was his first public commission, and his solution ensured the survival of the building.

The astonishingly slender Torre di Piazza alongside has stood since the 12th century. Opposite is the elegant café Gran Caffè Garibaldi, which is next to Palladio's Loggia del Capitaniato (1571). The Loggia's upper rooms contain the city's council chamber.

🏛 Contrà Porti

Contrà (an abbreviation of *contrada*, or district) is the local dialect word for street. On the western side is a series of pretty Gothic buildings with painted windows and ornate balconies, including Palazzo Porto-Colleoni (No. 19). These houses reflect the architecture of Venice, a reminder that

Vicenza was part of the Venetian empire.

Several fine Palladian *palazzi* stand on this street. The Palazzo Thiene (No. 12) of 1545–50, the Palazzo Porto Barbarano (No. 11) of 1570, and the Palazzo Iseppo da Porto (No. 21) of 1552 all illustrate the sheer variety of Palladio's style – Classical elements are common to all three, but each is unique. The Palazzo Thiene reveals some intriguing details of Palladio's methods: though the building appears to be of stone, close inspection reveals that it is built of cheap lightweight brick, cleverly rendered to look like masonry.

🏛 Casa Pigafetta

Contrà Pigafetta. *No public access.*
This highly decorated Spanish Gothic building of 1481 has clover-leaf balconies, gryphon brackets and Moorish windows. The owner, Antonio Pigafetta, sailed round the world with Magellan in 1519–22, being one of only 20 men who survived the voyage.

🏛 Museo Civico

Piazza Matteotti 37–9. *Tel 0444 32 13 48.* 🕙 9am–5pm Tue–Sun.
🔴 1 Jan, 25 Dec. 🈂 ♿
This fine museum is housed in Palladio's Palazzo Chiericati, built in 1550. Inside is a fresco by Domenico Brusazorzi of a naked charioteer, representing the Sun, who appears to fly over the ceiling of the entrance hall. In the upstairs rooms are many great pictures. Among the Gothic altarpieces from local churches is Hans Memling's *Crucifixion* (1468–70), the central panel of a triptych whose side panels are now in New York.

In the later rooms are works by the local artist Bartolomeo Montagna (c.1450–1523), including his remarkable *Virgin Enthroned with Child, St John the Baptist and Saints Bartholomew, Augustine and Sebastian.*

🔒 Santa Corona

This impressive Gothic church was built in 1261 to house a thorn from Christ's Crown of Thorns, donated by Louis IX of France. In the Porto Chapel is the tomb of Luigi da Porto (died 1529), author of the novel *Giulietta e Romeo*, upon which Shakespeare based his

Brusazorzi's ceiling fresco in the large entrance hall of the Museo Civico

famous play. Notable paintings include Giovanni Bellini's *Baptism of Christ* (c.1500–5) and Paolo Veronese's *Adoration of the Magi* (1573). In the cloister the Museo Naturalistico-Archeologico exhibits natural history and archaeology.

San Lorenzo

The portal of this church is a magnificent example of Gothic stone carving, decorated with figures of the Virgin and Child, and St Francis and St Clare. The frescoes inside are damaged, but there are fine tombs. The cloister, north of the church, is a flower-filled haven of calm.

The elegant Villa Rotonda, most famous of all Palladio's works

The beautiful cloister of the church of San Lorenzo

Palazzo Leoni Montanari

Contra' Santa Corona 25. **Tel** *800 57 88 75.* ☐ *10am–6pm Tue–Sun.*

This Baroque building was completed around 1720, commissioned by Giovanni Leoni Montanari, who had made his fortune producing and selling cloth. Today the Palazzo houses an art gallery renowned for its collections of Venetian paintings and Russian icons.

Monte Berico

Basilica di Monte Berico. **Tel** *0444 55 94 11.* ☐ *daily.*

Monte Berico is the green, cypress-clad hill to the south of the city to which wealthy Vicenzans once escaped in the summer to enjoy cooler air and bucolic charms. The wide avenue linking the city to the basilica on top of the hill features shady colonnades with many shrines along the route. The Baroque basilica was built in the 15th century

and is dedicated to the Virgin who appeared during the 1426–8 plague to declare that Vicenza would be spared.

Many pilgrims still travel to the lovely church, where Bartolomeo Montagna's moving *Pietà* fresco (1572) makes an impact within the ornate interior. Other attractions include a fossil collection in the cloister, and Veronese's fine painting *The Supper of St Gregory the Great* (1572) in the refectory. The large canvas was cut to ribbons by bayonet-wielding soldiers during the revolutionary outbursts of 1848 and painstakingly restored.

Villa Valmarana

Via dei Nani 2. **Tel** *0444 32 18 03.* ☐ *10am–noon, 3–6pm Tue–Sun (Nov–mid-Mar: 10am–noon, 2–4pm Sat & Sun).* **www**.villavalmarana.com

The wall alongside the Villa Valmarana, built in 1688 by Antonio Muttoni, is topped by the figures of dwarfs, which give this building its alternative name –

The Baroque hilltop church, the Basilica di Monte Berico

ai Nani (at the Dwarfs). Inside the villa, the walls are covered with frescoes by Tiepolo, in which pagan gods float on clouds watching scenes from the epics of Homer and Virgil. In the separate Foresteria (guest house), the frescoes with themes of peasant life and the seasons, painted by Tiepolo's son, Giandomenico, are equally decorative but more earthily realistic.

The villa can be reached by a 10-minute walk from the basilica on Monte Berico. Head downhill along Via M d'Azeglio to the high-walled convent on the right where the road ends, then take the Via San Bastiano. There is also a bus service from town.

Villa Rotonda

Via della Rotonda 45. **Tel** *0444 32 17 93.* **Villa** ☐ *mid-Mar–4 Nov: Wed.* **Garden** ☐ *10am–noon, 3–6pm Tue–Sun (5 Nov–mid-Mar: 10am–noon, 2:30–5pm Tue–Sun).* **www**.villalarotonda.it

With its regular, symmetrical forms, this is the epitome of Palladio's architecture, and the most famous of all his villas. The design is simple yet satisfying, as is the contrast between the green lawns, white walls and terracotta roof tiles. Built between 1550 and 1552, it has inspired lookalikes in cities as far away as Delhi and St Petersburg. Fans of *Don Giovanni* will recognize locations used in Joseph Losey's 1979 film. The villa can be reached by bus from town, or on foot, following the path that passes the Villa Valmarana.

Vicenza: Teatro Olimpico

Europe's oldest surviving indoor theatre, the Teatro Olimpico is an elegant and remarkable structure, largely made of wood and plaster and painted to look like marble. Fashionable architect Andrea Palladio *(see pp24–5)* began work on the design in 1579, but he died the following year without finishing it. His pupil, Vincenzo Scamozzi, took over the project and completed the theatre in time for its ambitious opening performance of Sophocles' tragic drama, *Oedipus Rex*, on 3 March 1585.

Bacchantes
Euripides' Greek tragedy is still performed using Scamozzi's versatile scenery.

Main ticket office

★ **Odeon Frescoes**
The gods of Mount Olympus, after which the theatre is named, decorate the Odeon, a room used for music recitals.

Anteodeon
Oil lamps from the original stage set are now displayed in the theatre's Anteodeon, whose frescoes (1595) depict the theatre's opening performance.

★ **Stage Set**
Scamozzi's scenery represents the Greek city of Thebes. The streets are cleverly painted in perspective and rise at a steep angle to give the illusion of great length.

STAR SIGHTS

- ★ Stage Set by Vincenzo Scamozzi
- ★ Odeon Frescoes

Courtyard Sculptures
The courtyard of the former castle is decorated with sculpture donated by members of the Olympic Academy, the learned body that built the theatre.

Armoury Gateway
This stone gateway, with its military-style carvings, leads from Piazza Matteotti into the picturesque theatre courtyard.

The auditorium was designed by Palladio to resemble the outdoor theatres of ancient Greece and Rome, such as the arena at Verona *(see p195),* with a semi-circle of "stone" benches (actually made of wood) and a ceiling painted to portray the sky.

Costume Designs for Sofonisba
Ancient Greek vases inspired the costumes for this tragedy (1562) by Palladio's patron, GG Trissino.

Façade Statues
The toga-clad figures are portraits of sponsors who paid for the theatre's construction.

The medieval town of Treviso, built around ancient canals

Treviso ❾

👥 81,700. 🚌 FS ℹ️ *Via Sant'Andrea 3 (0422 54 76 32).* 🛒 *Tue & Sat am.*

Full of attractive balconied houses overlooking willow-fringed canals, Treviso is a rewarding city for visitors. Comparisons are often made with Venice, but Treviso has its own distinctive character. A good place to explore the architecture is the main street, Calmaggiore, which links the cathedral with the rebuilt 13th-century town hall, the **Palazzo dei Trecento**. The tradition of painting the exterior of the houses dates back to the medieval period, and this form

of decoration, applied to brick and timber, compensated for the lack of suitable building stone. The bustling **fish market** also dates back to medieval times. It is held on an island in the middle of Treviso's river Sile so that the remains of the day's trading can be flushed away instantly.

🏛 Duomo
Treviso's cathedral, founded in the 12th century, was reconstructed in the 15th, 16th and 18th centuries. Inside is Titian's *Annunciation* (1570), but it is upstaged by the striking *Adoration of the Magi* fresco (1520) of Titian's arch rival, Il Pordenone. Other memorable works are *The Adoration of*

the Shepherds fresco by Paris Bordone, and the monument to Bishop Zanetti (1501) by Pietro Lombardo and his sons.

🏛 Museo Civico
Piazzetta M Botter 1. **Tel** *0422 54 48 64.* ⬜ *9am–12:30pm, 2:30–6pm Tue–Sun.* ⬛ *public hols.* 📷 ♿
The Museo Civico houses an archaeology collection and a picture gallery in the restored convent of Santa Caterina dei Servi. The best works are Lorenzo Lotto's *Portrait of a Dominican* (1526), Titian's *Portrait of Sperone Speroni* (1544) and Bassano's *Crucifixion* as well as Tomaso da Modena's 14th-century frescoes of the life of St Ursula.

🏛 San Nicolò
Nestling near the 16th-century town wall is the bulky Dominican church of San Nicolò, full of tombs and frescoes, including some by Lorenzo Lotto. There is a gigantic painting of St Christopher by Antonio da Treviso and the piers of the nave bear vivid portraits of saints by Tomaso da Modena. The latter also painted the humorous pictures of monks (1352) on the walls of the chapter house (*Sala del Capitolo*), which has a separate entrance through the Seminario Vescovile.

TREVISO TOWN CENTRE

Duomo and Battistero di San Giovanni ①
Museo Civico ⑤
Palazzo dei Trecento ③

Pescheria (fish market) ④
San Nicolò ②

Key to Symbols *see back flap*

Conegliano ❿

35,300. 🚌 FS ℹ️ *Via XX Settembre 61 (0438 21 230).* 📅 *Fri.* **Shops closed** *Mon am.*

Conegliano lies between the Prosecco-producing vineyards and those that produce fine red wine *(see pp240–41)*. Wine makers from both areas learn their craft at Conegliano's renowned wine school. The town's winding and arcaded main street, Via XX Settembre, is lined by 15th- to 18th-century *palazzi*, some decorated with external frescoes, some in Venetian Gothic style. The **Duomo** contains a gorgeous altarpiece by Cima da Conegliano (1460–1518) showing the *Virgin and Child with Saints* (1493). This was commissioned by the religious brotherhood whose headquarters, the Scuola di Santa Maria dei Battuti *(flagellants)*, stands beside the Duomo.

Reproductions of Cima's paintings are displayed in the **Casa di Cima**, the artist's birthplace. His detailed landscapes were based on the hills around the town; they can still be seen from the gardens surrounding the **Castelvecchio** (old castle). A small museum of local history is housed in the castle.

🏛️ Casa di Cima
Via Cima. **Tel** *0438 21 660.* ⏰ *3–6pm Sat & Sun (Apr–Sep: 4–7pm).* ♿

♟️ Castelvecchio
Piazzale Castelvecchio 8. **Tel** *0438 228 71.* ⏰ *Museum: Tue–Sun (Nov: Sat & Sun only); gardens: daily (except Nov).* ♿

A mythical statue outside the theatre in Conegliano's Via XX Settembre

The foundations of Roman buildings in Concordia, near Portogruaro

Portogruaro ⓫

26,000. 🚌 FS ℹ️ *Via Cimetta 1 (0421 735 58).* 📅 *Thu am.* **Shops closed** *Mon.* **www**.portogruaro turismo.it

Situated on the main road linking Venice to Trieste, Portogruaro is the medieval successor to the Roman town of Concordia Sagittaria. Finds from Concordia, including statues, tomb inscriptions and mosaics, are displayed in the town's **Museo Concordiese**. These objects were unearthed in the modern village of Concordia, 2 km (1 mile) south of Portogruaro, where the footings of ruined Roman buildings can be seen all around the church and baptistry.

🏛️ Museo Concordiese
Via Seminario 26. **Tel** *0421 726 74.* ⏰ *daily.* 🚫 *1 Jan, 25 Dec.* ♿

Caorle ⓬

11,700. 🚌 ℹ️ *Calle delle Liburniche 18. (0421 810 85).* 📅 *Sat am.*

Like Venice, Caorle was built among the swamps of the Venetian lagoon by refugees fleeing the Goths in the 5th century. Today it is a fishing village and a busy beach resort perched on the edge of a huge expanse of purpose-built lagoons, carefully managed to encourage fish to enter and spawn. The young are then fed and farmed.

The area is also of great interest to naturalists for the abundant bird life of the reed-fringed waters. The town's 11th-century **Duomo** is worth a visit for its Pala d'Oro, a gilded altarpiece made up of 12th- and 13th-century Byzantine panel reliefs.

Local fishermen at work in the village of Caorle

Mestre ⓭

179,000. 🚌 📅 *Wed & Fri am.*

Mestre, the industrial offspring of Venice, is often favoured by visitors as a relatively less expensive base for exploring the region than Venice or other towns. Flying into Venice's Marco Polo airport *(see pp278–9)* you cannot miss the factories and oil terminals that surround Mestre and its neighbour, Marghera, vital to the region's economy.

Street-by-Street: Padua ⑭

The city centre of Padua (Padova) is one of the liveliest in northern Italy, thanks to a large student population and to the two street markets, one specializing in fruit and the other in vegetables. These take place every day except Sunday around the vast Palazzo della Ragione, the town's medieval law court and council chamber. The colonnades round the exterior of the *palazzo* shelter numerous bars, restaurants and shops selling meat, game, cheeses and wine.

Palazzo del Capitanio
Built between 1599 and 1605 for the head of the city's militia, the tower incorporates an astronomical clock made in 1344.

Piazza dei Signori
is bordered by attractive arcades which house small speciality shops, interesting cafés and old-fashioned wine bars.

Corte Capitaniato, a 14th-century arts faculty (open for concerts), contains frescoes which include a rare portrait of Petrarch.

Loggia della Gran Guardia
Now used as a conference centre, this fine Renaissance building, dating from 1523, once housed the Council of Nobles.

PIAZZA CAPITANIATO

VIA SAN CLEMENTE

PIAZZA DEI SIGNORI

VIA MONTE DI PIETA

VIA MANIN

PIAZZA DEL DUOMO

VIA SONCIN

VIA SONCIN

VIA VANDELLI

The Palazzo del Monte di Pietà has 16th-century arcades and statues enclosing a medieval building.

★ Duomo and Baptistry
The 12th-century baptistry of the Duomo contains one of the most complete medieval fresco cycles to survive in Italy, painted by Giusto de' Menabuoi in 1378 and now restored.

KEY

– – – Suggested route

| 0 metres | 75 |
| 0 yards | 75 |

★ **Caffè Pedrocchi**
Built like a Classical temple, the Caffè Pedrocchi has been a famous meeting place for students and intellectuals since it opened in 1831.

VISITORS' CHECKLIST

220,000. FS Piazza Boschetti. Piazzale Stazione 13a. **Tel** 049 875 20 77. Mon–Sat (Prato della Valle). **Shops closed** Mon am (clothes), Wed pm (food). concert season (Oct–Apr). **www**.turismopadova.it

Palazzi Communali
This complex, which houses the city's council offices, has a 13th-century defensive tower.

The Palazzo della Ragione, the "Palace of Reason", was, in medieval times, the city court of justice. Its interior is covered with magnificent astrological frescoes.

Padua University
Founded in 1222, this is the second oldest university in Italy. The main building dates back to the 16th century.

★ **Piazza delle Erbe**
There are good views on to the market place from Palladio's 16th-century loggia, which runs alongside the Palazzo della Ragione.

STAR SIGHTS

★ Duomo and Baptistry

★ Caffè Pedrocchi

★ Piazza delle Erbe

Exploring Padua

Padua is an old university town with an illustrious academic history. Rich in art and architecture, it has two particularly outstanding sights. The first is the Scrovegni Chapel *(see pp180–81)* in the north of the city, which is renowned for Giotto's lyrical frescoes. Close to the railway station, it forms part of the Eremitani museums complex. The second is the Basilica di Sant'Antonio, one of Italy's most popular pilgrim shrines, which forms the focal point for a number of sights in the south of the city *(see p182)*. A combined museum ticket is available.

Sundial on the façade of the Palazzo della Ragione

Detail from the Egyptian room, upper floor of the Caffè Pedrocchi

🚋 Caffè Pedrocchi

Via VIII Febbraio 15. *Tel* 049 878 12 31.
◯ *daily (Jun–Oct: Tue–Sun).* **Museo del Risorgimento e dell'Età Contemporanea** *Tel* 049 820 50 07. ◯
9.30am–12.30pm, 3:30–6pm Tue–Sun.
◯ *Aug.* ◻ www.caffepedrocchi.it
Grand cafés have long played an important role in the intellectual life of northern Italy, and many philosophical issues have been thrashed out at the Caffè Pedrocchi since it first opened in 1831. Politics superseded philosophy when it became a centre of the Risorgimento movement, dedicated to liberating Italy from Austrian rule; it was the scene of uprisings in 1848, for which several student leaders were executed. Later it became famous as the café that never closed its doors. These days people come to talk, read, play cards or watch the world go by as they eat and drink.

The upstairs rooms, decorated in Moorish, Egyptian and Greek styles, are now the premises of a museum.

🚋 Palazzo del Bo (University)

Via VIII Febbraio 2. *Tel* 049 827 51 11.
◯ *Tue, Thu & Sat am, Mon, Wed & Fri pm (may vary, phone to check).*
◻ ◻
Named after a tavern called *Il Bo* (the ox), the historic main university building is mostly

used today for graduation ceremonies. Originally it housed the medical faculty, renowned throughout Europe. Among its famous teachers and students was Gabriele Fallopio (1523–62), after whom the Fallopian tubes are named.

Elena Lucrezia Corner Piscopia was the first female graduate in 1678 – long before women could study at many of Europe's other universities. Her statue is on the staircase leading to the upper gallery of the 16th-century courtyard.

Visitors on the tour are shown the pulpit Galileo used when he taught here from 1592 until 1610. They also see the world's oldest surviving anatomy theatre (1594), viewing the room from the centre looking up.

🚋 Palazzo della Ragione

Piazza delle Erbe. *Tel* 049 820 50 06.
◯ *Tue–Sun.* ◯ *1 Jan, 1 May, 25 Dec.* ◻ ◻ ◻
The "Palace of Reason", also known as the "Salone" by locals, was built to serve as Padua's law court and council chamber in 1218. The vast main hall was originally frescoed by the celebrated artist Giotto, but fire destroyed his work in 1420. The frescoes that survive today are by the relatively unknown Nicola Miretto, though their astrological theme is fascinating.

The Salone is breathtaking in its sheer size. It is Europe's biggest undivided medieval hall, 80 m (260 ft) long, 27 m (90 ft) wide and 27 m (90 ft) high. The scale is reinforced by the wooden horse displayed at one end – a massive beast, copied from Donatello's Gattamelata statue *(see p183)* in 1466 and originally made to be pulled in procession during Paduan festivities.

The walls are covered in Miretto's frescoes (1420–25), a total of 333 panels depicting the months of the year with appropriate gods, zodiacal signs and seasonal activities.

Also within the *palazzo* is the Stone of Shame, on which bankrupts were exposed to ridicule before they were sent into exile.

The 16th-century galleried anatomy theatre in the Palazzo del Bo

Eremitani Museums

This major museum complex occupies a group of 14th-century monastic buildings attached to the church of the Eremitani, a reclusive Augustinian order. The admission ticket includes entry to the Scrovegni Chapel (*see pp180–81*), which stands on the same site, overlooking the city's Roman amphitheatre, and to the Archaeology Museum, the Bottacin Museum of coins and medals, and the Medieval and Modern Art Museum, all of which are housed around the cloisters.

The tomb of the Volumni family in the archaeological collection

EREMITANI CHURCH

Alongside the museum complex is the Eremitani church (1276–1306), with its magnificent roof and wall tombs. Interred here is Marco Benavides (1489–1582), a professor of law at the city university, whose mausoleum was designed by Ammannati, a Renaissance architect from Florence. Sadly missing from the church are Andrea Mantegna's celebrated frescoes of the lives of St James and St Christopher (1454–7), which were destroyed during a bombing raid in 1944. Two scenes from this magnificent work survive in the Ovetari Chapel, south of the sanctuary. *The Martyrdom of St James* was reconstructed from salvaged fragments, and *The Martyrdom of St Christopher* was removed carefully and stored elsewhere before the bombing. Otherwise only photographs on the walls remain to hint at the quality of the lost works.

THE MUSEUMS

The highlight of the rich archaeological collection is the temple-like tomb of the Volumni family, dating from the 1st century AD. Among several other Roman tombstones from the Veneto region is one to the young dancer, Claudia Toreuma – sadly, a fairly dull inscribed column rather than a portrait. The collection also includes some fine mosaics, along with several impressive life-size statues depicting muscular Roman deities and toga-clad dignitaries. For most visitors the Renaissance bronzes are likely to be

Angels in Armour (15th century) by Guariento in the Art Museum

the most appealing feature of the museum, especially the comical *Drinking Satyr* by Il Riccio (1470–1532).

Coin collectors should make a point of visiting the Bottacin Museum. Among the exhibits there is an almost complete set of Venetian coinage and some very rare examples of Roman medallions.

The Modern Art Museum is currently closed to the public. However, the massive Medieval Museum is well worth a visit. It covers the history of Venetian art, with paintings from Giotto to the 1700s. Another museum looks at Giotto and his influence on local art, using the Crucifix from the Scrovegni Chapel as its centrepiece. The Crucifix is flanked by an army of angels (late 15th century) painted in gorgeous colours by the artist Guariento. Another 15th-century painting worth a look is *Portrait of a Young Senator* by Giovanni Bellini.

Early 14th-century crucifix on loan from the Scrovegni Chapel

VISITORS' CHECKLIST

Piazza Eremitani 8.
Tel 049 820 45 50.
9am–7pm Tue–Sun.
Only chapel open Mon.
1 Jan, 1 May, 25 & 26 Dec.
www.turismopadova.it

Padua: Scrovegni Chapel

Enrico Scrovegni built this chapel in 1303, hoping thereby to spare his dead father, a usurer, from the eternal damnation wished upon him by the poet Dante in his *Inferno*. The chapel is filled with harmonious frescoes of scenes from the life of Christ, painted by Giotto between 1303 and 1305. As works of great narrative force, they exerted a powerful influence on the development of European art.

The Nativity
The naturalism of the Virgin's pose marks a departure from Byzantine stylization, as does the use of natural blue for the sky, in place of celestial gold.

Expulsion of the Merchants
Christ's physical rage, the cowering merchant and the child hiding his face are all typical of Giotto's style.

The Coretti
Giotto painted the two panels known as the Coretti as an exercise in perspective, creating the illusion of an arch with a room beyond.

View towards altar

| West entrance | North side | Altar | South side | West entrance |

GALLERY GUIDE

It is compulsory to book your visit to the Scrovegni Chapel in advance, since there are strict limits on the number of visitors allowed in the chapel at any one time. Prior to entry, all visitors must spend 15 minutes in a "decontamination chamber", and the duration of the visit to the chapel is also limited to 15 minutes. An explanatory film is shown while you wait in the chamber. The rest of the Eremitani complex is also worth a visit.

KEY

- Episodes of Joachim and Anna
- Episodes from the Life of Mary
- Episodes from the Life and Death of Christ
- The Virtues and Vices
- The Last Judgment

The Last Judgment
This scene fills the entire west wall of the chapel. Its formal composition is closer to the Byzantine tradition than some of the other frescoes, with parts probably painted by assistants. A model of the chapel is shown, being offered to the Virgin by Scrovegni.

View towards entrance

Mary is Presented at the Temple
Giotto sets many scenes against an architectural background, using the laws of perspective to give a sense of three dimensions.

Injustice
The Virtues and Vices are painted in monochrome. Here Injustice is symbolized by scenes of war, murder and robbery.

Lament over the Dead Christ
Giotto's figures express their grief in different ways, some huddled, some gesturing wildly.

GIOTTO

The great Florentine artist Giotto (1266–1337) is regarded as the father of Western art. His work, with its sense of pictorial space, naturalism and narrative drama, marks a decisive break with the Byzantine tradition of the preceding 1,000 years. He is the first Italian master whose name has passed into posterity, and although he was regarded in his lifetime as a great artist, few of the works attributed to him are fully documented. Some may have been painted by others, but his authorship of the frescoes in the Scrovegni Chapel need not be doubted.

The lofty interior of Padua's
16th-century duomo

🛈 **Duomo and Baptistry**
Baptistry *Tel 049 65 69 14.*
⏱ *10am–6pm daily.* ● *Easter,*
25 Dec. 📷 📷
Padua's duomo was commis-
sioned from Michelangelo in
1552, but his designs were
altered during the construction.
Of the 4th-century cathedral
which stood on the site, the
domed Romanesque baptistry
still survives, with its frescoes
by Giusto de' Menabuoi
(c.1376). The frescoes cover
biblical stories, such as the
Creation, Christ's Passion,
Crucifixion and Resurrection
and the Last Judgment.

🛈 **Basilica di Sant'Antonio**
Piazza del Santo. *Tel 049 822 56 52.*
This exotic church, with its
minaret-like spires and Byzantine domes, is also known as
Il Santo. It was begun in 1232
to house the remains of St
Anthony of Padua, a preacher
who modelled himself on St
Francis of Assisi. Although he
was a simple man who reject-
ed worldly wealth, the citizens
of Padua built one of the most
lavish churches in Christendom
to serve as his shrine.

The outline reflects the
influence of Byzantine architecture; a cone-shaped central
dome is surrounded by a
further seven domes, rising
above a façade that combines
Gothic with Romanesque
elements. The interior is
more conventional, however.
Visitors are kept away from
the high altar, which features
Donatello's magnificent reliefs
(1444–5) on the miracles of St
Anthony, and his statues of the
Virgin, the Crucifixion and
several Paduan saints. There is
access to St Anthony's tomb
in the north transept, which is
hung with offerings and photographs of people who have
survived serious illness or car
crashes
with the
saint's
help. The
walls
around

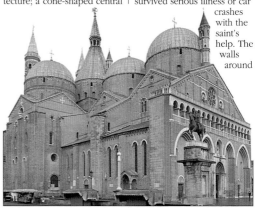

The Basilica di Sant'Antonio and Donatello's statue of Gattamelata

The Brenta Canal

The River Brenta, between Padua and the Venetian
Lagoon, was canalized in the 16th century. Flowing
for a total of 36 km (22 miles), its potential as a
transport route was quickly realized, and fine villas
were built along its length. Today, these elegant
buildings can still be admired. Three open their doors
to the public: the Villa Foscari at Malcontenta, the Villa
Widmann-Foscari at Mira and the Villa Pisani at
Stra. They can be visited either on an 8- to
9-hour guided tour from Padua to
Venice (or vice versa) along the river
on a motor launch, or by bus, a
cheaper and faster alternative.

The picturesque town of Mira
on the Brenta Canal   *Dol*

Fiessa d'Artico ●   S11

◄— *PADOVA*

🚏 ①

KEY

▬▬ Tour route

═══ Roads

🚏 Boat stops

Villa Pisani ①
This 18th-century
villa features
an extravagant
frescoed ceiling
by Tiepolo.

the shrine are decorated with large marble reliefs depicting St Anthony's life, carved in 1505–77 by various artists, including Jacopo Sansovino and Tullio Lombardo. These are rather cold by comparison with the *Crucifixion* fresco (1380s) by Altichiero da Zevio in the opposite transept. This pageant-like painting of every-day scenes from medieval life shows depictions of people, animals and plants.

One of four stone bridges spanning the canal around Prato della Valle

⋔ Statue of Gattamelata

Near the entrance to the basilica stands one of the great Renaissance works. This gritty portrait of the mercenary soldier Gattamelata (whose name means "Honey Cat") was created in 1443–52, honouring a man who in his life did great service to the Venetian Republic. Donatello won fame for the monument, the first equestrian statue made of this size since Roman times.

⛩ Scuola del Santo and Oratorio di San Giorgio

Piazza del Santo. **Tel** 049 822 56 52. ◯ 9am–12:30pm, 2:30–7pm daily (to 5pm in winter). ● 1 Jan, 25 Dec. 🎫 (combined ticket).

These two linked buildings contain excellent frescoes, in-cluding the earliest documented paintings by Titian. These comprise two scenes from the life of St Anthony in the Scuola del Santo, executed in 1511. The delightful saints' lives and scenes from the life of Christ in the San Giorgio oratory are the work of two artists, Altichiero da Zevio and Jacopo Avenzo, who painted them in 1378–84.

🌿 Orto Botanico

Via Orto Botanico 15. **Tel** 0498 27 21 19. ◯ Apr–Oct: 9am–1pm, 3–7pm daily; Nov–Mar: 9am–1pm Mon–Sat. 🎫 ♿

Founded in 1545, Padua's botanical garden is the oldest in Europe, and it retains much of its original appearance; one of the palm trees dates to 1585. Originally intended for the cultivation of medicinal plants, the pathways now spill over with exotic foliage, shaded by ancient trees. The gardens were used to cultivate the first lilacs (1565), sunflowers (1568) and potatoes (1590) grown in Italy.

⛩ Prato della Valle

The Prato (field) claims to be the largest public square in Italy, and its elliptical shape reflects the form of the Roman theatre that stood on the site.

St Anthony of Padua used to preach sermons to huge crowds here, but subsequent neglect saw the area turn into a malaria-ridden swamp. The land was drained in 1767 to create the canal that now encircles the Prato. Four stone bridges cross the picturesque channel, which is lined on both sides by statues of 78 eminent citizens of Padua. On Saturdays there is a market.

Villa Foscari ③ Also known as the Malcontenta, this villa was built by Palladio in 1560 and is decorated with magnificent frescoes by Zelotti.

Oriago

S11

LAGUNA VENETA

Canale Nuovissimo

S309

Fusina

VENEZIA

Villa Widmann-Foscari ② Built in 1719, but altered in the 19th century, the interior is decorated in a French Rococo style.

0 kilometres 4

0 miles 2

TIPS FOR PASSENGERS

🚌 **Padua to Venice.** **Wed, Fri and Sun, Mar–Oct. Dep** bus station, Piazza Boschetti, 8:15am. **Arr** Piazza San Marco 6:30pm.
🚌 **Venice to Padua.** **Tue, Thu and Sat, Mar–Oct. Dep** Piazza San Marco 9am. **Arr** bus station, Piazza Boschetti 6:30pm.

Booking necessary through a local travel agent or www.ilburchiello.it **Ticket includes** bus between Padua and Stra, boat tour and guide, entrance to two villas (ticket for Villa Pisani not included). Return trip (not included in cost) by train or bus (approx. 45 mins).

The Euganean Hills, formed by ancient volcanic activity

Euganean Hills ⓫

🏃 10,000. ℹ️ Viale Stazione 60, Montegrotto Terme (049 892 83 11).

The Euganean Hills, remnants of long-extinct volcanoes, rise abruptly out of the Veneto plain and offer plenty of walking opportunities. Hot springs bubble up out of the ground at Abano Terme and Montegrotto Terme where scores of establishments offer thermal treatments, ranging from mud baths to immersion in the hot sulphurated waters. Spa cures such as these date back to Roman times, and visitors can see extensive remains of the Roman baths and theatre at Montegrotto.

🔒 Abbazia di Praglia

Via Abbazia di Praglia, Bresseo di Teolo. Tel 049 999 93 00. ⬤ Mar–Oct: 3:30–5:30pm Tue–Sun; Nov–Feb: 2:30–4:30pm Tue–Sun. 🎫 Donations welcome. www.praglia.it

The Benedictine monastery at Praglia, 6 km (4 miles) west of Abano Terme, is a peaceful haven in the tree-clad hills. The monks have long been growing herbs commercially and there is a shop selling aromatic wares. They also lead guided tours of parts of the abbey and the Renaissance church (1490–1548), with its beautiful cloister.

🏛 Casa di Petrarca

Via Valleselle 4, Arquà Petrarca. Tel 0429 71 82 94. ⬤ Tue–Sun. ⬤ most public hols. 🎫 📷

The picturesque town of Arquà Petrarca, on the southern edge of the Euganean hills, was once simply Arquà. Its name changed in 1868 to honour the medieval poet Francesco Petrarca, or Petrarch (1303–74), who lived here in his old age. He had often sung the praises of the well-tended landscape of olive groves and vineyards, and spent his last few years in a house frescoed with scenes from his poems. The house still contains the poet's desk and chair, his bookshelves and his mummified cat. Petrarch is buried in a sarcophagus in the piazza in front of the church.

🏯 Villa Barbarigo

Valsanzibio. Tel 049 805 92 24. ⬤ Mar–Nov: 10am–1pm, 2pm–sunset. 🎫 📷 ♿

To the north of Arquà is the Villa Barbarigo at Valsanzibio, the only one of scores of villas, built by wealthy Paduans, regularly open to the public. The villa itself is of a simple design compared with the Baroque garden. Planted from 1669, it is full of variety, with fountains, statues and lakes.

The house of the poet Petrarch in the town of Arquà Petrarca

Montagnana ⓰

🏃 12,000. FS 🚌 ℹ️ Piazza Trieste 15 (0429 813 20). ⬤ Thu am. Shops closed Mon am & Wed pm.

Medieval brick walls encircle this town, extending for 2 km (1 mile), pierced by four gateways and defended by 24 towers. Just inside the castellated Padua Gate is the town's archaeological museum. The Gothic-Renaissance Duomo contains Paolo Veronese's Transfiguration (1555). Outside the city walls is Palladio's Villa Pisani (c.1560). Now rather neglected, its façade features the original owner's name (Francesco Pisani) in bold letters below the pediment.

Antique market in Montagnana

Este ⓱

🏃 17,600. FS 🚌 ℹ️ Via Guido Negri 9 (0429 600 462). ⬤ Wed & Sat am. Shops closed Mon am (clothes) & Wed pm (food).

Excavations at Este have uncovered impressive remains of the ancient Ateste people, who flourished from the 9th century BC until they were conquered by the Romans in the 3rd century BC. The archaeological finds, including funerary urns, figurines, bronze vases and jewellery, are on display in the excellent Museo Nazionale Atestino, set within the walls of the town's 14th-century castle. The museum also displays examples of Roman and medieval art, and pieces of local pottery, famous since the Renaissance period, and still produced.

⬫ Museo Atestino
Palazzo Mocenigo. *Tel* 0429 20 85.
⬤ daily. ⬤ 1 Jan, 1 May, 25 Dec. 🗺
🔖 www.atestino.beniculturali.it

Monselice ⑱

🏚 17,000. FS 🚌 🛈 *Via del Santuario 6 (0429 78 30 26).*
🛒 Mon & Fri. **Shops closed** Tue am (clothes), Wed pm (food).

The town of Monselice stands at the foot of two hills, one of which has been quarried extensively for rich deposits of crystalline minerals. The other is topped by ruined **Castle Rocca**, now a nature reserve. It is worth walking up the cobbled Via del Santuario as far as **San Giorgio**, to see its exquisite inlaid marble work.

Other features on the way up are the 13th-century cathedral and the statue-filled Baroque gardens of the Villa Nani that can be glimpsed through the villa gates. Nearby is **Ca' Marcello**, a 14th-century castle featuring period furnishings, suits of armour, frescoes and tapestries.

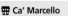

Marble inlay detail from San Giorgio

🏰 Ca' Marcello
Via del Santuario. *Tel* 0429 729 31.
⬤ Apr–Nov: Tue–Sun; Dec–Mar: groups only; book in advance. 🗺
🔖 www.castellodimonselice.it

The sanctuary of San Giorgio on the hill top at Monselice

Polesine and Rovigo ⑲

FS 🚌 🛈 *Piazza Matteotti 1, Porto Viro (0426 63 30 12).*

Polesine is the flat expanse of fertile agricultural land, crisscrossed by canals and subject to flooding, between the river Adige and the Po. The Po Delta is now a national park and has a wealth of fascinating birdlife, including egrets, herons and bitterns.

The most scenic areas are around Scardovari and Porto Tolle, on the south side of the Po. Companies in Porto Tolle offer canoe and bicycle hire and half-day boat cruises.

The modern city of Rovigo has one outstanding monument, the splendid octagonal church called **La Rotonda** (1594–1602), decorated with paintings and statues in niches.

Environs
Adria, 22 km (14 miles) east of Rovigo, gave its name to the Adriatic Sea and was once a Greek and later an Etruscan port. A programme of silt deposition, undertaken to increase Adria's agricultural potential, left the city dry, apart from a 24-km (15-mile) canal. Among the exhibits on display in the **Museo Archeologico** is a complete iron chariot dating from the 4th century BC.

⬫ Museo Archeologico
Via Badini 59, Adria. *Tel* 0426 216 12. ⬤ daily. ⬤ 1 Jan, 1 May, 25 Dec 🗺

Chioggia ⑳

🏚 56,000. 🚌 FS 🚢 🛈 *Lungomare Adriatico 101. (041 40 10 68).*
🛒 Thu. www.chioggiaturismo.it

Chioggia is the principal fishing port on the lagoon and the bustling, colourful **fish market** is a good reason to come here early in the day (open every morning except Monday). Many visitors enjoy the gritty character of the port area, with its smells, its vibrantly coloured boats and the tangle of nets and tackle. The town also has numerous inexpensive restaurants which serve fresh fish in almost every variety. Eel, crab and cuttlefish are the local specialities. There is a beach area at Sottomarina, on the western part of the island. Worth seeking out for a special visit is Carpaccio's *St Paul* (1520), the artist's last known work, which is permanently housed in the church of **San Domenico**.

Net mending in the traditional way, Chioggia

VERONA AND LAKE GARDA

V erona is one of northern Italy's most alluring cities, its noble palaces, quiet cloisters and ancient streets every bit as romantic as you would expect of Romeo and Juliet's city. On its doorstep are the well-known vineyards of Soave, Bardolino and Valpolicella, set against the rugged slopes of the Little Dolomites. To the west lie the beautiful shores of Lake Garda, a mere 30 minutes' drive from Verona by car, but a world away in atmosphere.

Set within the curves of the river Adige, Verona has been a prosperous and cosmopolitan city since the Romans colonized it in 89 BC. It stands astride two important trade routes – the Serenissima, connecting the great port cities of Venice and Genoa, and the Brenner Pass, used by commercial travellers crossing the Alps from northern Europe. This helps to explain the Germanic influence in Verona's magnificent San Zeno church, or the realism of the paintings in the Castelvecchio museum, owing more to Dürer than to Raphael.

Verona's passion and panache, however, are purely Italian. Stylish shops and cafés sit amid the impressive remains of Roman monuments. The massive Arena amphitheatre fills with crowds of 20,000 or more, who thrill to opera beneath the stars. All over the city, art galleries and theatres testify to a crowded calendar of cultural activities.

Italy's largest lake, Lake Garda, is renowned for its beautiful scenery. The broad southern end of the lake, with its waterfront promenades, is very popular with Italian and German visitors. Those in search of peace can escape to the heights of the Monte Baldo mountain range, rising above the eastern shore. The ridge marks the western edge of the mountainous region north of Verona. Here is the great plateau of Monti Lessini, with its little river valleys that fan out southwards to join the river Adige.

Giardino Giusti in Verona, one of Italy's finest Renaissance gardens

◁ Fishing boats outside Rocca Scaligera castle, Sirmione

Exploring Verona and Lake Garda

Verona makes an excellent touring base, with lofty
mountains, castles and vineyards all within easy
reach of the city. Lake Garda, whose western shore
is actually over the border in Lombardy, is a popular
destination for excursions from Verona. The many
resort towns have excellent hotels, harbourside fish
restaurants and lakeside gardens, and the lake is
perfect for watersports such as windsurfing or dinghy
racing. Less exhausting are the steamer excursions,
offering mid-lake views of entrancing beauty.

SIGHTS AT A GLANCE

Bolca **6**
Bosco Chiesanuova **8**
Garda **10**
Gardone Riviera **15**
Giazza **7**
Grezzana **2**
Malcesine **17**
Montecchio Maggiore **4**
Peschiera **11**
Riva del Garda **16**
Salò **14**
Sant'Anna d'Alfaedo **9**
*Sirmione Peninsula
pp206–7* **13**
Soave **3**

Solferino **12**
Valdagno **5**
Verona pp192–203 **1**

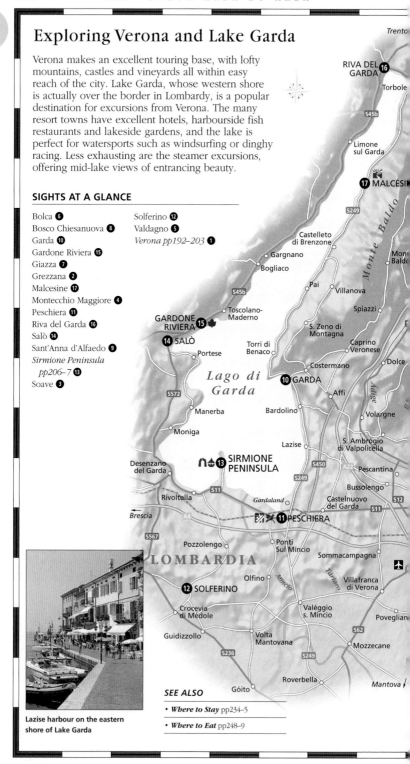

Lazise harbour on the eastern
shore of Lake Garda

SEE ALSO

• *Where to Stay* pp234–5

• *Where to Eat* pp248–9

GETTING AROUND

The roads around Verona are heavily used by commercial vehicles and commuter traffic, so expect delays, especially during morning and evening rush hours. Motorways are faster, even though those in this region are among the oldest in Italy. There are good rail services linking Verona with Lake Garda to the west and with Bolzano to the north. The Brenner pass also runs northwards from Verona. For information on ferries across Lake Garda, see p204.

The green pastures of Bolca, an area rich in fossil remains

Trento

Monte Sparavieri
1976m

Corno d'Aquilio
1546m

M o n t i   L e s s i n i

Staro   S46

Recoaro
Terme   S246

Montagna
Spaccata

Ongaro   S46

Malo

Selvavecchia

7 GIAZZA

5 VALDAGNO   Orolo

Priabona

SANT'ANNA
D'ALFAEDO   **8** BOSCO
CHIESANUOVA   Selva
di Progno

Vaggimàl

Cerro
Veronese

6 BOLCA

Castelgomberto

Agno

Trissino

Negrar   Stallavena

Badia
Calavena

Chiampo

S. Giovanni
Ilarione   Chiampo   S246   Sovizzo

Tregnano

Arzignano   S11

2 GREZZANA

Castagnè

Céllore   MONTECCHIO
MAGGIORE   **4**   Alte Ceccato

Arbizzano   Santa Maria
in Stelle

V E N E T O

Vicenza   A4

Poiano   Montório

S. Zeno

Costalunga

1 VERONA   S. Martino
Buon Albergo   **3** SOAVE

San Bonifacio   S11

San Giovanni
Lupatoto   Àdige   S12

ttapietra   S434   Zévio

0 kilometres		10
0 miles		5

KEY

═══ Motorway

═══ Major road

─── Secondary road

┄┄┄ Minor road

─── Scenic route

⊷⊷ Main railway

┈┈┈ Minor railway

═══ Regional border

△ Summit

A vineyard in spring on the hillsides around Verona

The 14th-century Castello Romeo, on a hill overlooking Montecchio

Verona ❶

See pp192–203.

Grezzana ❷

🏛 9,680. 🚌 🚆 1st Wed & 3rd Fri each month.

In Grezzana itself, seek out the 13th-century church of Santa Maria which, though frequently rebuilt, retains its robustly carved Romanesque font and its beautiful campanile of gold, white and pink limestone.

Environs:
Grezzana is in the foothills of the scenic Piccole Dolomiti or Little Dolomites. Close to the town, at nearby Cuzzano, is the 17th-century Baroque **Villa Allegri-Arvedi**. To the south, in Santa Maria in Stelle, is a Roman nymphaeum (a shrine to the nymphs who guard the fresh-water spring) next to the church (known as the Pantheon).

🏚 **Villa Allegri-Arvedi**
Cuzzano di Grezzana. **Tel** 045 90 70 45. ◻ for groups only (book by phone). 📷 🔖 **www**.villarvedi.it

Soave ❸

🏛 6,200. 🚌 🚆 Foro Boario 1 (045 619 07 73). 🚆 Tue am.

Soave is a heavily fortified town ringed by 14th-century walls. Its name is familiar all over Europe because of the light and dry white wine that is produced and exported from here in great quantity. Visitors will see few vineyards around the town, since they are mainly located in the hills to the north, but evidence of the industry can be seen in the gleaming factories on the outskirts, where the Garganega grapes are crushed and the fermented wine bottled. Cafés and wine cellars in the town centre provide plenty of opportunity for sampling the excellent local wine.

The city walls rise up the hill to the dramatically sited **Rocca Scaligera**, an ancient castle enlarged in the 14th century by the Scaligeri rulers of Verona. It has been furnished in period style.

♠ **Rocca Scaligera**
Via Castello Scaligero. **Tel** 045 768 00 36. ◻ Tue–Sun. 📷

Rocca Scaligera, the ancient castle in Soave

Montecchio Maggiore ❹

🏛 20,000. 🚌 🚆 Via Pietro Ceccato 88, Alta di Montecchio (0444 69 65 46). 🚆 Fri am.

Visitors to industrialized Montecchio Maggiore come principally to see the two 14th-century castles on the hill above the town. Although these are known as the **Castello di Romeo** and the **Castello di Giulietta** (which includes a restaurant), there is no evidence that they belonged to Verona's rival Capulet and Montague families *(see p199)*, but they look romantic and provide lovely views over the vineyard-clad hills to the north.

♠ **Castello di Romeo**
Via Castelli 4. ◻ Sat & Sun. 📷
♠ **Castello di Giulietta**
Via Castelli 4. **Tel** 0444 69 61 72. ◻ Wed–Sun. ◉ Sat & Sun pm.

The dramatic gorge of Montagna Spaccata, north of Valdagno

Valdagno ❺

🏛 28,000. 🚌 🚆 Viale Trento 4–6 (0445 40 11 90). 🚆 Tue & Fri am.

A scenic drive of 20 km (12 miles) from Montecchio Maggiore leads to Valdagno, a town of woollen mills and 18th-century houses. Just northwest is the Montagna Spaccata, its rocky bulk split by a dramatic 100-m (330-ft) deep gorge and waterfall.

Fossilized plant remains found in the rocks near Bolca

Bolca ❻

🗺 *500.* 🚌 ℹ *Via Villa Bolca (045 656 00 13).* **Shops closed** *Mon am (clothes), Wed pm (food).*

Pretty Bolca sits at the centre of the Monti Lessini plateau, looking down the valley of the river Alpone and encircled by fossil-bearing hills. The most spectacular finds have been transferred to Verona's Museo Civico di Scienze Naturali *(see p203)*, but the local **Museo di Fossili** still has an impressive collection of fish, plants and reptiles preserved in the local basalt stone. A circular walk of 3 km (2 miles) from the town (details available from the museum) takes in the quarries where the fossils were found.

🏛 **Museo di Fossili**
Via San Giovanni Battista. **Tel** *045 656 50 88.* ◯ *9am–noon, 2–6:30pm daily (Nov–Feb: 10am–noon, 2–5pm).* 🌐 **www**.lapesciara.it

Giazza ❼

🗺 *150.* 🚌 **Shops closed** *Wed pm (food).*

The small town of Giazza has an almost Alpine appearance. Its **Museo dei Cimbri** covers the history of the Tredici Comuni (the Thirteen Communes). In reality there are far more than 13 little hamlets dotted about the plateau, many of them settled by Bavarian farmers who migrated from the German side of the Alps in the 13th century. Cimbro, their German-influenced dialect, has now almost completely disappeared, but other traditions survive. For example, their huge mountain horns, *tromboni*, are still part of local festivities.

🏛 **Museo dei Cimbri**
Via dei Boschi, 62. 📠 *045 784 70 50.* ◯ *3–6pm Fri–Sun.* 🌐 📷 🏠 **www**.cimbri.it

Bosco Chiesanuova ❽

🗺 *3,000.* 🚌 ℹ *Piazza della Chiesa 34 (045 705 00 88).* 🛒 *Sat am.*

One of the principal ski resorts of the region, Bosco Chiesanuova is well supplied with hotels, ski lifts and cross-country routes. To the east, near Camposilvano, is the picturesque **Valle delle Sfingi** (valley of the sphinxes), so called because of its landscape of large and impressive rock formations.

Sant'Anna d'Alfaedo ❾

🗺 *2,500.* 🚌 ℹ *in Bosco Chiesanuova.* 🛒 *Wed am.*

Distinctively alpine in character, Sant'Anna d'Alfaedo is noted for the stone tiles used to roof local houses. The hamlet of Fosse, immediately to the north, is a popular base for walking excursions up the **Corno d'Aquilio** (1,546 m/5,070 ft), a mountain which boasts one of the world's deepest pot-holes, the **Spluga della Preta**, 850 m (2,790 ft) deep.

More accessible is another natural wonder, the **Ponte di Veia**, just south of Sant'Anna, a great stone arch bridging the valley. Prehistoric finds have been excavated from the caves at either end. This spectacular natural bridge is one of the largest of its kind in the world.

The town of Giazza, spectacularly situated on the Monti Lessini plateau

Verona ❶

Dragon carving on Duomo façade

Verona is a vibrant and self-confident city, the second biggest in the Veneto region (after Venice) and one of the most prosperous in northern Italy. Its ancient centre boasts many magnificent Roman remains, second only to those of Rome itself, and *palazzi* built of *rosso di Verona*, the local pink-tinged limestone, by the city's medieval rulers. Verona has two main focal points, the massive 1st-century AD Arena and the Piazza Erbe with its colourful market, separated by a maze of narrow lanes lined with some of Italy's most elegant boutiques.

Verona as seen from the Museo Archeologico

Verona's rulers

In 1263 the Scaligeri began their successful 127-year rule of Verona. They used ruthless tactics in their rise to power, earning nicknames like Mastino (Mastiff) and Cangrande (Big Dog), but once in power the Scaligeri family brought peace to a city racked by civil strife and inter-family rivalry. They proved to be relatively just and cultured rulers – the poet Dante was welcomed to their court in 1301–4 and dedicated his *Paradise*, the final part of the epic *Divine Comedy*, to Cangrande I.

Verona fell to the Visconti of Milan in 1387, and a succession of outsiders – Venice, France and Austria – followed before the Veneto was united with the rest of Italy in 1866.

Key to Symbols *see back flap*

0 metres	500
0 yards	500

Fruit and vegetable stall in a side street of old Verona

For hotels and restaurants in this region see pp234–5 and pp248–9

⚜ Castelvecchio

Corso Castelvecchio 2. **Tel** 045 806
26 11. ⏲ 8:30am–7:30pm daily
(from 1:30pm Mon); 9am–7pm
public hols. ⬤ 1 Jan, 25 & 26 Dec.
🈹 🄿 📷

This spectacular castle, built
by Cangrande II between
1355 and 1375, has been
transformed into one of the
Veneto's finest art galleries.
Various parts of the medieval
structure have been linked
together using aerial walk-
ways and corridors, designed
by Carlo Scarpa to give striking
views of the building itself,
as well as the exhibits
within, which are
excellent and varied.
    The first section
contains a wealth of
late Roman and early
Christian material,
including a 7th-century
silver plate that shows
armoured knights

in combat, 5th-century
brooches and glass painted
with a portrait of Christ the
Shepherd in gold. The
martyrdom scenes depicted
on the carved marble
sarcophagus of Saints Sergius
and Bacchus (1179) are
gruesomely realistic.
    The following section, which
is devoted to medieval and
early Renaissance art, vividly
demonstrates the influence of
northern art on local painters,
suggesting strong links with
Verona's neighbours across
the Alps. Here, instead of the
serene saints and virgins of
Tuscan art, the emphasis is on
brutal realism. This is summed
up in the 14th-century
Crucifixion with Saints, which
depicts the torture
musculature of Christ
and the racked faces
of the mourners in
painful detail. Far
more lyrical is a
beautiful 15th-
century painting
by Stefano da
Verona called *The
Madonna of the
Rose Garden*. This
contains many
allusions to popular
medieval fables,
including the figure
of Fortune with her
wheel. In the
painting the Virgin sits in a
pretty garden alive with
decorative birds and angels
gathering rosebuds.
    Other Madonnas from the
15th century, attributed to
Giovanni Bellini, are displayed
among the late Renaissance
works upstairs. Jewellery,
suits of armour, swords and
shield bosses feature next,
some dating back to the 6th
and 7th centuries when

**Cangrande I's horse
in ceremonial garb**

VISITORS' CHECKLIST

🏙 261,000. ✈ Villafranca 14 km
(9 miles). 🚆 🚌 Piazzale 25
Aprile (045 800 08 61). 🚏 Piazza
Cittadella. 🚌 Via degli Alpini 9
(045 806 86 80). 🗓 daily.
Shops closed Wed pm (food),
Mon am (department & clothing
stores). 🍷 Vinitaly – Italy's largest
wine fair (Apr); Festival della Lirica
(opera festival) (end Jun–Aug);
Estate Teatrale Veronese, including
Shakespeare Festival (end Jun–
Aug). **www**.tourism.verona.it

Verona was under attack
from Teutonic invaders from
beyond the Alpine range.
    After the armour room, take
the walkway that leads out
along the river flank of the
castle, with its dizzying
views of the swirling
waters of the river
Adige and the
Ponte Scaligero
(*see p194*).
    Next, turning a
corner, one finds
Cangrande I, his
equestrian statue
dramatically
displayed out of
doors on a plinth.
This 14th-century
statue once graced
Cangrande's tomb
(*see p198*). It is
possible to study every detail
of the horse and rider draped
in their ceremonial garb.
Despite Cangrande's cherubic
cheeks and inane grin, his
face is compelling.
    Beyond lie some of the
museum's celebrated
paintings, notably Paolo
Veronese's *Deposition* (1565)
and a portrait attributed by
some to Titian, by others
to Lorenzo Lotto.

SIGHTS AT A GLANCE

Arco dei Gavi ④
Arena ⑦
Castelvecchio ③
Duomo ⑫
Giardino Giusti ⑱
Museo Archeologico ⑯
Museo Civico di Scienze
    Naturali ⑲
Museo Lapidario Maffeiano ⑤
Piazza Erbe ⑨
Piazza dei Signori ⑧
Ponte Scaligero ②
San Fermo Maggiore ⑥
San Giorgio in Braida ⑬
Sant'Anastasia ⑪
Santa Maria Antica ⑩
Santa Maria in Organo ⑰
Santo Stefano ⑭
San Zeno Maggiore ①
Teatro Romano ⑮

Courtyard of Castelvecchio

Around the Arena

Most visitors to Verona first arrive at Piazza Brà, a large, irregularly shaped square with a public garden. On the north side is an archway known as the Portoni della Brà. Dominating the eastern side of the piazza is the Roman Arena, Verona's most important monument, still in use today for operatic performances. The piazza is ringed with 19th-century buildings resembling ancient temples and historical landmarks.

Ponte Scaligero, part of the old defence system of Castelvecchio

🏛 Ponte Scaligero

This medieval bridge was built by Cangrande II between 1354 and 1376. The people of Verona love to stroll across it to ponder the river Adige in all its moods, or to admire summer sunsets and distant views of the Alps. Such is their affection for the bridge that it was rebuilt after the retreating Germans blew it up in 1945, an operation that involved dredging the river to salvage the medieval masonry. The bridge leads from Castelvecchio *(see p193)* to the Arsenal on the north bank of the Adige, built by the Austrians between 1840 and 1861 and now fronted by public gardens. Looking back from the gardens it is possible to see how the river was used as a natural moat to defend the castle, with the bridge providing the inhabitants with an escape route.

🏛 Arco dei Gavi and Corso Cavour

Dwarfed by the massive brick walls of Castelvecchio, the monumental scale of this Roman triumphal arch is now hard to appreciate. Originally the arch straddled the main Roman road into the city, today's Corso Cavour. But French troops who were occupying Castelvecchio in 1805 damaged the monument so much that a decision was made to move it to its present, less conspicuous position just off the Corso in 1933.

Continuing up Corso Cavour, there are some fine medieval and Renaissance palaces to see (especially Nos. 10, 11 and 19) before the Roman town gate, the **Porta dei Borsari**, is reached. The gate dates from the 1st century BC, but looking at the pedimented windows and niches it is easy to see what influenced the city's Renaissance architects.

The Roman Arco dei Gavi, 1st century AD

🏛 Museo Lapidario Maffeiano

Piazza Brà 8. **Tel** 045 590 087. ☐ 8:30am–7:30pm daily (from 1:30pm Mon). ⬤ 1 Jan, 25 & 26 Dec. 🖾
This "museum of stone" displays all kinds of architectural fragments hinting at the last splendour of the Roman city. There are many carved funerary monuments, and a large part of the collection consists of Greek inscriptions collected by the museum's 18th-century founder, Scipione Maffei.

🔒 San Fermo Maggiore

Stradone San Fermo. **Tel** 045 59 28 13. ☐ Mar–Oct: 10am–6pm; Nov–Feb: 10am–4pm. ⬤ Nov–Feb: Mon. 🖾 🗖
San Fermo Maggiore consists of not one but two churches. This can best be appreciated from the outside, where the eastern end is a jumble of rounded Romanesque arches below with pointed Gothic arches rising above. The lower church, now rather dank due to frequent flooding, dates from 1065, but the upper church (1313) is more impressive. It has a splendid ship's keel roof and lots of medieval fresco work. Frescoes from the 14th century, just inside the main door, are by Stefano de Zevico. They show the fate meted out to four Franciscan missionaries who journeyed to India in the mid-14th century. Nearby is the Brenzoni mausoleum (1439) by Giovanni di Bartolo with Pisanello's *Annunciation* fresco (1426) above. In the south aisle is an unusually ornate pulpit of 1396 with saints in canopied niches above, surrounded by frescoes of the Evangelists and Doctors of the Church.

The apse of the lower church of San Fermo Maggiore

The Arena

Verona's amphitheatre, completed around AD 30, is the third largest in the world, after Rome's Colosseum and the amphitheatre at Capua, near Naples. Originally, the Arena could hold almost the entire population of Roman Verona, and visitors came from across the Veneto to watch mock battles and gladiatorial combats. Since then, the Arena has been used for public executions, fairs, theatre performances, bullfighting and opera.

VISITORS' CHECKLIST

Piazza Brà. **Tel** *045 800 51 51.*
🕐 *8:30am–7:30pm daily (from 1:30pm Mon; last adm 6:30pm). Closes earlier on performance days.* ⬤ *1 Jan, 25 Dec.* 🎟 📷 ♿ *partial. Operas & concerts (see pp256–7).* **www**.arena.it

Interior
The interior has survived virtually intact, maintained by the Arena Conservators since 1580.

The façade of the Arena seen from Piazza Brà

The elliptical amphitheatre is 139 m (456 ft) long and 110 m (361 ft) wide.

Gladiators and wild beasts entered the arena from both sides.

Stone seats in 44 tiers

Below ground were cages for lions, tigers and other wild beasts, and a maze of passages.

Blood Sports
Prisoners of war, criminals and Christians died in their thousands in the name of entertainment.

Opera in the Arena
Today, performances of Verdi's Aida *and other popular operas can attract a capacity crowd of 25,000.*

Street-by-Street: Verona

Since the days of the Roman empire, the Piazza Erbe has been the centre of Verona's commercial and administrative life. Built on the site of the ancient Roman forum, it is an enjoyably chaotic square, bustling with life. Shoppers browse in the colourful market at stalls sheltered from the sun by wide-brimmed umbrellas. The massive towers and *palazzi* of the Scaligeri rulers of Verona have retained their medieval feel, even though they have been altered and adapted many times.

★ **Piazza dei Signori**
This square is bordered by individual Scaligeri palazzi linked by Renaissance arcades and carved stone archways.

Statue of Dante
Dante, the medieval poet, stayed in Verona as a guest of the Scaligeri during his period in exile from his native Florence. His statue (1865) looks down on Piazza dei Signori.

The 17th-century Palazzo Maffei is surmounted by a balustrade supporting statues of gods and goddesses.

Colonna di San Marco (1528) is surmounted by St Mark's Lion, the symbol of Venetian rule.

The fountain of 1368 is topped by a figure known as the Madonna of Verona; in fact, the statue is Roman and probably symbolizes Commerce.

Torre dei Lamberti, 84 m (275 ft) high

Piazza Erbe
Verona's medieval herb market is now lined with art galleries, up-market boutiques and inviting pavement cafés.

Palazzo della Ragione
The medieval Palace of Reason features an elegant Renaissance staircase. It leads from the exterior courtyard into the magistrates' rooms on the upper floor.

CORSO SANT' ANASTASIA

PIAZZA DEI SIGNORI

PIAZZA ERBE

VIA CAPPELLO

Via Sottoriva is lined with arcaded medieval houses and typifies the heart of the old city.

Sant'Anastasia
Carved hunchbacks (gobbi), crafted in 1495, form the unusual supports for the holy water stoups in this church.

PIAZZA SANT ANASTASIA

VIA DON BASSI

VIA SOTTORIVA

LUNGADICE DONATELLI

ADIGE

2 STELLE

SANTA MARIA IN CHIAVICA

ALETTO

SCALIGERI

ARCHE

SCALIGERI

VIA PONTE NUOVO

PIAZZA FRANCESCO VIVIANI

VIA CRISTO

VIA NIZZA

VIA STELLA

★ Scaligeri Tombs
In this masterpiece of 14th-century Gothic funerary art, soldier saints stand guard around the tombs, a reminder of the military prowess of Verona's powerful medieval rulers.

Santa Maria Antica is a little Romanesque church which dates back to the 7th century. The canopied tomb of Cangrande I rises above the entrance.

PONTE NUOVO

Ponte Nuovo
The "new bridge" (1540) spans the river Adige, linking the hills on the east bank of the city with Verona's historic centre.

0 metres	100
0 yards	100

Casa di Giulietta
The House of Juliet looks the part, with its marble balcony and romantic setting, although there is no evidence linking this house with the romantic legend.

KEY

– – – Suggested route

STAR SIGHTS

★ Piazza dei Signori

★ Scaligeri Tombs

Central Verona

The streets of this ancient city centre owe their grid-like layout to the order and precision of the Romans. At the heart is the lively Piazza Erbe, where crowds shop in the ancient market place. The fine *palazzi*, churches and monuments date mostly from the medieval period.

An elegant café in the spacious Piazza dei Signori

Piazza Erbe

Piazza Erbe is named after the city's old herb market. Today's stalls, shaded by huge umbrellas, sell everything from lunchtime snacks of herb-flavoured roast suckling pig in bread rolls to fresh-picked fruit or delicious wild mushrooms.

The **Venetian lion** that stands on top of a column to the north of the square marks Verona's absorption in 1405 into the Venetian empire. The statue-topped building that completes the north end of Piazza Erbe is the baroque **Palazzo Maffei** (1668), now converted to shops and luxury apartments. An assortment of boutiques and cafés lines the edge of the square.

The **fountain** that splashes away quietly in the middle of the piazza is often overlooked amid the competing attractions of the market's colourful stalls. Yet the statue at the fountain's centre dates from Roman times, a reminder that this long piazza has been in almost continuous use as a market place for 2,000 years.

Piazza dei Signori

Torre dei Lamberti *Tel* 045 927 30 27. ☐ 8:30am–7:30pm daily (Mar–Oct: to 8:30pm Sat–Thu, 11pm Fri). 📷

Stonework detail, Piazza dei Signori

In the centre of Piazza dei Signori is a 19th-century **statue of Dante**, who surveys the surrounding buildings with an appraising eye. His gaze is fixed on the grim **Palazzo del Capitano**, home of Verona's military commander, and the equally intimidating **Palazzo della Ragione**, the palace of Reason, or law court, both built in the 14th century. The Palazzo della Ragione is not quite so grim within. The courtyard has a handsome external stone staircase, added in 1446–50. Fine views of the Alps can be had by climbing the 84-m (275-ft) **Torre dei Lamberti**, which rises from the western side of the courtyard.

Behind the statue of Dante is the pretty Renaissance **Loggia del Consiglio**, or council chamber, with its frescoed upper façade (1493) and statues of Roman worthies born in Verona. These include Catullus the poet, Pliny the natural historian and Vitruvius the architectural theorist.

The piazza is linked to Piazza Erbe by the Arco della Costa, or the arch of the rib, whose name refers to the whale rib hung beneath it, put up here as a curiosity in the distant past.

🔒 Santa Maria Antica

This tiny Romanesque church is almost swamped by the bizarre Scaligeri tombs built up against its entrance wall. Because Santa Maria Antica was their parish church, the Scaligeri rulers of Verona chose to be buried here, and their tombs speak of their military prowess *(see p207)*.

Over the entrance to the church is the impressive tomb of Cangrande I, or Big Dog (died 1329), topped by his equestrian statue. This statue is a copy; the original is now in the Castelvecchio *(see p193)*. The other Scaligeri tombs are next to the church, surrounded by an intricate wrought-iron fence featuring the ladder motif of the family's original name *(della Scala*, meaning "of the steps"). Towering above the fence are the spire-topped tombs of Mastino II, or Mastiff (died 1351) and

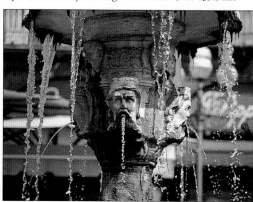

The fountain in Piazza Erbe, erected in the 14th century

Cansignorio, meaning Noble Dog (died 1375). These two tombs are splendidly decorated with Gothic pinnacles. In their craftsmanship and design there is nothing else in European funerary architecture quite like these spiky, thrusting monuments.

Plainer tombs nearer the church wall mark the resting place of other members of the Scaligeri family – Mastino (died 1277) who founded the Scaligeri dynasty, having been elected mayor of Verona in 1260, and two who did not have dog-based names: Bartolomeo (died 1304) and Giovanni (died 1359).

🔒 Sant'Anastasia

Tel 045 592 813. ⏰ *Mar–Oct: 9am–6pm Tue–Sat, 1–6pm Sun; Nov–Feb: 1–5pm Tue–Sun.* 📷 ♿ ⍉

A huge church, Sant'Anastasia was begun in 1290 and built to hold the massive congregations who came to listen to the rousing sermons preached by members of the fundamentalist Dominican order. The most interesting aspect of the church

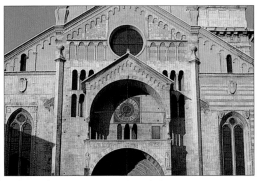

The façade of the Duomo, Santa Maria Matricolare

is its Gothic portal, with its faded 15th-century frescoes and carved scenes from the life of St Peter Martyr. Inside, the two holy water stoups are supported on realistic figures of beggars, known as *i gobbi*, the hunchbacks (the one on the left carved in 1495, the other a century later).

Off the north aisle is the sacristy, home to Antonio Pisanello's fresco, *St George and the Princess* (1433–8). Despite being badly damaged, the fresco still conveys something of the aristocratic grace of the Princess of Trebizond, with her noble brow and her ermine-fringed cloak, as St George prepares to mount his horse in pursuit of the dragon.

🔒 Duomo

Tel 045 595 627. ⏰ *Nov–Feb: 10am–1pm, 1:30–4pm Tue–Fri, 1–5pm Sat & Sun; Mar–Oct: 10am–5:30pm Mon–Fri, 1:30–5:30pm Sat & Sun.* ♿ 📷 ⍉

Visitors to Verona's cathedral pass through a magnificent

The lofty, Romanesque interior of Sant'Anastasia

Romanesque portal carved by Nicolò, one of the master masons who carved the façade of San Zeno (*see pp200–1*). Here he sculpted the sword-bearing figures of Oliver and Roland, knights whose exploits in the service of Charlemagne were celebrated in medieval poetry. Nearby, stand saints and evangelists with bold staring eyes and flowing beards. To the south there is a second Romanesque portal carved with Jonah and the Whale (removed for restoration) and comically grotesque caryatids (load-bearing figures).

The highlight is Titian's *Assumption* (1535–40) in the first chapel on the left. Further down is the entrance to the Romanesque cloister with excavated remains of earlier churches on the site. It leads to the baptistry, known as San Giovanni in Fonte (St John of the Spring). This 8th-century church features a huge marble font carved in 1200.

ROMEO AND JULIET

The tragic story of Romeo and Juliet, written by Luigi da Porto of Vicenza in the 1520s, inspired countless poems, films, ballets and dramas. At the **Casa di Giulietta** (Juliet's house), No. 27 Via Cappello (tel: 045 803 43 03), Romeo is said to have climbed to Juliet's balcony. In reality this is a restored 13th-century inn. The run-down **Casa di Romeo** is in Via delle Arche Scaligere, while the so-called **Tomba di Giulietta** (tel: 045 800 03 61) is in a crypt below the cloister of San Francesco al Corso on Via del Pontiere. The stone sarcophagus is empty and rather plain, but the setting is atmospheric. Juliet's house is open 8:30am–7:30pm daily (from 1:30pm Mon), her tomb 9am–7pm.

The lovers *Romeo and Juliet* from a 19th-century illustration

Verona: San Zeno Maggiore

Stone façade detail

Built between 1120 and 1138 to house the shrine of Verona's patron saint, San Zeno is northern Italy's most ornate Romanesque church. The façade is embellished with marble reliefs of biblical scenes, matched in vitality by bronze door panels showing the miracles of San Zeno. Beneath an impressive rose window, a graceful porch canopy rests on two slim columns. A brick campanile soars to the south, while a squat tower to the north is said to cover the tomb of King Pepin of Italy (777–810).

Nave Ceiling
The nave has a magnificent example of a ship's keel ceiling, so called because it resembles the inside of an upturned boat. This ceiling was constructed in 1386 when the apse was rebuilt.

Striped brickwork is typical of Romanesque buildings in Verona. Courses of local pink brick are alternated with ivory-coloured tufa.

Altarpiece
Andrea Mantegna's three-part altarpiece (1457–59) depicts the Virgin and Child with various saints. The painting served as an inspiration to local artists.

★ Cloister
North of the church the fine, airy cloister (1293–1313) has rounded Romanesque arches on one side and pointed Gothic arches on the other.

STAR FEATURES

★ Cloister

★ West Doors

★ Crypt

For hotels and restaurants in this region see pp234–5 and pp248–9

BRONZE DOOR PANELS

The 48 bronze panels of the west doors are primitive but forceful in their depiction of biblical stories and scenes from the life of San Zeno. Those on the left date from 1030 and survive from an earlier church on the site; those on the right were made 100 years later. Huge staring eyes and Ottoman-style hats, armour and architecture feature prominently, and the meaning of some scenes is not known – the woman suckling two crocodiles, for example.

Descent into limbo   **Christ in Glory**   **Human head**

VISITORS' CHECKLIST

Piazza San Zeno. **Tel** 045 59 28 13. 🚌 31, 32, 33 from Castel-vecchio. ⏰ 8:30am–6pm daily (from 1pm Sun); Nov–Feb: 10am–1pm, 1:30–4pm Tue–Sat, 1–5pm Sun & pub hols. ✝ times vary. 🚫 during mass. 📷 ♿ 🚫

The campanile, started in 1045, reached its present height of 72 m (236 ft) in 1173.

Rood Screen
Marble statues of Christ and the Apostles, dating from 1250, are ranged along the sanctuary rood screen.

Nave and Main Altar
The nave of the church is modelled on an ancient Roman basilica, the Hall of Justice. The main altar is situated in the raised sanctuary where the judge's throne would have stood.

The rose window symbolizes the Wheel of Fortune: figures around the rim show the rise and fall of human fortunes.

Marble side panels, carved in 1140, depict events from the life of Christ to the left of the doors, and scenes from the Book of Genesis to the right.

★ **West Doors**
Each of the wooden doors has 24 bronze plates joined by bronze masks, nailed on to the wood to look like solid metal. A bas relief above the doors depicts San Zeno vanquishing the devil.

★ **Crypt**
The vaulted crypt contains the tomb of San Zeno, appointed eighth bishop of Verona in AD 362, who died in AD 380.

Across the Ponte Romano

The Ponte Romano, or Roman Bridge, links Verona's city centre to the eastern bank of the river Adige. This upmarket residential district is dotted with fine palaces, gardens and churches, and offers good views back on to the towers and domes of the medieval city.

View from the Teatro Romano across the river Adige

🏛 Teatro Romano

Rigaste Redentore 2. *Tel 045 800 03 60.* ☐ *8:30am–7:30pm daily (from 1:30pm Mon; also open Mon am on public hols).* 🖼 🕭

When this theatre was built, in the 1st century BC, the plays performed would have included satirical dramas by such writers as Terence and Plautus. The tradition continues with open-air performances at the annual Shakespeare festival.

The theatre is built into a bank above the river Adige. The views over the city must have been as entrancing to Roman theatre-goers as the events on stage. Certainly it is for the views that the theatre is best visited today, since little is left of the original stage area, though the semi-circular seating area remains largely intact.

In the foreground of the view is one of three Roman bridges that brought traffic into the city. The only one to have survived, this had to be painstakingly reconstructed after being blown up in 1945 by retreating German soldiers who were attempting to delay the advance of Allied troops. Of the five arches, the two nearest to the theatre are least altered.

🏛 Museo Archeologico

Rigaste Redentore 2. *Tel 045 800 03 60.* ☐ *8:30am–7:30pm daily (from 1:30pm Mon; also open Mon am on public hols).* 🖼

A lift carries visitors from the Teatro Romano up through the cliffs to the monastery above. This is now converted into an archaeological museum in which panoramic city views vie for attention with the range of exhibits.

The first part of the museum displays well-restored mosaics, one of which depicts the kind of gory gladiatorial combat that once went on in Verona's amphitheatre *(see p195).* Such barbaric performances, seen as a legitimate way of disposing of criminals and prisoners of war, finally came to an end in the early 5th century following a decree from the Christian Emperor Honorius.

In the little monastic cells to the side of this room, visitors can see a bronze bust of the first Roman emperor, the

Augustus Caesar, Museo Archeologico

young Augustus Caesar (63 BC–AD 14), who succeeded in outmanoeuvring his opponents, including Mark Antony and Cleopatra, to become the sole ruler of the Roman world in 31 BC. The subject of the female bust in the adjoining cell is unknown. Next comes the tiny cloister, littered with mosaics and ancient masonry fragments, and a warren of ancient rooms used to display pottery, glass, inscriptions and tombstones. Labelling stops after a while, leaving visitors to puzzle out the nature and age of exhibits for themselves.

🔒 Santo Stefano

This is one of the city's oldest churches; the original, long-demolished building was constructed in the 6th century. It served as Verona's cathedral until the 12th century when the Duomo was built *(see p199)* on the opposite bank of the Adige. Visitors to Santo Stefano are afforded a striking view of the Duomo across the river, taking in the Romanesque apse and the bishop's palace alongside. Santo Stefano itself was rebuilt at the same time by Lombard architects and given its octagonal red brick campanile, but the original apse survives.

Inside the church there is a Byzantine-influenced arrangement of a stone bishop's seat and bench, and a gallery with 8th-century carved capitals. The apse (which is often locked) is even older, dating back to the original 6th-century building. In the crypt there are fragments of 13th-century frescoes and a 14th-century statue of St Peter.

Towering above the church to the east is Castel San Pietro, strikingly fronted by flame-shaped cypress trees. The present castle was built in 1854 under Austrian rule, but it stands on the ruins of an earlier castle which was built by the Visconti of Milan when the Milanese captured Verona in 1387.

Figure of St Peter, Santo Stefano

🔒 San Giorgio in Braida

San Giorgio is a rare example in Verona of a domed Renaissance church. It was begun in 1477 by Michele Sanmicheli, an architect best known for his military works. Sanmicheli also designed the classically inspired altar, which is topped by Paolo Veronese's *Martyrdom of St George* (1566). This celebrated painting is outshone by the calm and serene *Virgin Enthroned between St Zeno and St Lawrence* (1526) by Girolamo dai Libri. This work has a beautifully detailed background landscape and a lemon tree growing behind the Virgin's throne.

Marquetry cockerel in Santa Maria in Organo

🔒 Santa Maria in Organo

Some of the finest inlaid woodwork to be seen in Italy is in this church. The artist was Fra Giovanni da Verona, an architect and craftsman who worked for nearly 25 years, from 1477 to 1501, on these stunning examples of illusionistic marquetry. The seat backs in the choir and cupboard fronts in the sacristy are full of entertaining detail. By clever interpretation of perspective, Fra Giovanni gave depth to flat landscapes, depicted city views glimpsed through an open window, and created "cupboard interiors" stacked with books, musical instruments or bowls of fruit. Most charming of all are the little animal pictures – look out for the rabbit on the lectern and the owl and the cockerel in the sacristy.

Fossilized fish from Verona's natural history museum

🏛 Museo Civico di Scienze Naturali

Lungadige Porta Vittoria 9. **Tel** 045 807 94 00. ◯ 9am–5pm Mon–Thu, 9am–1pm Sat, 2–6pm Sun and public hols. ● 1 Jan, Easter, 1 May, 25 Dec. 🔲 🔲

Verona's natural history museum contains an outstanding collection of fossils, which can be enjoyed by experts and newcomers alike. Whole fish, trees, fern leaves and dragonflies are captured in extraordinary detail. The fossils were found in rock in the foothills of the Little Dolomites north of the city during quarrying for building stone *(see Bolca, p191)*.

Human prehistory is represented by finds from ancient settlements round Lake Garda, and there are reconstructions of original lake villages. On the upper floor, cases full of stuffed birds, animals and fish provide an extensive account of today's living world, making this a good museum for visiting with children.

🍀 Giardino Giusti

Via Giardino Giusti 2. **Tel** 045 803 40 29. ◯ summer: 9am–8pm; winter: 9am–sunset. ● 25 Dec. 🔲 ♿

Hidden among the dusty façades of the Via Giardino Giusti is the entrance to one of Italy's finest Renaissance gardens. They were laid out in 1580 and, as with other gardens of the period, artifice and nature are deliberately juxtaposed. The lower garden of clipped box hedges, gravel walks and potted plants is contrasted with an upper area of wilder woodland, the two parts linked by stone terracing.

Past visitors have included the English traveller Thomas Coryate who, writing in 1611, called this garden "a second paradise". The diarist John Evelyn, visiting 50 years later, thought it the finest garden in Europe. Today the garden makes an excellent, picturesque spot for a quiet picnic.

Italianate topiary and statuary in the Giardino Giusti

Around Lake Garda

Garda, the largest and easternmost of the Italian
Lakes, is a favourite summer playground for sports
lovers. Strong winds make ideal conditions for windsurfing and sailing, there are numerous yacht harbours
and artificial beaches, and luxury hotels offer tennis
and horse-riding facilities. The less energet-
ic can explore the lake and shore by
steamer, while the magnificent scenery
of snow-capped peaks and
spectacular sunsets
will appeal to
every visitor.

RIVA DEL GARDA

• TORBOLE

LIMONE SUL GARDA •

• MALCESINE

• ASSENZA

• BRENZONE

• CASTELLETTO

GARGNANO •

BOGLIACO •

La Gardesana

TOSCOLANO MADERNO •

GARDONE RIVIERA •

SALÒ •

PORTESE •

• TORRI DEL BENACO

• GARDA

MANERBA •

MONIGA •

• BARDOLINO

• LAZISE

• SIRMIONE

DESENZANO •

• PESCHIERA DEL GARDA

Malcesine
*The streets of this town
are full of character,
clustering beneath an
imposing medieval
castle.*

Desenzano
*With its lively harbour
and palm-fringed
promenades, Desenzano
is the main terminus for
steamer excursions.*

Bardolino gave its name to the
well-known red wine.

The Sirmione peninsula is
best seen from the lake.

KEY

•••• Steamer routes

•••• Car ferry

0 kilometres   10

0 miles   5

Torri del Benaco
*Built by the Republic of
Venice in 1452, the Hotel
Gardesana was originally
used to host the meetings
of the Council.*

LA GARDESANA

This is the name given to the 143-km (89-mile) perimeter road that hugs the lake shore. For much of its route the road is cut through solid rock, sometimes following a narrow ledge in the cliff face, sometimes passing through tunnels (around 80 in total). The switchback route offers spectacular views at every turn, particularly at Gargnano, and there are numerous viewing points. Places of interest along La Gardesana include the splendid 18th-century gardens of Palazzo Bettoni at Bogliaco and the castle at Riva del Garda.

The scenic road to Limone

LAKE TRIPS

Lake Garda's ferries are still called steamers, even though they are diesel-powered today. The major towns around the southern rim of the lake all have jetties where visitors can buy a ticket and board the boat for a leisurely cruise. Gardens and villas that are otherwise hidden from view can be seen from the water. A trip from one end of the lake to the other takes approximately 2 hours 20 minutes by hydrofoil, and four hours by steamer. Catamarans also operate around the southern end of the lake.

The hydrofoil operating out of Desenzano harbour

Lake Garda steamer at dusk near Peschiera

Garda ❿

🏛 3,400. 🚌 🛈 Piazzetta Donatori di Sangue 1 (045 627 03 84). 🔼 Fri am. **Shops closed** Wed pm (food). www.tourism.verona.it

Numerous pavement cafés brighten the streets around the central Palazzo dei Capitani, built in the 15th century for the use of the Venetian militia. In a different vein, a series of prehistoric rock engravings features along the Strada dei Castei, an old route above the town.

Peschiera ⓫

🏛 8,900. 🚌 FS 🛈 Piazzale Bettelone 15. (045 755 16 73). 🔼 Mon am. **Shops closed** Wed in winter. www.tourism.verona.it

At Peschiera the River Mincio flows out of Lake Garda to join the River Po. The main site of interest is a fortress built in the 19th century. Named Fortezza del Quadrilatero because of its square shape, it replaced a 15th-century stronghold.

Environs
Just outside town are **Gardaland**, a theme park with a replica of the ancient Egyptian Valley of the Kings (free bus from Peschiera station), and **Parco Natura Viva**, a zoo with a safari park and models of dinosaurs.

🏛 **Gardaland**
Loc. Ronchi, 37014 Castelnuovo del Garda. **Tel** 045 644 97 77. ◯ end Mar–Sep: daily; Oct & Christmas period: Sat & Sun. 🈸 🈺

🦌 **Parco Natura Viva**
Nr. Bussolengo. **Tel** 045 717 01 13. ◯ mid-Mar–Nov: daily. ● Wed in Nov. 🈸 🈺 www.parconaturaviva.it

Solferino ⓬

🏛 2,118. 🚌 🔼 Sat pm. **Shops closed** Mon pm.

The battle of Solferino (1859) left 40,000 Italian and Austrian troops dead and injured, abandoned without medical care or burial. Shocked by such neglect, a Swiss man named Henri Dunant began a campaign for better treatment. The result was the first Geneva Convention, signed in 1863, and the establishment of the International Red Cross. In the town of Solferino there is a war museum and an ossuary chapel, lined with bones from the battlefield. There is also a memorial to Dunant built by the Red Cross with donations from member nations.

The ossuary chapel at Solferino, lined with skulls

For hotels and restaurants in this region see pp234–5 and pp248–9

Sirmione Peninsula ⑬

Charming Sirmione is a finger of land extending into the southern end of Lake Garda, connected to the mainland by a bridge. The Roman poet Catullus (born in 84 BC) owned a villa here: the ruins of the Grotte di Catullo lie among ancient olive trees at the northern tip. The Rocca Scaligera castle stands guard at the base of the peninsula, and beyond, the narrow streets of the village give way to peaceful lakeside walks and elegant spa hotels.

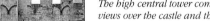

View Towards the Grotto
The high central tower commands views over the castle and the whole of the Sirmione peninsula.

★ Rocca Scaligera
The castle was built in the 13th century by the Scaligeri of Verona. It is cleverly designed to trap shipborne invaders, leaving them vulnerable to missiles dropped from the castle walls.

The main keep tower was used for bombarding attackers trapped below.

The moat, originally a complex defence system, is today home to carp.

Piazza Castello

Sirmione Old Town
Narrow stone-paved streets are packed with shops selling crafts and souvenirs.

Visiting the Peninsula
Cars must be parked before entering Sirmione, leaving the medieval streets for pedestrians.

STAR FEATURES

- ★ Rocca Scaligera
- ★ Grotte di Catullo

VISITORS' CHECKLIST

Viale Marconi 8 (030 91 61 14). **Rocca Scaligera** *Tel* 030 91 64 68. 8:30am–7pm Tue–Sun. 1 Jan, 1 May, 25 Dec. **www**.lombardia. beniculturali.it **Grotte di Catullo** *Tel* 030 91 61 57. 8:30am–7pm Tue–Sun (Nov–Feb: to 1pm). 1 Jan, 1 May, 25 Dec. Sat & Sun.

Lakeside Walk
Following the eastern shores of the peninsula, this pretty walk links the village to the Grotte di Catullo.

San Pietro
Founded in AD 765, on Sirmione's highest point, this church contains a 12th-century fresco of Christ in Majesty.

★ Grotte di Catullo
This complex of villas, baths and shops, built as a resort for wealthy Romans from the 1st century BC, lies ruined here. Finds are displayed in the Antiquarium building.

The inner harbour provided a haven for fishermen during lake storms and an anchorage for the castle fleet.

The drawbridge is heavily fortified, linking the castle to the mainland and offering an escape route to its inhabitants.

THE SCALIGERI

The Rocca Scaligera is one of many castles built throughout the Verona and Lake Garda region by the Scaligeri family *(see p192)*. During the turbulent 13th and 14th centuries, powerful military rulers fought each other incessantly in pursuit of riches and power. Despite the autocratic nature of their rule, the Scaligeri brought a period of peace and prosperity to the region, fending off attacks by the predatory Visconti family who ruled neighbouring Lombardy.

The Scaligeri ruler, Cangrande I

Salò

🏛 *10,000.* 🚉 🍽 *Sat am.*

Locals prefer to associate
this elegant town with
Gaspare da Salò (1540–1609),
the inventor of the violin,
rather than with Mussolini,
the World War II dictator.
Mussolini set up the so-called
Salò Republic in 1943 and
ruled northern Italy from here
until 1945, when he was shot
by the Italian resistance.

Happier memories are
evoked by Salò's buildings,
including the cathedral with
its unusual wooden altarpiece
(1510) by Paolo Veneziano.
The main appeal of the town
derives from its pastel-coloured
waterfront buildings, picturesque squares and alleyways,
and the lake views. Salò
marks the beginning of the
Riviera Bresciana, where the
shore is lined with villas and
grand hotels set in semi-
tropical gardens.

Gardone Riviera ⑮

🏛 *2,500.* 🚉 ℹ️ *Via Repubblica 8.
(0365 203 47).*

Gardone's most appealing
feature is the terraced public
park that cascades down the
hillside, planted with noble and
exotic trees. Equally exotic
are the Mediterranean
and African plants
in the **Hruska
Botanical
Gardens,**

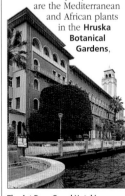

**The Art Deco Grand Hotel in
Gardone Riviera**

founded in 1910, which benefit
from the town's mild winters.
Gardone has long been a
popular resort – the magnificent 19th-century **Villa Alba**
(now a congress centre) was
built for the Austrian emperor
to escape the bitter winters of
his own country. The Art Deco
Grand Hotel on the waterfront
was built for lesser beings.

High above the town is the
Villa il Vittoriale, built for the
poet Gabriele d'Annunzio. His
Art Deco villa has blacked-out
windows (he professed to
loathe the world) and is full of
curiosities, including a coffin-
shaped bed. The garden has a
landlocked warship, the prow
raised high over Lake Garda.

🌸 **Hruska Botanical Gardens**
Via Roma. **Tel** 336 41 08 77.
⏱ Mar–Oct: 9am–7pm daily. 📷

🏛 **Villa il Vittoriale**
Via Vittoriale 12. **Tel** 0365 29 65
23. ⏱ Tue–Sun (garden daily).
⏱ 1 Jan, 24 & 25 Dec. 📷 📷
📷 💻 www.vittoriale.it

Valpolicella Wine Tour

This circular tour takes in the beautiful, remarkably varied scenery of the wine district that lies
between Verona and Lake Garda. On the shores of
Lake Garda itself, deep and fertile glacial soils
provide sustenance for the grapes that are
used to make Bardolino, a wine that is meant
to be drunk young *(see pp238–9)*. Inland,
the rolling foothills of the Lessini
mountains shelter hamlets
where lives and working
rhythms are tuned to the
needs of the vines. These
particular vines are grown
to produce the equally famed
Valpolicella, a red wine that
varies from light and fruity
to full-bodied.

TIPS FOR DRIVERS

Starting point: Verona.
Length: 45 km (28 miles).
Approximate driving time:
3 hours.
Stopping-off points: The main
village of the Valpolicella region,
San Pietro in Cariano, has cafés
and restaurants.

Affi ④
This wine-producing village is
surrounded by vineyards planted
in the sheltered basin of the
Adige Valley.

Bardolino ③
Famous for its light
red wine, Bardolino
hosts a grape festival
in September and has
numerous cellars
offering tastings.

KEY

▬▬ Tour route

═══ Other roads

Lazise ②
Lazise has long been the
chief port of Garda's eastern
shore, its picturesque
harbour and medieval
church guarded by a
14th-century castle.

Malcesine ⑰

🚶 3,500. 🚌 ⛴ Sat.

German visitors who come to Malcesine trace the journey taken by the poet Goethe in 1788. His travels were full of mishaps, and at Malcesine he was accused of spying and locked up.

From Malcesine, visitors can take the rotating **cable car** up to the broad ridge of Monte Baldo (1,745 m/5,725 ft). The journey takes 15 minutes, and on a clear day it is possible to see the distant peaks of the Dolomites, including the Brenta range. Footpaths for walkers are signposted at the top. The lower slopes are designated nature reserves; a good place to see the local flora is the **Riserva Naturale Gardesana Orientale**, just to the north of Malcesine, on the western side of Monte Baldo.

Looking across Lake Garda from Riva del Garda

Riva del Garda ⑯

🚶 13,600. 🚌 ℹ️ Largo Medaglie d'Oro (0464 55 44 44). 🗓️ 2nd Wed (& 4th Wed in summer). **Shops closed** Mon (non-food); Mon pm (food) & Sat pm in winter. www.gardatrentino.it

Riva's waterfront is overlooked by the moated **Rocca di Riva**, a former Scaligeri fortress. Inside is a museum with exhibits from the region's prehistoric lake villages, built by driving huge piles into the lake bed to support platforms. The lake is popular with windsurfers.

♣ Rocca di Riva
Piazza Cesare Battisti 3a. **Tel** 0464 57 38 69. 🕐 mid-Mar–Oct: Tue–Sun (Mon also in Jul–Sep). 📷 ♿ 🏠

Cloisters of San Giorgio in Valpolicella

Sant'Ambrogio di Valpolicella ⑤
Apart from red wine, this village is a source of the pink stone used for Verona's palaces.

Gargagnago ⑥
The Alighieri wine estate is owned by a direct descendant of the medieval poet Dante, and set around a 14th-century villa built by Dante's son.

Pedemonte ⑦
The Villa Santa Sofia wine estate operates out of a theatrical villa designed by Palladio, but never completed.

TRENTO

San Giorgio

San Floriano

San Pietro in Cariana

S12

• Pescantina

Adige

Biffi

PADOVA

S11

Verona ①
The city has numerous old-fashioned bars, called osterie, where visitors can go to sample local wine.

| 0 kilometres | 3 |
| 0 miles | 2 |

THE DOLOMITES

he name of the Dolomites conjures up a vision of spectacular mountains, as noble and awe-inspiring as the Alps. To the south of the region lie the cities of Feltre, Belluno and Vittorio Veneto. To the north is the renowned ski resort of Cortina d'Ampezzo. In between, travellers will encounter no more cities – just ravishing views, unfolding endlessly, and pretty hamlets tucked into remarkably lush and sunny south-facing valleys.

The Dolomites cover a substantial portion of the Veneto's land mass, and it is easy to forget, when visiting the cities of the flat Veneto plain, that behind them lies this range of mountains rising to heights of 2,000 m (6,500 ft) and more. Catering for an urban population hungry for fresh air and freedom, the towns and villages of the Dolomites have striven to balance the needs of tourism and nature.

Italian is the region's principal language, but in the northwest a German influence can sometimes be heard, reflecting the region's strong historic links with the Austrian Tyrol. Once ruled by the Hapsburgs, certain areas of the region only became part of Italy in 1918, after the break up of the Austro-Hungarian empire at the end of World War I. Some of that war's fiercest fighting took place in the Dolomites, as both sides tried to wrest control of the strategic valley passes linking Italy and Austria-Hungary. Striking war memorials in many villages and towns provide a sad reminder of that time.

Today the region is renowned for its winter sports facilities. International cross-country ski competitions were held in Cortina d'Ampezzo as early as 1902, and in 1956 the town hosted the Winter Olympics. Today, Cortina is considered to be Italy's most exclusive resort, the winter playground of film stars and royalty.

Outdoor café in the old town of Feltre

◁ Pleasure boats on Lake Misurina, looking towards the peaks of the Sorapiss

Exploring the Dolomites

The environment of the Dolomites is completely different from the industrialized Veneto plain. Huge areas are designated nature reserves, while others, accessible by chair lifts, allow visitors to enjoy the views and appetite-sharpening treks in the mountain meadows. Refuges, dotted along the high trails, offer dormitory accommodation and refreshments, while hamlets have comfortable hotels.

Titian's statue, Pieve di Cadore

Snow covers the peaks from October to May, and it is possible to ski all year round on Marmolada, at 3,343 m (10,970 ft) the highest peak in the Dolomites.

Mountain chalet near the stadium at Cortina d'Ampezzo

SIGHTS AT A GLANCE

Belluno ❺
Cortina d'Ampezzo ❶
The Dolomites (Dolomiti)
  pp216–17 ❹
Feltre ❼
Misurina ❷
Pieve di Cadore ❸
Valzoldana ❻
Vittorio Veneto ❽

0 kilometres   10

0 miles   5

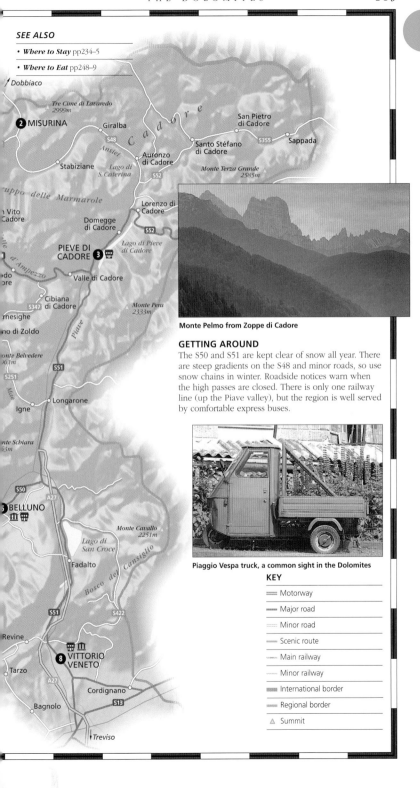

SEE ALSO

• *Where to Stay* pp234–5

• *Where to Eat* pp248–9

Dobbiaco

Tre Cime di Lavaredo
2999m

2 MISURINA

Giralba

San Pietro
di Cadore

Cadore

Anstei

Stabiziane

Auronzo
di Cadore

Santo Stéfano
di Cadore

S355

Sappada

*Lago di
S. Caterina*

552

Monte Terza Grande
2585m

ruppo delle Marmarole

Lorenzo di
Cadore

Vito
Cadore

Domegge
di Cadore

552

*Lago di Pieve
di Cadore*

**PIEVE DI
CADORE 3**

d'Ampezzo

do
re

Valle di Cadore

Cibiana
di Cadore

5347

Monte Pera
2333m

Piave

rnesighe

no di Zoldo

nte Belvedere
61m

551

S251

Longarone

Igne

nte Schiara
5m

S50

A27

5 BELLUNO

Monte Cavallo
2251m

*Lago di
San Croce*

Fadalto

Boscco del Cansiglio

551

S422

Revine

Tarzo

A27

8 VITTORIO
VENETO

Cordignano

S13

Bagnolo

Treviso

Monte Pelmo from Zoppe di Cadore

GETTING AROUND

The S50 and S51 are kept clear of snow all year. There are steep gradients on the S48 and minor roads, so use snow chains in winter. Roadside notices warn when the high passes are closed. There is only one railway line (up the Piave valley), but the region is well served by comfortable express buses.

Piaggio Vespa truck, a common sight in the Dolomites

KEY

▬▬▬	Motorway
▬▬▬	Major road
▭▭▭	Minor road
▬▬▬	Scenic route
▬▭▬	Main railway
▬▬▬	Minor railway
▬▬▬	International border
▬▬▬	Regional border
△	Summit

Cortina d'Ampezzo **❶**

🏔 *6,800.* 🚌 🛈 *Piazzetta San Francesco 8 (0436 3231).* 🛒 *Tue & Fri am.* **www.infodolomiti.it**

Italy's top ski resort, much favoured by the smart set from Turin and Milan, is well supplied with restaurants and bars. The reason for its popularity is the dramatic scenery, which adds an extra dimension to the pleasure of speeding down the slopes. Guests are surrounded by crags

Strolling along the Corso Italia in Cortina d'Ampezzo

Skiers at Cortina

and spires, which rise skyward, thrusting their weather-sculpted shapes above the trees.

As a consequence of hosting the 1956 Winter Olympics, Cortina has better-than-normal sports facilities. There is a ski jump and a bobsleigh run, the Olympic ice stadium holds skating discotheques, and there are several swimming pools as well as tennis courts and riding facilities.

During the summer months, Cortina becomes an excellent base for walkers. Information on the many trails and guided walks is available from the tourist office or, during the summer, from the Guides' office opposite.

Visitors can also take the cable car *Freccia nel Cielo* (Arrow in the Sky), which goes to a height of 3,243 m (10,639 ft) above sea level.

The Dolomite Road

The Strada Delle Dolomiti, or Dolomite Road, is one of the most beautiful routes anywhere in the Alps and is a magnificent feat of highway construction. It starts in the Trentino-Alto Adige region at Bolzano and enters the Veneto region at Passo Pordoi, at 2,239 m (7,346 ft) the most scenic of all the Dolomite passes. From here the route follows the winding S48 for another 35 km (22 miles) east to the resort of Cortina d'Ampezzo.

There are plenty of stopping places along the route where it is possible to stop and enjoy the spectacular views. In many of the ski resorts, cable cars will carry visitors up to alpine refuges (some with cafés attached) that are open from mid-June to mid-September. These refuges mark the start of a series of signposted walks.

Passo Pordoi ①
To the north of Passo Pordoi, the Gruppo di Sella rises to 3,152 m (10,340 ft).

← *BOLZANO*

TIPS FOR WALKERS

Starting point: Passo Pordoi.
Length (within the Veneto): 35 km (22 miles).
Approximate driving time: Two hours, but allow a full day to include the return journey and time to stop and enjoy the stunning scenery.
Stopping-off points: The small towns of Pieve di Livinallongo and Andraz have good cafés and restaurants.

KEY

🚌 Tour route

Other roads

View point

| 0 kilometres | | 5 |
| 0 miles | 2 | |

Arabba ②
Arabba is a pleasant resort with a cable car to Porta Vescovo (2,478 m/ 8,129 ft) to the south.

For hotels and restaurants in this region see p235 and p249

Misurina ❷

🏠 82. 🚌 ℹ️ *Via Misurina (0435 390 16)*. ◯ *Jul–Aug; late Dec–early Jan.* **www**.infodolomiti.it

Smaller and quieter than Cortina, Misurina nestles by the exquisite Lake Misurina. The lake's mirror-like surface reflects the peaks of Monte Sorapiss and the Cadini group. Take the toll road

One of the creeks flowing into Lake Misurina

that climbs northeast for 8 km (5 miles) to the Auronzo mountain refuge and to the base of the Tre Cime di Lavaredo peaks (2,999 m/9,840 ft).

Pieve di Cadore ❸

🏠 4,000. 🚌 ℹ️ *Piazza Municipio 13 (0435 316 44).* � *Wed am (at Tai).* **www**.infodolomiti.it

For centuries the Cadore forests supplied Venice with its timber. The main town of this vast mountainous region is Pieve di Cadore, primarily known as the birthplace of Titian. The humble **Casa di Tiziano** can be visited, and the nearby **Museo Archeologico** has exhibits of finds from the pre-Roman era.

Principally, though, this is a base for touring the scenic delights of the region. North

Titian's house at Pieve di Cadore

of Pieve the valley narrows to a dramatic ravine, and the road north to Comelica and Sesto is noted for its alpine scenery and its traditional balconied houses. Continuing northeast, the Piave river can be followed to its source, 8 km (5 miles) north of Sappada.

🏠 Casa di Tiziano
Via Arsenale 4. **Tel** 0435 322 62. ◯ *Jun–Sep: Tue–Sun (Aug): daily); Oct–May: by appointment.* 📷

🏛 Museo Archeologico Romano e Preromano
Palazzo della Magnifica Comunità Cadorina, Piazza Tiziano 2. **Tel** 0435 322 62. ◯ *Jun–Sep: Tue–Sun (Aug): daily); Oct–May: by appt.* 📷

Falzarego ⑤
War memorials record the fighting that took place here in 1914–18 on the frontier between Austria and Italy.

Cortina d'Ampezzo ⑥
Descending to Cortina, the view is dominated by the irregularly-shaped Cinque Torri (Five Towers).

Andraz ④
The partially restored Castello di Andraz, sitting on a rocky outcrop, was built in the 14th century to prevent banditry and to control the approach to the Passo Falzarego.

Pieve di Livinallongo ③
The chief town of the scenic Cordevole valley, Pieve offers spectacular views of dolomitic peaks and cliffs.

Visitors at Passo Falzarego, by the war memorials

The Dolomites ❹

The Dolomites are the most distinctive and beautiful mountains in Italy. They were formed of mineralized coral which was laid down beneath the sea during the Triassic era, and uplifted when the European and African continental plates dramatically collided 60 million years ago. Unlike the glacier-eroded saddles and ridges of the main body of the Alps, the pale rocks here have been carved by the corrosive effects of ice, sun and rain, sculpting the cliffs, spires and "organ pipes" that we see today. The eastern and western ranges of the Dolomites have slightly different characteristics; the eastern section is the more awe-inspiring, especially the Catinaccio (or Rosengarten) range which is particularly beautiful, turning rose pink at sunset.

Onion dome, a common local feature

STRADA DELLE DOLOMITI

One of the most spectacular routes through the Dolomites links Bolzano with Cortina d'Ampezzo (see p214). It follows the lie of the land, passing some of the greatest peaks, and the most majestic landscape.

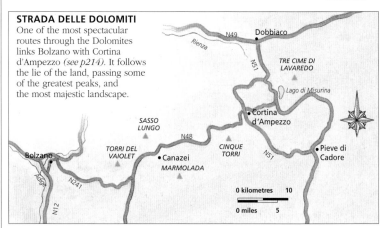

DISTINCTIVE PEAKS OF THE DOLOMITES

The peaks of the Dolomites include several with distinctive shapes and some of the highest mountains in the range. Many are easily identifiable and have been individually named.

Marmolada 3,343 m (10,968 ft)

Sasso Lungo 3,179 m (10,430 ft)

Cinque Torri 2,366 m (7,762 ft)

The Cinque Torri or *Five Towers rise from one base between Passo Falzarego and Cortina d'Ampezzo.*

Sasso Lungo *is a tall peak easily recognized by its distinctive scar. It is joined to the Sasso Piatto.*

Marmolada *is the highest peak in the Dolomite chain. A cable-car ascends to 3,000 m above the glacier.*

Lago di Misurina *is a large and beautiful lake lying beside the resort of Misurina. The crystal clear waters reflect the surrounding mountains, mirroring various peaks such as the distinctive and dramatic Sorapiss, in shimmering colours.*

Outdoor activities *in this area of dramatic landscapes include skiing in winter, and walking and rambling along the footpaths, and to picnic sites, in summer. Chair-lifts from the main resorts provide easy access up into the mountains themselves, transporting you into some breathtaking scenery.*

NATURE IN THE DOLOMITES

Forests and meadows support a breathtaking richness of wildlife in the region. Alpine plants, which flower between June and September, have evolved their miniature form to survive the harsh winds.

THE FLORA

Gentian roots *are used to make a bitter local liqueur.*

The orange mountain lily *thrives on sun-baked slopes.*

The pretty *burser's saxifrage grows in clusters on rocks.*

Devil's claw *has distinctive pink flower heads.*

THE FAUNA

The ptarmigan *changes its plumage from mottled brown in summer to snow white in winter for effective camouflage. It feeds on mountain berries and young plant shoots.*

The chamois, *a shy mountain antelope prized for its soft skin, is protected in the national parks, where hunting is forbidden.*

Roe deer *are very common as their natural predators – wolves and lynx – have now died out. Their keen appetite for tree saplings causes problems for foresters.*

Torri del Vaiolet
2,243 m
(7,375 ft)

Tre Cime di Lavaredo
2,999 m
(9,839 ft)

The Torri del Vaiolet *is part of the beautiful Catinaccio range, known for its colour.*

Tre Cime di Lavaredo *or Drei Zinnen dominate the valleys north of the Lago di Misurina.*

Belluno ❺

🏠 35,800. 🚇 ⌨ 🛈 Piazza Duomo
2 (0437 94 00 83). 🚌 Sat am.
Shops closed Mon am (clothes) &
Wed pm (food). **www**.infodolomiti.it

Façade and entrance to Palazzo dei Rettori in Belluno

Picturesque Belluno, capital of Belluno province, serves as a bridge between the two very different parts of the Veneto, with the flat plains to the south and the Dolomite peaks to the north. Both are encapsulated in the picture-postcard views to be seen from the 12th-century **Porta Rugo** at the southern end of Via Mezzaterra, the main street of the old town. Even more spectacular are the views from the campanile of the 16th-century **Duomo** which was designed by Tullio Lombardo, but rebuilt twice after damage by earthquakes.

The nearby baptistry contains a font cover with the figure of John the Baptist carved by Andrea Brustolon (1662–1732), whose elaborate furnishings decorate Ca' Rezzonico in Venice (see p126). Brustolon's works also grace the churches of **San Pietro** (two altarpieces) and **Santo Stefano** (crucifix and angels). On the same

Exterior fresco, Zoppe di Cadore

square is the 12th-century **Torre Civica**, all that survives of the Bishop's Palace, and the city's most elegant building, the Renaissance **Palazzo dei Rettori** (1491), once home to Belluno's Venetian rulers.

The **Museo Civico** is worth visiting for the archaeological exhibits, and the paintings by Bartolomeo Montagna (1450–1523) and Sebastiano Ricci (1659–1734). Just to the right of the museum is the town's finest square, the **Piazza del Mercato**, which features arcaded Renaissance palaces and a fountain built in 1410.

South of the town are the ski resorts of the Alpe del Nevegal. It is worth taking the chair lift in the summer

to the Rifugio Brigata Alpina Cadore (1,600 m/5,250 ft), which has superb views and a botanical garden specializing in alpine plants.

🏛 **Museo Civico**
Piazza Duomo 16. **Tel** 0437 94 48
36. ⬜ May–Sep: Tue–Sun;
Oct–Apr: daily. 🈺 📷 ⬜

Valzoldana ❻

🚌 from Longarone. 🛈 Via Roma
10, Forno di Zoldo (0437 78 73 49).

The wooded Zoldo valley is a popular destination for walking holidays. Its main resort town is Forno di Zoldo and the surrounding villages are noted for their Tyrolean-style alpine chalets and hay-lofts. Examples built in wood on stone foundations can be

BELLUNO

Duomo ②
Museo Civico ④
Palazzo dei Rettori ③
Piazza del Mercato ⑦
Porta Rugo ①
San Pietro ⑥
Santo Stefano ⑧
Torre Civica ⑤

0 metres   500
0 yards   500

Key to Symbols
see back flap

seen at Fornesighe, 2 km (1 mile) northeast of Forno di Zoldo, and on the slopes of Monte Penna at Zoppe di Cadore, 8 km (5 miles) north.

If there is time, a circular tour is a good way to explore the area. Drive north on the S251, via Zoldo Alto to Selva di Cadore, then west via Colle di Santa Lucia (a favourite viewpoint for photographers). From here take the S203 south through the lakeside resort of Alleghe. The route passes through wonderful scenery with woodland, flower-filled meadows and pretty mountain hamlets which complement the splendour of the rocky crags.

The southernmost town of the area is Agordo, nestling in the Cordevole Valley. From here, a spectacularly scenic route follows the S34 north-east to the Passo Duran (1,605 m/5,270 ft), descending to Dont, close to the starting point of the tour. Wayside shrines mark the route and it is worth stopping on the way down to visit village shops selling local woodcarving. Take care when driving along this narrow and winding road.

Selva di Cadore from Colle di Santa Lucia, northwest of Valzoldana

Palazzo Guarnieri, one of the Renaissance palaces in Feltre

Feltre ❼

🚶 19,600. 🚉 🚌 ℹ️ *Piazzetta Trento e Trieste 9 (0439 25 40).* 🛍️ *Tue & Fri am.* **Shops closed** *Mon am (clothes), Wed pm (food).* **www**.infodolomiti.it

Feltre owes its venerable good looks to the vengeful Holy Roman Emperor, Maximilian I. He sacked the town twice, in 1509 and in 1510, at the outbreak of the war against Venice waged by the League of Cambrai (*see p44*). Despite the destruction of its buildings and the murder of most of its citizens, Feltre remained

stoutly loyal to Venice, and Venice repaid the debt by rebuilding the town after the war. Thus the main street of the old town, Via Mezzaterra, is lined with arcaded early 16th-century houses, most with steeply pitched roofs to keep snow from settling.

Follow the steep main street to the striking Piazza Maggiore, where it is possible to see the remains of Feltre's medieval castle, the church of **San Rocco** and a fountain by Tullio Lombardo (1520).

On the eastern side of the square is Via L Luzzo, a beautiful street lined with Renaissance palaces, one of which houses the **Museo Civico**. The museum displays a fresco by the local artist Lorenzo Luzzo, who was known as Il Morto da Feltre (The Dead Man of Feltre), a nickname given to him by his contemporaries because of the deathly pallor of his skin.

🏛️ **Museo Civico**
Palazzo Villabruna, Via Luzzo 23. **Tel** *0439 88 52 41.* 🕐 *Thu–Sun.* 🔴 *pub hols.* 📷 **www**.comune.feltre.bl.it

Vittorio Veneto ❽

🚶 30,000. 🚉 🚌 ℹ️ *Viale della Vittoria 110 (0438 572 43).* **Shops closed** *Tue (clothes), Wed pm (food).* 🔴 *Mon.* **www**.visittreviso.it

Two separate towns, Ceneda and Serravalle, were merged and renamed Vittorio Veneto in 1866 to honour the unification of Italy under King Vittorio Emanuele II. The town later gave its name to the last decisive battle fought in Italy in World War I. The **Museo della Battaglia** in the Ceneda quarter, the commercial heart of the town, commemorates this. Serravalle is more picturesque, with many fine 15th-century *palazzi* and pretty arcaded streets. Franco Zeffirelli shot scenes for his film *Romeo and Juliet* in this town that sits at the base of the rocky Meschio gorge. To the east, via Anzano, the S422 climbs up to the Bosco del Cansiglio, a wooded plateau.

🏛️ **Museo della Battaglia**
Piazza Giovanni Paolo I. **Tel** *0438 576 95.* 🕐 *Tue–Sun.* 📷

Vittorio Veneto old town and river

TRAVELLERS' NEEDS

WHERE TO STAY

Venice's perennial attraction to romantics and art lovers means it has an astonishing number of hotels for its size, many of them in former *palazzi*. On the mainland, ancient cities abound with hotels and *pensioni*, often housed in magnificent old buildings and extravagantly decorated. Those in the smaller towns are often run by families who take pride in their reputation.

Lake Garda is a long-established resort area with many hotels to choose from, and the mountainous north of

Logo for the Italian Youth Hostel Association

the region is an all-year-round holiday area with accommodation of all types. Here you can find self-catering in a small farmhouse at very reasonable cost, and there are also numerous idyllically situated and well-equipped campsites.

Budget options in the cities include self-catering flats, hostels and dormitory accommodation, and the mountains offer simple refuges for enthusiastic walkers. For more information on hotels in Venice and the Veneto, see the listings on pages 228–35.

WHERE TO LOOK

Unlike most other cities, Venice has hardly any "undesirable" addresses. You will pay considerably more for a hotel in the immediate vicinity of the Piazza San Marco, but in such a compact city even apparently outlying areas such as Cannaregio or Santa Croce *(see pp14–15)* are never far from places of interest. Addresses in Venice are immensely confusing *(see p282)*, but a map reference for each hotel on the main islands is given in the listings. The maps referred to are to be found on pages 290–301.

Most visitors feel it is worth splashing out for a few nights' stay in Venice itself, despite the high cost, though an increasing number are choosing to stay in Verona or Padua instead and

Outside the Hotel Marconi *(see p229)* on the busy Riva del Vin

"commute" into Venice by train. Do not be tempted by the relatively low prices of the Mestre hotels, unless you are prepared to stay in a sprawling industrial town. Remember, too, that if you are travelling by car you will have to pay stiff parking charges at the Piazzale Roma car park or one of its satellites for the duration of your stay in Venice *(see p280)*.

Many of the hotels in minor inland towns of the Veneto cater primarily for business travellers, but if you plan to explore the region you will find some lovely villa hotels in the countryside. Padua and Verona have a number of hotels, but those in Verona are fully booked for months ahead in the summer opera season, so forward planning is essential. Further north there is more choice. The

hotels are geared to holiday-makers, with lovely gardens, swimming pools and sports facilities. But bear in mind that Italians as well as foreign tourists flock to the lakes and mountains, so it is always advisable to plan your trip and book in advance.

HOTEL PRICES

Hotel charges were de-regulated in 1994, so that hotels are free to charge what they feel the market will bear rather than being tied to the tariffs determined by their star rating. Venice is an expensive place to stay and nowadays can hardly be said to have a "low season" with the benefits of lower or negotiable prices. It is difficult but not impossible to find a basic double room for less than €50. Occasionally you can find some cheaper

Hotel Europa e Regina *(see p229)* overlooking the Grand Canal

◁ Pavement cafés line the Riva del Vin by the Grand Canal

rooms from November to February, when the weather is often superb. But remember that many hotels close out of season. Some re-open for Carnival – and raise their prices accordingly.

July and August are the most expensive months at the resorts along Lake Garda. In the Dolomites winter is the high season, when skiers flock to the area, and the hotels may close during the summer.

Single room rates are higher than individual rates for two people sharing a double room. Prices include tax.

HIDDEN EXTRAS

If you are travelling on a budget, try to avoid hotels with inclusive breakfast as this rarely good value for money. You are expected to tip at least €1 for room service and bellboys, even if service is included in the price of the room. Laundry services are usually expensive, as are drinks from the minibar and telephone calls from hotel rooms. Check all the rates when you make the booking. Some small hotels in Venice, and most in holiday areas like Lake Garda, may expect you to take full- or half-board during the high season.

HOTEL GRADINGS AND FACILITIES

Italian hotels are classified by a rating system from one to five stars. However, each province sets its own level for grading, so standards for each category may vary from one area to another. Some hotels may not have a restaurant, but those which do sometimes welcome non-residents who wish to eat.

Air-conditioning is rare in old buildings. Although the thick stone walls provide good insulation against the summer's heat, if you cannot tolerate high temperatures it is well worth choosing air-conditioned accommodation in Venice during the hottest months. Under Italian law, central heating remains off, whatever the temperature outside, until 1 November. This is something that is worth remembering if you plan a late-October trip.

Children are welcome everywhere but smaller hotels have limited facilities. Although Venice is not thought to be child-friendly, it can be an excellent holiday for families. The Lido is a good base as children will have access to the beach and probably a garden.

WHAT TO EXPECT

Hotels are obliged by law to register you with the police, so they will ask for your passport when you arrive. They may need to keep it for a few hours, but make sure you take it back, because you will need identification to change money or travellers' cheques. Italian

Terrace, Hotel Bauer (see p229)

Excelsior Palace (see p233)

hotel rooms are not "cosy": carpets are rare, the storage space is usually very limited and luxuries such as tea-making facilities are unknown, even in four- and five- star establishments. The decor may be simple and Italian taste can be rather different from what you are used to. However, hotel staff will be friendly and charming, and the standard of cleanliness is high. The bathrooms are, almost without exception, spotlessly clean, even when they are shared.

Less expensive hotels are unlikely to have bathtubs; showers are considered more hygienic and more economical on water. Rooms without a bathroom usually have a washbasin and towels are provided.

Breakfast is very light – a cup of coffee and a brioche (a plain or cream- or jam-filled pastry), though hotels generally include fruit juice, bread rolls and jam as well. It is always cheaper to have breakfast in a bar.

With the exception of Venice, where the only sounds are water-borne or human, Italian towns can be very noisy. If you are a light sleeper, ask for a room that is away from the street, or come equipped with earplugs to deaden traffic sounds and church bells.

Check-out time is usually noon in four- and five-star hotels and between ten and noon in small establishments. If you stay longer you will be asked to pay for an extra day.

The Palazzo Abadessa is set in beautiful gardens (see p232)

BOOKING AND PAYING

Book at least two months in advance if you want to stay in a particular hotel in the high season; some people book as far as six months or a year ahead in Venice itself. The local tourist office will have listings of all the hotels in the area, and they will be able to advise you on the best hotels in each star category. Hotels above the €50 price bracket usually take credit cards, but check which cards are accepted when you make your reservation. You can generally pay the deposit by credit card, or by sending an international money order.

Under Italian law, a booking is valid as soon as the deposit is paid and confirmation is received. As in restaurants, you are required by law to keep your hotel receipts until you leave the country.

DISABLED TRAVELLERS

Facilities for the disabled are limited throughout Italy, and Venice poses its own particular problems, with many stepped bridges across the canals. A list of tour

The conveniently located Hotel La Fenice *(see p228)*

operators that specialize in holidays for the disabled can be obtained from ENIT, the Italian State Tourist Board *(see p271)*. For further advice, see p269.

HOTELS IN HISTORIC BUILDINGS

Many of Venice's hotels are housed in buildings of historical or artistic interest, for example in Gothic *palazzi*. Some of the best are included in the listings below. In the Veneto there are also

some attractive villa hotels – see the **Relais and Châteaux** guide for more details.

SELF-CATERING

Self-catering flats in Venice proper are fairly easy to find. **International Chapters** handle some holiday lets within the city, as do **Tailor Made Tours** and **Vacanze in Italia**. You could also try a Venetian agent, such as **Sant'Angelo** or **Centro Immobiliare NG**, although they may prefer to deal with longer rentals.

DIRECTORY

HOTELS IN HISTORIC BUILDINGS

Relais & Châteaux
Tel 0800 2000 0002.
www.relaischateaux.com

SELF-CATERING

Centro Immobiliare NG
Rio Terra Canal, Dorsoduro 3066. **Map** 6 D2.
Tel 041 522 09 32.

International Chapters
51a St John's Wood High Street,
London NW8 7NJ.
Tel 020 7722 0722.

Sant'Angelo
Campo Sant'Angelo,
San Marco 3818.
Map 6 F2.
Tel 041 522 15 05.

Tailor Made Tours
22 Church Rise,
London SE23 2UD.
Tel 020 8291 9736.

Vacanze in Italia
www.homeabroad.com

Venice Rentals
90 Sea Street,
Suite 121, N. Weymouth,
MA 02191 USA.
Tel 617 472 5392.
www.venicerentals.com

BUDGET ACCOMMODATION

Associazione Italiana Alberghi per la Gioventù
Fondamenta dei Tolentini,
Santa Croce.
Map 1 C5.
Tel 041 520 44 14.

Foresteria Valdese
Campo Santa Maria Formosa, Castello 5170.
Map 7 C1.
Tel 041 528 67 97.
www.foresteriavenezia.it

Ostello Venezia
Fondamenta delle Zitelle,
Giudecca 86. **Map** 7 B5.
Tel 041 523 82 11.
www.ostellovenezia.it

Santa Fosca
Fmta Diedo, Cannaregio 2372. **Map** 2 F3.
Tel 041 71 57 75.
www.santafosca.it

CAMPSITES AND MOUNTAIN REFUGES

Club Alpino Italiano
Via Petrella 19, 20124 Milan. *Tel* 02 205 72 31.
www.cai.it

Marina di Venezia
Via Montello 6,
Punta Sabbioni.
Tel 041 530 09 55.
www.marinadivenezia.it

San Nicolò
Riviera San Nicolò 65, Lido.
Tel 041 526 74 15.
www.campingsannicolo.it

Touring Club Italiano
Tel 02 852 61.
www.touringclub.it

WATERBORNE ACCOMMODATION

Boat and Breakfast
Giudecca 212A, 30133.
Tel 335 666 6241.
www.venicevacation rentals.it

Navigador
Tel 348 814 61 23.
www.navigador.com

Venice Rentals offers a variety of accommodation, from small apartments on the Lido to a palatial home on the Grand Canal. Other options might be a simple conversion or a luxurious and spacious villa with a swimming pool. Prices reflect these variations, and they also fluctuate according to the time of year. Low-season prices for four people start at about €500 per week.

Detail on the Hotel Danieli *(see p231)*

BUDGET ACCOMMODATION

One- or two-star budget hotels charging from €20 to €40 per person per night are generally small, family-run places. These used to be known as *pensioni*, but the term is no longer used very much officially. However, many places retain the name and the personal character that has made them so popular. They rarely offer breakfast and have very few rooms with private bathrooms. You should not expect particularly high standards of service. A variation on these *pensioni* are *affittacamere*, or rented rooms. These are even smaller establishments, and they also offer excellent value for money.

Accommodation in hostels and dormitories is sometimes available at convents and religious institutions, such as the **Foresteria Valdese** and **Santa Fosca**. It is often possible to book these rooms through the local tourist offices. The **Associazione Italiana Alberghi per la Gioventù** (Italian Youth Hostel Association) has lists of youth hostels throughout the whole of Italy. The main youth hostel in Venice is the beautifully situated **Ostello Venezia** on the Giudecca island. It is essential to book well ahead if you want to stay in July or August.

Lists and booking forms for youth hostels are available through the Italian Tourist Board or from local offices. The Venice office also produces a simple typed list of all kinds of hostel accommodation in Venice itself.

CAMPSITES AND MOUNTAIN REFUGES

There are good campsites throughout the region, concentrated mainly on the mainland to the north of Venice, on the shores of Lake Garda and in the northern mountains. Among the best are **Marina di Venezia** and **San Nicolò**. A list of campsites and mountain refuges can be obtained from ENIT *(see p271)* or local tourist offices. Most huts in the mountain districts are owned by the **Club Alpino Italiano**, based in Milan, which can provide

full information. Some huts offer just a bed for the night, whereas others may have staff who prepare meals and drinks. The **Touring Club Italiano** publishes annually a list of campsites: *Campeggi e Villaggi Turistici in Italia*.

A suitcase boat transporting visitors' luggage to a hotel

WATERBORNE ACCOMMODATION

Venice and the Veneto offer a vast selection of accommodation ranging from basic to luxurious. However, there are options for guests who are looking for something a little different.

For a city that is based on water there is surprisingly little in the way of floating lodgings. The options that are available often represent good value for money and are a more exciting alternative to a standard hotel room.

Roberto Terzi operates a Turkish schooner, **Navigador**, as a sumptuous bed and breakfast. The boat sleeps between six and eight people, although there is a larger schooner, Udachi, which sleeps 20. Both boats are capable of making trips around the lagoon.

Another company catering to the nautically minded is **Boat & Breakfast**. Guest stay in a 1930s yawl moored on the tranquil southern side of the Giudecca. There are seven beds in three cabins, which have all been beautifully decorated. At the front of the ship is an authentic 60s kitchen and on deck there is a hammock, which is perfect for lazing in on sunny days.

The Ostello Venezia, situated on the Giudecca

Venice's Best Hotels

Hotels in Venice range from the luxurious and renowned, which are mainly clustered along the Grand Canal, to simple, family-run places in the quieter parts of the city. Wherever you stay, you will be within easy reach of the main attractions, with restaurants and shops close at hand. All the hotels shown on this map have something special to recommend them, whether it is the waterside position, a garden or a quiet location away from the crowds. Always book well in advance, and remember that many Venetian hotels are shut at some stage in winter. The hotels shown here are the best in their particular style or price range.

Hotel Rossi
A comfortable establishment on the busy Lista di Spagna, the Hotel Rossi is good value. (See p232.)

Cannaregio

San Polo and Santa Croce

Dorsoduro

Al Sole
Situated beside a tranquil canal, this Gothic palazzo is away from the main tourist haunts, but within easy reach by foot or water of all the sights. (See p230.)

0 metres	500
0 yards	500

Agli Alboretti
This charming hotel in a central location has attractive rooms and a garden courtyard. (See p231.)

Gritti Palace
One of Venice's most famous hotels, the Gritti offers rooms and service of impeccable standard in an historic palazzo on the Grand Canal. (See p229.)

Giorgione
*This high-class, spacious hotel, with its excellent
facilities, offers every modern comfort at lower
prices than others of similar
calibre.* (See p232.)

Marconi
*This efficiently run hotel,
housed in an old palazzo, has
views of the Grand Canal and
the Rialto Bridge.* (See p229.)

Castello

San Marco

La Residenza
*This family-run hotel offers good value for
money and is away from the crowds. It has
frescoed public rooms and antiques, but
the bedrooms are more simple.* (See p230.)

Flora
*A flower-filled garden is just
one of the attractions of this
delightful hotel.* (See p228.)

Londra Palace
*Tchaikovsky once
stayed in this
grand palazzo
with its views
to San Giorgio
Maggiore. Today's
guests appreciate
the welcoming bar
and restaurant.*
(See p231.)

Choosing a Hotel

The hotels listed here have been selected across a wide price range for facilities, good value, and location. All rooms have private bath and TV, and most have Internet access. It is wise to confirm disabled accessibility when booking. The hotels are listed by area. For information on other types of accommodation, *see pp222–25*.

PRICE CATEGORIES
The following price ranges are for a double room per night, including breakfast, tax and service.
€ Under €100
€€ €100–€200
€€€ €200–€300
€€€€ €300–€400
€€€€€ Over €400

VENICE

SAN MARCO Locanda ai Bareteri   🖥 W   €€
Calle di Mezzo 4966, 30124 **Tel** *041 523 22 33* **Fax** *041 244 34 50* **Rooms** *12*   **Map** *7 B1*

Located in a quiet back alley, only a few minutes walk from the Mercerie shopping district and St. Mark's Square, this comfortable bed and breakfast offers air conditioning and Internet facilities to its guests. It is also close to the *vaporetto* landing stage at Rialto. **www.bareteri.com**

SAN MARCO Locanda Fiorita   🖥 W   €€
Campiello Novo e dei Morti 3457/A, 30124 **Tel** *041 523 47 54* **Fax** *041 522 80 43* **Rooms** *10*   **Map** *6 F2*

This welcoming hotel offers lovely spacious rooms decorated with 18th-century style furniture and fitted out with all mod cons. It is located just off the delightful Campo S. Stefano, and is in an ideal position for visiting the major art collections such as the Accademia gallery and privately run Palazzo Grassi. **www.locandafiorita.com**

SAN MARCO Monaco and Grand Canal   📶 ♿ 🍴 🖥 W   €€
Calle Vallaresso 1332, 30124 **Tel** *041 520 02 11* **Fax** *041 520 05 01* **Rooms** *99*   **Map** *7 B3*

Incorporating the carefully restored Ridotto theatre, this elegant hotel also has a renowned restaurant on the Grand Canal. The rooms are a little small and not all have canal views, however, each is beautifully furnished and has all modern facilities. A modern annexe nearby has larger rooms. **www.hotelmonaco.it**

SAN MARCO Santo Stefano   📶 🖥 W   €€
Campo Santo Stefano 2957, 30124 **Tel** *041 520 01 66* **Fax** *041 522 44 60* **Rooms** *11*   **Map** *6 F3*

A charming hotel that occupies a tall narrow building overlooking Campo Santo Stefano – popular with children in the afternoon. The rooms are fully equipped, though several are quite small. It is only a 10-minute walk to Piazza San Marco or the Rialto district. Wi-Fi access is available in the lobby. **www.hotelsantostefanovenezia.com**

SAN MARCO Al Gambero   🖥   €€€
Calle dei Fabbri 4687, 30124 **Tel** *041 522 43 84* **Fax** *041 520 04 31* **Rooms** *30*   **Map** *7 B2*

Gondolas glide beneath the windows of this guesthouse, conveniently set halfway between Rialto and Piazza San Marco. The rooms have been decorated in an old-fashioned style, and offer a full range of services. Good restaurants and shops abound in the neighbouring alleys. **www.locandaalgambero.com**

SAN MARCO Al Gazzettino   🍴 🖥 W   €€€
Calle di Mezzo 4971, 30124 **Tel** *041 528 65 23* **Fax** *041 522 33 14* **Rooms** *10*   **Map** *7 A3*

This long-standing hotel was named after the adjacent premises of the popular local newspaper, *Il Gazzettino*, which has since moved to the mainland. The walls of the ground-floor *trattoria* are covered with pages from the paper. The location is excellent, close to both Rialto and St. Mark's, and the atmosphere is friendly. **www.algazzettino.com**

SAN MARCO Antico Panada   📶 ♿ 🖥 W   €€€
Calle Specchieri 646, 30124 **Tel** *041 520 90 88* **Fax** *041 520 96 19* **Rooms** *48*   **Map** *7 A2*

Located in a quiet street, very close to the main sights, the Panada occupies a converted 17th-century mansion. The cosy bar is decorated with historic mirrors, possibly made by the craftsmen who once had their workshops in this district. The continental breakfast buffet features delicious pastries. **www.hotelpanada.com**

SAN MARCO Flora   📶 🖥 W   €€€
Via XXII Marzo 2283a, 30124 **Tel** *041 520 58 44* **Fax** *041 522 82 17* **Rooms** *43*   **Map** *7 A3*

This tiny hotel is squeezed in a narrow alley off one of the major fashion-shopping streets, close to Piazza San Marco and the *vaporetto* landing stages. The rooms are a little cramped, but well equipped. A small but pleasant garden can be enjoyed when the weather is fine, and there is a wellness centre. Book in advance. **www.hotelflora.it**

SAN MARCO La Fenice & des Artistes   📶 🍴 🖥 W   €€€
Campiello Fenice 1936, 30124 **Tel** *041 523 23 33* **Fax** *041 520 37 21* **Rooms** *70*   **Map** *7 A2*

In a quiet square alongside the renowned opera house La Fenice, this pretty hotel is furnished with antiques and period-style fittings. The staff are very helpful. The premises consist of two buildings joined by a patio, and there is an atmospheric bar for a relaxing apéritif as the day draws to a close. **www.fenicehotels.com**

Key to Symbols *see back cover flap*

SAN MARCO Bauer   €€€€

Campo San Moisè 1459, 30124 **Tel** *041 520 70 22* **Fax** *041 520 75 57* **Rooms** *117*   **Map** *7 A3*

This deluxe hotel is right in the heart of Venice amidst top-name boutiques. The Bauer also boasts wonderful Grand Canal views from many of its rooms, extending across to the Salute church, and gondolas can be hired outside the front door. The waterfront restaurant does a gourmet buffet. **www.bauerhotels.com**

SAN MARCO Concordia   €€€€

Calle Larga San Marco 367, 30124 **Tel** *041 520 68 66* **Fax** *041 520 67 75* **Rooms** *50*   **Map** *7 B2*

Crammed in between the souvenir shops and near to the Piazza, this excellent family-managed hotel has many rooms with good views. It is furnished with impeccable period pieces. The top-notch restaurant specializes in seasonal produce. It is best to book well in advance. **www.hotelconcordia.it**

SAN MARCO Rialto   €€€€

Riva di Ferro 5149, 30124 **Tel** *041 520 91 66* **Fax** *041 523 89 58* **Rooms** *79*   **Map** *7 A1*

This rambling establishment has good family rooms, excellent facilities and a canalside restaurant in the summer months. Its marvellous position at the foot of the Rialto bridge ensures spectacular views from many of its rooms, and the *vaporetto* is very convenient. **www.rialtohotel.com**

SAN MARCO Europa e Regina   €€€€€

Calle Larga XXII Marzo 2159, 30124 **Tel** *041 240 00 01* **Fax** *041 523 15 33* **Rooms** *185*   **Map** *7 A3*

This splendid establishment was the home of the 18th-century artist Tiepolo. Occupying an inspiring position on the Grand Canal, close to Piazza San Marco, it has beautifully decorated spacious rooms and sumptuous public areas. The excellent al fresco waterside restaurant is recommended. **www.westin.com/europaeregina**

SAN MARCO Gritti Palace   €€€€€

Santa Maria del Giglio 2467, 30124 **Tel** *041 79 46 11* **Fax** *041 520 09 42* **Rooms** *91*   **Map** *7 A3*

Ernest Hemingway described this sumptuous 15th-century palace as "the best hotel in a city of great hotels". It combines deluxe standards with a superb setting on the magnificent Grand Canal. Service is meticulous and a meal at the waterside restaurant is highly recommended. **www.luxurycollection.com/grittipalace**

SAN MARCO Luna Hotel Baglioni   €€€€€

Calle Larga dell'Ascension 1243, 30124 **Tel** *041 528 98 40* **Fax** *041 528 71 60* **Rooms** *104*   **Map** *7 B3*

This sophisticated and surprisingly spacious hotel once hosted knights en route to the Holy Land. The breakfast room is particularly sumptuous with chandeliers and frescoes by pupils of Tiepolo. Close to San Marco, this is an excellent base for sightseeing. **www.baglionihotels.com**

SAN MARCO San Clemente Palace   €€€€€

Isola di San Clemente 1, 30124 **Tel** *041 244 50 01* **Fax** *041 244 58 00* **Rooms** *200*

A special haven well away from the bustle of Venice, the luxury San Clemente has its own island, complete with vast gardens, swimming pool, and conference and fitness centre. The superb rooms are wonderfully spacious and light-filled. A private launch ferries guests back and forth to San Marco. **www.sanclemente.thi.it**

SAN POLO Al Campaniel   €

Calle del Campaniel 2889, 30125 **Tel** *041 275 07 49* **Fax** *041 275 07 49* **Rooms** *4*   **Map** *6 E2*

Right next to the San Tomà *vaporetto* stop, this cosy and spotless guesthouse in a quiet street is run by a Spanish-Venetian couple. Guests have tea- and coffee-making facilities in their rooms, otherwise a handy self-contained apartment is available for families who would prefer self-catering. **www.alcampaniel.com**

SAN POLO Alex   €

Rio Terrà Frari 2606, 301 25 **Tel** *041 523 13 41* **Fax** *041 523 13 41* **Rooms** *11*   **Map** *6 E1*

Not all rooms have private bathroom facilities, and there is no air conditioning, but this friendly and simple family-run hotel is great value for money. Situated in the vicinity of the Frari church, it is also handy for the Rialto markets. The closest *vaporetto* stop is Piazzale Roma or San Tomà. Wi-Fi is available in most rooms. **www.hotelalexinvenice.com**

SAN POLO Hotel Marconi   €€

Riva del Vin 729, 30125 **Tel** *041 522 20 68* **Fax** *041 522 97 00* **Rooms** *26*   **Map** *7 A1*

A popular hotel with English-speaking tourists, the Marconi has a wonderful street café on the lively Grand Canal next to the Rialto bridge. A refurbished 16th-century palace with an opulent reception area, its rooms are a little disappointing and cramped. It is essential to reserve in advance. **www.hotelmarconi.it**

SAN POLO Locanda Sturion   €€

Calle del Sturion 679, 30125 **Tel** *041 523 62 43* **Fax** *041 522 83 78* **Rooms** *11*   **Map** *7 A1*

Situated very close to the Grand Canal, the Sturion's central location, beautiful views and a history going back to the 13th century, all add to its appeal. This friendly hotel is very good value for money. Breakfast is served in a stylish room dominated by a Murano glass chandelier. **www.locandasturion.com**

SAN POLO Pensione Guerrato   €€

Calle drio la Scimia 240/A, 30125 **Tel** *041 522 71 31* **Fax** *041 241 14 08* **Rooms** *19*   **Map** *3 A5*

This former *osteria* (tavern) claims it was established in 1288. The rooms are charming, although some share bath facilities. There is a lovely breakfast, and the location is excellent, virtually in the middle of the Rialto market. Discounted rates can sometimes be negotiated. The hotel also has two apartments. **www.pensioneguerrato.it**

SANTA CROCE Al Sole

Fondamenta Minotto 136, 30135 **Tel** *041 244 03 28* **Fax** *041 72 22 87* **Rooms** *51*   **Map** *5 C1*

Book well in advance to stay in this lovely 14th-century palace, with a marble-floored reception area and photogenic façade. The courtyard is a blaze of scented blooms in summer. The inviting rooms have views over the canal or a private garden. Close to Piazzale Roma for buses and *vaporetti*. **www.alsolehotels.com**

SANTA CROCE B&B Al Gallion

Calle Gallion 1126, 30135 **Tel** *041 524 47 43* **Fax** *041 275 81 26* **Rooms** *3*   **Map** *2 D5*

Perfect for visitors arrriving by either road or rail, B&B Al Gallion is only 5 minutes walk from Piazzale Roma and the railway station. Its spotless, great value rooms are located in a 16th-century palace in a quiet neighbourhood. The staff often have great tips on visiting the city. **www.algallion.com**

SANTA CROCE Hotel Falier

Salizzada San Pantalon 130, 30135 **Tel** *041 71 08 82* **Fax** *041 520 65 54* **Rooms** *19*   **Map** *5 C1*

This friendly hotel boasts a wisteria-filled garden that will delight summer visitors. The pleasant rooms are well equipped. A brief walk from the transport hub of Piazzale Roma, the Falier is close to San Rocco and other attractions. The staff are extremely friendly and helpful. Breakfast is included. **www.hotelfalier.com**

SANTA CROCE San Simeon Ai Due Fanali

Campo San Simeon Grande 946, 30135 **Tel** *041 718 490* **Fax** *041 244 87 21* **Rooms** *16*   **Map** *2 D5*

Formerly a monastery, this pleasant building stands close to the church of the same name, and on the outside wall is a huge bas relief of St. Simeon. Several rooms have retained their timber rafters and there is a roof terrace with panoramic views. Conveniently placed for both Piazzale Roma and the railway station. **www.aiduefanali.com**

SANTA CROCE San Cassiano - Ca' Favretto

Calle della Rosa 2232, 30135 **Tel** *041 524 17 68* **Fax** *041 72 10 33* **Rooms** *35*   **Map** *2 F4*

One of the city's favourite upmarket hotels, Ca' Favretto opens directly onto the Grand Canal, and guests can disembark at the private landing stage. In fact this is easier than arriving by land due to the labyrinth of alleys that need to be navigated to reach it! Elegance and attention to service are trademarks. **www.sancassiano.it**

CASTELLO Corte Campana

Calle del Rimedio 4410, 30122 **Tel** *041 523 36 03* **Fax** *041 523 36 03* **Rooms** *3*   **Map** *7 C1*

Corte Campana offers friendly lodgings close to Campo S. Maria Formosa and San Marco. The rooms are spacious, light-filled and overlook a pretty courtyard. They also have a TV and free Internet access. Two self-catering flats in the same building are also available. Closed 10–31 Jan, 5–25 Aug. **www.cortecampana.com**

CASTELLO Foresteria Valdese

Calle Lunga S. Maria Formosa 5170, 30122 **Tel** *041 528 67 97* **Fax** *041 241 62 38* **Rooms** *21*   **Map** *7 C1*

Remember to book well ahead to get a room in the welcoming Foresteria Valdese. Run by the Waldensian and Methodist community, it offers dormitory accommodation as well as cosy private guest rooms, several of which are en suite. Breakfast is served at a long table in a refectory atmosphere. **www.foresteriavenezia.it**

CASTELLO Casa per Ferie 'S. Maria della Pietà'

Calle della Pietà 3701, 30122 **Tel** *041 244 36 39* **Fax** *041 241 15 61* **Rooms** *15*   **Map** *8 D2*

Founded by the Franciscans in 1346 as a home for abandoned children and single mothers, this is now a friendly hotel behind Vivaldi's church. The peaceful rooms are spotless, although the bathrooms are shared. There is a superb panoramic terrace, which is lovely in summer. Book ahead in peak periods. **www.pietavenezia.org**

CASTELLO La Residenza

Campo Bandiera e Moro 3608, 30122 **Tel** *041 528 53 15* **Fax** *041 523 88 59* **Rooms** *15*   **Map** *8 E2*

La Residenza started life as a 14th-century *palazzo* built in the Venetian Gothic style. The bedrooms are elegant and comfortable, with period furnishings. The common areas boast frescoed ceilings and antique furniture. A few minutes' walk from the bustling Riva Schiavoni waterfront. **www.venicelaresidenza.com**

CASTELLO Locanda La Corte

Calle Bressana 6317, 30121 **Tel** *041 241 13 00* **Fax** *041 241 59 82* **Rooms** *16*   **Map** *3 C5*

The inviting rooms in this converted 16th-century palace, the former residence of an ambassador, are tastefully furnished. In the summer, guests can enjoy breakfast in a charming courtyard. Water taxis can pull up at the entrance, otherwise public transport is close by at the Fondamente Nuove. **www.locandalacorte.it**

CASTELLO Pensione Wildner

Riva degli Schiavoni 4161, 30122 **Tel** *041 522 74 63* **Fax** *041 241 46 40* **Rooms** *16*   **Map** *8 D2*

This small family-run hotel with immaculate rooms has a lovely roof terrace where guests can enjoy a leisurely buffet-style breakfast, along with wonderful views over St. Mark's Basin to the island of San Giorgio. The novelist Henry James stayed here in 1881 while working on *Portrait of a Lady*. **www.veneziahotels.com**

CASTELLO Liassidi Palace Hotel

Ponte dei Greci 3405, 30122 **Tel** *041 520 56 58* **Fax** *041 522 18 20* **Rooms** *26*   **Map** *8 D1*

This ultra-modern establishment near the Greek church St George successfully blends an old palace with modern, stylish facilities. There's a lovely entrance courtyard, pleasant bars with canal views and attractively decorated bedrooms. The staff can be a little abrupt at times. **www.liassidipalacehotel.com**

Key to Price Guide *see p228* **Key to Symbols** *see back cover flap*

CASTELLO Paganelli ⬚ ♿ ♨ ▤ Ⓦ   €€€

Riva degli Schiavoni 4182, 30122 **Tel** *041 522 43 24* **Fax** *041 523 92 67* **Rooms** *22*   **Map** *8 D2*

This hotel has an excellent location on the San Marco waterfront, close to ferry services. There are wonderful views from the front rooms, which are furnished in a formal style but are cosy all the same. The accommodation in the annexe (*dipendenza*) is quieter but less attractive. Babysitting can be arranged. **www.hotelpaganelli.com**

CASTELLO Londra Palace ⬚ ♨ ▤ Ⓦ   €€€€

Riva degli Schiavoni 4171, 30122 **Tel** *041 520 05 33* **Fax** *041 522 50 32* **Rooms** *53*   **Map** *8 D2*

Elegance, excellent service and spacious rooms characterize this luxury hotel. Located close to the monument to King Vittorio Emanuele on the broad bustling Riva a short stroll from the Piazza, it has splendid views over the water. It was here that Tchaikovsky composed his Fourth Symphony. **www.hotelondra.it**

CASTELLO Hotel Danieli ⬚ ♨ ▤ Ⓦ   €€€€€

Riva degli Schiavoni 4196, 30122 **Tel** *041 522 64 80* **Fax** *041 520 02 08* **Rooms** *225*   **Map** *7 C2*

The Danieli is the epitome of luxury. It was the palace of the Dandolo family and has strong literary and musical connections. The reception rooms are lit by resplendent Venetian glass chandeliers. There are two wings, one built in the 1940s and an older section (the first choice for guests). **www.luxurycollection.com/danieli**

DORSODURO Agli Alboretti ⬚ ♨ ▤   €€

Rio Terrà Foscarini 884, 30123 **Tel** *041 523 00 58* **Fax** *041 521 01 58* **Rooms** *23*   **Map** *6 E4*

Set in a peaceful spot close to the Accademia and Zattere for *vaporetto* transport, this cosy hotel is popular with English-speaking guests. The bedrooms are very attractive if a little small. A garden is available in the summer, and there's a good restaurant. Closed 7 Jan–mid-Feb. **www.aglialboretti.com**

DORSODURO Istituto Artigianelli ⬚ ♿ ♨ ♨ ▤ Ⓦ   €€

Rio Terrà Foscarini 909/A, 30123 **Tel** *041 522 40 77* **Fax** *041 528 62 14* **Rooms** *80*   **Map** *6 E4*

A restored 15th-century monastery, this religious institution has bright rooms with en-suite bathrooms. It is located close to the sunny Zattere as well as the Accademia gallery. Winter guests share the premises with students, so reserving well in advance is essential. **www.donorione-venezia.it**

DORSODURO Istituto Canossiano ⬚ ♿ Ⓦ   €€

Fondamenta delle Romite 1323, 30123 **Tel** *041 240 97 11* **Fax** *041 240 97 12* **Rooms** *60*   **Map** *6 D3*

This vast modernised convent hosts both university students and tourists in its simple but adequate rooms. There's a midnight curfew and breakfast is available from a vending machine. The Istituto is located a short distance from the Zattere waterfront. Closed 10 days in Aug, one week at Christmas. **www.romite1323.com**

DORSODURO Locanda Ca' Zose ▤   €€

Calle del Bastion 193/B, 30123 **Tel** *041 522 66 35* **Fax** *041 522 66 24* **Rooms** *12*   **Map** *6 F4*

This guesthouse is run by two local sisters, and is just around the corner from the Guggenheim collection and La Salute *vaporetto* stop. The comfortable, well-equipped rooms are tastefully furnished and several have enchanting canal views. **www.hotelcazose.com**

DORSODURO Locanda San Barnaba ♿ ▤   €€

Calle del Traghetto 2785-2786, 30123 **Tel** *041 241 12 33* **Fax** *041 241 38 12* **Rooms** *13*   **Map** *6 D3*

A wonderful place to come back to after a hard day's sightseeing, this converted palace has a roomy foyer and a pretty garden for summer guests. Only metres from the Ca' Rezzonico ferry stop. The spotless rooms are named after the plays of Venice's own Carlo Goldoni. **www.locanda-sanbarnaba.com**

DORSODURO Montin ♨ ▤   €€

Fondamenta Eremite 1147, 30123 **Tel** *041 522 71 51* **Fax** *041 520 02 55* **Rooms** *11*   **Map** *6 D3*

Well off the beaten track, but only a few minutes' walk from the lovely Zattere. The simply furnished rooms, most with en suite bathrooms, are in a Venetian apartment block situated above a renowned restaurant, overlooking a lovely canal. Montin offers a pleasant stay, but breakfast is extra. **www.locandamontin.com**

DORSODURO Pausania ▤   €€

Fondamenta Gherardini 2824, 30123 **Tel** *041 522 20 83* **Fax** *041 522 29 89* **Rooms** *24*   **Map** *6 D3*

This hotel has elegant light-filled rooms with modern facilities, and a common Internet point is available. There is a delightful veranda for breakfast, flanked by a spacious garden. Located on the Rio San Barnaba canal, Pausania is handy for Campo S. Margherita where nightlife is guaranteed. **www.hotelpausania.it**

DORSODURO Pensione La Calcina ♨ ▤   €€

Zattere ai Gesuati 780, 30123 **Tel** *041 520 64 66* **Fax** *041 522 70 45* **Rooms** *27*   **Map** *6 E4*

Book well in advance for this marvellous guesthouse as it is very popular. Everything is perfect here, starting from the waterside terrace, the pleasant breakfast room, the pretty rooms and the exquisite service. Sunsets over the Lagoon Islands are memorable. Five apartments are also available nearby. **www.lacalcina.com**

DORSODURO Pensione Accademia Villa Maravegie ♿ ▤ Ⓦ   €€€

Fondamenta Bollani 1058, 30123 **Tel** *041 521 01 88* **Fax** *041 523 91 52* **Rooms** *27*   **Map** *6 E3*

After traversing the pretty garden, where an excellent buffet breakfast can be enjoyed, it's the courtesy of the staff that is memorable. This beautiful 17th-century villa was once the Russian embassy and provides a tranquil haven from the hustle and bustle of the city's main sights. **www.pensioneaccademia.it**

DORSODURO Ca' Pisani ⬚⬚⬚⬚⬚⬚⬚ €€€€
Rio Terrà Foscarini 979a, 30123 **Tel** *041 240 14 11* **Fax** *041 277 10 61* **Rooms** *29*   **Map** *6 E4*

This converted 15th-century palace is well located for the Accademia galleries and the Peggy Guggenheim Collection. The historic atmosphere is complemented by stunning modern design, a roof terrace and a relaxing Turkish bath. Closed 3 weeks Jan. **www.capisanihotel.it**

CANNAREGIO Al Gobbo €
Campo S. Geremia 312, 30121 **Tel** *041 71 50 01* **Fax** *041 71 47 65* **Rooms** *12*   **Map** *2 D4*

This modest but reliable hotel has some rooms overlooking bustling Campo San Geremia. It is located a short walk from the railway station. The immaculately kept premises are comfortable and cool (some rooms have air conditioning), and continental breakfast is served in the rooms. Closed 3 weeks Jan, Nov–Dec. **www.albergoalgobbo.it**

CANNAREGIO Al Saor ⬚ €
Calle Zotti 3904/A, 30125 **Tel** *041 296 06 54* **Fax** *041 713 287* **Rooms** *3*   **Map** *3 A4*

This friendly guesthouse close to the Ca' D'Oro is run by a local family who serve home-made cookies for breakfast. All guests have access to kitchen facilities, and there is a fully equipped apartment available for self-catering families. Trips in the owners' rowing boat are also on offer. **www.alsaor.com**

CANNAREGIO Abbazia ⬚⬚⬚ €€
Calle Priuli di Cavalletti, 68, 30121 **Tel** *041 71 73 33* **Fax** *041 71 79 49* **Rooms** *50*   **Map** *1 C4*

Near the railway station and just off busy Lista di Spagna, with its host of shops, the Abbazia is an oasis of peace. It has a lovely garden where drinks are served in summer. The rooms are comfortable if not huge, a reflection of the building's original purpose as a monastery. **www.abbaziahotel.com**

CANNAREGIO Ai Mori d'Oriente ⬚⬚⬚⬚ €€
Fondamenta della Sensa 3319, 30121 **Tel** *041 71 10 01* **Fax** *041 71 42 09* **Rooms** *22*   **Map** *2 F3*

This attractive hotel overlooks a peaceful canal in the Cannaregio neighbourhood and guests arriving by water can disembark directly at the front door, which is lit by candles in the evening. Behind the lovely Byzantine-style façade are stylish if somewhat small rooms, but the bathrooms are divine. **www.hotelaimoridoriente.it**

CANNAREGIO Hotel Rossi ⬚⬚ €€
Lista di Spagna 262, 30121 **Tel** *041 71 51 64* **Fax** *041 71 77 84* **Rooms** *14*   **Map** *2 D4*

Reserve well in advance for this pleasant family hotel, located in a quiet alleyway. Rooms here are simple but modern – though only some have bathrooms – and offer excellent value for money. The service is professional and friendly, and breakfast is included. **www.hotelrossi.ve.it**

CANNAREGIO Giorgione ⬚⬚⬚ €€€
Calle dei Proverbi 4587, 30125 **Tel** *041 522 58 10* **Fax** *041 523 90 92* **Rooms** *76*   **Map** *3 B5*

This highly recommended hotel has been completely refurbished. The Giorgione is extremely comfortable and well situated – only a 10-minute walk from Piazza San Marco, and 5 minutes from the lively Rialto market. Several suites have terraces with wonderful views looking over the city's rooftops. **www.hotelgiorgione.com**

CANNAREGIO Palazzo Abadessa ⬚⬚⬚ €€€
Calle Priuli 4011, 30131 **Tel** *041 241 37 84* **Fax** *041 521 22 36* **Rooms** *15*   **Map** *3 A4*

The garden is the first thing that strikes you on arriving at this beautifully restored *palazzo*. From the atmospheric entrance hall, with thick carpets and chandeliers, elegant staircases lead to spacious and well-equipped rooms furnished with antiques. It really is like spending time in a private palace. **www.abadessa.com**

CANNAREGIO Continental ⬚⬚⬚⬚ €€€€
Lista di Spagna 166, 30121 **Tel** *041 71 51 22* **Fax** *041 524 24 32* **Rooms** *93*   **Map** *2 D4*

This sizeable modern hotel caters mainly to large groups. It boasts a restaurant with panoramic views of the Grand Canal. Many rooms also have views of the canals, while others overlook a shady square. The hotel's location is especially good for one of the city's main tourist shopping districts. **www.hotelcontinentalvenice.com**

THE LAGOON ISLANDS Ca' del Borgo and Ca' Alberti ⬚⬚⬚ €€
Piazza delle Erbe 8, Malamocco, 30126 **Tel** *041 77 07 49* **Fax** *041 77 07 44* **Rooms** *20*

Well off the beaten track, this charming 15th-century villa with a private garden is in the fishing village of Malamocco on the Venice Lido. It is a 30-minute trip to Venice but only minutes to the sea wall and a bicycle ride to the beaches. An open fireplace ensures a cosy ambience in the winter months. **www.cadelborgo.com**

THE LAGOON ISLANDS Monastero di San Giorgio ⬚⬚ €€
Isola di San Giorgio, 30124 **Tel** *041 241 47 17* **Fax** *041 520 65 79* **Rooms** *5*   **Map** *8 D4*

Visitors who desire peace and quiet should head to the island of San Giorgio. This heaven of shade and greenery is just across St Mark's Basin and is well served by *vaporetto*. A simple breakfast is shared with the hospitable monks, although there are also self-catering apartments.

THE LAGOON ISLANDS Residenza Junghans ⬚⬚ €€
Ramo Terzo della Palada 394, Giudecca, 30133 **Tel** *041 521 08 01* **Fax** *041 521 09 72* **Rooms** *59*

Modern architecture is a rare thing in Venice, but this former industrial island has been transformed into a showcase of bright sleek structures such as this hotel. Rooms are simply but adequately furnished. Frequent ferries to the railway and bus stations are nearby. Breakfast for groups only. Closed Christmas. **www.residenzajunghans.com**

THE LAGOON ISLANDS Locanda Cipriani   🏚 🗏   €€€
Piazza Santa Fosca 29, Torcello, 30012 **Tel** *041 73 01 50* **Fax** *041 73 54 33* **Rooms** *6*

Illustrious guests at this comfortable old-style *locanda* on the island of Torcello have included Hemingway and the British royal family. The rooms are comfortably furnished and a range of reading matter is on hand. It is advisable to book well in advance. Closed 6 Jan–6 Feb. **www.locandacipriani.com**

THE LAGOON ISLANDS Villa Mabapa   🏚 🕭 🏚 🗏 🅿 🅦   €€€
Riviera San Nicolò 16, Lido di Venezia, 30126 **Tel** *041 526 05 90* **Fax** *041 526 94 41* **Rooms** *67*

This 1930s villa, originally built as a private residence, has been converted into a comfortable guesthouse. An attractive shady garden welcomes guests back from sightseeing expeditions. Close to the *vaporetto* landing stages, it is situated on a promenade overlooking the lagoon. **www.villamabapa.com**

THE LAGOON ISLANDS Bauer Palladio Hotel   🏚 🕭 🏚 🅦   €€€€
Fondamenta San Giovanni 33, Giudecca 30133 **Tel** *041 270 38 06* **Rooms** *50*

Part of the Bauer Hotel Group in Venice, this establishment takes you away from the city crowds. There is a pretty garden and several indoor spaces with plush armchairs. The rooms are quietly elegant, and the spa is a haven of pampering and relaxation. Closed mid-Nov–mid-Mar. **www.bauerhotels.com**

THE LAGOON ISLANDS Excelsior Palace   🏚 🏚 🏊 🏚 🗏 🅿 🅦   €€€€€
Lungomare Marconi 41, Lido di Venezia, 30126 **Tel** *041 526 02 01* **Fax** *041 526 72 76* **Rooms** *197*

Luxury and flamboyance are combined at this superb historic beachfront hotel, where the *cabanas* are styled like Arab tents. The service and facilities are all excellent. This hotel is packed with VIPs and *paparazzi* during the Film Festival in late summer. Closed Nov–mid-Mar. **www.ho10.net**

THE LAGOON ISLANDS Hotel Cipriani   🏚 🏚 🏊 🏚 🗏 🅦   €€€€€
Giudecca 10, 30133 **Tel** *041 520 77 44* **Fax** *041 520 39 30* **Rooms** *95*   **Map** *7 C5*

Set in luxurious gardens occupying the eastern tip of one of the Lagoon Islands, the Cipriani has been one of the world's great hotels since it opened in 1963. The bedrooms and suites are furnished with tasteful opulence. The terrace restaurant is renowned and the outdoor pool a bonus. Closed Nov–mid-Mar. **www.hotelcipriani.com**

THE VENETO PLAIN

ASOLO Hotel Duse   🏚 🗏 🅦   €€
Via R. Browning 190, 31011 **Tel** *042 35 52 41* **Fax** *042 395 04 04* **Rooms** *14*

Located right in the centre of Asolo, this charming small hotel represents good value for money. The rooms are attractively decorated, although some of them are rather cramped as is the entrance hall. Most have views over the main square or over the rooftops. The staff are helpful and friendly. **www.hotelduse.com**

ASOLO Villa Cipriani   🏚 🏚 🏚 🗏 🅿 🅦   €€
Via Canova 298, 31011 **Tel** *042 352 34 11* **Fax** *042 395 20 95* **Rooms** *31*

This exceptionally comfortable hotel is in a 16th-century villa in which Robert Browning once lived. A popular feature is its beautiful garden, which has a lovely view over the countryside. It also has a fine restaurant serving Venetian specialities and a good wine list. A great base for exploring the area. **www.villaciprianiasolo.com**

ASOLO Al Sole   🏚 🏚 🏚 🗏 🅿   €€€
Via Collegio 33, 31011 **Tel** *042 395 13 32* **Fax** *042 395 10 07* **Rooms** *23*

The orange façade of this hotel is decorated with green shutters. Many of the rooms overlook the main square and the old town walls. The public rooms are slightly impersonal, but the bedrooms and suites are spacious and well furnished. The lovely terrace is ideal for breakfast or a pre-dinner drink. Closed Christmas–mid-Jan. **www.albergoalsole.com**

BASSANO DEL GRAPPA Victoria   🏚 🕭 🗏 🅿 🅦   €
Viale Diaz 33, 36061 **Tel** *042 450 36 20* **Fax** *042 450 31 30* **Rooms** *21*

Just outside the city walls, the pleasant Victoria has comfortable, simply-furnished rooms with private bathrooms featuring hydromassage baths. It is a busy hotel that can occasionally be noisy. However, it is ideally placed for sightseeing, being a short walk from Palladio's bridge and the historic town centre. **www.hotelvictoria-bassano.com**

BASSANO DEL GRAPPA Bonotto Hotel Belvedere   🏚 🕭 🏚 🗏 🅿 🅦   €€
Piazzale G Giardino 14, 36061 **Tel** *042 452 98 45* **Fax** *042 452 98 49* **Rooms** *83*

Standing in one of Bassano's main squares, this busy hotel is the best equipped in the area, and the location is good for exploring the city. Rooms are comfortable and pretty, and the service is excellent. The hotel has a modern restaurant and spacious reception rooms and bar. **www.bonotto.it**

BASSANO DEL GRAPPA Ca' Sette   🏚 🕭 🏚 🗏 🅿 🅦   €€
Via Cunizza da Romano 4, 36061 **Tel** *042 438 33 50* **Fax** *042 439 32 87* **Rooms** *19*

This Venetian villa has been attractively converted into a stylish hotel. Ca' Sette is on the outskirts of the city in a formal garden and surrounded by olive groves. Rooms are all individually decorated, some with original frescoes. The restaurant offers creative cuisine, including a vegetarian menu. **www.ca-sette.it**

CHIOGGIA Grande Italia   🛏 🍴 📺 🗎 🅿 W   €€

Rione S. Andrea 597, 30015 **Tel** *041 40 05 15* **Fax** *041 40 01 85* **Rooms** *56*

This unpretentious old-fashioned hotel at the head of the main street has a Liberty-style façade. It has elegant, comfortable rooms and an up-to-date wellbeing centre. Grande Italia is conveniently situated for boats running to Venice. Closed Nov. **www.hotelgrandeitalia.com**

CONEGLIANO Il Faè   🖥 🏋 🅿   €

Via Faè1, San Pietro di Feletto, 31020 **Tel** *043 878 71 17* **Fax** *043 878 78 17* **Rooms** *8*

This comfortable guesthouse is in a converted farmhouse amongst hills and vineyards. It has good views over the foothills of the Alps and is a 10-minute drive from Conegliano. The hosts also offer activities for their guests including cookery classes. Closed 3 weeks Jan. **www.ilfae.com**

PADUA Augustus Terme   🛏 🍴 🖥 🏋 📺 🗎 🅿 W   €€

Viale Stazione 150, Montegrotto Terme, 35036 **Tel** *049 79 32 00* **Fax** *049 79 35 18* **Rooms** *120*

A big, comfortable hotel with opulent rooms and a vast restaurant. It has spacious, welcoming public areas, as well as tennis courts.The wellbeing and beauty centre, along with the hot thermal springs, are the real focal point of this pleasant complex. **www.hotelaugustus.com**

PADUA Plaza   ♿ 🍴 📺 🗎 🅿 W   €€

Corso Milano 40, 35139 **Tel** *049 65 68 22* **Fax** *049 66 11 17* **Rooms** *130*

An established and efficiently run hotel with a deservedly good reputation. Though its 1970s exterior appears somewhat unattractive, inside it offers up-to-date technology and all modern comforts. The Plaza provides a full range of services and a thoroughly warm welcome. **www.plazapadova.it**

PORDENONE Palace Hotel Moderno   🛏 🍴 🏋 📺 🗎 🅿   €€

Viale Martelli 1, 33170 **Tel** *043 42 82 15* **Fax** *043 452 03 15* **Rooms** *96*

A comfortable, refurbished traditional hotel with a good range of facilities in all its bedrooms. It is centrally located close to the station. The restaurant (which is under separate management) specializes in traditional cuisine, particularly fish dishes. Amenities include a fitness room, sauna and an Internet room. **www.palacehotelmoderno.it**

SARCEDO Casa Belmonte   ♿ 🖥 🏋 🅿   €€€

Via Belmonte 2, 36030 **Tel** *044 588 48 33* **Fax** *044 588 41 34* **Rooms** *6*

A small hotel set on the top of a hill surrounded by vineyards and olive groves. The rooms are luxuriously decorated with antiques and rich drapes. Breakfast is served outside in the summer or in the conservatory. There is a large pool for the guests. A good base from which to explore the Palladian villas. **www.casabelmonte.com**

TREVISO Ca' del Galletto   📺 ♿ 🍴 🖥 🏋 🗎 🅿 W   €

Via Santa Bona Vecchia 30, 31100 **Tel** *042 243 25 50* **Fax** *042 243 25 10* **Rooms** *67*

Set in its own grounds and only a 10-minute walk from the city walls, Ca' del Galletto's bedrooms are spacious and modern, though slightly lacking in charm. However, the friendly staff and excellent sports facilities, as well as the peaceful surroundings, make for a pleasant stay. **www.hotelcadelgalletto.it**

TREVISO Il Focolare   🏋 🗎 W   €€

Piazza Ancillotto 4, 31100 **Tel** *042 25 66 01* **Fax** *042 25 66 01* **Rooms** *14*

One of Treviso's best budget hotels, Il Focolare is clean, welcoming and situated in the heart of the historic centre. The rooms are rather small, as are the bathrooms, but the location makes up for it. There is an excellent restaurant opposite which serves traditional Treviso dishes. **www.albergoilfocolare.net**

VICENZA Casa San Raffaele   🛏 ♿ 🏋 🗎 🅿   €

Viale X Giugno 10, 36100 **Tel** *044 454 57 67* **Fax** *044 454 22 59* **Rooms** *29*

This tranquil hotel is set in charming surroundings with excellent views of the slopes of Monte Berico. The comfortable rooms are all en suite. Friendly staff and simple style can be found at this centrally located establishment. No high season means that this is one of the best budget choices in the area.

VICENZA Campo Marzio   🛏 🍴 🗎 🅿 W   €€€

Via Roma 27, 36100 **Tel** *044 454 57 00* **Fax** *044 432 04 95* **Rooms** *35*

A stylish boutique hotel with good facilities, just a short stroll from the city centre and the principal Palladian sites. The bedrooms are large and beautifully furnished – each one with its own individual decor and wireless Internet connection. Campo Marzio is situated in a peaceful location. **www.hotelcampomarzio.com**

VERONA AND LAKE GARDA

GARDA Locanda San Vigilio   🍴 🖥 🏋 🗎 🅿   €€€€

San Vigilio, 37016 **Tel** *045 725 66 88* **Fax** *045 627 81 82* **Rooms** *7*

One of the loveliest hotels on Lake Garda, the San Vigilio exudes Old World charm and is set in peaceful grounds with a small church dedicated to the saint of the same name. Comfort and service live up to expectations, and there is a private beach and free mooring for boats. Closed mid-Nov–Mar. **www.locanda-sanvigilio.it**

Key to Price Guide *see p228* **Key to Symbols** *see back cover flap*

MALCESINE Sailing Center Hotel

Via Gardesana 187, 37018 **Tel** *045 740 00 55* **Fax** *045 740 03 92* **Rooms** *32*

A modern hotel just outside town, away from the crowds. Rooms are cool and pleasant, and there is a tennis court and private beach. The hotel offers low-key service and immaculate grounds. Its lakeside setting makes it an ideal base for guests keen on watersports. Closed mid-Oct–Mar. **www.hotelsailing.com**

PESCHIERA DEL GARDA Peschiera

Via Parini 4, 37010 **Tel** *045 755 05 26* **Fax** *045 755 04 44* **Rooms** *30*

The hotel is set in its own verdant grounds and has lofty, cool bedrooms. There are fine lake views, though some of the rooms look out onto the equally pretty hills. There is a sun terrace and a private swimming pool. The hotel can arrange riding in the hills or golf at the course nearby. **www.hotel-peschiera.com**

TORRI DEL BENACO Hotel Gardesana

Piazza Calderini 20, 37010 **Tel** *045 722 54 11* **Fax** *045 722 57 71* **Rooms** *34*

The 15th-century harbour master's house overlooking Lake Garda has been converted into a friendly, comfortable hotel. Its spectacular location means that there are views of the castle from the restaurant terrace, while rooms on the third floor have wonderful views of the lake. Closed Nov–Feb. **www.hotel-gardesana.com**

VERONA Il Torcolo

Vicolo Listone 3, 37121 **Tel** *045 800 75 12* **Fax** *045 800 40 58* **Rooms** *19*

This small, family-run hotel is a few minutes' walk from the Arena, making it a popular destination during the opera season. Though some of the reception areas are rather cramped, the guest rooms are pretty and traditional. Il Torcolo has its own breakfast terrace. Closed 2 weeks end Jan, 5 days Christmas. **www.hoteltorcolo.it**

VERONA Due Torri Hotel

Piazza Sant'Anastasia 4, 37121 **Tel** *045 59 50 44* **Fax** *045 800 41 30* **Rooms** *90*

Standing alongside a beautiful church in the heart of medieval Verona, this sumptuous 14th-century building is one of Italy's most eccentric hotels. Each bedroom is decorated and furnished in the style of a different era. The public areas are equally opulent in this unique establishment. **www.duetorrihotels.com**

THE DOLOMITES

BELLUNO Albergo Cappello e Cadore

Via Ricci 8, 32100 **Tel** *043 794 02 46* **Fax** *043 729 23 19* **Rooms** *31*

Centrally situated, Cappello e Cadore is popular with skiers in winter and walkers in summer. The rooms are comfortable, with independent heating and air conditioning. Most overlook the square, but a few have panoramic views of the mountains. **www.albergocappello.com**

CORTINA D'AMPEZZO Montana

Corso Italia 94, 32043 **Tel** *043 686 04 98* **Fax** *043 61 99 20 01* **Rooms** *31*

Montana is conveniently situated in the town centre, close to the main shops. The area is pedestrianized, making the hotel quiet and a popular choice. Some of the rooms are rather small, although all are attractively decorated and bathrooms have hydromassage baths. Good value for money. **www.cortina-hotel.com**

CORTINA D'AMPEZZO Menardi

Via Majon 110, 32043 **Tel** *0436 24 00* **Fax** *0436 86 21 83* **Rooms** *49*

This rather old-fashioned hotel on the outskirts of Cortina has been in the same family since 1900. It is tastefully furnished with antiques and has a welcoming atmosphere. Service is attentive and excellent. There is also an annexe behind the main building. Half-board only. Closed 10 Apr–10 Jun, 10 Sep–1 Dec. **www.hotelmenardi.it**

FOLLINA Villa Abbazia

Via Martiri della Liberta, 31051 **Tel** *043 897 12 77* **Fax** *043 897 00 01* **Rooms** *18*

This delightful 17th-century villa has been tastefully restored by the Zanon family. The spacious rooms are all individually decorated in an English country house style. A small garden makes a wonderful place to relax or enjoy a drink in the early evening. A good base from which to explore the area. **www.hotelabbazia.it**

PIEVE D'ALPAGO Albergo Dolada

Via Dolada 21, 32010 **Tel** *043 747 91 41* **Fax** *043 747 80 68* **Rooms** *7*

A small, stylish hotel with an excellent restaurant much patronized by Venetians. The bedrooms are modern and bright, each decorated in a colour of the rainbow. Most have good views over the surrounding countryside. In the restaurant creative dishes are prepared following a seasonal menu. Closed 3 weeks Jan. **www.dolada.it**

SAPPADA Haus Michaela

Borgata Fontana 40, 32047 **Tel** *043 546 93 77* **Fax** *043 56 61 31* **Rooms** *18*

Located in a small ski resort at the foothills of the Dolomites, Haus Michaela's rooms are simply decorated, spacious and comfortable. Facilities include a pool, a fitness centre and a sauna. A good spot for a family holiday in summer and winter. The restaurant serves up hearty mountain dishes. Closed Apr–mid-May, Oct–Nov. **www.hotelmichaela.com**

RESTAURANTS, CAFES AND BARS

Restaurants in Venice and the Veneto serve predominantly Italian food from the region, with the emphasis in Venice very much on fish. Wherever you go, you will find the cooking simple, with dishes that make full use of the traditional local ingredients.

Most Venetians eat lunch *(pranzo)* around 12:30pm and dinner *(cena)* from 8pm, though restaurants start serving dinner earlier to cater for the many foreign visitors.

Egyptian detail, Caffè Pedrocchi

Restaurants may be closed for several weeks during the winter and also for two to three weeks during the staff summer holidays. Closing dates are included in the listings, but avoid disappointment by asking your hotel to phone first to confirm that the restaurant is open. Finding restaurants can be confusing in Venice, so use the map references provided. The restaurants listed on pages 242–49 are some of the best across all price ranges.

El Gato restaurant, Chioggia, famous for its fish *(see p247)*

TYPES OF RESTAURANTS

Italian eating places have a bewildering variety of names, and the differences between them can be considerable. A *ristorante* is smarter than a *trattoria* or an *osteria*, for example, and is likely to be more expensive. Nowadays, there is also a growing number of fast-food joints and *tavola calda* establishments, which have no cover or service charge. A *birreria* and a *spaghetteria* are more down-market eating places that sell beer, pasta dishes and snacks; you will mainly find these outside Venice itself. A good *pizzeria* will use wood-fired ovens efor the pizza; if this is the case it will normally be open only in the evenings.

If you do not want to eat a full meal at lunchtime you can always stop in a bar or café for a snack. For further information on light meals see page 250.

OPENING TIMES AND CLOSING DAYS

Opening times are virtually the same throughout Venice and the Veneto: from noon to 2:30pm for lunch, and from 7:30pm to 10:30pm for dinner. Under Italian law all restaurants close one day a week and some close for an additional evening as well; closing days are staggered so there is always somewhere open in the area. Individual restaurants' closing days are given in the listings.

The main bar of the historic Caffè Pedrocchi *(see p178)*

VEGETARIAN FOOD

Italians find it difficult to understand vegetarianism, but if you eat fish you should have no difficulty eating well. If not, there is still a variety of meatless dishes since many starters *(antipasti)*, soups and pasta sauces are vegetable-based. Salads and vegetables are always good, and most places will be happy to serve an omelette *(frittata)* or a selection of cheese.

FIXED-PRICE MENUS

In the days when Italy was building its tourist industry all restaurants had to supply a fixed-price menu. This has largely fallen into abeyance, particularly outside the main tourist centres. Restaurants may often have the so-called *menu turistico* pinned up in the street, but not on offer inside. Such menus, if you do find them, are usually boring and offer no opportunity to sample the wonderful variety of the local cuisine. If money is tight it is far better to have a good pasta dish and some salad, which is acceptable in all but the grandest places.

The *menu gastronomico* is a fixed-price menu consisting of six or seven courses, which allows you to sample the full range of a chef's specialities.

HOW MUCH TO PAY

Transport charges can add as much as 30 per cent to the price of basic commodities coming into Venice, which partly explains the high cost of eating. In cheaper eating places and *pizzerie* you can have a two-course meal with half a litre of wine for around €10–15. Three-course meals average about €18–25, and in up-market restaurants you can easily pay €50–70. In the Veneto, prices are lower, except for stylish restaurants in Verona and along Lake Garda during the summer.

Nearly all restaurants have a cover charge *(pane e coperto)*, usually €1–3. Many also add a 10 per cent service charge *(servizio)* to the bill *(il conto)*, so always establish whether or not this is the case. Where leaving a tip is a matter of your own discretion, 12–15 per cent is acceptable.

Restaurants are obliged by law to give you a receipt *(una ricevuta fiscale)*. Scraps of paper with an illegible scrawl are illegal, and you are within your rights to ask for a proper bill. The preferred form of payment is cash, but many restaurants will accept payment by major credit cards. Check which cards are accepted when booking.

MAKING RESERVATIONS

Whatever the price range, Venice's best restaurants are always busy, so it is best to reserve a table, especially if you are making a long boat trip to get there. If restaurants do not accept bookings, try to arrive early to avoid queuing.

DRESS CODE

Italians like to dress up in general, and dining out is no exception. However, this does not mean that women have to wear evening attire at a restaurant, or that men have to wear a tie, and you will rarely feel under-dressed without a jacket. Smart casual clothes are the general rule for both men and women.

Eating under the loggia of Treviso's Palazzo dei Trecento *(see p174)*

READING THE MENU

Both lunch and dinner in a restaurant follow the same pattern and usually start with an *antipasto*, or hors d'oeuvres (seafood, olives, beef carpaccio, ham, salami), followed by the *primo* (soup, rice or pasta). The main course, or *secondo*, will be fish or meat, either served alone or accompanied by vegetables *(contorni)* or a salad *(insalata)*. These are never included in the price of the main course.

To finish, there will probably be a choice of fruit *(frutta)*, a pudding *(dolce)* or cheese *(formaggio)*, or a combination of all three. Coffee – Italians always have an *espresso*, never a *cappuccino* – is ordered and served right at the end of the meal, often with a *digestivo*. In cheaper restaurants, the menu *(il menu)* may be chalked up or the waiter may simply recite the day's special dishes at your table.

CHOICE OF WINE

House wines are usually local *(see pp240–41)*. Cheaper restaurants will have a limited wine list, but at the top of the scale there should be a wide range of Italian wines and a selection of foreign vintages.

CHILDREN

Children are welcome in restaurants, particularly in simple, family-run ones. Smart places may be less welcoming, particularly in the evenings. Special facilities such as high chairs are not commonly provided. Most restaurants will prepare a half-portion *(mezza porzione)* if requested, and some charge less for these smaller helpings.

SMOKING

Smoking in enclosed public spaces, including restaurants, is now banned in Italy. The ban does not extend to tables on outside terraces.

WHEELCHAIR ACCESS

Very few restaurants make special provision for wheelchairs, though a word when booking should ensure a conveniently situated table and assistance on arrival.

EATING ON A BUDGET

Eating out all the time can become very expensive, especially in Venice, a cheaper option is to make your own picnic. Most supermarkets stock a range of fresh washed salads, local cheeses and tasty cold cuts. The Coop chain has several outlets in Venice, including a flagship store at Piazzale Roma. Otherwise try Billa, which has store through-out the Veneto. Alternatively support the local shops, many of which will make large rolls from your choice of fillings.

There are plenty of lovely places to stop and enjoy an al fresco meal. In Venice the Park at Saint Elena is a shady spot even in summer. Verona has many picturesque squares and most towns will have a quiet park to stop and take a break.

A short break at Carnival

The Flavours of Venice and the Veneto

The cuisine of Venice and the Veneto reflects the region's varied landscape, from cattle-grazing and agricultural land to mountains and coastline. The most important sources of ingredients, however, are the waters – both inland and coastal – that yield a constant supply of fish and seafood. In general, the cooking is light, fresh and delicately flavoured, without heavy sauces. Fish may be simply grilled or poached with herbs, while *carpaccio* of raw beef is sliced to transparent thinness. The vibrant colours of dishes recall canvases by Tintoretto or Titian: bright yellow saffron or polenta, emerald green fresh peas, dark red radicchio and the blue-black stain of cuttlefish ink in *riso nero* risotto.

Saffron

Produce from the Veneto is loaded onto the Venetian canalside

VENETIAN FOOD

Food in Venice is almost always Italian, and many restaurants serve local specialities. There are very few ethnic eating places despite the city's long history as a trading port and home to foreign settlers. Foodstuffs have always been traded, starting with the local salt and fish. In the 15th and

16th centuries, when Venice was the prosperous gateway to the East, imported spices, pepper, raisins, pine nuts and sugar made their way into the diet. Recipes from the period cite ingredients such as ginger, nutmeg, saffron, cloves, cinnamon and coriander. The city's noble families liked their food to be appealing to the eye as well as the palate, and so they introduced fine, locally-made glassware to enhance the table. They served extravagant fare such as peacock, roasted whole with

spices and then garnished with gold leaf. A few traces of these exotic influences still appear in classic Venetian cooking, such as Asian-style sweet and sour combinations and the use of spices as well as herbs. *Baccalà* (dried salted cod) originally brought from the Baltic area, is still very popular, often cooked with milk or wine and garlic or onion. Superb vegetables are grown in market gardens on the islands of the lagoon, not least the delicious purple artichokes *(castraure)* from Sant' Erasmo.

Caper berries   **Marinated white anchovies**   **Olives wrapped in anchovies**   **Seafood cocktail**

Selection of Venetian *antipasti*, the perfect appetizer

REGIONAL DISHES AND SPECIALITIES

Antipasto di frutti di mare (a mixed seafood appetizer) is a special favourite in Venice, where the ingredients come fresh from the Adriatic. From lovely Lake Garda, *anguilla del pescatore* (stewed eel), *lavarelli al vino bianco* (lake fish in white wine) and *carpione* (a type of lake trout) are all fishy delights. Another fish speciality of the region is *baccalà alla veneziana*, made with dried salt cod. Pork and salamis feature throughout the area but in Friuli goose is often used as an alternative to pork, with succulent cured meat offerings such as *salame d'oca* (goose salami). Game is also found on the menu, together with sauerkraut and filling goulash, while desserts often have an Austrian flavour, too, such as *apfel strudel*. But the region is also proud of claiming as its own the voluptuous, classic Italian dessert *tiramisù*.

Asparagus

Sarde in Saor *is a Venetian speciality of fried sardines in a sweet and sour onion marinade, with pine nuts.*

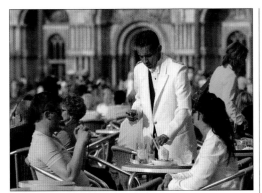
Enjoying an aperitif in the sunshine of St Mark's Square in Venice

FOOD OF THE VENETO

The region's staples have long been polenta and rice, although pasta is also popular. Polenta, made from ground maize (corn) that was originally imported from America in the 16th century, was always a peasant food. Today, it often accompanies a main course and can appear as a thick purée or be allowed to set into in a more solid form, when it can be cut into slices and grilled. The Veneto is one of Italy's main rice-growing regions. Rice was introduced from Spain by the Arabs, and the *vialone nano* variety grown around Verona is the favourite for risotto, giving a superbly creamy finish when cooked in stock with meat, fish or vegetables in season. A huge range of vegetables is grown in the Veneto. Bassano di Grappa is noted for its asparagus, and Treviso for a long variety of radicchio that is eaten raw, baked (*radicchio in forno*), grilled or in risotto. Soups are made from vegetables and beans, notably *pasta e fagiola* – a thick brown soup of highly-prized borlotti beans from Lamon, near Belluno. Fish comes from the inland rivers and Lake Garda, while farms produce chicken, duck, turkey and goose. Towards the mountains there are pigs for cured hams, salami and sausages like the pork *sopressa*, as well as veal, beef and dairy cattle, and wild game in season. An Austrian legacy is tasted in the dumplings and apple strudels of the Dolomites.

Fishing on the tranquil waters of Lake Garda

VENETIAN FISH DISHES

The catch from the region's waters includes sardines, mussels, clams, sea snails, squid, cuttlefish, eel, prawns, crab and lobster. These are served as *antipasti*, made into soups (*brodo di pesce*), and cooked in risottos or with pasta, such as the popular *spaghetti alle vongole* (with clams). Regional specialities include:

Bisato su l'aro Eel baked with bayleaf is a dish from Murano, where it was cooked in the glass furnaces.

Sarde in Saor Sardines in a sweet and sour sauce.

Moleche frite Soft-shelled crabs from the lagoon, coated with beaten egg and fried.

Seppie alla Veneziana Cuttlefish cooked in their own ink.

Zuppa di Cozze Mussels steamed with white wine, garlic and parsley.

Risi e bisi *mixes rice with fresh peas in a soft, moist risotto, sometimes with ham and Parmesan cheese.*

Fegato alla Venezia *is calf's liver served on a bed of sautéed onions. Grilled polenta is a good side dish.*

Tiramisù *(the name means "pick me up") is rich pudding of mascarpone, sponge fingers, coffee and marsala.*

What to Drink in Venice and the Veneto

Italy has been making wine for over 3,000 years, and production in the Veneto reflects this, with the largest output in Italy of superior DOC wines. The area produces an abundance of different wines, which include not only well-known names such as Soave, Valpolicella and Bardolino, but many others which are also excellent value for money. Although Italians tend to drink lighter wines with their food, the area is also noted for some excellent strong wines. Italy's famous *digestivo*, grappa, originated in this corner of the country, and meals are often preceded by an *aperitivo* or a glass of sparkling local Prosecco.

Grapes drying in Valpolicella

RED WINE

Red
Venegazzù   Masi's ripasso

Red wines in the veneto are produced mainly near Bardolino and Valpolicella between Verona and Lake Garda *(see pp208–9)*. Made predominantly from the Corvina grape, they are usually light and fruity, but quality can vary so it is worth looking for reliable names.

Valpolicella comes in several forms. In addition to the normal easy-drinking wine, it is available as a *ripasso*, boosted in colour and strength by macerating the skins of the grapes before pressing. Recioto della Valpolicella is very different, a rich, sweet wine made from selected air-dried grapes. Some Reciotos undergo further fermentation to remove the sweetness, producing the strong, dry Recioto Amarone. These are some of the strongest naturally alcoholic wines in the world and are delicious but expensive.

Excellent red wines are also made by producers such as Venegazzù and Maculan from the Cabernet Sauvignon and Merlot grapes.

Bardolino wine is light, fruity and garnet-red in colour.

Amarone is full-bodied, rich, full of fruit and very alcoholic.

READING WINE LABELS

Italian wines are classified by four quality levels. Starting at the top, DOCG status *(Denominazione di Origine Controllata e Garantita)* has been awarded to a small number of Italian growing areas, none of which are in the Veneto. Most quality wines – more than 250 in the whole of Italy – are in the DOC category (as above but without the "guarantee") and these can be relied on as good value, quality wines. The IGT *(Indicazione Geografica Tipica)* category corresponds to the popular French Vin de Pays. The final classification is *vino da tavola*, or table wine, but due to the inflexible Italian wine laws many superb wines appear in this category.

No vintage recommendations are given in the chart because almost all Veneto wines are made for young drinking.

WINE TYPE	RECOMMENDED PRODUCERS
White Wine	
Soave	Anselmi, Bertani, Col Baraca (Masi), Boscaini, CS di Soave, Masi, Pieropan, Scamperle, Tedeschi, Zenato, Zonin
Bianco di Custoza	Cavalchina, Le Tende, Le Vigne di San Pietro, Pezzini, San Leone, Tedeschi, Zenato
Breganze di Breganze	Maculan
Gambellara	CS di Gambellara, Zonin
Red Wine	
Bardolino	Alighieri, Bertani, Bolla, Boscaini, Guerrieri-Rizzardi, Masi, Tedeschi
Valpolicella	Alighieri, Allegrini, Bertani, Bolla, Boscaini, Guerrieri-Rizzardi, Masi, Tedeschi, Zenato
Ripasso Valpolicella (non-DOC)	Serègo Alighieri, Jago (Bolla), Le Cane (Boscaini), Le Sassine (Le Ragose), Campo Fiorin (Masi), Capitel San Rocco (Tedeschi)
Recioto and Recioto Amarone della Valpolicella	Serègo Alighieri, Allegrini, Masi, Quintarelli, Le Ragose, Tedeschi

WHITE WINE

The Veneto produces more white wine than red, and most of the region's whites are from vineyards around the hilltop town of Soave (see p190). These wines can be dull, but increasing numbers of producers are trying to raise Soave's image. Bianco di Custoza, a creamy, richer "super Soave" from the eastern shores of Lake Garda, is well worth trying. Breganze is a name to look out for, with Maculan a leader in making fresh, clean, inexpensive wines and world-class dessert wines. Gambellara is made mainly from Soave's Garganega grape and is seldom of poor quality. Venegazzù is another producer you can trust for good quality white wines.

Bianco di Custoza

White Recioto

Pieropan is a top quality producer of Soave. The single-vineyard wines from here are superb.

White vino da tavola wines range from pale and dry to sweet and golden coloured.

Venegazzù's Pinot Grigio wine is dry and goes well with Venetian seafood.

Puiatti's white Ribolla wine is fruity but dry. It is made in neighbouring Friuli.

APERITIFS AND OTHER DRINKS

Italian aperitifs tend to be wine-based, bitter, herb-flavoured drinks such as Martini and Campari. Less familiar are the herbal Punt e Mes, Cynar (made from artichokes), and the vivid orange Aperol, which is good mixed with white wine and soda. Crodino is a popular non-alcoholic choice. For settling the stomach after a good meal there are *amari* (bitters) and *digestivi*. Montenegro and Ramazzotti are well worth trying, and grappa, distilled from wine lees (see Bassano del Grappa p166), is another favourite. A local speciality, Trevisana, is mixed with an extract of the long red radicchio from Treviso. Italian brandy can be rather oily, but Vecchia Romagna is a reliable name.

Grappa

Crodino

PROSECCO

The Veneto's own sparkling wine, Prosecco is perfect as either a refreshing light *aperitivo* or with a meal. It originates in Conegliano (see p175), the home of Italy's greatest wine school, and comes in both *secco* (dry) or *amabile* (medium-sweet) forms, and as *frizzante* or *spumante* (semi and fully sparkling). An excellent accompaniment to both fruit and seafood, it is also the traditional base for Bellini, a delicious *aperitivo* of wine mixed with fresh white peach juice (see p92). This drink has bred several variants, such as Mimosa (with orange) and Tiziano (with red grape juice).

Prosecco

Bellini cocktail

SOFT DRINKS

Italian bottled fruit juices come in delicious flavours such as pear, apricot and peach. Many bars will squeeze you a *spremuta* of fresh orange (*arancia*) or grapefruit (*pompelmo*) juice on the spot. A *frullato* is an ice-cold mix of milk and fresh fruit.

Spremuta di arancia

COFFEE

Coffee is an essential part of Italian life. Milky *cappuccino* with chocolate powder is drunk at breakfast time, and tiny cups of strong black *espresso* throughout the day. If you like your coffee with milk, choose a *caffè con latte*, or with just a dash of milk, *caffè macchiato*. Black coffee that is not too strong is *caffè lungo*; a *doppio* has an extra kick and a *corretto* has a good measure of alcohol.

Espresso

Cappuccino

Choosing a Restaurant

The restaurants listed below have been selected across a wide price range for their fine food, good value and interesting location. They are listed alphabetically according to area, starting with San Marco in the centre of Venice. For more details on regional food and alternative places to eat, *see pp236–241*.

PRICE CATEGORIES
The following price ranges are for a three-course meal for one, including a half-bottle of house wine, cover charge, tax and service.

€ Under €25
€€ €25–€40
€€€ €40–€55
€€€€ €55–€70
€€€€€ Over €70

VENICE

SAN MARCO Bar all'Angolo   €
Campo Santo Stefano 3465, 30124 **Tel** *041 522 07 10*   **Map** 6 F2

Specializing in sandwiches of all kinds, this fun bar also offers light meals and salads. It is a great place for relaxing with a chilled glass of prosecco after a few hours of sightseeing, and it is certainly one of the cheapest eateries in the square. A great place for people-watching. Closed Sun; Jan.

SAN MARCO Devil's Forest Pub   €
Calle dei Stagneri 5185, 30124 **Tel** *041 520 06 23*   **Map** 7 B1

Always buzzing with life, this Venetian pub serves excellent dishes, such as pasta with prawn, pumpkin and radicchio sauce, that are good value for money. The kitchen closes at midnight but the dart games go on until much later. It is in the vicinity of the central square Campo San Bartolomeo.

SAN MARCO Rosticceria San Bartolomeo   €
Calle della Bissa 5424, 30124 **Tel** *041 522 35 69*   **Map** 7 B1

Popular with the locals, who pop in for the delicious deep-fried snack *mozzarella in carrozza*, Rosticceria San Bartolomeo also prepares a vast range of pasta, risottos and soups including *pasta e fagioli* (with beans). It is cheaper to order your food at the counter and find yourself a seat; otherwise restaurant-style seating is upstairs.

SAN MARCO Ai Assassini   €€
Rio Terà dei Assassini 3695, 30124 **Tel** *041 528 79 86*   **Map** 7 A2

Tucked away off the main thoroughfare, this friendly *osteria* attracts both locals and tourists alike. The menu changes on a daily basis and follows the seasons closely. It includes game and fish dishes and a great array of vegetables, such as *Treviso radicchio* in winter. Closed Sun; 3 weeks Jan.

SAN MARCO Cavatappi   €€
Campo della Guerra 525/526, 30124 **Tel** *041 296 02 52*   **Map** 7 B1

An inviting, modern wine bar that serves mouth-watering pasta dishes on elegant plates. Artichokes and smoked ricotta cheese are on offer, as well as tender roast meats and regional cheeses. Make sure you leave space for a dessert. Closed 9pm and all day Mon; all of Jan.

SAN MARCO Al Bacareto   €€€
Calle delle Botteghe 3447, 30124 **Tel** *041 528 93 36*   **Map** 6 F2

A cheerful family-run *osteria* that prides itself on serving traditional dishes such as *baccalà* (creamed salt cod) and *bigoli in salsa* (wholemeal spaghetti with onion and anchovies) along with delicious seafood. Outside tables let you enjoy good food while watching the world pass by on its way to nearby Palazzo Grassi. Closed Sun.

SAN MARCO Da Raffaele   €€€
Ponte delle Ostreghe 2347, 30124 **Tel** *041 523 23 17*   **Map** 7 A3

This well-established lively restaurant offers a vast range of regional dishes in an especially romantic setting. Dishes worth trying include *granseola* (spider crab) as an antipasto, and risotto with scampi and turbot as a main course. Closed Thu; Dec–late Jan.

SAN MARCO Le Bistrot de Venise   €€€
Calle dei Fabbri 4685, 30124 **Tel** *041 523 66 51*   **Map** 7 B2

This welcoming restaurant serves traditional Venetian cuisine as well as special dishes based on historic recipes. The desserts are definitely worth saving space for, and the wine list is truly international. A meeting place for local artists and poets, the Bistrot regularly holds cultural events in the afternoons and evenings. Closed Christmas.

SAN MARCO Osteria Enoteca San Marco   €€€
Frezzeria 1610, 30124 **Tel** *041 528 52 42*   **Map** 7 B2

This restaurant may be small, but the cuisine is ambitious and the wine list extensive. Favouring local and independent producers, the menu combines tradition and creativity in dishes that range from meat to seafood and game. A haven of good cooking among the many rip-off joints that abound in this neighbourhood.

Key to Symbols *see back cover flap*

SAN MARCO Ristorante all'Angelo   €€€

Calle Larga S. Marco 403, 30124 **Tel** *041 520 92 99*   **Map** *7 C2*

This wonderful bustling restaurant, situated below the hotel of the same name, is just off Piazza San Marco. It used to be a meeting point for great artists and scholars, and specializes in seafood such as Chioggia-style soup and grilled fish. For dessert, try the luscious *zuppa inglese* (trifle).

SAN MARCO Acqua Pazza   €€€€

Campo Sant'Angelo 3808/10, 30124 **Tel** *041 277 06 88*   **Map** *6 F2*

A winning blend of Mediterranean cuisine from Amalfi and Campania is on the menu at this bright restaurant that spreads into Campo Sant'Angelo during the summer. The crusty pizzas are hard to resist, though other offerings featuring capers, fresh tomato, aubergine (eggplant) and anchovies are memorable too. Closed Mon, 7 Jan–7 Feb.

SAN MARCO Ristorante alla Borsa   €€€€

Calle delle Veste 2018, 30124 **Tel** *041 523 54 34*   **Map** *7 A2*

Alla Borsa was named after the stock exchange formerly in the vicinity. The Stanziani family from Abruzzo have been serving Mediterranean food here since the 1700s. The best dish is fish baked with a flavoursome sauce of clams, capers and tomato. The extensive wine list is mainly Italian.

SAN MARCO Antico Martini   €€€€€

Campo San Fantin 1983, 30124 **Tel** *041 522 41 21*   **Map** *7 A2*

Located alongside the Fenice theatre, this smart restaurant boasts high-quality cuisine, a vast choice of wines and impeccable service. The lamb with balsamic sauce is just one of the many recommended dishes on the menu. An excellent choice for dinner.

SAN MARCO Centrale   €€€€€

Piscina Frezzaria 1659, 30124 **Tel** *041 296 06 64*   **Map** *7 A2*

A unique relaxing lounge-bar-restaurant close to the Fenice opera house, the Centrale serves innovative Mediterranean cuisine with an Asian flair. It is open until 2am every day with soft music, avant-garde art and romantic candle-lit tables. The impressive wine list has 800 labels, both Italian and foreign.

SAN MARCO Do Forni   €€€€€

Calle Specchieri 468, 30124 **Tel** *041 523 21 48*   **Map** *7 B2*

This is a large "show business" establishment where the guest book includes politicians and heads of state. The Do Forni has two dining rooms furnished in contrasting styles, one rustic but smart and the other more elegant. The mixed grilled fish is a house speciality that should not be missed. Book ahead.

SAN MARCO Grand Canal   €€€€€

Calle Vallaresso 1332, 30124 **Tel** *041 520 02 11*   **Map** *7 B3*

Perfect for stylish dining all year round, the Grand Canal has a winter dining room and a summer terrace with views of the island of San Giorgio Maggiore. The menu features traditional Venetian cuisine, including pasta made freshly every day, and wonderful fish and meat dishes. It is advisable to book in advance.

SAN MARCO Harry's Bar   €€€€€

Calle Vallaresso 1323, 30124 **Tel** *041 528 57 77*   **Map** *7 B3*

Known the world over as Ernest Hemingway's favourite watering hole in Venice, Harry's Bar is a hallowed institution as well as a cosy café. Coffee and toasted sandwiches can be ordered, or a Bellini cocktail. The renowned food on the menu includes *carpaccio* (raw marinated beef), a dish invented by the owner.

SAN POLO Al Nono Risorto   €

Sottoportego di Sior Bettina 2337, 30135 **Tel** *041 524 11 69*   **Map** *2 F5*

Going strong until late into the night, this busy pizzeria and modest restaurant has a pretty shady courtyard for summer dining. Located near the Rialto market area, it is popular with the locals, and booking is advisable at weekends. Closed Wed, Thu lunch; 3 weeks Jan, 1 week mid-Aug.

SAN POLO Osteria alla Patatina   €€

Ponte San Polo 2741A, 30123 **Tel** *041 523 72 38*   **Map** *6 E1*

Delicious battered vegetables, creamy *baccalà* (cod) and tender octopus are on display at the counter at this typically Venetian *osteria*. Locals drop in for a quick glass of wine accompanied by hot chips (*patatina*, hence the name of the place), though sit-down meals are also served. Closed Sun; 1 week mid-Aug.

SAN POLO Poste Vecie   €€€

Rialto Pescheria 1608, 30125 **Tel** *041 72 18 22*   **Map** *3 A5*

Poste Vecie claims to be the oldest restaurant in the city, and traces its history back to the 1500s. The entrance is from the fish market at Rialto, and the baked turbot is excellent, as are the home-made ravioli and *tagliolini* (ribbon pasta). The wine list and the dessert trolley cannot fail to impress. Closed Tue.

SAN POLO Trattoria alla Madonna   €€€

Calle della Madonna 594, 30123 **Tel** *041 522 38 24*   **Map** *7 A1*

In this well-known fish restaurant in the Rialto area, waiters dash around loaded with platters of traditional seafood, such as delicate *granceola* (spider crab) and *seppie in nero* (squid in black-ink sauce). Arrive early to avoid having to wait for a table. Closed Wed; Jan, 5–20 Aug, Christmas.

SAN POLO Da Fiore

Calle del Scaleter 2202, 30125 **Tel** *041 72 13 08*   **Map** 2 E5

An exclusive establishment hidden behind Campo San Polo, Da Fiore is probably the city's best restaurant. Seasonal produce is the rule. Gourmet diners appreciate the sea bass with balsamic vinegar, tuna with rosemary, and *molecche* (soft-shelled crabs). Leave room for a delicate fruit sorbet. Closed Sun, Mon; 3 weeks Jan, 3 weeks Aug.

SANTA CROCE Il Réfolo

Campo del Piovan 1459, 30135 **Tel** *041 524 00 16*   **Map** 2 E5

Set in a picturesque square on a canalside near San Giacomo dell'Orio, this modern establishment serves innovative gourmet pizzas and simple pasta meals. Il Réfolo belongs to the family who run the nearby Osteria da Fiore. Closed Mon, Tue lunch; Jan.

SANTA CROCE La Zucca

Calle del Megio 1762, 30135 **Tel** *041 524 15 70*   **Map** 2 E5

This pretty canalside restaurant is beloved of locals and tourists alike. Serving tasty meat dishes, plus vegetarian options, the menu focuses on traditional Veneto cuisine with some international variations. The pumpkin flan is famous and the puddings are exquisite. Booking is advisable. Closed Sun.

SANTA CROCE Antica Bessetta

Salizzada Ca' Zusto 1395, 30135 **Tel** *041 72 16 87*   **Map** 2 D5

This tiny, long-established restaurant is flanked by a famous narrow alley close to San Giacomo dell'Orio. It prides itself on Venetian cuisine such as *tagliolini con granseola* (thin ribbon pasta with spider crab). The selection of delicious desserts includes lemon mousse with strawberry purée. Closed Tue & Wed lunch.

CASTELLO Aciugheta

Campo SS Filippo e Giacomo 4357, 30122 **Tel** *041 522 42 92*   **Map** 7 C2

Popular with the young local crowd for apéritifs, this place remains busy until the early hours of the morning. Sleek and modern, it serves light salads and snacks for lunch, as well as excellent pasta dishes. The outdoor seating is the perfect way to watch the world go by. Only a few minutes' walk from Piazza San Marco.

CASTELLO L'Olandese Volante

Campo San Lio 5658, 30122 **Tel** *041 528 93 49*   **Map** 7 B1

An extended stop for a cold beer and light meal at this laid-back pub known as the "Flying Dutchman" is always rewarding. The tasty salads have names of ships such as the *Galeone*, which is a concoction of prawn and egg, while the rolls are named after pirates! Extensive outdoor seating. Closed Sun am.

CASTELLO Alla Rivetta

Ponte San Provolo 4625, 30125 **Tel** *041 528 73 02*   **Map** 7 C2

This tiny place with a mouth-watering window display of glistening fish is squeezed in at the foot of a busy bridge only minutes' walk from St Mark's Square. Popular with gondoliers as well as tourists, it has been serving delicious fresh seafood and pasta for years. Closed Mon; 25 Jul–mid-Aug.

CASTELLO Trattoria Giorgione

Via Garibaldi 1533, 30122 **Tel** *041 522 87 27*   **Map** 8 F3

A great neighbourhood *trattoria* serving flavoursome traditional-style fish meals (such as fish lasagne) and delicious risotto. The jovial owner entertains diners with Venetian folk songs and guitar music. Set on an animated avenue beyond the Arsenale. Closed Wed; 2 weeks Nov.

CASTELLO Osteria Ae Due Porte

Corte delle Due Porte 6492, 30122 **Tel** *041 520 88 42*   **Map** 4 D5

The fragrance of the fish cooking on the huge grill at this quiet family-managed restaurant in the back streets of Castello often wafts out over the adjoining square. Ae Due Porte has an attractive timber-panelled interior. Only open for lunch. Closed Sat, Sun; 1 week mid-Aug, 1 week Christmas.

CASTELLO Al Mascaron

Calle Lunga S. Maria Formosa 5225, 30122 **Tel** *041 522 59 95*   **Map** 7 C1

Advance booking is essential here as this restaurant has become very popular. Both cramped and chaotic at times, this old style *osteria* does memorable fish and pasta meals, washed down by house wine served in short glasses as dictated by tradition. Closed Sun, 20 Dec–mid-Jan.

CASTELLO Da Remigio

Salizzada dei Greci 3416, 30122 **Tel** *041 523 00 89*   **Map** 8 D2

Since this is a favourite with Venetians and seating is limited, you should book ahead. A memorable seafood meal is guaranteed, and should include the creamy *risotto ai frutti di mare* (seafood risotto). Conclude with a *sgroppino*, a lemon sorbet and prosecco delight. Closed Mon dinner, Tue; Christmas–20 Jan, 2 weeks Jul–Aug.

CASTELLO Al Covo

Campiello della Pescaria 3968, 30122 **Tel** *041 522 38 12*   **Map** 8 E2

This hidden gem tucked away behind the Arsenale boat stop is run by husband and wife team Cesare and Diane Benelli. Cesare is the chef and the focus is on fish dishes of the highest quality. Save room for one of Diane's desserts. Closed Wed, Thu; 2 weeks Jan, 1 week Aug.

Key to Price Guide *see p242* **Key to Symbols** *see back cover flap*

DORSODURO Improntacafé

Crosera San Pantalon 3815, 30123 **Tel** *041 275 03 86*   **Map** *6 D2*

A trendy wine bar in the city's university district, Improntacafé is a good place to hang out. You can spend hours watching passers-by thanks to the vast windows. As well as decent wines, you will also find plates of pasta and salads at very reasonable prices. Open until 2am. Closed Sun; 10–25 Aug, Christmas, first week Jan.

DORSODURO Pizzeria ai Sportivi

Campo S. Margherita 3052, 30123 **Tel** *041 521 15 98*   **Map** *6 D2*

Summertime diners at this busy pizzeria can enjoy outdoor seating in one of the city's most delightful squares, Campo S. Margherita. The long menu includes specialities such as pizza with Treviso red chicory, radicchio and mouthwatering buffalo mozzarella cheese. Booking is advisable.

DORSODURO Pizzeria Ae Oche

Fondamenta Zattere 1414, 30123 **Tel** *041 520 66 01*   **Map** *6 E4*

This lively pizzeria (part of a small Venetian chain) attracts young and old locals, as well as tourists, with its great selection of pizzas. Ae Oche also offers a decent restaurant menu in a wonderful waterside setting overlooking the Giudecca canal. Closed Christmas.

DORSODURO Taverna San Trovaso

Fondamenta Priuli 1016, 30123 **Tel** *041 520 37 03*   **Map** *6 E3*

This bustling restaurant just around the corner from the Accademia gallery is extremely popular with English-speaking tourists, so book a table in advance or be prepared to queue. Pizzas are a staple, along with simple but flavoursome pasta, fish and meat dishes. There is also a good range of desserts. Closed Mon.

DORSODURO Cantinone Storico

Fondamenta Bragadin 660, 30123 **Tel** *041 523 95 77*   **Map** *6 E4*

Situated near the Peggy Guggenheim Collection and Accademia, this pleasant trattoria serves a wonderful *risotto terra mare* (a blend of seafood, vegetables and porcini mushrooms), complemented by a good selection of wines from their cavernous cellar. Book ahead for a table outside. Closed Sun.

DORSODURO La Rivista

Rio Terrà Foscarini 979/A, 30123 **Tel** *041 240 14 25*   **Map** *6 E4*

A modern, welcoming establishment close to the Accademia, La Rivista also does light salads and cold platters for lunch. Imaginative meat, pasta and vegetable dishes are also on the menu, as are divine desserts such as wild-berry cream. The menu changes on a monthly basis. Closed Mon.

DORSODURO Ai Gondolieri

San Vio 366, 30123 **Tel** *041 528 63 96*   **Map** *6 F4*

Close to the Guggenheim Collection, this restaurant is located in elegant wood-panelled premises where regional meat and vegetable specialities are served with flair. The stewed chicken with polenta and white truffles from Piedmont is especially recommended. Book ahead. Closed Tue; lunchtime Aug.

DORSODURO L'Avogaria

Calle dell'Avogaria 1629, 30123 **Tel** *041 296 04 91*   **Map** *5 C3*

This modern stylish restaurant close to the Zattere is run by a young, creative team. They specialize in food from Puglia, such as delectable stuffed calamari and tasty *tiedda*, a summer dish made with rice, mussels and potatoes. Wines are from all over Italy. Closed Tue; 1 week Jan, 2 weeks Jul–Aug.

DORSODURO Agli Alboretti

Rio Terrà Antonio Foscarini 884, 30123 **Tel** *041 523 00 58*   **Map** *6 E4*

Agli Alboretti is welcoming during the winter and refreshing in summer, when you can eat outside under the pergola. The cooking has innovative touches and the menu changes monthly to follow the seasons. Try one of their speciality *risotti*, such as beer and beetroot. Closed Wed & Thu lunch; 3 weeks Jan.

CANNAREGIO Brek

Lista di Spagna 124, 30121 **Tel** *041 244 01 58*   **Map** *2 D4*

This vibrant self-service restaurant close to the railway station serves freshly prepared food all day long. It is handy for a quick sandwich or pastry with a coffee or a longer sit-down meal, and the reasonable prices make it accessible to all pockets. Tasty pasta and meat dishes are prepared while you wait.

CANNAREGIO La Cantina

Strada Nuova 3689, 30121 **Tel** *041 522 82 58*   **Map** *2 F4*

This jovial wine bar opens on to the bustling thoroughfare Strada Nuova. Mouthwatering snacks and substantial dishes are prepared on the spot with fresh seafood, roast meats, cheeses and cold cuts to accompany the excellent range of wines. Closed Sun; 2 weeks Jan, last week Jul, first week Aug.

CANNAREGIO Pizzeria Al Faro

Ghetto Vecio 1181A, 30121 **Tel** *041 275 07 94*   **Map** *2 D3*

A pleasant neighbourhood pizzeria run by international staff who prepare crunchy pizzas heaped with delicious toppings. Pasta and meat dishes are also on the menu. Tables are set out under the shady trees in the square for most of the year. Closed Tue; 2 weeks Nov.

CANNAREGIO Trattoria da Gigio   €€
Rio Terrà San Leonardo 1594, 30121 **Tel** *041 71 75 74*   **Map** *2 D3*

During the week this busy *trattoria* is filled with stallholders from the nearby produce market, which adds to the lively atmosphere. On the menu you will find fresh seafood dishes and huge fillet steaks. The friendly service is another pleasant plus. Closed Sun, Mon lunch.

CANNAREGIO Osteria Da Rioba   €€€
Fondamenta della Misericordia 2553, 30121 **Tel** *041 524 43 79*   **Map** *2 F3*

This pleasant restaurant is set on a lively canalside in the Cannaregio neighbourhood. Specialities include *baccalà alla vicentina* (stewed cod) and tasty seafood risotto, along with a variety of meat dishes. The wine list is short but very well rounded. Closed Mon.

CANNAREGIO Osteria Giorgione   €€€
Calle Larga dei Proverbi 4582A, 30121 **Tel** *041 522 17 25*   **Map** *3 B4*

A cosy, sophisticated establishment with a good wine list. Giorgione serves seasonal fish specialities such as *carpaccio alle tonno*, while meat eaters will enjoy the *fegato alla veneziana* (Venetian-style liver with onions). Temptation comes in the form of scrumptious desserts, such as hot chocolate flan with ice cream. Closed Mon.

CANNAREGIO Fiaschetteria Toscana   €€€€€
Salizzada San Giovanni Grisostomo 5719, 30131 **Tel** *041 528 52 81*   **Map** *3 B5*

Along with a superb wine list, the Busatto family serve fresh seafood such as a delicious warm octopus salad, followed by turbot in caper sauce. Do book ahead – this is one of Venice's leading stylish restaurants. Closed Tue & Wed lunch; late Jul–Aug.

CANNAREGIO Vini Da Gigio   €€€€€
Fondamenta San Felice 3628A, 30121 **Tel** *041 528 51 40*   **Map** *3 A4*

Here you will find an elegant atmosphere and refined dishes based on seasonal produce. Risotto with prawns or grilled cuttlefish often feature on the menu, along with delicious duck and local artichokes. There is also a vast wine list to choose from. Advance booking is advisable. Closed Mon, Tue; mid-Jan–5 Feb, 2 weeks Aug.

THE LAGOON ISLANDS Food & Art   €
Campazzo di Dentro 554, Giudecca, 30133 **Tel** *041 241 14 13*

Something of a workers' canteen in the midst of the boatbuilding yards on the Giudecca, this place guarantees the cheapest meal in Venice. Diners help themselves to a good selection of salads and vegetables, and there's always a mountain of pasta with meat or tomato sauces. Open Mon–Fri lunch, 7–9pm Mon–Thu.

THE LAGOON ISLANDS Ai Cacciatori   €€
Mazzorbo 23, 30012 **Tel** *041 73 01 18*

A reasonably priced traditional *trattoria* on the island adjoining Burano, this establishment serves tasty dishes with fresh fish, such as *gnocchi* with crab. In the autumn months, duck and game also feature prominently on the menu. Only minutes from the ferry stop on Mazzorbo. Closed Mon; first week Jan–first week Feb.

THE LAGOON ISLANDS Da Romano   €€€
Via Galuppi 221, Burano, 30012 **Tel** *041 73 00 30*

It is advisable to book ahead to avoid disappointment since this is the leading restaurant on the island of Burano. A wide range of fish is served in traditional Venetian fashion, under the watchful eye of a descendant of the original 19th-century owner. Closed Sun dinner, Tue; mid-Dec–Jan.

THE LAGOON ISLANDS Trattoria Busa alla Torre Da Lele   €€€
Campo S. Stefano 3, Murano, 30141 **Tel** *041 73 96 62*   **Map** *4 E2*

Tables from this superb restaurant occupy a good part of the charming square, which is a marvellous setting. Come hungry as there's a lot to taste. Start with fragrant *granseola* (spider crab) and proceed with fish-stuffed ravioli and *fritto misto* (mixed fried seafood). Desserts include nougat delights and *tiramisu*. Open for lunch only.

THE LAGOON ISLANDS Ai Pescatori   €€€€€
Via Galuppi 371, Burano, 30012 **Tel** *041 73 06 50*

The menu at this welcoming establishment focuses on ancient Burano recipes, such as *broeddo* (fish soup), and fresh seafood such as crayfish or cuttlefish served in black sauce with *tagliolini* (ribbon pasta), and accompanied by tiny, tasty local artichokes. Winter diners can also enjoy game dishes. Extensive wine list. Closed Tue; 2 weeks Jan.

THE LAGOON ISLANDS Cipriani   €€€€€
Giudecca 10, 30122 **Tel** *041 520 77 44*

A courtesy launch ferries guests from the San Marco waterfront to this exclusive island hotel with two restaurants for a unique meal. The food and service at both the formal Fortuny and the more relaxed Cip are impeccable and the views stunning. Children under eight are not admitted and there is a strict dress code. Closed Nov–Mar.

THE LAGOON ISLANDS Harry's Dolci   €€€€€
Fondamenta San Biagio 773, Giudecca, 30133 **Tel** *041 522 48 44*   **Map** *5 C5*

A divine veranda on the Giudecca waterfront, far from the bustle of San Marco, gives diners a leisurely view of the craft plying the broad canal. Famous for its pastries and *gelati* (ice creams), this elegant restaurant also serves superb meals. Booking recommended. Closed Mon dinner, Tue; Nov–Apr.

Key to Price Guide *see p242* **Key to Symbols** *see back cover flap*

THE LAGOON ISLANDS Locanda Cipriani   🖼📧 ©©©©©
Piazza Santa Fosca 29, Torcello, 30012 **Tel** *041 73 01 50*

A fisherman's inn in the 1930s, this charming exclusive island restaurant has a lovely shady courtyard where guests can enjoy dishes made with fresh produce from the kitchen garden. The risotto and seafood *fritto misto* (fried fish platter) are both excellent. Closed Tue; 6 Jan–6 Feb.

THE VENETO PLAIN

ASOLO Villa Cipriani   🖼📧 ©©©©©
Via Canova 298, 31011 **Tel** *042 352 34 11*

Set in one of the grand hotels of the Veneto, this restaurant leads out on to the hotel gardens with breathtaking views of the verdant hills below. Local and seasonal ingredients are used in the creative cuisine, with dishes such as ricotta *gnocchi* with rosemary sauce.

BASSANO DEL GRAPPA Osteria Trinità   🚻🖼 ©
Via San Giorgio 17, 36061 **Tel** *042 450 37 00*

A traditional *osteria* serving Veneto dishes such as *pasta e fagioli* (a bean and pasta soup served tepid). *Baccalà* (cod) is served as an antipasto in the form of pâté and eaten with bread. Home-made desserts and a good selection of wine, including good local choices sold as *vino sfuso* (by the glass). Closed Sat lunch, Wed.

CAORLE Duilio   🚻🖼📧 ©©©
Via Strada Nuova 19, 30021 **Tel** *042 18 10 87*

A spacious restaurant with a nautically inspired decor, where fish-based regional cuisine is the house speciality. Do not miss the *broeto alla Duilio*, a wine-drenched mixed fish soup. Less boozy is the grilled sole, although it is just as delicious. Closed Mon in winter; early Jan–early Feb.

CASTELFRANCO Barbesin   🖼📧 ©©©
Via Circonvallazione Est 41, 31033 **Tel** *042 349 04 46*

A restaurant serving regional dishes, including risotto with asparagus or porcini mushrooms. However, it is the local radicchio that predominates. Other dishes include a generous mixed grill and *baccalà alla vicentina* (cod prepared according to a local recipe). Closed Wed dinner, Thu; 1–15 Jan, 3 weeks Aug.

CHIOGGIA El Gato   🚻🖼📧 ©©©
Campo Sant'Andrea 653, 30015 **Tel** *041 40 02 65*

Classic cooking based on seafood in an elegant setting. El Gato, one of the oldest restaurants in town, is located next to a 14th-century bell tower, and the outdoor tables look out on to Chioggia's main square. Inside there are three dining rooms. Closed Mon.

CONEGLIANO Al Salisa   🖼📧 ©©©
Via XX Settembre 24, 31015 **Tel** *043 82 42 88*

An elegant restaurant set in a medieval house with a pretty veranda for al fresco dining. The traditional menu includes snails and home-made pasta served with a range of vegetarian sauces. The *guanciale di vitello* (veal) and the exemplary wine list guarantee a feast. Closed Tue dinner, Wed.

DOLO Alla Posta   🚻🖼📧 ©©©©
Via Ca' Tron 33, 30031 **Tel** *041 41 07 40*

This outstanding fish restaurant, in an old Venetian posthouse overlooking the town's main canal, prepares regional specialities with fresh ingredients and well-blended flavours. On the menu you will find dishes such as lobster served with steamed vegetables. Closed Wed.

GRANCONA Isetta   🚻🖼📧 ©©©
Via Pederiva 96, 36040 **Tel** *044 488 99 92*

This pretty little restaurant, just 15 minutes' drive from Vicenza, serves regional food with the emphasis on grilled meats and good puddings, based on recipes handed down by the owner's grandmother, Isetta. Set in the Berici Hills, the restaurant also offers accommodation in ten rooms. Closed Tue dinner, Wed; 1 week Jan, 2 weeks Aug.

MIANE Da Gigetto   🖼📧 ©©©
Via De Gaspari 5, 31050 **Tel** *043 896 00 20*

Traditional Venetian cuisine served with flair awaits at this restaurant. The menu is seasonal, and in the autumn the pumpkin and mushroom dishes are particularly good. Game dishes such as hare and deer are also served in the winter. The wine cellar is enormous. Closed Mon dinner, Tue; 2 weeks Jan, 3 weeks Aug.

NOVENTA PADOVANA Boccadoro   🚻📧 ©©©
Via della Resistenza 49, 35027 **Tel** *049 62 50 29*

A family-run restaurant offering good Paduan food in surroundings that have an air of relaxed elegance. The *bigoli* pasta with goose sauce is well worth sampling, as is the guinea fowl with *radicchio au gratin*. The service is exemplary. Closed Tue dinner, Wed; 3 weeks Aug, 27 Dec–6 Jan.

ODERZO Dussin   ©©
Via Maggiore 60, Località Piavon, 31046 **Tel** *042 275 21 30*

Good-value traditional cuisine is served in Dussin. Fish is a speciality, with such dishes as seafood risotto and grilled tuna. However, the home-made desserts are something special. The setting is tranquil, the restaurant being situated just outside the town centre. Closed Mon dinner, Tue; 10 days Aug.

PADUA La Braseria   ©©
Via Tommaseo 48, 35121 **Tel** *049 876 09 07*

A friendly restaurant with good cooking. Typical Veneto dishes include penne with porcini and smoked bacon, but the chef (from Basilicata) also offers southern specialities. The *battuta siciliana* is a non-fried variation of the beef cutlet. The *crème brûlée* is also excellent. Closed Sat lunch, Sun; 1 week Aug.

PADUA Antico Brolo   ©©©
Corso Milano 22, 35100 **Tel** *049 66 45 55*

This quietly chic restaurant delivers appropriately elegant food, for example ravioli stuffed with courgette flowers. Veal's head cooked in vinegar and onion is the house's speciality. The menu includes a well-rounded wine list. Good for families and groups. Closed Mon lunch.

ROVIGO Trattoria Al Sole   ©
Via Bedendo Nino 6, 45100 **Tel** *042 52 29 17*

An old-fashioned *trattoria* serving unpretentious, traditional local cuisine. The tripe broth and the *baccalà alla vicentina* (salt cod) are two favourites. Home-made traditional cakes are served for pudding. The service is friendly and prompt. Closed Sun.

TREVISO Toni del Spin   ©©
Via Inferiore 7, 31100 **Tel** *042 254 38 29*

A homely restaurant serving regional fare. Though busy serving office workers at lunchtime, this *trattoria* slows down in the evenings, offering a more intimate experience. House specialities include pasta and *fagioli* (beans), the ubiquitous *risotto al radicchio*, tripe and *tiramisu*. Closed Sun & Mon lunch; last week Jul–15 Aug.

TREVISO Osteria all'Antica Torre   ©©©
Via Inferiore 55, 31100 **Tel** *042 258 36 94*

Here, outstanding wines accompany superb local cuisine. In season, radicchio is used in many ways, including in the making of the grappa. However, fish is the main contender on the menu, with imaginative dishes such as cuttlefish risotto. Art exhibitions are also held here. Closed Sun & Mon dinner; 3 weeks Aug.

VICENZA Taverna Aeolia   ©©©
Piazza Conte da Schio 1, Costozza di Longare, 36023 **Tel** *044 455 50 36*

This restaurant is housed in an elegant villa with a beautiful frescoed ceiling. The menu is especially strong in creative meat dishes, with kangaroo, bison and frog all available to choose from. Vegetarians can enjoy the lemon risotto, and a children's menu is also available. Closed Tue; 1–15 Jan.

VICENZA Rosso Aragosta   ©©©©
Piazzetta Porta Padova 65–67, 36100 **Tel** *044 450 61 23*

A stylish restaurant within the city walls serving nothing but fish. Dishes include a mixed plate of scampi and squid, or roast turbot on a bed of potatoes and olives. The mint and liquorice *semifreddo* (ice-cream dessert) will help you to digest the generous portions. Closed Sat lunch, Sun, Mon lunch; Aug.

VERONA AND LAKE GARDA

BREGANZE Al Toresan   ©©
Via Zabarella 1, 36042 **Tel** *044 587 32 60*

In the autumn the locals flock here for the delicious wild-mushroom dishes. Mushrooms come in every shape and form: stuffed, as filling for ravioli, and grilled. The cooking is hearty and complemented by the local wines, of which the reds are particularly good. Closed Thu; 3 weeks Aug.

LAKE GARDA Antica Locanda Mincio   ©©©
Via Michelangelo Buonarroti 12, Valeggio sul Mincio, 37067 **Tel** *045 795 00 59*

Once a staging post, this is now a delightful restaurant, with frescoed walls and open fireplaces serving good regional food. The shaded seating outside overlooks the river. Specialities include trout and eels caught in the nearby Lake Garda. Closed Wed, Thu; 2 weeks Feb, 2 weeks Nov.

LAKE GARDA Locanda San Vigilio   ©©©©
Localita San Vigilio, Garda, 37016 **Tel** *045 725 66 88*

This excellent restaurant overlooking Lake Garda has been welcoming guests with a good selection of wines and food for five centuries. Nowadays, it has an astounding range of freshwater fish and seafood dishes. The spacious garden has shady olive trees. Closed mid-Nov–Mar, though the restaurant occasionally opens during this period.

Key to Price Guide *see p242* **Key to Symbols** *see back cover flap*

MONTECCHIO DI CROSARA Alpone €€€

Via Pergola 17, 37030 **Tel** *045 617 53 87*

A refined restaurant offering a seasonal-inspired menu. In the spring, try dishes based on mushrooms or cherries. Also on offer is an *à la carte* menu with *gnocchi, crespelle* (pancakes) and grilled vegetables. End your meal with a plate of local cheeses served with a variety of chutneys and jams. Closed Sun dinner, Tue; 2 weeks Jan, 2 weeks Aug.

MONTECCHIO DI CROSARA Grazioso €€€

Via Cabalao 12, 37030 **Tel** *045 745 02 22*

Black-truffle risotto is a good choice in this restaurant situated in the heart of the Soave wine-producing region. Other dishes worth trying in this friendly, informal setting include stuffed duck thigh in an Amarone wine sauce or tagliatelle with quail sauce. Closed Sun dinner, Mon; 3 weeks Jan, 3 weeks Aug.

VERONA Ristorante Greppia €€

Vicolo Samaritana 3, 37121 **Tel** *045 800 45 77*

Run by the Guizzardi family since 1975, this restaurant, named after the local word for a feeding trough, offers superb food. As well as delicious, freshly made pasta, there is a memorable *bollito misto* (boiled-meats platter): diners choose their meat from a trolley. Booking recommended. Closed Mon; 2 weeks Jun.

VERONA Al Bersagliere €€€

Via Dietro Pallone 1, 37121 **Tel** *045 800 48 24*

Traditional Veronese food served in a friendly atmosphere is available at the centrally located Al Bersagliere. A superb wine cellar hosts wine-tasting evenings, while the garden offers respite for those dining with children. Dishes include *pastisada* (meat stew) and *bigoli con l'anatra* (pasta with duck). Closed Sun; 2 weeks Jan, 10 days mid-Aug.

VERONA Arche €€€€

Via Arche Scaligere 6, 37121 **Tel** *045 800 74 15*

This long-established fish restaurant opened for business in 1879. It is perfectly situated next to Romeo's house, a location that only adds to its charm. On the menu: smoked oysters with horseradish and caviar, and marinated rock lobster. Closed Sun, Mon lunch; 2 weeks Jan.

VERONA Il Desco €€€€€

Via Dietro San Sebastiano 5–7, 37121 **Tel** *045 59 53 58*

One of Italy's finest restaurants, set in a 16th-century *palazzo*, Il Desco truly deserves its two Michelin stars. Dishes include pumpkin and Amarone wine risotto and the famous aubergine ravioli. The gourmet menu offers a staggering seven courses. Closed Sun, Mon (except dinner Jul, Aug, Dec); 2 weeks Jun, 2 weeks Christmas.

THE DOLOMITES

BELLUNO Ristorante Taverna €€

Via Cipro 7, 32100 **Tel** *043 72 51 92*

Centrally placed and popular with the locals, the Taverna specialises in grilled meat, game and traditional dishes. Try *schiz*, a type of fresh cheese that has been oven-baked, and *pastin*, a tasty blend of minced meats flavoured with juniper berries. Closed Sun.

BELLUNO Terracotta €€

Via Garibaldi 61, 32100 **Tel** *043 794 26 44*

Regional specialities in this friendly restaurant include pork wrapped in Parma ham with a grain mustard sauce. The menu changes each month. Views from the restaurant are limited, but there is a pretty wisteria-covered pergola. An extensive wine list suits all budgets. Closed Tue; Aug.

CORTINA D'AMPEZZO Ristorante Pizzeria Croda Cafè €€

Corso Italia 163, 32043 **Tel** *043 686 65 89*

In the traffic-free centre of Cortina d'Ampezzo, this conveniently placed establishment serves up affordable meals. These range from traditional dishes such as *polenta con funghi* to good pizzas. When it's time for dessert, *frutti di bosco* (summer berries) is a good bet, accompanied by a scoop of ice cream. Closed Tue.

CORTINA D'AMPEZZO Baita Fraina €€€

Località Fraina 1, 32043 **Tel** *043 636 34*

This lovely wood-panelled mountain restaurant features a terrace with panoramic views and a large play area for children. The pasta dishes are good, as are the game dishes, which include *tagliata di cervo* (venison). There is an excellent wine list and a choice of over 100 types of grappa. Closed Mon low season; May–Jun, Oct–Nov.

PASSO FALZAREGO Rifugio Col Gallina €€

Passo Falzarego 2, 32043 **Tel** *043 629 39*

A cosy chalet with lodgings high above Cortina d'Ampezzo and snowbound in winter, this *rifugio* serves hearty alpine fare in a wonderful Dolomite setting. Try the delicious polenta with melted cheese or the home-made *casunziei* (ravioli stuffed with beetroot and covered with poppy seeds). Closed mid-Apr–mid-Jun, mid-Sep–mid-Dec.

Bars and Cafés in Venice

Many bars in Venice draw their trade from tourists and are busy throughout the day, as visitors ease their aching feet and consult their guide-books. Custom is swelled mid-morning and around lunchtime as the Venetians drop in for a drink or snack. Cafés range from basic one-room bars patronized by local workmen, to opulent coffee houses in old-world style, such as **Caffè Quadri** and **Caffè Florian**. Even the humblest establishment provides a continuous range of refreshments and you can enjoy anything from a morning coffee or lunchtime beer, to an aperitif or a final brandy before bed. Bars also serve snacks throughout their opening hours: freshly baked morning pastries and lunchtime sandwiches, rolls, cakes, biscuits and sometimes home-made ice cream. Wine bars often have a wide range of traditional Venetian snacks, and so make good places to stop for lunch.

BARS

Italians will often stop for breakfast in a bar on their way to work. This normally consists of a *cappuccino* (milky coffee) and a *brioche* (a plain, jam- or cream-filled pastry). **Pasticceria Dal Mas**, on the main route from the station to the Rialto, is much favoured by early morning commuters.

A wide range of alcoholic drinks is on offer, and you can ask for a glass of wine or beer on tap. Beer from the keg is called *birra alla spina* and comes in three different sizes: *piccola, media* and *grande*. Italian and imported bottled beers are also available, though the latter can be expensive. All bars serve glasses of mineral water and it is acceptable to request a glass of tap water (*acqua del rubinetto*), which will be free. Most bars also serve delicious freshly squeezed fruit juices (*una spremuta*) and milkshakes made with fruit (*un frullato*). Italian bottled juices are good and are available in unusual flavours such as apricot and pear.

All bars serve a range of sandwiches (*tramezzini*) and filled rolls (*panini*), and often have toasted sandwiches and pizzas as well. Some double as cake-shops (*pasticceria*), and these have a tempting range of calorie-filled delights on display to eat in or take away. If you are near the Accademia, seek out the tiny **Pasticceria Vio** for wonderful cakes, or for an expensive treat, go to **Harry's Dolci** on the Giudecca (*see p246*).

Bear in mind that sitting down to drink in a bar or café can cost a lot more than standing at the bar, as there is a table charge, which can be high. This rises proportionally as you draw nearer San Marco. Some bars, particularly in the less tourist-frequented areas, have a stand-up counter only. All have a lavatory (*il bagno* or *il gabinetto*), though you may have to ask at the desk for the key. It is also worth noting that bars and cafés tend to shut earlier here than in other parts of Italy, particularly in winter.

The normal procedure is to choose what you want to eat or drink, then ask for it and pay at the cashdesk. You will be given a receipt (*lo scontrino*) which you present at the bar. If they are busy, a small tip will usually speed things up. If you decide to sit down, either inside or at an outside table, your order will be taken by a waiter who will bring the bill when he delivers the drinks. You should expect to pay double or more for this, but you can stretch your drink out for as long as you like.

WINE BARS

There is an old tradition in Venice called *cichetti e l'ombra*, meaning "a little bite and the shade". The little bite ranges from a slice of bread and *prosciutto crudo* (raw cured ham), meatballs or fried vegetables, to sardines and *baccalà* (salt cod). The shade is a glass of wine, so called because the gondoliers used to snatch a glass in the shade away from the glare of the sun on the water. Wine bars serving these snacks and a range of wines are numerous and heavily populated by locals. Many, such as **Do Mori**, are in the crowded alleys off the Rialto, but one of the nicest is the **Cantina del Vino già Schiavi** near the Ponte San Trovaso.

CAFES AND ICE CREAM PARLOURS

Coffee houses have played their part in the history of the Veneto – notably Padua's Caffè Pedrocchi (*see p178*) – and a visit to Venice would not be complete without a drink at the historic **Caffè Florian** or **Caffè Quadri**. It is a hard decision whether to take a table outside and watch the crowds or to experience the elegant charm of the interior rooms, with their atmosphere of past eras. The prices are sky-high, but you can take your time and be entertained by the resident orchestras.

Harry's Bar (*see p92*), is another world-famous bar and café. In summer it is crammed with foreigners and the prices are always high, but for a treat, sip a Bellini, a mixture of Prosecco and fresh white peach juice, in the place where it was invented.

The cafés along the Zattere, with their lovely views across the Giudecca Canal, make good places to pause, and the prices are much lower. Many Venetian squares have cafés with tables outside. There are several in the Campo Santo Stefano, or try **Bar Colleoni** in Campo Santi Giovanni e Paolo (San Zanipolo). **Il Caffè** is the nicest in Campo Santa Margherita.

Venetian ice cream is definitely among the best in Italy, with ice cream shops (*gelaterie*) serving a wide selection of seasonal flavours, some unique to Venice. The Venetians eat ice cream all year round, often instead of pudding or as the finale to the evening stroll, or *passeggiata*. It comes as either a cone *(un cono)* or a cup *(una coppa)* and it is normal to have at least three flavours. **Paolin** on Campo Santo Stefano is one of the best ice cream shops. You could also try **Il Doge**, which is in Campo Santa Margherita, and **Nico** on the Zattere, where you will find *gianduiotto*, a rich chocolate-based Venetian speciality. Make certain you buy ice cream made on the premises, *artigianato* or *produzione propria*, and experiment with what is clearly seasonal; the high-summer fruit ices such as melon, peach and apricot are delightfully refreshing.

DIRECTORY

SAN MARCO

Bar Gelateria Paolin
Campo Santo Stefano,
San Marco 2962A.
Map 6 F3.

Caffè Florian
Piazza San Marco,
San Marco 56/59.
Map 7 B2.

Caffè Quadri
Piazza San Marco,
San Marco 120–24.
Map 7 B2.

Harry's Bar
Calle Vallaresso,
San Marco 1323.
Map 7 B3.

Hostaria ai Rusteghi
Campiello del Tentor,
San Marco 5513.
Map 7 B1.

Osteria Terrà Assassini
Rio Terrà degli Assassini,
San Marco 3695.
Map 7 A2.

Rosa Salva
Calle Fiubera, San Marco
951. **Map** 7 B1.

Vino Vino
Ponte delle Veste,
San Marco 2007.
Map 7 A3.

SAN POLO AND SANTA CROCE

Al Prosecco
C. San Giacomo dell'Orio,
S. Croce 1503. **Map** 2 E5.

Bar Dogale
Campo dei Frari, San Polo
3012. **Map** 6 E1.

Do Mori
Calle Do Mori,
San Polo 429.
Map 3 A5.

CASTELLO

Bar Colleoni
Campo Santi Giovanni
e Paolo, Castello 6811.
Map 3 C5.

Bar Gelateria Riviera
Ponte de la Pietà,
Riva degli Schiavoni 4153.
Map 8 D2.

Bar Mio
Via Garibaldi,
Castello 1820.
Map 8 F3.
Bar Orologio
Campo Santa Maria
Formosa, Castello 6130.
Map 7 C1.

Caffè al Cavallo
Campo Santi Giovanni
e Paolo, Castello 6823.
Map 3 C5.

La Boutique del Gelato
Campo San Lio,
Castello 5727.
Map 7 B1.

Snack & Sweet
Salizzada San Lio,
Castello 5689.
Map 7 B1.

DORSODURO

Accademia Foscarini
Rio Terra A Foscarini,
Dorsoduro 878/C. 0
Map 6 E4.

Ai do Draghi
Calle della Chiesa,
Dorsoduro 3665.
Map 6 F4.

Al Chioschetto Zattere
Dorsoduro 1406A.
Map 6 D4.

Bar Gelateria Causin
Campo Santa Margherita,
Dorsoduro 2995.
Map 6 D2.

Bar Gelateria Il Doge
Campo Santa Margherita,
Dorsoduro 3058A.
Map 6 D2.

Bar Gelateria Nico
Zattere ai Gesuati,
Dorsoduro 922.
Map 6 D4.

Bar Pasticceria Vio
Rio Terrà della Toletta,
Dorsoduro 1192.
Map 6 D3.

Cantina del Vino già Schiavi
Ponte San Trovaso,
Dorsoduro 992.
Map 6 E4.

Il Caffè
Campo Santa Margherita,
Dorsoduro 2963.
Map 6 D3.

Soto Sopra
Calle San Pantalon,
Dorsoduro 3740.
Map 6 D2.

CANNAREGIO

Alla Bomba
Calle dell'Oca,
Cannaregio 4297.
Map 3 A5.

Bar Algiubagio
Fondamente Nuove,
Cannaregio 5039.
Map 3 C4.

Bar Gelateria Solda
Campo Santi Apostoli,
Cannaregio 4440.
Map 3 B5.

Caffè Pasqualigo
Salizzada Santa Fosca,
Cannaregio 2288.
Map 2 F4.

Enoteca Boldrin
San Canciano,
Cannaregio 5550.
Map 3 B5.

Il Gelatone
Rio Terrà Maddalena,
Cannaregio 2063.
Map 2 F3.

Osteria da Alberto
Calle Larga
Giacinto Gallina,
Cannaregio 5401.
Map 3 C5.

Pasticceria Dal Mas
Lista di Spagna,
Cannaregio 150/A.
Map 2 D4.

THE LAGOON ISLANDS

Bar della Maddalena
Mazzorbo.

Bar Ice
Campo San Donato,
Murano.
Map 4 F2.

Bar La Palanca
Fondamenta Santa
Eufemia, Giudecca 448.
Map 6 D5.

Bar Palmisano
Via Baldassare Galuppi,
Burano.

Bar Trono di Attila
Torcello.

Harry's Dolci
Fondamenta San Biagio,
Giudecca 773.
Map 6 D5.

Lo Spuntino
Via Baldassare
Galuppi, Burano.

SHOPS AND MARKETS

The narrow streets of Venice are lined with beautifully arranged windows that cannot fail to tempt shoppers, and the city has the additional bonus of being truly pedestrianized. Few cities of similar size have such a wide variety of goods to browse through as you explore the fascinating and diverse neighbourhoods. There is still a strong

Piece of traditional Murano glass

artisan tradition in Venice, and alongside glass and lace you will find high-quality fashion and leather goods, antiques and jewellery. In the Veneto, which is one of Italy's most prosperous regions, every town boasts a wide range of shops, and many have seasonal speciality markets. In country areas you can buy wine and olive oil direct from the producers.

Display of jewellery in a shop window in the Frezzeria

WHEN TO SHOP

Generally, shops open around 9 or 9:30am and close for lunch at 12:30 or 1pm, with the exception of food shops and markets, which are in business from 8am. In the afternoon stores are open from 3:30pm to 7:30pm in winter, and 4pm to 8pm in summer. In Venice, many stores aimed directly at tourists are open all day and even on Sundays, as are big out-of-town supermarkets and hypermarkets – useful if you are self-catering in the region.

Monday is usually the traditional closing day in northern Italy though, again, this does not apply to all shops in Venice itself. The smaller towns in the Veneto often have very variable opening hours, with perhaps food shops closing on Mondays but ironmongers and clothes shops closing on Wednesdays. Shops and markets in the Veneto are

often closed for two or three weeks during the national holiday time in August.

The best time for finding bargains is during the January and July sales: look out for window signs with the words *saldi* or *sconti*.

WHERE TO SHOP IN VENICE

The glittering Mercerie (see p95), which runs from Piazza San Marco to the Rialto, has been the main shopping street since the Middle Ages and, together with the parallel Calle dei Fabbri, is still a honey pot for the crowds. West of San Marco, the zigzagging Frezzeria is full of interesting and unusual shops. The main route from the Piazza to the Accademia Bridge is lined with up-market speciality stores, while the streets north of Campo Santo Stefano (see p93) are another excellent trawling ground for quality souvenirs and gifts.

Across the Grand Canal, the narrow streets from the Rialto southwest towards Campo San Polo (see p101) are lined with a wide variety of less

A colourful display of T-shirts with the "Venezia" logo

expensive stores, while near the station the bustling Lista di Spagna and the route along the Strada Nova towards the Rialto cater for the everyday needs of ordinary Venetians.

The islands of Murano and Burano (see pp150–51) are *the* places to buy traditional glass and lace.

HOW TO PAY

Major credit cards are usually accepted in the main stores for larger purchases, but cash is preferred for small items, and smaller shops will want cash. Travellers' cheques are also accepted, though the rate that you will get is less favourable than at a bank.

By law, shopkeepers should give you a receipt (*ricevuta fiscale*), which you should keep until you are some distance away from the store (legally this is 600 m). If a purchased item is defective, most shops will change the article or give you a credit note, as long as you show the till receipt. Cash refunds are not usually given.

VAT EXEMPTION

Visitors from non-European Union countries can reclaim the 19 per cent sales tax (IVA) on goods exceeding €160 from the same shop. Ask for an invoice when you buy the goods and inform the shop that you intend to reclaim the tax. The invoice must be stamped at customs as you leave Italy. The shop will reimburse the tax in euros once they have received the stamped invoice.

Designer clothes shop in Treviso

FASHION AND ACCESSORIES

In Venice, the big names in fashion are all found near San Marco. **Armani, Gucci, Missoni and Roberto Cavalli** all have stylish shops just off the Piazza. For really innovative and outrageous designs visit **Fiorella** in Campo Santo Stefano. The stalls at the foot of the Ponte delle Guglie on Strada Nuova sell a range of good value leather shoes and a wide variety of traditional Venetian slippers in a stunning range of colourful velours. For a genuine gondolier's shirt, take a look in **Emilio Ceccato**.

FABRICS AND INTERIOR DESIGN

Venice has long been famed for sumptuous brocades, fine silks and figured velvets. **Trois** sells silks by the metre, including the gossamer-fine pleated silks invented by Fortuny for his Delphos dresses *(see p94)*, and **Il Canapè** has wonderful designer silks and other fabrics in its shop near Campo San Pantalon. The famous house of **Rubelli** has its headquarters at Palazzo Corner Spinelli near Campo Sant'Angelo. Here you will find a variety of rich brocades and velvets. **Color Casa**, in San Polo, has equally lovely textiles at slightly lower prices. **Luigi Bevilacqua**, at Ponte della Canonica, sells beautiful brocades, velvets, damasks and other luxury fabrics, all woven on 17th-century hand-operated looms.

MASKS AND COSTUMES

You can buy cheap, mass-produced masks all over the city, but a genuine one is a good souvenir, and you will be spoilt for choice. **Papier Maché** in Castello specializes in traditional mask-making and their designs are absolutely stunning. Near Campo San Polo **Tragicomica** sells costumes and masks, as well as Commedia dell'Arte figures. You will find these at **Leon d'Oro** on the Frezzeria too, where they also make string puppets. Dorsoduro has several workshops; **Mondonovo**, just off Campo Santa Margherita, has a marvellous selection of masks and costumes. In the weeks leading up to Carnival, maskmakers are, of course,

A typical Venetian mask

extremely busy, but at other times of the year many workshops welcome visitors and are pleased to show you their craft *(see p31)*.

GLASS

The best place to buy glass is on the island of Murano, where it has been made since the 13th century *(see p151)*. All the main manufacturers have their furnaces and showrooms here, catering to mainstream taste. Some manufacturers also have showrooms in Venice itself.

On Murano, **Seguso** and **Barovier e Toso** make glass to traditional designs with good simple lines. Another option is **Totem-il Canale**, which has an excellent selection of both traditional and contemporary designs. **Venini** has shops near San Marco; it represents the top end of the market and some of its designs are very pleasing. For other important glass designware, go to **Ma.Re** in Frezzeria.

JEWELLERY

Venice's smartest jewellers are **Missiaglia** and **Nardi**, both in the arcades of Piazza San Marco. Shops on the Rialto Bridge sell cheaper designs, and this is a good place to find bracelets and chains, whose price is determined by the weight of the gold. For inexpensive, pretty Venetian glass earrings, necklaces and bracelets try **FGB** in Campo Santa Maria Zobenigo.

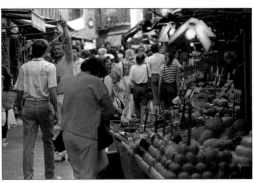
Wide range of fruit and vegetables for sale in the Rialto market

A typical general food store in the San Marco area

DEPARTMENT STORES

Department stores are not as common in Italy as in many other countries. The main chain store in Venice is Coin, which sells everything from umbrellas to tableware. Oviesse and Upim are cheaper supermarket-style options. You will find branches of these in other towns in the Veneto.

Treasure trove in one of the art shops on Murano

BOOKS AND GIFTS

The best general bookshop in Venice is **Goldoni**, which also sells maps. **Filippi Editori Venezia** stocks fac-simile editions of old books and books about Venice. **Fantoni** is a specialist art

bookshop, and English books are sold at **Cafoscarina 3**, **Libreria Marco Polo** and **Libreria Emiliana**.

Handmade marbled and dragged paper are typically Venetian, and used as book covers and made up into writing desk equipment. **Paolo Olbi** has a wide range of papers, while **Alberto Valese-Ebru** uses a distinctive marbling technique on fabrics as well as paper. For watercolour views of Venice, try the stalls in Campo dei Santi Apostoli.

The San Barnaba area has several art and craft shops where you can buy unusual gifts and souvenirs. **Signor Blum** on the Campo San Barnaba has charming carved and painted wooden objects and toys. Another carver, **Livio de Marchi**, makes large whimsical wooden ornaments. **Gilberto Penzo** offers boat models – you can even buy a kit to make your own. **L'Arte di Alesia** sells interesting papier mâché objects and masks. For unusual trinkets and ornaments, browse in **Officina Veneziana**.

MARKETS AND FOOD SHOPS

One of the delights of Venice is a morning spent exploring the food markets and shops around the Rialto. Fruit and vegetable stalls

sprawl to the west of the bridge and the Pescheria, or fish market, lies right beside the Grand Canal (see p100). The neighbouring streets are full of unusual and excellent food shops. Olive oil, vinegar and dried pasta, which comes in many colours, shapes and flavours, are all good choices if you are looking for food to take home. **Aliani (Casa del Parmigiano)** is a superlative cheese shop right by the vegetable market, where you can also buy a selection of fresh pasta, salamis and ready-made dishes for a picnic.

On Ruga Rialto, the **Drogheria Mascari** has a fine range of coffees, teas, dried fruits and nuts. **Pasticceria Tonolo** is one of Venice's best pasticcerie, selling traditional sweetmeats, as well as cakes and biscuits.

Viale Santa Maria Elisabetta, the main shopping street of the Lido

DIRECTORY

FASHION AND ACCESSORIES

Armani
Calle Goldoni, San Marco 4412. **Map** 7 A2.
Tel 041 523 47 58.

Emilio Ceccato
Sottoportico di Rialto, San Polo 16/17.
Map 7 A1.
Tel 041 522 27 00.

Fiorella Gallery
Campo Santo Stefano, San Marco 2806.
Map 6 F3.
Tel 041 520 92 28.

Gucci
Calle Larga XXII Marzo, San Marco 2102.
Map 7 A3.
Tel 041 277 73 01.

Missoni
Calle Vallaresso, San Marco 1312. **Map** 7 B3.
Tel 041 520 57 33.

Roberto Cavalli
Calle Vallaresso, San Marco 1314. **Map** 7 B3.
Tel 041 520 57 33.

Stalls at the foot of Ponte delle Guglie
Strada Nuova, Cannaregio. **Map** 2 D3.

FABRICS AND INTERIOR DESIGN

Annelie
Calle Lunga San Barnaba, Dorsoduro 2748.
Map 6 D3.
Tel 041 520 32 77.

Color Casa
Calle della Madonneta, San Polo 1990.
Map 6 F1.
Tel 041 523 60 71.

Il Canapè
Calle San Pantalon, Dorsoduro 3736.
Map 6 D2.
Tel 041 714 264.

Luigi Bevilacqua
Ponte della Canonica, San Marco 337B.
Map 7 C2.
Tel 041 528 75 81.

Rubelli
Campiello del Teatro, San Marco 3877.
Map 7 B2.
Tel 041 523 61 10.

Trois
Campo San Maurizio, San Marco 2666.
Map 6 F3.
Tel 041 522 29 05.

MASKS AND COSTUMES

Atelier Pietro Longhi
Rio Terrà Frari, San Polo 26046.
Map 6 E1.
Tel 041 714 478.

Leon d'Oro
Frezzeria, San Marco 1770. **Map** 7 A2.
Tel 041 520 33 75.

Mondonovo
Rio Terrà Canal, Dorsoduro 3063.
Map 6 D3.
Tel 041 528 73 44.

Papier Maché
Calle Lunga Santa Maria Formosa, Castello 5175.
Map 7 C1.
Tel 041 522 99 95.

Tragicomica
Calle dei Nomboli, San Polo 2800.
Map 6 F1.
Tel 041 72 11 02.

GLASS

Barovier e Toso
Fondamenta Vetrai 28, Murano. **Map** 4 E3.
Tel 041 73 90 49.

Ma.Re
Frezzeria, San Marco 1586–8. **Map** 7 B3.
Tel 041 241 26 87.

Seguso
Fondamenta Vetrai 143, Murano.
Map 4 E2.
Tel 041 73 94 23.

Totem-il Canale
Campo Carità, Dorsoduro 8786.
Map 6 E3.
Tel 041 522 36 41.

Venini
Piazzetta dei Leoncini, San Marco 314. **Map** 7 B2.
Tel 041 522 40 45.

JEWELLERY

FGB
Campo Santa Maria Zobenigo, San Marco 2514. **Map** 7 C1.
Tel 041 523 65 56.

Missiaglia
Procuratie Vecchie, San Marco 125. **Map** 7 B2.
Tel 041 522 44 64.

Nardi
Procuratie Nuove, Piazza San Marco, San Marco 69/71. **Map** 7 B2.
Tel 041 522 57 33.

BOOKS AND GIFTS

Alberto Valese-Ebru
Campiello Santo Stefano, San Marco 3471. **Map** 6 F3. *Tel 041 523 88 30.*

Cafoscarina 3
Calle Foscari, Dorsoduro 3259. **Map** 6 D2.
Tel 041 522 18 65.

Cartoleria Accademia
Rio Terrà Carità, Dorsoduro 1044. **Map** 6 E3.
Tel 041 520 70 86.

Cartoleria Testolini
Calle dei Fabbri, San Marco 4745. **Map** 7 A1.
Tel 041 522 30 85.

Daniela Porto
Rio Terrà dei Nomboli, San Polo 2753. **Map** 6 E1.
Tel 041 523 13 68.

Fantoni
Salizzada San Luca, San Marco 4119. **Map** 7 A2. *Tel 041 522 07 00.*

Filippi Editori Venezia
Calle Casselleria, Castello 5284.
Map 7 C1.
Tel 041 523 69 16.

Gilberto Penzo
Calle dei Saoneri, San Polo 2681. **Map** 6 E1.
Tel 041 524 61 39.

Goldoni
Calle dei Fabbri, San Marco 4742. **Map** 7 A1.
Tel 041 522 23 84.

L'Arte di Alesia
Ponte San Barnaba, Dorsoduro 2806.
Map 6 D3.
Tel 041 523 08 25.

Libreria Emiliana
Calle Goldoni, San Marco 4487. **Map** 7 A2.
Tel 041 522 07 93.

Libreria Marco Polo
Salizzada San Lio, Castello 5469. **Map** 7 B1.
Tel 041 522 63 43.

Libreria della Toletta
Sacca della Toletta, Dorsoduro 1214. **Map** 6 D3. *Tel 041 523 20 34.*

Livio de Marchi
Salizzada San Samuele, San Marco 3157/A. **Map** 6 E2. *Tel 041 528 56 94.*

Officina Veneziana
Calle San Pantalon, Dorsoduro 3752/A. **Map** 6 D2. *Tel 041 720 313.*

Paolo Olbi
Calle della Mandola, San Marco 3653. **Map** 6 F2.
Tel 041 528 50 25.

Signor Blum
Campo San Barnaba, Dorsoduro 2840.
Map 6 D3.
Tel 041 522 63 67.

FOOD SHOPS

Aliani (Casa del Parmigiano)
Erberia Rialto, San Polo 214/5. **Map** 3 A5.
Tel 041 520 65 25.

Drogheria Mascari
Ruga Rialto, Calle dei Spezieri San Polo 381. **Map** 3 A5. *Tel 041 522 97 62.*

Pasticceria Tonolo
Calle San Pantalon, Dorsoduro 3764.
Map 6 D2.
Tel 041 523 72 09.

What to Buy in the Veneto

Glass is the most popular Venetian souvenir, but there are many other possibilities, ranging from Carnival masks and ceramics to fabrics and lace. For food lovers there is a wide selection of local olive oils, honey, wines and preserves. In the Veneto many food producers sell direct to the public, while different craft and food specialities are found in individual towns and islands.

Modern vase of opaque glass

Traditional glass with gold overlay

Two-coloured goblet

Venetian Glass

In traditional rich colours of blue and claret, or in striking modern designs, you will find anything from scent bottles to chandeliers.

Gift box covered in marbled paper

Address book

Venetian Marbled Paper

Marbled paper is a Venetian speciality. The sheets of paper are dipped into liquid gum before adding the paint. You can buy a large range of stationery items covered in the paper, as well as paper by the individual sheet. Each sheet of marbled paper is unique.

Pretty trinket box

Sheets of marbled paper

Delicate lace collar from Burano

Crafts from the Veneto

The ancient patterns of Burano lace are used to great advantage on table linen and to trim exquisite lingerie. Handpainted vases, plates and bowls are produced in the picturesque old town of Bassano del Grappa.

Decorated ceramic vase from Bassano

Silver spoon with Venetian lion finial

Masks *(see pp30–31)*
Mask designs range from Commedia dell'Arte motifs to modern abstracts from young designers, and many are intricate and colourful. They are available all year, but at Carnival time you can buy them from street stalls.

Carnival mask

Red and gold mask

Clothing
As everywhere in Italy, stylish designer shops abound. Clothes for children are particularly bright and inventive. Velvet slippers, which are made in rich jewel-like colours, are worn at home as well as to dress up in at Carnival time.

Velvet slippers

Colourful child's sweater

Pasta
Attractively packaged dried pasta comes in many colours, shapes and flavours. Tomato, herb and spinach are the most popular varieties, but beetroot, garlic, artichoke, salmon, squid, and even chocolate can also be found in many shops.

Artichoke   **Beetroot**   **Squid**   **Pasta shapes**

Amaretto biscuits

Balsamic vinegar and extra virgin olive oil

Panettone

Delicacies from the Veneto
Panettone is the light yeast cake, flavoured with vanilla and studded with currants and candied peel, that is traditionally eaten at Christmas. Other local delicacies include olive oil from the shores of Lake Garda, vinegars, mountain honey from Belluno, fruit-flavoured liqueurs, grappa from Bassano (see p166), and after-dinner Amaretto biscuits.

Orange liqueur   **Lime liqueur**   **Pear liqueur**

ENTERTAINMENT IN THE VENETO

Venice was once one of Europe's liveliest night-time cities, and today it still has an impressive range of special events throughout the year. At every season there are some splendid festivals unique to Venice, and in late summer the normal city diet of opera, theatre and concerts is

Poster advertising the Film Festival

augmented by the International Film Festival and the Biennale, which rank among the best world-class cultural events. The day-to-day evening entertainment in Venice itself now tends to be far less frenetic than in the heyday of the Republic *(see pp46–7)*, but there

are a few clubs and discos, and many more across the causeway in Mestre. Or you could have a little flutter at the casino.

Whatever you choose, your enjoyment will be enhanced by the idyllic backdrop of Venice itself. The ultimate and quintessential Venetian romantic experience is, of course, a gondola ride by moonlight *(see p284)*. However, an evening's entertainment could more usually comprise the traditional stroll, or *passeggiata*, followed by a drink at a bar or café in one of the squares or amid the floodlit splendours of the Piazza San Marco.

PRACTICAL INFORMATION

Information about what's on in Venice can be found in *Leo Bussola*, a free bilingual Italian and English booklet published quarterly by the Tourist Board. *2Night* is a free fortnightly publication with listings of concerts and events. Another publication, *Un Ospite di Venezia* (A Guest in Venice), comes out fortnightly during the summer and monthly in the winter, and is available from most hotels. The Venetian newspaper *Il Gazzettino* also lists cinema performances, rock concerts and discos under *Spettacoli*. Posters advertising forthcoming cultural events are displayed all over town.

For details of events and festivities in the other towns and cities in the Veneto, ask at the local tourist offices. Regional newspapers also often have listings of what is on in their area.

Music and coffee at Caffè Florian, Piazza San Marco *(see p251)*

BOOKING TICKETS

Booking in advance is not part of the Italian lifestyle, where decisions are made on the spur of the moment. If you want to be certain of a seat you will have to visit the box office in person, as they usually do not take bookings over the telephone. You may

also have to pay an advance booking supplement, or *prevendita*, which is usually about 10 per cent of the price of the seat.

The price of a theatre ticket starts at about €16, though prices are likely to be five times as much for star-name performances. Tickets for popular music concerts are normally sold through record and music shops whose names are displayed on the publicity posters.

Whereas tickets for classical concerts are sold on the spot for that day's performance, opera tickets are booked months ahead. There are very few ticket touts, so it is almost impossible to obtain tickets when the box office has sold out. The **Goldoni** box office is open 10am–1pm and 3–7pm.

La Fenice opera house before the 1996 fire *(see p93)*

CINEMA AND THE FILM FESTIVAL

There are four cinemas in Venice, mainly showing dubbed versions of international films. These are known as *prima visione* (first run). The **Giorgione Movie d'Essai** shows "art-house" films as well as the usual commercial fare. You will find these listed in *Il Gazzettino*.

The annual Film Festival, which takes place in August and September, is one of the major world cinema showcases and has been running since 1932. Screenings are held in the **Palazzo del Cinema** on the Lido, the Giorgione and the **Arena di Campo San Polo**, an open-air cinema. Tickets are sold to the public direct from the cinema on the day of performance. Programmes can be obtained in advance from the tourist office, and you will see posters for the festival displayed all over the city.

Outdoor entertainment in the courtyard of the Doge's Palace

Gondolier serenading on the Grand Canal

MUSIC AND THEATRE

Like many Italian cities, Venice makes good use of the most magnificent churches as concert halls. La Pietà *(see p112)* was Vivaldi's own church and is still used for concerts, as are the churches of the Frari *(see pp102–3)* and **San Vidal**. Other concerts are held from time to time in Scuola di San Giovanni Evangelista *(see p104)* and the Palazzo Prigioni Vecchie, the old prison attached to the Doge's Palace *(see pp84–9)*. In the summer, the garden of Ca' Rezzonico *(see p126)* is also used as an outdoor concert hall, as is the Doge's Palace's courtyard, albeit occasionally.

La Fenice *(see p93)*, one of Italy's most charming opera houses and the main local venue for major operas, suffered a disastrous fire in early 1996. It re-opened in November 2004 and now shares the opera, classical music and ballet programme with **Teatro Malibran**.

Venice's principal theatre is **Teatro Goldoni** where, not surprisingly, the repertoire is mainly drawn from the 250 or more comic works written by the Venetian dramatist Carlo Goldoni (1707–93). Most performances are staged in Italian and run from November to June.

At Carnival time in February *(see pp30–31)*, the whole city takes on a party atmosphere as it is invaded by merrymakers in fancy dress. Many theatrical and musical events take place, both in theatres and in the streets and *campi*.

FACILITIES FOR THE DISABLED

Access for disabled people is difficult everywhere in Venice, and theatres are no exception, although concerts are often held in easily accessible churches. PalaFenice and Teatro Malibran guarantee obstacle-free entrance for the disabled if contacted one week in advance (fax: 041 786 50). For more advice, see page 269.

Masked reveller at Carnival time *(see pp30–31)*

THE BIENNALE AND OTHER EXHIBITIONS

Venice is without doubt one of the leading art exhibition centres in Europe, offering shows on themes ranging from art history to photography, and frequently playing host to the world's major travelling exhibitions.

Exhibit by Larry Rivers at the 1992 Biennale exhibition

There are excellent facilities for such exhibitions, and these include the Doge's Palace, the Museo Correr, the Palazzo Grassi, the Querini-Stampalia, the Peggy Guggenheim and the Fondazione Cini. *Un Ospite di Venezia* will give details, as will the tourist office and posters around the city.

One of the best and largest exhibitions is the Biennale, an international display of contemporary and avant-garde art which was first begun in 1895. It is held from June to September in odd-numbered years. The main site is the Giardini Pubblici *(see p121)*, where the specially built pavilions represent about 40 different countries. Another branch of the exhibition showing the work of less established artists, takes place around the city in venues such as the old rope factory in the Arsenale *(see p119)*. The Biennale also organizes architecture, theatre, dance and music festivals.

CASINOS, CLUBS AND DISCOS

If you want to gamble or play roulette during your visit to Venice, there is a magnificent casino housed in the **Palazzo Vendramin-Calergi** on the Grand Canal *(see p61)* and you can sweep up to the stately entrance by gondola.

The **Centrale Restaurant Lounge** is the best-known late-night club. Open until 2am, it has live music in smart surroundings. A few other bars also feature live bands, including **Paradiso Perduto** in Cannaregio. Discos are few and far between in Venice. You could try **Piccolo Mondo**, near the Accademia; **Café Blue**, near Piazzale Roma; or alternatively go to the mainland, where Mestre has a few discos to choose from. You will find these clubs advertised in the *Spettacoli* listings in *Il Gazzettino*.

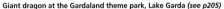

Placido Domingo singing at the Verona Festival

SPORT AND CHILDREN

Venetians are very keen on rowing and sailing. There are several clubs in the city, and the tourist office will be able to give you information. Most of the other sporting facilities are on the Lido, where you can ride, swim, cycle, and play golf or tennis.

In the city itself, there are few attractions for young children, but the mainland is more promising. Around Lake Garda there are plenty of watersports and a theme park, Gardaland *(see p205)*.

MUSIC AND THEATRE IN VERONA

Verona has two exceptional venues for theatre and music: the superb Arena *(see p195)*, and the 1st-century Teatro Romano *(see p202)* on the far side of the River Adige. Both stage open-air performances during the summer months.

The Arena is a popular site for rock concerts and is internationally renowned for its summer opera season. The Teatro Romano stages a succession of ballets and drama, including a Shakespeare Festival, in Italian translation. Tickets for the Teatro can be ordered by post; they are also sold at the box office at the Arena. Tickets to some events are free. Information about all the entertainment is given in the Verona newspaper, *L'Arena*.

OPERA AT THE ARENA

Almost everyone will enjoy the experience of hearing opera in the magnificent open-air setting of the Arena. Real opera buffs should be aware, however, that Verona performances are very much "opera for all". You should be prepared for less-than-perfect acoustics, noisy audiences, and even small children running about. The opera season runs from the first week in July until the beginning of September, and every year features a lavish production of Verdi's *Aida*. Performances start at 9pm, as dusk is falling, and it is customary to buy one of the little candles that are on sale. Ten minutes before the "curtain

Giant dragon at the Gardaland theme park, Lake Garda *(see p205)*

◁ **Venice's colourful Marriage with the Sea festival**

Aida, performed annually in Verona's Roman Arena

goes up", the whole Arena becomes a breathtaking sight, with a sea of flickering lights.

During the intervals, most people eat the picnics they have brought with them, or buy *panini* and ice creams. Glass bottles are not allowed in the Arena, so if you are taking a drink make sure it is in a plastic bottle. Be warned that toilets are few and far between and are most likely to have lengthy queues during the intervals.

Ticket prices are high, though there are some concessions. An unreserved, un-numbered, backless seat in the *gradinata*, or tiers, is €21, while the *poltrone*, literally "armchairs", either on the steps or in the stalls, range from €85 to €160. If you decide to get a cheap seat, arrive at least 2 hours before the performance and sit halfway down the tiers, where the acoustics are better. You can hire an air cushion for about €3. Numbered seats

are more comfortable, but seats lower in the Arena can be very hot and airless and the view of the stage can be restricted. You may well prefer to sacrifice comfort for fresh air and a bird's-eye view. Unless you have a seat in the best stalls with the glitterati, there is no need to dress up.

Visitors flock to Verona to attend the opera season, so you need to book accommodation well in advance.

DIRECTORY

MUSIC AND THEATRE

San Vidal
Campo San Vidal,
San Marco 2862/B.
Map 6 E3.

Teatro La Fenice
Campo San Fantin,
San Marco 1965.
Tel 041 24 24.
www.teatrolafenice.it

Teatro Goldoni
Calle Goldoni,
San Marco 4650/B.
Map 7 A2.
Tel 041 240 20 11.
www.teatrostabile
veneto.it

Teatro Malibran
Corte del Milion,
Cannaregio 5873.
Map 7 B1.
Tel 041 24 24.
www.teatrolafenice.it

CINEMAS

Arena di Campo San Polo
Campo San Polo,
San Polo. **Map** 6 F1.
Tel 041 524 13 20.

Giorgione Movie d'Essai
Rio Terra dei Franceschi,
Cannaregio 4612.
Map 7 A2.
Tel 041 522 62 98.

Multisala Astra
Via Corfù 9, Lido.
Tel 041 526 57 36.

Palazzo del Cinema
Lungomare G Marconi,
Lido. *Tel 041 272 65 01.*

CASINOS, CLUBS AND DISCOS

Café Blue
Calle della Scuola,
Dorsoduro 3778. **Map** 5
C1. *Tel 041 522 76 13.*

Centrale Restaurant Lounge
Piscina Frezzeria, San Marco
1659/B. **Map** 7 A2.
Tel 041 296 06 64.

Palazzo Vendramin-Calergi
Strada Nuova, Cannaregio
2040. *Tel 041 529 71 11.*
www.casinovenezia.it

Paradiso Perduto
Fondamenta della
Misericordia, Cannaregio
2540. **Map** 1 C4.
Tel 041 72 05 81.

Piccolo Mondo
Calle Corfù, Dorsoduro
1056/A. **Map** 6 E3.
Tel 041 520 03 71.

SPORTS

Cycling
Bruno Lazzari
21/B Gran Viale, Lido.
Tel 041 526 80 19.

Golf
Alberoni
Lido. *Tel 041 73 13 33.*
www.circologolfvenezia.it

Rowing
Canottieri Bucintoro
Punta Dogana,
Dorsoduro 15. **Map** 7 B4.
Tel 041 520 56 30.
www.bucintoro.org

Tennis
Tennis Club Venezia
Lungomare
G Marconi 41/d, Lido.
Tel 041 526 03 35.

VERONA OPERA

Main box office
Tel 045 800 51 51.
www.arena.it

Ticket agent
Vertours, Galleria Pellicciai
13, 37121 Verona.
Tel 045 929 82 00.
www.vertours.com

SPECIALIST HOLIDAYS AND OUTDOOR ACTIVITIES

The Veneto's rich cultural heritage and wide range of natural landscapes makes it a perfect location for numerous specialist holidays and outdoor excursions. The city of Venice hosts a dazzling array of study courses and craft workshops, including traditional mask-making and glass-blowing. It is also an unforgettable location in which to learn Italian. Outside of the city, the region's coastal and inland waterways provide space for many types of boating as well as more active watersports and bird-watching. The towering mountains in the alpine hinterland are challenging walking and climbing country, while in the winter there is skiing, facilitated by an excellent network of cable cars and lifts. Between mountain and sea are gentle hills, perfect for horse-riding enthusiasts and home to various relaxing local spas.

Skiing in the mountains

ARTS AND CRAFTS

Each summer the **Venice in Peril Fund** organises a series of lectures on the precious heritage of the city, aimed at history of art enthusiasts.

More practical courses are given by expert local craftspeople to anyone wishing to discover the intricacies of a range of crafts. Following a centuries-old tradition of glass-making, the **Scuola del Vetro Abate Zanetti** prides itself on teaching traditional and contemporary methods and styles at its premises on the island of Murano, the heart of the city's glass trade. Glass-making is also on offer through the craft organisation Confartigianato, as are lessons in furniture restoration. Techniques for repairing stucco and marble work can be learned at the well-established **European School for Heritage Crafts and Professions** set in the grounds of Villa Fabris near Vicenza.

IED Venezia offers a range of workshops and courses in fields such as photography and art throughout the summer. Lessons in crafting papier-mâché carnival masks are given at the dynamic **Ca' Macana** workshop and can be followed in several different European languages.

Year-round courses in oil and watercolour painting, as well as printmaking, are run by the friendly atelier **Bottega del Tintoretto**. A larger institution, with a vast range of open-air painting and graphics classes, is the **Scuola Internazionale di Grafica**. Courses on old textiles are occasionally held at **Palazzo Mocenigo**, home to the Centro Studi di Storia del Tessuto e del Costume. Even the ancient intricate art of lace-making is still demonstrated, by its few remaining expert practitioners, at the **Museo del Merletto** on the distant and colourful island of Burano.

COOKERY COURSES AND WINE TASTING

Visitors wishing to discover the secrets of the local cusine should try one of the cookery courses on offer in Venice. Most include a shopping visit to the fish and fresh produce market at Rialto followed by the preparation of a meal using seasonal ingredients. The enthusiastic young chefs at **Venice & Veneto Gourmet** cater to groups. Alternatively, longer intensive classes are held, often by Michelin-starred chefs, at the exclusive Hotel Cipriani *(see p233)*. In the hills outside Verona a magnificent country estate hosts tempting cooking classes run by **Tasting Places**. The Rome-based organisation **Delicious Italy** can arrange for residential cooking lessons around the Veneto that focus specifically on regional specialities.

Lessons on wine appreciation are organised by **Millevini**, a well-stocked winery at the foot of the Rialto bridge.

Cookery courses at Tasting Places

Students gaining practical experience in restoration techniques

Climbing in the spectacular Dolomites

WALKING AND CLIMBING

During the summer and autumn months keen walkers and trekkers should head straight up to the imposing Dolomites, where hundreds of kilometres of clearly marked pathways wind their way through brightly flowered meadows and spectacular rocky landscapes. Easy access combined with a network of high-altitude refuge huts make this a very accessible activity. For walkers who require extra assistance, **Cortina Guides** can provide specialist help with their team of friendly experts. **Club Alpino Italiano** offers qualified alpine guides for such climbs as the *via ferrata* routes, as well as for more general walking tours. The club has branches in all major towns, so it is not difficult to find help when needed. UK-based **Colletts Mountain Holidays** also offers a good range of walking and climbing trips.

WATER SPORTS

A quick glance at a map reveals the many coastal and inland waterways along the Veneto's Adriatic coast. It is unsurprising that water sports are a speciality here. It is possible to explore the region at your own pace by hiring a motor boat from **Cristiano Brussa**. (Customers will need to demonstrate some experience in handling craft.) Another truly unique holiday can be experienced on a houseboat in the lagoon, exploring its myriad islands and waterways. **Italiabella** have a fleet anchored at Chioggia, while **Houseboat Holidays Italia** are based at Porto Levante in the Po Delta. For those who have never sailed before, or would like a more relaxed trip, **Il Bragozzo** arrange day trips on the Venice Lagoon, with an experienced sailor at the helm.

In Venice there are many opportunities to take advantage of the waterways. A good sense of balance and plenty of energy are required for rowing in the traditional standing-up style. Clubs such as the **Bucintoro** on the Zattere, active since 1882, welcome visitors and provide lessons for novices. Sailing enthusiasts, on the other hand, can contact one of the city's clubs: those keen on old-style wooden craft with colourful sails should contact the **Associazione Vela al Terzo**, or for sleek modern yachts there is the prestigious **Compagnia della Vela**, which is based on the island of San Giorgio.

Further afield Lake Garda is the place for windsurfers. Schools such as **Surfsegnana**, at Torbole in the northern reaches of the lake, offer a good range of courses and holidays. The lake also guarantees superb swimming, especially off Sirmione in the south, where the bleached rocks and crystal clear water are reminiscent of the Caribbean. A string of yellow-sand beaches lines the Adriatic coast of the Veneto. Well frequented in summer by the locals, the Veneto seaside resorts also cater to the needs of overseas visitors. Caorle and Jesolo, close to Venice, are very popular, as is Rosolina Mare and Albarella, which is near the Po Delta. The Venice Lido is also a very pleasant place to swim, although a fee is charged to use the beach huts. For a free public beach head along to the Alberoni.

Lastly, for those in search of a more challenging experience, there is white-water rafting and canoeing at Valstagna on the Brenta River. The experienced crew at **Ivan Team** can arrange a craft, with all the necessary equipment, and transport.

Windsurfing near Torbole Lago di Garda Veneto

LANGUAGE COURSES

One of the best and most beautiful places to learn the Italian language is in Venice. Visitors who are keen to take part in a course should enrol in Italian for Foreigners at the **Centro Linguistico Ateneo** of the Ca' Foscari University. Classes are in an atmospheric modernised *palazzo* and are supplemented by access to well-stocked multimedia labs with all manner of support material. Another centrally located school is the **Istituto Venezia**, which offers a good range of lessons, as well as arranging for concerts, cultural initiatives and excursions. Accommodation is either homestays or self-catering flats.

WINTER SPORTS

A winter holiday in the breath-taking Dolomite mountains can include an extraordinary range of activities. Wrapped up warm and plastered with high-factor sun protection cream, visitors in need of relaxation can laze on the sun decks in the ski resorts. Those in search of exciting downhill skiing can head for Arabba, which has a superb series of cable cars to whisk skiers up to the snow fields, including the Marmolada glacier. Val Zoldana, dominated by the magnificent Civetta and Pelmo mountains, is another excellent location. If a chic ambience is important, you must stay at Cortina d'Ampezzo, which hosted the Winter Olympics in 1956 and now boasts excellent modern ski facilities and lifts, including the Tofana cable car. All the resorts are managed by **Dolomiti Superski**, which includes 12 ski areas and an amazing 1,200 km (750 miles) of pistes all covered by a single pass. Slopes for intrepid snow-boarders are also included.

Toddlers to adults, beginners to more advanced skiers, and anyone in between can attend the ski school run by the qualified ski instructors of the **Scuola Sci** which is found at all the main centres.

Cortina d'Ampezzo, Alleghe and Val Zoldana also have indoor ice rinks, which make a refreshing change to the high energy of the slopes.

Experienced skiers wishing to get away from the pistes can join a group accompanied by a local alpine guide to explore the more secluded slopes. Snow-shoeing is also undergoing a revival. Guides and modern equipment can be found at all the major resorts. There is superb cross-country skiing in the Veneto. The vast undulating Asiago plateau north of Vicenza has hundreds of kilometres of prepared tracks for both classical and skating techniques. Contact the **Consorzio Turistico** for information about the main centres, such as Campolongo and Enego, which all have top-level facilities. Further west is the Monti Lessini above Verona, where pistes fan out from Bosco Chiesanuova; the best source of information is the **Lessinia Turistsport**.

SPA HOLIDAYS

As the ancient Romans discovered to their delight, naturally occurring spas are dotted across the Veneto, and visitors can pamper body and mind with a soak in a thermal pool or with a relaxing massage. Abano-Montegrotto Terme in the Euganean Hills has numerous hotels with steaming outdoor and indoor pools, catering to both long-term and day visitors. The **Consorzio Terme Euganee** can help organise your holiday.

Further afield, on the southern shore of Lake Garda, is the state-of-the-art spa facilities at **Terme di Sirmione**, which continue a tradition going back to the 1500s.

BIRDWATCHING

Pink flamingoes flock in spectacular numbers to the sprawling **Po Delta Park** in the winter months, though the local waterfowl are worth visiting at any time of year. Also, on the western edge of the Venice Lagoon, located on the Romea road that links Mestre with Chioggia, is the wetland reserve **Oasi Valle Averto**, run by the World Wide Fund for Nature. This reserve is accessible by bus.

Horse riding at Salten Jenesien

HORSERIDING AND GOLF

The rolling Euganean Hills east of Venice together with the foothills of the Dolomites have plenty of quiet roads and lanes suitable for horse riding. Several agriturismo establishments, such as **Il Faè** near Conegliano and **Le Frassanelle** beyond Padua, keep stables and all the facilities needed for riding holidays. Le Frassanelle also has access to a golf course.

Many of the other notable golfing facilities in the Veneto are to be found in the hinterland. These include a course in the lovely garden premises of **Golf Club Villa Condulmer** at Mogliano. However, for a game with a difference, visitors can play a few rounds at the **Circolo Golf Venezia** at Alberoni, situated on the Venice Lido.

Cable car and downhill slopes in the Dolomite mountains

DIRECTORY

COOKERY COURSES AND WINE TASTING

Delicious Italy
Via Angelo Piliziano 58,
Rome. *Tel 064 547 61 23.*
www.deliciousitaly.com

Millevini
San Marco 5362, Venice.
Map 7 B1.
Tel 041 520 60 90.

Tasting Places London
Tel +44 (0)2089 645 333.
www.tastingplaces.com

Venice & Veneto Gourmet
Tel 335 522 97 14.
www.veniceveneto
gourmet.com

ARTS AND CRAFTS

Bottega del Tintoretto
Fondamenta dei Mori,
Cannaregio 3400, Venice.
Map 2 F3.
Tel 041 72 20 81.
www.tintorettovenezia.it

Ca' Macana
Calle delle Botteghe,
Dorsoduro 3172, Venice.
Map 6 D3.
Tel 041 277 61 42.
www.camacana.com

European School for Heritage Crafts and Professions
Villa Fabris, Via Trieste 43,
Thiene. *Tel 044 537 23 29.* www.villafabris.eu

IED Venezia
Palazzo Querini Stampalia,
Campo S. Maria Formosa,
Castello 5252, Venice.
Map 7 C1. *Tel 041 277 11 64.* www.ied.it

Museo del Merletto
Piazza Galuppi 187,
Burano, Venice.
Tel 041 73 00 34.
www.museicivici
veneziani.it

Palazzo Mocenigo
Santa Croce 1992,
Venice. **Map** 2 F5.
Tel 041 72 17 98.
www.museicivici
veneziani.it

Scuola del Vetro Abate Zanetti
Calle Briati 8/b, Murano,
Venice. **Map** 4 F2.
Tel 041 273 77 11.
www.abatezanetti.it

Scuola Internazionale di Grafica
Calle del Cristo, Cannaregio
1798, Venice. **Map** 2 E4.
Tel 041 72 19 50.
www.scuolagrafica.it

Venice in Peril Fund
Unit 4, Hurlingham
Studios, Ranelagh
Gardens, London, UK.
Tel (44) 020 7736 6891.
www.veniceinperil.org

WALKING AND CLIMBING

Club Alpino Italiano
www.cai.it

Colletts Mountain Holidays
Harvest Mead, Great
Hormead, Buntingford,
Herts., UK.
Tel (44) 01763 289 660.
www.colletts.co.uk

Cortina Guides Office
Corso Italia 69/a,
Cortina d'Ampezzo.
Tel 043 686 85 05.
www.guidecortina.com

WATER SPORTS

Associazione Vela al Terzo
www.velaalterzo.it

Bucintoro Rowing Club
Zattere, Dorsoduro 263,
Venice. **Map** 7 A4.
Tel 041 520 56 30.
www.bucintoro.org

Compagnia della Vela
S. Marco 2, Venice.
Map 7 A3.
Tel 041 520 08 84.
www.compvela.com

Cristiano Brussa
Ponte delle Guglie,
Cannaregio 1030, Venice.
Map 2 D3.
Tel 041 275 01 96.
www.cristianobrussa.com

Houseboat Holidays Italia
Via C. Colombo 36/A,
Porto Levante,
Porto Viro.
Tel 042 666 60 25.
www.houseboat.it

Il Bragozzo
Tel 388 182 60 10.
www.ilbragozzo.it

Italiabella
Viale delle Terme 163,
Abano Terme.
Tel 049 66 72 01.

Ivan Team
Via Oliero di Sotto 85,
Valstagna.
Tel 042 455 82 50.
www.ivanteam.com

Surfsegnana
Foci del Sarca, Torbole.
Tel 046 450 59 63.
www.surfsegnana.it

LANGUAGE COURSES

Centro Linguistico Ateneo
Campiello San Sebastiano,
Dorsoduro 1686, Venice.
Map 5 C3.
Tel 041 234 97 13.
www.unive.it/cli

Istituto Venezia
Campo S. Margherita,
Dorsoduro 3116a, Venice.
Map 6 D2.
Tel 041 522 43 31.
www.istitutovenezia.com

WINTER SPORTS

Consorzio Turistico Asiago 7 Comuni
Viale Trento Trieste 19,
Asiago.
Tel 042 446 41 37.
www.asiago7comuni.to

Dolomiti Superski
www.dolomitisuperski.
com

Lessinia Turistsport
www.leturispo.it

Scuola Sci Alleghe Civetta
Corso Italia 20, Alleghe.
Tel 043 772 37 16.
www.scuolascialleghe
civetta.it

Scuola Sci Arabba
Via Boè 14, Livinallongo.
Tel 043 67 91 60.
www.scuolasciarabba.com

Scuola Sci Cortina d'Ampezzo
Corso Italia 67, Cortina
d'Ampezzo.
Tel 043 629 11.
www.scuolascicortina.com

SPA HOLIDAYS

Consorzio Terme Euganee
Largo Marconi 8,
Abano Terme.
Tel 049 866 66 62.
www.abanomonte
grottosi.it

Terme di Sirmione
Piazza Virgillo 1, Sirmione.
Tel 030 916 81.
www.termedisirmione.com

BIRDWATCHING

Oasi Valle Averto
Lugo di Campagnalupia.
Tel 041 518 50 68.
www.wwf.it/oasi

Po Delta Park
Visitors Centre Ca'
Vendramin, Taglio di Po.
Tel 042 638 09 04.
www.parcodeltapo.org

HORSERIDING AND GOLF

Circolo Golf Venezia
Strada Vecchia 1, Alberoni,
Lido di Venezia.
Tel 041 73 13 33.
www.circologolfvenezia.it

Golf Club Villa Condulmer
Via della Croce 3, Zerman
di Mogliano, Veneto.
Tel 041 45 70 62.
www.golfvillacondulmer.
com

Il Faè
Via Fae, S. Pietro di Feletto.
Tel 043 878 71 17.
www.ilfae.com

Le Frassanelle
35030 Rovolon.
Tel 049 875 12 34.
www.frassanelle.it

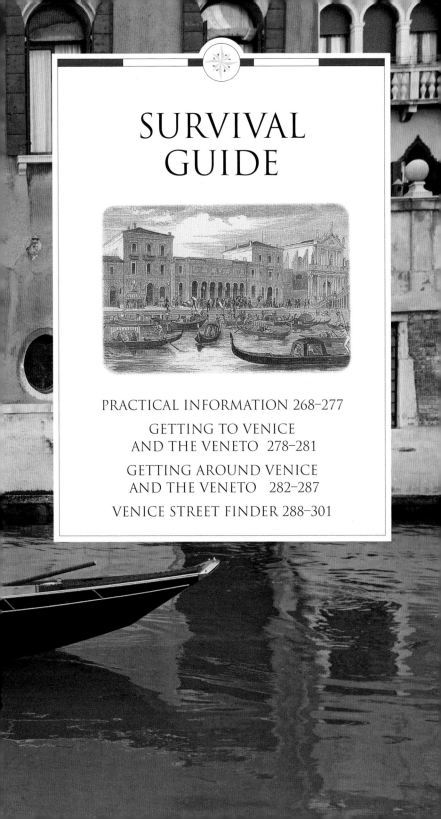

SURVIVAL GUIDE

PRACTICAL INFORMATION

ENTE NAZIONALE
ITALIANO PER IL TURISMO
Tourist Board logo

The wealth of art and architecture found in Venice and the cities of Padua, Verona and Vicenza can dazzle and overwhelm. Avoid cultural overload by sightseeing in the morning, relaxing over lunch as the Italians do and shopping or visiting churches in the late afternoon. In the Veneto, restoration of buildings and artworks is an ongoing process, and you may often see the sign *chiuso per restauro* (closed for restoration). Always check opening hours in advance with individual museums or the tourist office. Italians also enjoy visiting their art cities, so public holidays and weekends often mean larger crowds. To make the most of your stay, take a tour by bus or on foot with a qualified guide who can explain the key sights and history. For lovers of outdoor pursuits, the Veneto also has areas of outstanding natural beauty along its coast and inland, in the hills and mountains.

Tourists shopping and sightseeing on Venice's Rialto Bridge

WHEN TO GO

July and August can get very hot and sticky in Venice and the Veneto towns. For a cooler, quieter time, visit in winter, spring and autumn. However, be aware that Venice is often subject to *acqua alta* (tidal flooding) in autumn (*see Walking, p282*), and the whole of the Veneto experiences thick fog in winter.

Most places around Lake Garda close during winter, while the Dolomites have two distinct seasons: December–March for skiing and snow-related activities, and June–September for hiking. Hotels, guesthouses and restaurants tend to cease trade between these times.

VISAS AND PASSPORTS

All visitors need a valid passport. European Union (EU) residents and visitors from the United States, Canada, Australia and New Zealand do not need visas for stays of up to three months. However, a visa may be needed for longer stays – check with your embassy – and is required for business or study related trips.

By law, all visitors to Italy must register with the police within three days of arrival; all hotels will request your passport on checking-in for such purpose.

The **Ministero degli Affari Esteri** (Foreign Office) or any *questura* (police station) can provide information on any visa requirements (*see p273*).

CUSTOMS INFORMATION

Duty free are as follows: non-EU residents can bring in either 200 cigarettes, 50 cigars, 100 cigarillos or 250 grams of tobacco; 1 litre of alcohol above 22 per cent vol;

4 litres of wine; 50 grams of perfume. Allowances for EU residents are almost unlimited, providing that the goods are for personal use only.

The tax refund system (*Imposta sul Valore Aggiunto*) for non-EU residents is complicated; it is worth reclaiming only if you have spent at least €160 in one establishment. Ask the cashier to fill out the form for you, and when leaving the country take the goods in your carry-on luggage for approval at the airport tax refund office. The website of the **Agenzia delle Dogane** (Italian customs) provides further information.

TOURIST INFORMATION

All major towns in the Veneto have excellent tourist offices. In high season, Venice, Verona and Padua also have several information points at railway stations and key sights. The offices in smaller towns may be of limited help. Tourist offices in Venice have city maps, *vaporetto* maps, lists of accommodation options and other literature. Travel agents and hotels are also good sources for information on the city, tours and local events (*see pp32–5*). In Venice, *Eventi e Manifestazioni* is a useful free booklet with listings information; its equivalent in Verona is *Carnet Verona*. Both are available from tourist information offices.

AZIENDA
PROMOZIONE
TURISTICA

A Tourist
Information
sign

To obtain information prior to travelling, contact **ENIT** (Italian State Tourist Board) in your home country. An array of publications and maps can also be downloaded from each city's tourist board website.

ADMISSION PRICES

Most museums, art galleries and archaeological sites charge an entry fee, but there are usually concessions for children, students and senior citizens over 65. Venice's civic museums pass, valid for six months, is available from any of the sights included in the deal or online at **Venice Connected**. You can also purchase a VENICEcard online from **Hello Venezia**. This pass includes entry to museums and churches, and savings on other admission fees, *vaporetto* tickets and car parking. However, you must buy the card at least 15 days in advance for discounted rates to apply.

Verona has the Verona Card (€15 for 2 days or €20 for 5 days), which covers entry to the main churches, museums and monuments, as well as travel on the city buses. The card is available from Verona's tourist office and any of the participating sights.

Some churches in smaller towns may not charge an admission fee.

OPENING HOURS

Due to ongoing restoration of many aging palaces, museums and galleries, opening hours are subject to change. The tourist office can supply a list of opening times or, if you are in Venice, you can also consult the booklets *Eventi e Manifestazioni* or **Un Ospite di Venezia**, which are available from most hotels. Museums are often shut on Mondays.

Churches are usually open mid-morning and late afternoon. Most Venetian churches are managed by **Chorus**, which sells a useful pass for multiple church entries.

Most food shops open at 8am, while other stores open at 9 or 10am. All close for an long lunch break from 12:30pm to around 4pm, then stay open

Basilica di Sant'Antonio in Padua

until about 7:30pm. However, in tourist areas, no lunch break is observed. Many supermarkets in the larger towns stay open all day, seven days a week.

ETIQUETTE

Any attempt by foreign visitors to speak Italian is always appreciated by the locals. Few people speak English in the Veneto, but hotel receptionists are usually helpful and will readily make any enquiries and reservations on your behalf.

To avoid offence, always dress decently, particularly if visiting churches, where bare shoulders and shorts are considered unsuitable. Photography is forbidden in most churches. Being drunk in a public place is frowned upon, and smoking is banned in all public buildings, including restaurants and bars, as well as on *vaporetti*. Feeding the pigeons in Piazza San Marco is illegal, and if caught, you may be fined.

PUBLIC CONVENIENCES

There are few public toilets in the Veneto, although Venice is better served. Public conveniences in Venice are usually signed and cost €1. You can also use the toilets at railway stations and in cafés and bars. Ask for *il bagno* (the bathroom) or *il gabinetto* (the toilet). Public toilets are always short of paper, so it is a good idea to carry tissues with you.

TAXES AND TIPPING

Like other EU countries, Italy has a form of Value Added Tax (VAT), which is called *Imposta sul Valore Aggiunto* (IVA); see *Customs Information*. The standard rate of IVA on goods and services is 20 per cent. Hotels generally include the tax in the room rate.

Always keep a few euros close to hand for hotel staff such as porters and chambermaids. In restaurants you may like to round up the bill, though a service charge is often already added. Italian taxi drivers do not expect a tip, and there is no need to tip a gondolier.

TRAVELLERS WITH SPECIAL NEEDS

Venice's many stepped bridges make it difficult for the wheelchair-bound to get around the city; in addition, many bridge lifts are being removed, further limiting disabled access.

Normal *vaporetti* (such as line 1) are accessible to wheelchairs since the deck is on the same level as the landing stages, and there is reserved space on board. Water taxis (*see p283*), however, are hazardous for wheelchair users and should be avoided.

The Venezia Accessibile information pack details a wide range of barrier-free itineraries, with maps and route instructions. It also shows places of interest that can be visited by or have special facilities for the disabled, and how to reach them by *vaporetto* or by land. Venezia Accessibile is available at tourist offices or downloadable from the **Informahandicap** website.

A mechanically operated wheelchair ramp across a bridge

TRAVELLING WITH CHILDREN

Italians love children, and while hotels and restaurants may not always be equipped for young visitors, they will be happy to accommodate them. Most restaurants have high chairs and will serve children simple meals such as pasta with olive oil or tomato sauce. It is best to request a cot at your hotel in advance of your visit. A holiday-let apartment *(see pp224–5)* is an excellent solution if you need kitchen access and play space. A useful website, **Italy Family Hotels** allows you to search and book accommodation for specifically child-friendly hotels throughout the Veneto and the country.

Venice is a wonderland for children, but it can also be very tiring for both kids and parents. It is best to invest in family passes or boat travel, so you can hop on and off at will. Limit the number of art galleries and museums you visit, and opt instead for more hands-on activities, such as glass-blowing demonstrations. Seek out the city's parks and play-grounds – such as Sant'Elena and Cannaregio, near the Ponte delle Guglie. In the summer, your kids can play with the local children on the Lido beaches; at other times of year, they can run

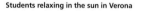
Students relaxing in the sun in Verona

around and let off steam in the neighbourhood squares.

Most sights throughout the Veneto offer discounted admission for families.

STUDENT TRAVELLERS

Full-time students who are in possession of a valid **International Student Identity Card (ISIC)** will usually get reductions on museum entry fees and other charges across the Veneto. However, occasionally this is restricted to students residing in the EU. The Rolling VENICEcard, available to 14- to 29-year-olds for a small fee, provides a package of useful information on the city. This includes alternative itineraries, fashionable haunts and lists of shops, hotels, theatres and restaurants offering card-holder discounts. The pass also offers a reduced-price travelcard for the *vaporetti*. The Rolling VENICEcard is available online at Hello Venezia *(see p269)*, or at any *vaporetto* boarding point in Venice.

SENIOR TRAVELLERS

Travellers over 65 years of age are entitled to free entry to state-run museums and archaeological sites. In addition, discounted entry fees are available at many locally managed museums and historical sites through-out the Veneto. Photographic identification, such as a passport or driver's licence, needs to be shown upon entry as proof of age.

Like its younger "Rolling" version, the VENICEcard is a good pass to purchase, as it offers information on Venice's sights and transport savings as well as free entry to the Casino di Venezia *(see p260)*. It is available from Hello Venezia *(see p269)*, and the main vaporetto stops.

If you are planning to do a fair amount of train travel while in

the Veneto, you might want to consider purchasing a **Carta d'Argento**. This card entitles people over 60 to discounts of 15 per cent on first and second class train tickets. Yearly membership to the Carta d'Argento costs €30 for those over 60 years of age and is free to seniors who are over 75 years old. This can be applied for at the main train stations and travel agencies.

The clock of San Giacomo di Rialto in San Polo, Venice

TIME

Italy is one hour ahead of Greenwich Mean Time (GMT). Daylight saving time is between April and October. For all official purposes, the Italians use the 24-hour clock.

ELECTRICITY

Electrical current in Italy is 220V AC, with two-pin, round-pronged plugs. Most hotels graded above three stars have electrical points for shavers (check the voltage first) and hairdryers in all bedrooms.

CONVERSION CHART

Imperial to Metric
1 inch = 2.54 centimetres
1 foot = 30 centimetres
1 mile = 1.6 kilometres
1 ounce = 28 grams
1 pound = 454 grams
1 pint = 0.6 litres
1 gallon = 4.6 litres

Metric to Imperial
1 centimetre = 0.4 inches
1 metre = 3 feet, 3 inches
1 kilometre = 0.6 miles
1 gram = 0.04 ounces
1 kilogram = 2.2 pounds
1 litre = 1.8 pints

RESPONSIBLE TOURISM

Italy is very aware of ethical and environmental issues. There are many projects to help its citizens live more sustainably and there are also steps visitors can take to enjoy the Veneto responsibly.

It should be easy to recycle as every town operates a *raccolta differenziata* (separate waste collection), with individual containers for glass, paper and plastic.

Organic, Fairtrade and local food is widely accessible in the Veneto. A range of organic products are available at the many **Coop** super-markets dotted around the region; they stock Fairtrade items too. Venice also has the **Rialto Biocenter** supermarket. Located in the vicinity of the Rialto Bridge in San Polo, the Biocenter is a modestly sized

Fruit and vegetables stalls at Rialto market

health food shop that stocks everything from tofu and whole-wheat pasta to incense and natural cosmetics. In addition to the famous Rialto markets (*see p100*), where you can buy fruit, vegetables and fish, farmers' markets and organic fairs are held regularly at Piazzale Roma. Some resident groups buy direct from growers on the island of **Sant'Erasmo**, who deliver by boat.

Buy your souvenirs at local artisan workshops, which help the community maintain the skills needed to make these regional products. Venice is known in particular for hand-blown glass.

DIRECTORY

EMBASSIES AND CONSULATES

Australia
Via Antonio Bosio, 5, Rome. *Tel 06 852 721.*
www.italy.embassy.gov.au

Canada
25 Riviera Ruzzante, 35123 Padova.
Tel 06 854 442 911.
www.canada.it

New Zealand
Via Clitunno 44, Rome 00198.
Tel 06 853 7501.
www.nzembassy.com/ italy

United Kingdom
Piazzale Donatori di Sangue 2–5, Mestre.
Tel 041 505 59 90.
http://ukinitaly.fco.gov. uk/en

United States
Via Principe Amedeo 2/10 20121 Milan.
Tel 06 852 541.
http://italy.usembassy.gov

VISAS AND PASSPORTS

Ministero degli Affari Esteri
www.esteri.it/visti

CUSTOMS INFORMATION

Agenzia delle Dogane
www.agenziadogane.it

TOURIST INFORMATION

ENIT UK
Tel 020 7408 1254.
www.enit.it

ENIT USA
Tel 212 245 48 22.
www.italiantourism.com

Padua Tourist Board
Railway station.
Tel 049 875 20 77.
www.turismopadova.it

Venice Tourist Board
Piazza San Marco 1.
Map 7 B2.
Piazzale Roma.
Map 1 B5.
Ferrovia Santa Lucia.
Map 1 B4.
Tel 041 529 87 11
(for all offices).
www.turismovenezia.it

Verona Tourist Board
Via degli Alpini 9.
Tel 045 806 86 80.
www.tourism.verona.it

Vicenza Tourist Board
Piazzale dei Signori 8.
Tel 044 454 41 22.
www.vicenzae.org

ADMISSION PRICES

Hello Venezia
Tel 041 24 24.
www.hellovenezia.com

Venice Connected
www.veniceconnected. com

OPENING HOURS

Chorus
Tel 041 275 04 62.
www.chorusvenezia.org

Un Ospite di Venezia
www.unospitedivenezia.it

TRAVELLING WITH CHILDREN

Italy Family Hotels
www.italyfamilyhotels. it/en

TRAVELLERS WITH SPECIAL NEEDS

Informahandicap
Tel 041 274 81 44.
www.comune.venezia.it/ informahandicap

STUDENT TRAVELLERS

International Student Identity Card (ISIC)
www.isic.org

SENIOR TRAVELLERS

Carta d'Argento
www.trenitalia.com

RESPONSIBLE TOURISM

Coop
Piazzale Roma.
Map 1 B5.
Tel 041 296 06 21.

Rialto Biocenter
Calle della Regina, Santa Croce 2264. **Map** 2 F5.
Tel 041 523 95 15.

Sant'Erasmo Growers
Tel 041 528 29 97.

Personal Security and Health

Venice is one of the safest cities in Europe, and visitors are unlikely to encounter any unpleasant situations. Violent crime is very rare, and petty crime is minimal in comparison with other main urban centres. Nevertheless, it is wise to take a few simple precautions, particularly against pickpockets, both in Venice and throughout the Veneto. Always leave valuables and important documents in the hotel safe, and carry only the minimum amount of money necessary for the day.

Make sure you take out adequate travel insurance before leaving for Italy, as it is very difficult to obtain once you are in the country.

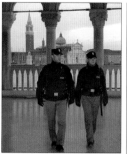

Two Venetian *polizia* on the Riva degli Schiavoni

POLICE

The *vigili urbani*, or municipal police, are most often seen in the streets regulating traffic and enforcing local laws. Their uniform is blue in winter and white in summer. The *carabinieri*, with red striped trousers, are the armed military police, responsible for public law and order. The *polizia*, or state police, wear blue uniforms with white belts and berets. They specialize in serious crimes. Any of these forces should be able to help you in an emergency.

In the event of theft, go to the nearest **questura** (police station) and make a statement. If there is a language problem, consult your nearest consulate (*see p271*).

WHAT TO BE AWARE OF

Always keep your valuables and personal documents in a safe place when travelling. It is also wise to keep a photocopy of all vital papers, including your passport, separately. Try not to attract the attention of pickpockets and bag-snatchers by having your bag unzipped, particularly at railway stations, markets and on public transport. In Venice, take care while waiting at the *vaporetto* landing stages, and be especially vigilant when people are jostling to get on board. On crowded boats, hold your handbag or rucksack in front of you.

Rented cars and vehicles with foreign number plates are favourite targets of car thieves. Always lock the car before you leave it, and never leave valuables on display inside.

Venice is fairly uneventful after dark, and you can generally stroll through the streets without any threat. There is no red-light quarter or any area that could be described as unsavoury, though the beaches are best avoided at night.

Women alone in Venice are unlikely to encounter anything more troublesome than the Latin roving eye; however, in the evening it is best to stick to well-trodden and well-lit routes. Elsewhere in the Veneto, particularly in the less touristy towns, unescorted females are likely to attract more attention.

Make sure you take only official taxis, which have the licence number clearly displayed (*see p287*). Avoid unauthorized taxi drivers, who may not be insured and almost invariably overcharge. Airports are their favourite haunts.

IN AN EMERGENCY

In the event of an emergency, call 112 or 113 to get hold of the **Soccorso Pubblico** (public assistance). Dialling 115 alerts the **Vigili del Fuoco** (fire brigade). If you are in need of urgent medical attention, go to the *Pronto Soccorso* (emergency) department of the nearest main hospital. There are often queues, so be prepared to wait. Doctors and hospital staff in tourist localities usually speak at least some English.

If you need an **Ambulanza** (ambulance), phone 118. In Venice, this will get you an ambulance boat; in the Dolomites, you will be connected to the *Soccorso Alpino* (mountain rescue). If necessary, a helicopter will be sent. If you do not speak Italian, use simple English to explain where you are and what the problem is.

All towns have a Guardia Medica service, with a doctor on duty for urgent problems at night time and weekends. Ask the tourist office for the relevant phone numbers. In tourist resorts, the Guardia Medica is generally available on site and 24-hours a day in season.

Police boat

Ambulance boat

LOST AND STOLEN PROPERTY

If you lose anything valuable, such as your passport, contact your consulate at once *(see p271)*. Items lost on public transport in Venice and Mestre end up at the **ACTV Oggetti Rinvenuti** offices – the one in Piazzale Roma is for items left on the *vaporetti*, the one in Mestre is for items lost on buses.

There are no railway lost property offices, so if you leave anything on a train, contact the lost property office – **Oggetti Rinvenuti** – in the nearest town.

In the event of stolen property, go to the nearest *questura* (police station; *see Police*) to make a statement. Take your passport with you for identification purposes.

Pharmacy sign

HOSPITALS AND PHARMACIES

Standards of health care in Italy are on a par with those in the UK and the US. Should you need a doctor, ask your concierge or look in the yellow pages, under *Medici*. If you have a serious medical complaint or allergy, it might be wise to bring a letter, preferably translated, from your doctor at home. Most doctors in the region speak some English.

Pharmacies *(farmacie)* are generally open 9am–12:30pm and 4–7:30pm Monday–Friday, and 9am–noon on Saturdays. All towns offer a 24-hour pharmacy service *(farmacia di turno)*, with a night-time and Sunday rota. You will find the rota posted on the doors of all pharmacies. Opening times can also be found in the local newspapers or, if you are in Venice, in the booklet *Un Ospite di Venezia (see p271)*. Italian pharmacists are well trained to deal with minor ailments and can sell many

drugs without needing a doctor's prescription. If you are taking prescribed medication, take enough supplies or a prescription including the generic name of the medication – pharmacies can usually distribute the local equivalent. Many of the words for minor complaints and remedies are similar in Italian, for example *aspirina* (aspirin), *tranquillante* (tranquillizer), and *lassativo* (laxative).

Dentists are expensive in Italy. You can find the nearest one in the yellow pages, under *Dentisti medici chirurghi*, or ask your hotel receptionist to give you a recommendation.

MINOR HAZARDS

Inoculations are not needed for the Veneto, but it is wise to take high-factor sunscreen, especially if you plan on travelling in spring or summer. Insect repellent is a must in the summer, as mosquitoes can be irksome in Venice. An electric gadget, available from pharmacies or department stores, will repel insects in your room for up to 12 hours. Tap water is safe to drink, as is the water from fountains, unless a sign warns that it is *non potabile* (undrinkable).

TRAVEL AND HEALTH INSURANCE

Visitors from the EU are entitled to reciprocal state medical care in Italy. Before you travel, obtain a European Health Insurance Card (EHIC), from the post office or online, which covers you for emergency medical treatment. You may wish to take out additional medical insurance as the EHIC does not cover repatriation costs.

Australia also has a reciprocal medical agreement with Italy, but other visitors from outside the EU should take out a comprehensive medical insurance policy. For claims, make sure you keep all receipts for medical treatment and any medicines prescribed.

Purchasing additional travel insurance before leaving home is recommended. If you intend to do any winter sports you will need extra cover.

DIRECTORY

POLICE

Questura
Venice: Fondamenta di S Chiara.
Map 1 B5. **Tel** 041 271 55 11.
Padua: Piazzetta G Palatucci 5.
Tel 049 83 31 11.
Verona: Lungadige Galtarossa 11.
Tel 045 809 04 11.
Vicenza: Viale Mazzini 213.
Tel 044 433 75 11.

IN AN EMERGENCY

General Emergency (Soccorso Pubblico)
Tel 112 or 113.

Fire (Vigili del Fuoco)
Tel 115.

Ambulance (Ambulanza)
Tel 118.

LOST PROPERTY

ACTV Oggetti Rinvenuti
1st Floor, Garage Comunale,
Piazzale Roma. **Map** 5 B1.
Tel 041 272 21 79.
Via Martiri della Libertà, Mestre.
Tel 041 272 27 23.

Oggetti Rinvenuti
Venice: **Tel** 041 274 82 25.
Padua: **Tel** 049 820 49 25.
Verona: **Tel** 045 805 78 81.
Vicenza: **Tel** 044 422 10 30.

HOSPITALS

Venice: Campo Santi Giovanni
e Paolo. Map 3 C5.
Tel 041 529 41 11.
Padua: Via Giustiniani 2.
Tel 049 821 11 11.
Verona: Piazzale Stefani 1.
Tel 045 812 11 11.
Vicenza: Via Rodolfi 37.
Tel 044 475 31 11.

PHARMACIES

Venice: Campo San Polo.
Map 6 F1. **Tel** 041 522 06 75.
Padua: Via Daniele Manin, 67.
Tel 049 875 83 63.
Verona: Piazza delle Erbe 20.
Tel 045 800 62 64.
Vicenza: Corso San Felice e
Fortunato 117. **Tel** 044 43211 82.

DENTISTS

Venice: **Tel** 041 63 01 37.
Padua: **Tel** 049 872 16 38.
Verona: **Tel** 045 803 46 88.
Vicenza: **Tel** 044 456 49 80.

Banking and Local Currency

Visitors to the Veneto have a number of options available to them for changing money. Banks tend to give more favourable rates than bureaux de change, hotels and travel agents, but the paperwork is usually more time-consuming. Alternatively, you can use a credit card for purchasing goods and services. If using a debit card, check with your bank about fees for overseas withdrawals before departing from home.

The waiting area of a bank in Vicenza

BANKS AND BUREAUX DE CHANGE

It is a good idea to acquire some euros before you arrive in Italy. Changing foreign currency at a bank can be a frustrating process because it involves endless form-filling and queuing. You must apply first at the window displaying the *cambio* sign, then move to the *cassa* to obtain your euros. If in doubt, ask a member of staff in order to avoid waiting in the wrong queue.

For security reasons, most banks have electronic double doors with metal detectors, allowing only one person in at a time. Metal objects and bags should first be deposited in lockers situated in the foyer. Press the button to open the outer door, step in and wait for it to close behind you. The inner door will then open automatically.

Banks are usually open from 8:30am–1:30pm Monday to Friday. Most also open for an hour in the afternoon. They are closed at weekends and public holidays, and they also close early the day before a major holiday. One of the

main banks in Venice is the **Cassa di Risparmio di Venezia**.

Bureaux de change stay open longer and work seven days a week. The exchange offices at Venice's Stazione Venezia Santa Lucia *(see p280)*, Marco Polo Airport and Antonio Canova Airport at Treviso *(see p279)*, stay open until the evening and at weekends.

Exchange rates vary from place to place, but banks usually offer the best deal. Some hotels also offer a currency exchange service; rates tend to be poor, but the commission is modest.

If you need to have money sent to you in Italy, banks in your home country can wire money to an Italian bank, but this can take up to a week. For a swifter money-transfer service, try **Travelex**, the Italian agent for Western Union.

CREDIT AND DEBIT CARDS

Credit cards are widely accepted throughout Italy and can be very useful, particularly for hotel and restaurant bills, shopping, car hire, booking tickets by telephone and emergency situations. **VISA**, **MasterCard** and **American Express** are the most popular. Be aware that most credit cards levy a surcharge on overseas transactions. Some establishments require a minimum expenditure to accept credit card payment, so always make sure that you have enough cash just in case.

To avoid your card being unnecessarily blocked, notify your bank of your travel plans before you set off. If your credit card is lost or stolen, contact the relevant emergency telephone number immediately. The card will be blocked, and any unauthorized payments

will then be refused. Keep a copy of your credit card number in a safe place, separate from the actual card, in case of loss. Prepaid credit cards are also a safe option.

Travellers' cheques are another safe way to carry money. They are still accepted at leading exchange offices, though these may charge hefty commissions to convert them into currency.

ATMS

Most banks have an ATM *(bancomat)* that will accept debit and major credit cards (VISA, MasterCard and American Express). Cash dispensers will be located throughout the main cities. Instructions are given in different languages. You will need to enter your personal PIN number for a cash withdrawal. Be aware that a percentage charge will usually be applied by your home bank for this service.

Always take precautions to ensure that your PIN number remains a secret, and make sure nobody is looking over your shoulder as you type it in when using an ATM.

DIRECTORY

BANKS AND BUREAUX DE CHANGE

Cassa di Risparmio di Venezia
Campo Manin, San Marco.
Map 7 A6.
Tel 041 529 11 11.

Travelex
Riva del Ferro, Rialto,
San Marco 5126.
Map 7 A1.
Tel 041 528 73 58.

CREDIT AND DEBIT CARDS

For lost or stolen cards:
American Express
Tel 06 7290 0347.

MasterCard
Tel 800 870 866 *(freephone).*

Visa
Tel 800 877 232 *(freephone).*

THE EURO

The euro (€) is the common currency of the European Union. It came into general circulation on 1 January 2002, initially for 12 participating countries, including Italy. The previous Italian currency, the lira, was phased out by March 2002. EU members using the euro as their sole official currency are known as the Eurozone. Several EU members have opted out of joining this common currency.

Euro notes are identical throughout the Eurozone countries, each one including designs of fictional architectural structures. The coins, however, have one side identical (the value side) and one side with an image unique to each country. Notes and coins are exchangeable in each participating country.

Bank Notes

Euro bank notes have seven denominations. The €5 note (grey in colour) is the smallest, followed by the €10 note (pink), €20 note (blue), €50 note (orange), €100 note (green), €200 note (yellow) and €500 note (purple). All notes show the 12 stars of the European Union.

€5 note

€10 note

€20 note

€50 note

€100 note

€200 note

€500 note

€2 coin €1 coin 50 cents 20 cents 10 cents

Coins

The euro has eight coin denominations: €1 and €2; 50 cents, 20 cents, 10 cents, 5 cents, 2 cents and 1 cent. The €2 and €1 coins are both silver and gold in colour. The 50-, 20- and 10-cent coins are gold. The 5-, 2- and 1-cent coins are bronze.

5 cents

2 cents

1 cent

Communications and Media

Although there are still plenty of public telephones throughout the Veneto, mobile phone networks are far-reaching, efficient and relatively low priced. Most hotels offer an Internet or Wi-Fi service to their guests; if not, Internet points are easy to find in the region, even in small towns. Foreign-language newspapers and magazines are on sale in all cities and main towns, and satellite TV has a vast range of foreign-language programmes from around the world. There are post offices located in all towns and villages for buying stamps and sending letters and parcels.

Telephones in a call centre run by Venetian Navigator

REACHING THE RIGHT NUMBER

To ring Italy from the UK and Ireland dial 00 39 then the number, including the full area code. From the US and Canada dial 0 11 39, and from Australia dial 00 11 39.

- Dialling code for
  Venice   041
  Verona   045
  Vicenza   0444
  Padua   049
  Treviso   0422
- International directory
  enquiries   176
- International operator
  assistance   170
- Telegrams and cables in
  Italy and abroad 186
- *See also* Emergency
  Numbers, p273.

INTERNATIONAL AND LOCAL TELEPHONE CALLS

A wide range of phonecards *(carte telefoniche prepagate)* are available at newsagents and tobacconists *(tabacchi)*. The latter are easily recognized thanks to the black-and-white "T" sign they display. For making local and Italian calls, the best option is a Telecom card; simply remove the dotted corner before inserting it into the phone. For overseas calls, specify the country you will be calling, so the vendor can advise you on the best card. To use these, call the toll-free number displayed on the card, enter the bar code information, then proceed with the overseas number. A recording will tell you how much credit is left before each call. These cards expire three months after the first call you make.

If you opt to use the phone in your hotel room, ask beforehand about the charges, which tend to be steep. A cheaper option is to use the privately owned call centres that are scattered around main cities.

Any Italian number must be prefixed by its full area code (including the "0"), even if it is a local number. Similarly, do not drop the "0" from in front of the area code when dialling an Italian number from abroad. The only numbers that do not require the "0" are those for the emergency services *(see p273)*, mobile phones (which start with a "3") and toll-free numbers (which begin with an "8").

MOBILE PHONES

Mobile phones are extremely useful when travelling abroad. If you have a tri-band/GSM phone it should work in Italy, but check with your mobile provider that this is the case before you leave. Your handset will need to have "roaming" activated in order to use it abroad and be aware that you will be charged extra for making and receiving calls while away. Reasonably priced prepaid phone-

Tabacchi sign

cards can be used for long-distance calls from a mobile *(see International and Local Telephone Calls)*. Alternatively, you might want to consider purchasing an Italian mobile phone or a SIM card through one of the major companies such as **TIM**, **Wind** and **Vodafone**. You will need to show your passport for identification. Take note that to activate your SIM card you will need to make a short call to a landline or another mobile phone, and that the cards usually expire 12 months after the last top-up.

PUBLIC TELEPHONES

You can find the silver-and-orange Telecom public telephones on the streets and squares of all the main towns in the Veneto, as well as at railway and bus stations. In Venice there are public telephones at most *vaporetto* landing stages and in privately owned call centres. Coin-operated phones have virtually been phased out in favour of phones that take phonecards.

Computer terminals at an Internet café

INTERNET AND EMAIL

Across the Veneto, Wi-Fi or Internet points are available in most hotels although a time-related fee may be charged.

Internet cafés are found in every city and most small towns. The main ones in Venice are **Venetian Navigator** and **Teleradiofuga**. Wi-Fi is available in many outdoor spaces in Venice and Padua for a fee; the municipality of Verona offers free Wi-Fi in some public areas. To access these Wi-Fi services you must register with **Venice Connected**, **Padua WiFi** or, if in Verona, at **URP** or a local library.

Post Office sign

POSTAL SERVICE

In summer, anything sent from Venice to destinations abroad takes some time to arrive, as thousands of postcards are sent from the city every day. For important communications, use the *Posta Prioritaria* (priority mail) or ask for a *Raccomandata* (registered post), which can be traced.

Stamps (*francobolli*) are available from post offices and tobacconists. Post office hours are usually 8:30am–2pm Monday to Friday (but main city offices close at 6pm) and 8:30am–noon on Saturdays.

Large items to be sent abroad must be in a rigid cardboard box, which can be purchased at most post offices. You will also need to fill in a customs declaration form. Small items can be sent in a padded envelope. The postal system offers a well-priced tracked courier service, *Paccocelere*, for sending packages both within Italy and overseas.

For a rapid worldwide delivery, consider a private courier. Both **DHL** and **UPS** have bases in Venice and the Veneto.

NEWSPAPERS AND MAGAZINES

The local daily newspapers *Il Gazzettino* and *La Nuova Venezia* have separate editions for Padua, Venice, Verona and Vicenza as well as covering national and some international news. Local event listings can be found in the dailies and also in *Eventi e Manifestazioni* (Venice) and *Carnet Verona* (see p268). European and US newspapers and magazines such as *The Guardian* and *Time*, are available at large newsagents (such as those found at main railway stations) a day or two after publication.

TELEVISION AND RADIO

In Italy there are three state TV channels – Rai 1, Rai 2 and Rai 3 – and a myriad of private channels. Satellite and cable TV transmit foreign channels such as CNN in English and BBC World Service in many languages.

The main radio stations, also run by Rai, are Radio 1, Radio 2 and Radio 3. The frequencies vary depending on where you are in the Veneto and if you have a digital or analogue radio. Visit www.raiway.it for more details.

GETTING TO VENICE AND THE VENETO

The easiest way to reach the Veneto is by air. Direct flights link Venice to other major European cities, and there are several inter-continental flights available too, although visitors travelling from outside Europe must transfer at Milan or Rome. Venice's Marco Polo airport, located 10 km (6.5 miles) north of the city, is supplemented by smaller airports at Treviso, 40 km (29 miles) northwest of Venice, and Verona, which is useful for Lake

Alitalia aircraft

Garda. The Italian rail network is far-reaching, and both Venice and Verona train stations have excellent links with all the other Veneto towns and major European cities. Car drivers must bear in mind toll charges on European motorways and heavy traffic. Visitors to Venice itself will have to leave their cars in one of the large car parks on the outskirts of the city because cars are not allowed in the centre. Parking fees are high.

View of the lagoon from Venice's Marco Polo airport

ARRIVING BY AIR

Venice is served by two airports: **Marco Polo** at Campalto, which is the closest to the city, and **Antonio Canova** at Treviso, a short distance inland. These airports receive both low-cost and commercial flights from cities in the United Kingdom and other European countries. Direct flights from the UK to Venice are operated by **British Airways**, **easyJet** and **Jet2**, whereas the national Italian carrier **Alitalia** flies via Rome.

Few intercontinental flights operate, but it is possible to fly direct from New York to Venice with **Delta Airlines**. Visitors from outside Europe can take a flight to London, Amsterdam, Frankfurt or Paris and connect to Venice or Treviso from there. **Emirates** also flies to Marco Polo Airport from Dubai, which is

the stopover of choice for many travellers from Australia and Asia on long-haul flights.

Most charter flights operate to Antonio Canova airport, as does the low-cost airline **Ryanair**.

Valerio Catullo airport is 12 km (7.5 miles) west of Verona. It is perfectly placed for visitors to Lake Garda and the Dolomites. Alitalia and low-cost airlines, such as Ryanair, have regularly scheduled flights to Verona.

TICKETS AND FARES

The best deals on tickets are usually found on the Internet. However, these offers are usually only available to those who book well in advance and avoid travelling over the peak periods: Christmas, New Year and Easter, as well as the European school holidays during July and August.

Remember to have a credit card to hand when booking online. If you wish to book a flight during your stay in the Veneto, travel agents such as **Bucintoro Viaggi** offer a good service.

For visitors who prefer the convenience of a package holiday, Venice is either offered as a single destination or as part of a two- or three-city holiday alongside Florence and Rome. Taking a package holiday with a tour operator may be less costly than going independently. It is always worth comparing the costs, however, particularly if you intend to travel off-season, when charter flights are at their cheapest. Transfers from the airport are usually included in the price of the holiday.

In the Veneto, most tour operators tend to concentrate on Venice alone, though some offer packages to Verona or tours of the wider region, taking in the most popular villas, museums and art galleries.

ON ARRIVAL

Passengers on flights originating within the EU do not need to pass through customs. Intercontinental flight passengers need to have both their passports and visas ready to show staff. For visa information, see p268.

A *vaporetto* boarding point along the Grand Canal

MARCO POLO AIRPORT (VENICE)

The facilities available at Marco Polo Airport include a tourist information kiosk, hotel reservation service, car-hire offices, post office, self-service restaurant and currency exchange office.

The most exciting entry from the airport in to Venice is by vaporetto. **Alilaguna** operate *vaporetti* terminal routes A, B, O and R that travel to Venice and the Lido, departing regularly from 6:10am to around midnight daily. The journey to Venice takes about an hour; tickets start at €12 per person, depending on your destination, and are available from the boarding point on the quayside, a short stroll away. The vaporetto stops at several *landing stages*, including San Marco, San Zaccaria and Fondamente Nuove. Water taxis operating from the airport to San Marco take about half the time but will cost around €100. There is also a €10 surcharge at night. Beware of water-taxi touts, who will charge you more than the official fare.

The less spectacular – but quicker and cheaper –alternative to the lagoon crossing is by an **ATVO** bus to Piazzale Roma. This service meets all scheduled flights and costs around €3.50. Cheaper still (€2.50) is the **ACTV** public bus No. 5 to Piazzale Roma, which departs every 30 minutes and makes several stops along the way. There is also a land taxi rank in front of the airport. The journey takes 15 minutes, and the drop-off point is Piazzale Roma.

ANTONIO CANOVA AIRPORT (TREVISO)

This small but modern airport receives low-cost flights from cities in the UK and other European countries. It has a tourist information office, foreign exchange and cafés.

To reach Venice, take a shuttle service to Piazzale Roma; this costs €5 and takes about 45 minutes. Or, you can take a public bus No. 6 for €1, which runs to Treviso station, from where there is a regular rail service to Venice.

VALERIO CATULLO AIRPORT (VERONA)

Verona airport receives flights from cities in the UK, other European countries and Africa. The bus service to Verona town centre, which links up with scheduled flights, costs about €5. In summer there is usually a direct minibus to localities on Lake Garda.

ARRIVING BY SEA

Minoan Lines and **Anek** run large ferries with cabins and vehicle decks from several ports in Greece most months of the year. A grand way to travel, the Istrian peninsula and the Dalmatian coast are linked to Venice through the summer by fast catamarans and ferries run by operators such as **Venezia Lines**, **Atlas** and **Commodore Cruises**.

Venice is also a key port for state-of-the-art cruise ships bound for the Mediterranean. Companies stopping here include **P&O Cruises** and **MSC Crociere**.

Both ferries and cruise ships dock at **Venezia Terminal Passeggeri**, a large terminal near Tronchetto that spreads along the lagoon and canalside from the Stazione Marittima basin to Santa Marta and San Basilio. Most of the six terminal sections have full passenger facilities, including cafés, ATMs, duty-free shops, waiting halls and information points.

An automated people mover carries passengers from the central part of the terminal to Piazzale Roma in minutes. However, for cruise passengers it is usually more convenient to travel by the shuttle buses that are provided by the individual cruise companies as they pull up at boarding points. The ACTV bus No. 6 also links the main terminal entrance with Piazzale Roma. Santa Marta and San Basilio are served by ACTV *vaporetto* lines Nos. 61 and 62, which terminate at the Lido.

The terminal is spread over a large area, so it is important for departing passengers to be clear about which section their ferry or ship leaves from. The terminal's website is very helpful, with clear maps.

Cruise ship moored at Venezia Terminal Passeggeri

Stamp ticket here

Machine for validating train tickets

ARRIVING BY COACH

Long-distance regional and
international coaches use
Piazzale Roma as their
terminus in Venice. Regular
lines run by **SITA** link Venice
with Padua, while services
run by **Dolomiti Bus** travel
to various localities in the
Dolomite Mountains. For
Europe-wide routes, try
Eurolines, which offers a
good-value multi-day pass
and pick-ups from Piazzale
Roma, or the slightly more
costly **Busabout**, with similar
routes but pick-ups outside
Venice. Tickets can be
purchased at the office in
Piazzale Roma or online in
advance of your travels.

ARRIVING BY TRAIN

The **Stazione Venezia Santa
Lucia**, Venice's railway station,
is a modern, well-equipped
station located at the western
end of the Grand Canal.
Santa Lucia is the terminus
for trains from Paris, Munich,
Innsbruck, Vienna, Geneva,
Zurich and other European
cities. Passengers travelling
from London will have to

change in Paris or Ostend.
Fast intercity trains link
Venice with Verona, Bologna,
Milan, Rome and other major
Italian cities.

If the ticket office is closed,
it is possible to purchase train
tickets from the automatic
machines in the station. They
display instructions in six
languages and accept notes,
coins and some credit cards.
Electronic display screens
give up-to-date information
on arrivals and departures,
as well as notice of any
delays. Facilities include
a tourist information office,
hotel reservation service,
telephones, bank, currency
exchange office, left-luggage
storage, self-service restaurant
and café, and a shop that
sells international newspapers
and magazines.

Just below the steps of the
station are *vaporetti* landing
stages with lines to all parts of
the city. There are also water
taxis, a gondola service and
porters. The bus and coach
terminal and the land taxi
rank are located in Piazzale
Roma, a short walk away.

Trenitalia offers reduced-
price tickets for travel throughout Italy and Europe if you
buy them in advance online.
Europe-wide train passes such
as **Eurail** (no age limit) and
InterRail (for those under 26
years of age) are accepted;
however, you will have to
pay a supplement to travel
on the fast trains.

The German **DB Bahn**
and the Austrian **OEBB** also
provide rail links between
Venice, Verona, Munich and
Innsbruck. Tickets for these
services can be purchased
online or on board.

ORIENT-EXPRESS

Operating between March
and November, the Venice
Simplon **Orient-Express**
travels between London
and Venice, stopping at
Paris, Innsbruck and Verona
en route. A one-way journey
with cabin from London
to Venice is the ultimate
romantic experience, but
it can cost as much as ten
times the price of a low-
cost flight. Prices are more
reasonable for a return
trip. Visit the website for
further information.

Orient-Express logo

ARRIVING BY CAR

To drive your own car in Italy
you will need an international
Green Card and your vehicle
registration documents. Also,
check your car insurance to
ensure you are fully covered
to drive abroad. European
Union nationals who do not
have the standard pink-
coloured driving licence
will also need an Italian
translation of their licence,
available from most motoring
organizations and Italian
tourist offices. Requirements
for visitors from non-EU
countries vary, so check with
your insurance company
before leaving for Italy.

The toll-paying A4 *auto-
strada* (motorway), links Turin
to Venice via Padua, Verona
and Vicenza – simply take the
relevant exit for your destination. The A27 from Venice
leads north beyond Vittorio
Veneto towards the Dolomites.

In Venice, parking is
prohibitively expensive. The
closest car parks to the city
centre are at Piazzale Roma or
on the Tronchetto, linked to
Venice by *vaporetto* and bus.
There are cheaper car parks
at Fusina and San Giuliano,
near Mestre *(see city map)*.

For more information on
driving in Italy (including
rules of the road), *see p287.*

Eurostar train travelling through the countryside in the Veneto

CAR HIRE

All the major international car-hire companies, such as **Hertz**, **Avis** and **Europcar**, have offices in the Veneto, both at airports and at the main train stations. It is worth doing an online search to find the best price or, if you fly with a low-cost carrier, check out the deals they offer. Always make sure that quoted prices include collision damage waiver, theft protection, unlimited mileage, a breakdown service and *Imposta sul Valore Aggiunto* (Value Added Tax; *see p269*).

To hire a car you must be over 25 and have held a licence for at least a year. You will also need to show your passport and a credit card. Visitors from outside the EU need an international licence, though not all hire firms insist on this. Vehicles are usually supplied with a full tank of fuel, so try to refill it before returning the car to avoid inflated costs. Child seats need to be booked in advance.

Vaporetto boarding point and water-taxi rank at Stazione Venezia Santa Lucia

PORTERS IN VENICE

Unless you are staying very close to your arrival point, you will need to take a *vaporetto* to the boarding point nearest to your hotel. Porters *(portabagagli)* are very expensive; not only do you have to pay their boat fare, you must also pay for each item of luggage, which are charged an adult fare. In addition to the *vaporetto* fares, the cost of a porter handling two suitcases could easily amount to €40.

DIRECTORY

ARRIVING BY AIR

Alitalia
Tel 06 22 22.
www.alitalia.it

Antonio Canova Airport (Treviso)
Tel 042 231 51 11.
www.trevisoairport.it

British Airways
Tel 199 712 266.
www.britishairways.com

Delta Airlines
Tel 848 780 376.
www.delta.com

easyJet
www.easyjet.com

Emirates
Tel 02 9148 3383.
www.emirates.com

Jet2
www.jet2.com

Marco Polo Airport (Venice)
Tel 041 260 92 60.
www.veniceairport.it

Ryanair
www.ryanair.com

Valerio Catullo Airport (Verona)
Tel 045 809 56 66.
www.aeroportoverona.it

TICKETS AND FARES

Bucintoro Viaggi
Campo S Luca, San Marco 4267c, Venice. **Map** 7 A2.
Tel 041 521 06 32.
www.bucintoroviaggi.com

TRANSPORT FROM THE AIRPORT

ACTV
Tel 041 2424. www.actv.it

Alilaguna
Tel 041 240 17 01.
www.alilaguna.com

ATVO
Tel 042 138 36 72.
www.atvo.it

ARRIVING BY SEA

Anek
www.anekitalia.com

Atlas
www.atlas-croatia.com

Commodore Cruises
www.commodore-cruises.hr

Minoan Lines
www.minoanlines.it

MSC Crociere
http://msccrociere.crocierissime.it

P&O Cruises
www.pocruises.com

Venezia Lines
www.venezialines.com

Venezia Terminal Passeggeri
www.vtp.it

ARRIVING BY COACH

Busabout
www.busabout.com

Dolomiti Bus
www.dolomitibus.it

Eurolines
www.eurolines.com

SITA
www.sitabus.it

ARRIVING BY TRAIN

DB Bahn
www.bahn.de

Eurail
www.eurail.com

InterRail
www.interrailnet.com

OEBB
www.oebb.at

Orient-Express
www.orient-express.com

Stazione Venezia Santa Lucia
Map 1 C5.
Tel 041 78 56 70.

Trenitalia
Tel 89 20 21.
Disabled Passengers:
Tel 199 303 060.
www.trenitalia.it

CAR HIRE

Venice
Avis *Tel 041 523 73 77.*
www.avisautonoleggio.it
Europcar *Tel 041 523 86 16.* www.europcar.it
Hertz *Tel 041 528 40 91.*
www.hertz.com

Padua
Avis *Tel 049 864 7661.*
Europcar *Tel 049 65 78 77.*
Hertz *Tel 049 875 22 02.*

Verona
Avis *Tel 045 800 66 36.*
Europcar *Tel 045 927 31 61.*
Hertz *Tel 045 800 08 32.*

Vicenza
Avis *Tel 044 432 16 22.*
Europcar *Tel 044 428 00 42.*
Hertz *Tel 044 423 17 28.*

PORTERS IN VENICE

Tel 041 715 272.

GETTING AROUND VENICE AND THE VENETO

Venice is a small city, and most of the main sights can be covered comfortably on foot. Cars are not allowed, instead pedestrians stroll the avenues and narrow passageways. To avoid getting lost in the maze of alleys and squares, use the Street Finder *(see pp288–301)*. The iconic gondola is the most romantic way to see the city from the canals and the lagoon. However, the excellent network of *vaporetti*, is more affordable. The boats also travel across the lagoon to the outlying islands. For those in a hurry, a water taxi is the fastest means of travelling across Venice. Day trips to the Veneto can be made by train or bus, and most of the cities can easily be explored on foot. For longer stays, a car is more practical as it offers complete independence to enjoy the countryside.

GREEN TRAVEL

Most Venetian motor boats and ferries run on diesel; however, efforts are under way to switch to a less polluting fuel. At least one battery-operated *vaporetto* is in service, and an eco-friendly Alilaguna *vaporetto* offers trips to and from the airport *(see p279)*. This boat was designed to minimize wave damage in the canals.

Other cities in the Veneto are served by large fleets of buses powered by clean methane gas.

Car-hire companies Hertz and Europcar *(see p281)* offer some "ecological" vehicles with reduced CO_2 emissions.

There are also a number of bicycle tours that operate in the Veneto. See local tourist offices for details.

FINDING YOUR WAY AROUND VENICE

Venice's system of addresses can be very confusing. All buildings are numbered by the *sestiere* (administrative district) in which they fall rather than the street. A typical address might read, for example, "San Marco 2517" or "Cannaregio 3499". In order to locate an address, therefore, it is essential to establish the name of the actual street or square or, failing that, the nearest landmark. Do not hesitate to ask for assistance, as Venetians are very helpful. Translations of Venetian words commonly used in place names can be found on *p288*.

WALKING

The absence of traffic makes exploring Venice on foot a great pleasure. Wear comfortable footwear as a day's sightseeing can be tiring. You will have to contend with the constant flow of other tourists, especially around San Marco and Rialto, where the narrow alleys become extremely con-gested. An unwritten Venetian rule is to keep to the right and avoid stopping on bridges and in narrow streets. However, most tourists never venture beyond San Marco, so it may be little more than a matter of minutes before you find yourself with only a few locals for company.

You need to allow just 45 minutes to cross the city from north to south on foot – provided you do not lose your way, though that is half the fun. The Street Finder and City maps in this guide will help you find your way around.

An ornate Venetian door knocker

As the city is so compact, you are never far from the yellow signs that give directions to the main sights. Venice has countless *campi* (squares) that open out from narrow alleys. Many of these are equipped with public benches, and weary tourists can enjoy a drink in an open-air café.

In July and August, when temperatures are at their highest, avoid walking in the middle of the day, unless you have a broad-rimmed sun hat. From October there is a risk of high tides *(acqua alta)*, which cause flooding across the city, starting with Piazza San Marco. Duckboards are laid out in the square, however, and along main thoroughfares. If you are not equipped with wellington boots, you can buy cheap knee-high plastic shoe covers from local shops.

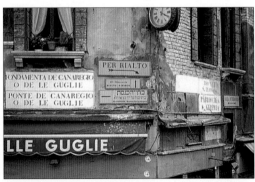

A plethora of confusing signs in Cannaregio

GUIDED TOURS

Tours with English-speaking guides in Venice and the outlying islands can be booked through tourist offices and travel agencies such as Viaggi Bucintoro *(see p281)*. One popular water tour takes you down the Grand Canal in a sleek *vaporetto*, with running commentary about the palaces en route. Other tours are on foot, visiting the city's main monuments. Costs range from €18 to €40 and can be booked at the Venetian tourist office *(see p271)*. Tours operated by the tourist board usually start at the main office in Piazza San Marco. The boat trips begin at various boarding points, mainly around the San Marco area.

In Verona and Padua, half-day tours are organized by each town's tourist office. Boat trips along the Brenta Canal between Venice and Padua *(see pp182–3)* are available from March to late October.

GONDOLAS

Gondolas are a luxury form of transport used only by tourists (apart from Venetians on their wedding day). There are a number of gondola ranks throughout the city and plenty of gondoliers in striped shirts and beribboned boater hats waiting for business on bridges and squares.

Before boarding, check the official tariffs and agree a price with the gondolier. Prices are

The romance of an early evening gondola ride

Crossing the Grand Canal by *traghetto*

posted on the **Gondoliers' Association** website, in the booklet *Un Ospite di Venezia (see p271)* and at gondola ranks. Official costs are around €80 for 40 minutes, rising to €100 from 7pm to 8am, but gondoliers are notorious for overcharging. Try bargaining – during the low season you may be able to negotiate a fee below the official rate and a journey shorter than the minimum of 40 minutes. Another way of cutting costs is to share a gondola – six is the maximum number of passengers.

Gondoliers all speak a smattering of English and have taken basic exams in Venetian history and art. Do not expect them to burst into "O Sole Mio", however; the most you are likely to hear are low cries of *oe* (watch out), *premi* (bear left) and *stai* (bear right) – the warning calls that have been echoing down the canals of Venice for centuries. If you want to go on a serenaded tour, travel agents regularly organize evening flotillas with accompanying musicians.

TRAGHETTI

Traghetti are gondola ferries that cross the Grand Canal at eight different points, providing an invaluable service for pedestrians. Surprisingly few tourists make use of this constant service, which costs only 50 cents. The points where the *traghetti* cross the Grand Canal are marked on the Street Finder maps *(see pp288–301)*. Yellow street signs show the way to the *traghetti*, illustrated with a little gondola symbol. You will be expected to do as the Venetians do, and travel the short distance standing up.

WATER TAXIS

For those with plenty of funds, the fastest means of getting around Venice is by water taxi. These sleek motorboats, all equipped with a cabin, zip to and from the airport in only 30 minutes. There are 16 water-taxi ranks, including one at the Lido and one at Marco Polo Airport. Water-taxi companies include **Consorzio Motoscafi**, **Serenissima** and **Veneziana Motoscafi**. Tariffs are listed in the booklet *Un Ospite di Venezia (see p271)*. There are extra charges for luggage, waiting, night service and for booking a taxi.

A water taxi

DIRECTORY

GONDOLAS

Gondola Stands
S. Marco (Molo). *Tel 041 520 06 85.*
Rialto (Riva Carbon).
Tel 041 522 49 04.
Railway Station (San Simeone Piccolo). *Tel 041 71 85 43.*

Gondoliers' Association
Tel 041 528 50 75.
www.gondolavenezia.it

WATER TAXIS

Consorzio Motoscafi
Tel 041 522 23 03.

Serenissima
Tel 041 522 12 65.

Veneziana Motoscafi
Tel 041 716 000/124.

Getting Around Venice by Vaporetto

For visitors to Venice, the *vaporetti*, or waterbuses, provide an entertaining form of public transport, although most journeys within the city can usually be covered just as quickly on foot. These waterbuses also supply a useful service connecting outlying points on the periphery of Venice and a link with the islands in the lagoon. The main route through the city is the Grand Canal, and the most useful service from a visitor's point of view is the No. 1. This line operates from one end of the Grand Canal to the other and travels sufficiently slowly for passengers to admire the parade of palaces at the waterside *(see pp56–71).*

Sightseeing from a *vaporetto* on the Grand Canal

THE BOATS

The original *vaporetti* were steam-powered motor boats (*vaporetto* means "little steamer"); today they run on diesel. Although all the boats tend to be called *vaporetti*, strictly speaking, this word applies only to the large, wide boats used on the slow routes, such as the No. 1. These boats provide the best views. The *motoscafi* are the slimmer, smaller and faster boats, such as the No. 52. Some of them might look old and rusty, but they go at quite a pace. The two-tier *motonavi*, which look huge in comparison to the *vaporetti* or *motoscafi*, are used on routes to outlying islands and the Lido.

TICKETS AND FARES

Tickets for the *vaporetti* are the same price irrespective of the length of journey, making the service very straightforward to use. Moreover, a range of timed tickets and passes provides decent savings over the standard single ticket price, especially if purchased in advance online.

If you only want to cross the Grand Canal, you can buy a *traghetto* ticket for 50 cents *(see p283).* A 60-minute *vaporetto* ticket costs €6.50 and allows travel for one hour from the time of validation. There are also 12-hour (€16), 24-hour (€18), 36-hour (€23), 48-hour (€28) and 72-hour (€33) tickets that entitle the holder to unlimited travel on most lines and offer better value. A one-week pass costs €50.

IMOB (electronic smart-card) passes are available from all ticket offices, such as the ones at Piazzale Roma, Ferrovia, Rialto and San Marco, as well as from tobacconists and newsagents displaying the **ACTV** logo. Reduced-price tickets can be purchased online through **Venice Connected**. Holders of the Rolling VENICEcard *(see p270)* can buy a *Tre Giorni Giovane*, or 3-day youth pass, for €18 *(see City Map).*

Note that the Alilaguna (to and from Marco Polo Airport; *see p279*), Clodia (from Chioggia to San Zaccaria) and Fusina (from Le Zattere to Fusina) lines need separate tickets.

TIMETABLES

The *vaporetti* are renowned for their punctuality, and the Venetians boast they can set their watches by them. There is just one timetable, covering both weekdays and public holidays. The only restrictions concern rowing events such as the Vogalonga *(see p33)* and the Regata Storica *(see p35),* when services are partially suspended, and the *acqua alta* high-tide flooding, when some lines are limited due to low bridges.

The main routes run every 10 to 20 minutes until the early evening, then at slightly less frequent intervals. All services are reduced at night, particularly after 1am, but a night route operates along the Giudecca and down the Grand Canal and to Rialto every 20 minutes (every 40 minutes to the Lido) through to early morning, when normal timetables resume. All of the outlying islands have round-the-clock *vaporetto* services.

Details of all the main *vaporetto* lines are in the ACTV timetable, available at most boarding points or online.

A *vaporetto* or waterbus

The smaller, sleeker *motoscafo*

THE MAIN ROUTES

① This is the slow *vaporetto* down the Grand Canal, stopping at every boarding point. The route starts at Piazzale Roma and travels the length of the Grand Canal; then, from San Marco, it heads east to the Lido.

② The No. 2 is the faster route down the Grand Canal. The whole route goes in a loop, starting at San Zaccaria, continuing westwards along the Giudecca Canal to Tronchetto and Piazzale Roma, then down the Grand Canal back to San Zaccaria, and from there out to the Lido (summer only).

㊶ ㊷ The 51 and 52 lines skirt the periphery of Venice and extend to the Lido. The circular "Giracittà" route provides a scenic tour of Venice, though to do the whole circuit you have to change at Fondamente Nuove.

㊹ ㊸ Circular "Giracittà" lines taking in Murano. The No. 41 travels anti-clockwise, while the No. 42 goes clockwise.

⑤ The No. 5 is a tourist route connecting San Zaccaria and Murano.

㊶ ㊷ These routes are the fast way to reach the Lido from Piazzale Roma.

⑬ The No. 13 leaves from Fondamente Nuove and travels to the "garden" islands, including Vignole and Sant'Erasmo.

Ⓛ Departing from the Fondamente Nuove, the LN (Laguna Nord) line serves the main islands in the northern lagoon: Murano, Mazzorbo, Burano and Torcello, circling via Punta Sabbioni and the Lido, before returning to San Zaccaria.

Ⓝ The N (night-time) line services all stops from Piazzale Roma, cruising along the Grand Canal to Lido Santa Maria Elisabetta.

USING THE VAPORETTI

The service is run by ACTV (*Azienda Consorzio Trasporti Veneziano*). The waterbus system is constantly being modified, and thus, while every effort is made to keep the map on the inside back cover of this guide up to date, it may not reflect the most recent changes. If you are not sure which *vaporetto* to take to reach your destination, check with the boatman – the *vaporetti* crew tend to be very helpful.

Timetable and routes at a *vaporetto* boarding point

1 Tickets are available at most boarding points, some bars, shops and tobacconists displaying the ACTV sign. The price of a ticket is the same whether you are going one stop or doing the whole circuit. There are also a variety of special tickets available (*see Tickets and Fares, opposite*).

2 Signs on the boarding point tell you which lines stop there.

3 Tickets should be swiped against the automatic machines on the boarding points before each journey. Inspectors travel on the *vaporetti*, and there are steep fines for passengers without valid tickets. There are notices in English to this effect in all the *vaporetti*.

4 An indicator board at the front of each *vaporetto* gives the line number and main stops. (Ignore the large black numbers on the side of the boat.)

5 Each boarding point has its name clearly marked on a yellow board. Most stops have two landing stages, and it is quite easy, particularly if it is crowded and you can't see which way the *vaporetto* is facing, to board a boat travelling in the wrong direction. It is helpful to watch which direction the *vaporetto* is approaching from; if in doubt, check with the boatman on board.

Getting Around the Veneto

The Veneto has many famous and historical cities, most of which are a comfortable day trip from Venice by train or bus. The smaller towns that surround Lake Garda are accessible by local bus, while the city centres of Verona and Padua can be explored on foot. The public transport networks are excellent and reasonably priced, discouraging car travel especially as motorways can be congested and tourist traffic is banned in city centres. Nevertheless, cars are more convenient when touring the Dolomites. Travelling by taxi is very expensive.

TRAIN TRAVEL

Trenitalia, Italy's state railway, runs an extensive and efficient network throughout the Veneto. Trains are regular and mostly punctual, and the cost of travel is reasonable. The variety of train services range from the slow *regionale*, stopping at almost every station en route, through the various intercity trains to the high-speed Freccia and Eurostar, which link Venice with Verona and beyond. Reduced fares are available if you book in advance online, otherwise tickets are available at stations. There are facilities for disabled travellers on intercity services *(see p281)*.

MAIN TRAIN STATIONS

For information on Venice's Santa Lucia Station, see p280. The nearest mainland station to Venice is Mestre, which lies at the end of the causeway leading to Venice. It is also the junction for lines to Conegliano, Treviso, Calalzo and the Friuli region.

Verona lies at the intersection of the main railway lines from Venice to Milan and from Bologna to Munich. The main station, Porta Nuova, lies a short distance south of the city centre and is connected to it by frequent buses. Facilities include a tourist office, left luggage storage and a newsagent that sells bus tickets. The small Porta Vescovo station, serving local stations to the east of Verona, is used mainly by locals.

Padua (Padova) is only 30 minutes by train from Venice. The station is in the north of the town; buses and a tram leave from outside the station for the centre, which is only a ten-minute walk away. Padua's station houses many facilities including a tourist office, a left luggage office and a bureau de change. The main bus terminal, with services to Venice and other towns in the Veneto, is adjacent.

Vicenza, 55 minutes from Venice, is on the main railway line between Verona and Padua. The station is a five-minute stroll south of the city centre, and services here include left luggage, ticket offices, tourist information and currency exchange.

TICKETS AND FARES

Main train stations have both ticket offices and easy-to-use self-service machines, which have clear instructions in several languages and accept both cash and credit cards. Ticket offices at many small railway stations have been replaced by a simpler machine that accepts cash only. Tickets can also be purchased on board all trains, but be aware that they will then be subject to a considerable surcharge.

Remember to stamp your ticket in the yellow machines at the entrance to the platform or on the platform before boarding the train.

Booking is compulsory when travelling on all of the fast Freccia, Eurostar and Intercity trains; it is also advisable to book in advance on other trains, especially if you wish to travel at busy times. If you are travelling less than 200 km (125 miles) on a *regionale* (local) train, ask for a *biglietto a fasce chilometriche* (short-range ticket). Available from the ticket office, as well as from tobacconists and newsagents at railway stations, this ticket is stamped with the destination you require. Both outward and return portions of a ticket must be used within three days of purchase. Like all other tickets, a *biglietto a fasce chilometriche* must be validated by inserting it in one of the yellow machines at the entrance to the platforms.

All tickets can be purchased on the Trenitalia website, often with good discounts if booked well ahead of the travel date.

BUS TRAVEL

City buses are cheap and regular. Tickets, which must be bought prior to travel, are available from newsstands, tobacconists and shops that display the bus company's logo. A flat fee is charged for rides within the city and the suburbs. The ticket becomes valid only when time-stamped in the machine on board the bus.

An ATV bus in front of the Roman arena in Verona

It is normally cheaper and quicker to travel between towns by train – in some cases, the bus can take twice as long as the train. However, there are a few towns, such as Asolo (see p167), where your only choice of public transport is by bus. In most cases the bus departure point is near the train station. You can usually buy a ticket valid for 1, 2 or more hours of travel to cover longer distances.

Venice has excellent bus connections to the Veneto from the hub at Piazzale Roma, where the main ticket offices are located.

TAXIS

Travelling by taxi in the Veneto is not cheap. Meters show a fixed starting charge, then clock up every kilometre. There are extra charges for luggage, trips to the airports and journeys taken between 10pm and 7am, on Sundays and on public holidays. Taxi drivers do not necessarily expect a tip – Italians give small tips or none at all.

Take taxis only from the official ranks, not from touts at railway stations and airports. In Venice the taxi rank is in Piazzale Roma; in Padua, Verona and Vicenza, taxis can be found in the main squares.

DRIVING AND PARKING

Many of the main roads in the region are old, with only a couple of lanes, and traffic can be heavy. What looks like a short trip on the map may take much longer than you expect. For more details on road conditions, contact the **CIS (Centro Informazione Stradale)**. Drivers must pay a toll to travel on Italian motor-ways (autostrade). Payment can be made in cash or by pre-paid magnetic cards called Viacards. These are available from the offices of the **ACI (Automobile Club d'Italia)** and tobacconists.

Motorway service stations are open 24 hours a day.

Petrol stations are scarce in the countryside, and many do not accept credit cards. However, there are self-service petrol stations that accept notes.

The ACI provides an efficient 24-hour breakdown service also available to foreign visitors. The organization has reciprocal arrangements with affiliated associations in other countries, such as the AA and RAC in Britain.

Many cities in the Veneto have limited-traffic zones, and normally only residents and taxis can drive into the centre. Visitors can drive up to their hotel to unload their luggage, but they must then park on the outside of town and come in on foot or by bus. Some hotels have a limited number of parking permits, but this is no guarantee of a space. Your best bet is to telephone in advance and warn the hotel of your arrival.

Official parking areas are marked by blue lines, usually with meters. The *disco orario* (parking disc) system allows free parking for a limited period in certain areas. Car-hire companies provide the cardboard discs

Disco orario parking disc

to place on your windscreen, indicating the time of your arrival. If your car is towed away, phone the **Polizia Municipale** (municipal police).

RULES OF THE ROAD

Drive on the right and, generally, give way to the right. Seat belts are compulsory in the front and back, and children should be properly restrained. You must also carry a warning triangle in case of breakdown. On secondary roads the speed limit is 90 km/h (55 mph), on main roads it is 110 km/h (70 mph) and on motorways 130 km/h (80 mph), though these are lower in fog or heavy rain. Penalties for speeding include spot fines and points added to your licence. There are also drink-driving laws; the blood-alcohol limit is 0.05 per cent. The use of mobile phones is forbidden, unless hands-free.

DIRECTORY

TRAIN TRAVEL

Trenitalia
Tel 892 021.
www.trenitalia.com

BUS TRAVEL

Belluno
Dolomiti Bus: *Tel 043 721 71 11.*
www.dolomitibus.it

Padua
APS Holding: *Tel 049 824 11 11.*
www.apsholding.it

Verona
ATV: *Tel 045 805 78 11.*
www.atv.verona.it

Vicenza
Aziende Industriali
Municipalizzate:
Tel 044 439 49 09.
www.aimvicenza.it

DRIVING AND PARKING

ACI (Automobile Club d'Italia)
Emergencies *Tel 803 116.*
www.aci.it
Via Ca' Marcello 67/d, Mestre.
Tel 041 531 03 62.
Via degli Scrovegni 19, Padua.
Tel 049 65 48 80.
Via Valverde 34, Verona.
Tel 045 59 50 03.
Via Enrico Fermi 233, Vicenza.
Tel 0444 96 60 46.

CIS (Centro Informazione Stradale)
Tel 1518 (Italian only).

Polizia Municipale
Venice *Tel 041 274 70 70.*
Padua *Tel 049 820 51 00.*
Verona *Tel 045 807 84 11.*
Vicenza *Tel 044 439 49 09.*

Speed limit (on minor road)   **End of speed restriction**

Pedestrianized street – no traffic   **Give way 320 m (350 yd) ahead**

VENICE STREET FINDER

All the sights, hotels, restaurants, shops and entertainment venues in Venice have map references which refer you to this section of the book. The key map below indicates the areas of the city covered by the Street Finder, and includes the colour coding specific to each area. Following the map section is a complete index of street names (see pp298–301). The standard Italian spelling has been used on the maps throughout this book, but when exploring the city you will find that the street signs are often printed in Venetian dialect. Sometimes this means only a slight variation in the spelling (see the word Sotoportico/Sotoportego below), but some names look completely different. For example, Santi Giovanni e Paolo (see Map 3) is often signposted as "San Zanipolo". Major sights are labelled in Italian.

RECOGNIZING STREET NAMES

The signs for street (calle), canal (rio) and square (campo) will soon become familiar, but the Venetians have a colourful vocabulary for the maze of alleys which makes up the city. When exploring, the following may help.

FONDAMENTA S.SEVERO

Fondamenta
A street that runs alongside a canal, often named after the canal it follows.

RIO TERRA GESUATI

Rio Terrà A filled-in canal. Similar to a rio terrà is a piscina, which often forms a square.

SOTOPORTEGO E PONTE S.CRISTOFORO

Sotoportico or Sotoportego
A covered passageway.

SALIZADA PIO X

Salizzada A main street (formerly a paved street).

RIVA DEI PARTIGIANI

Riva A wide fondamenta, often facing the lagoon.

RUGAGIUFFA

Ruga A street lined with shops.

CORTE DEI DO POZZI

Corte
A courtyard.

RIO MENUO O DE LA VERONA

Many streets and canals in Venice often have more than one name: o means "or".

0 metres 500
0 yards 500

Murano
(Inset on map pages 3 & 4)

3   **4**

Murano

GRANDE

San Marco   *Castello*

7   **8**

KEY TO STREET FINDER

	Major sight
	Place of interest
	Railway station
	Ferry boarding point
	Vaporetto boarding point
	Traghetto crossing
	Gondola mooring
	Coach station
	Tourist information office
	Hospital with casualty unit
P	Parking
	Police station
	Church
	Synagogue
	Post office
	Railway line

SCALE OF MAP PAGES

0 metres	200
0 yards	200

SCALE OF MURANO INSET

0 metres	500
0 yards	500

1 A B C

1

1

Canale delle

2

Canale Colambola

FONDAMENTA DI SACCA SAN GIROLAMO
SACCA DI SAN GIROLAMO
CALLE LARGA DEI PENITENTI
FONDAMENTA CASE NUOVE
FONDAMENTA CARLO
Rio di San
FONDAMENTA
CALLE FERAU
CALLE DEL FORNER
CPLO DELLE COOPERATIVE
CALLE TINTORIA
C.D. PORPORA
Tre Archi
FONDAMENTA DEL
Canale di Cannaregio
FONDAMENTA DI SAN GIOBBE
Ponte dei Tre Archi
CALLE D. MADONNA
CALLE D. STP SCURO
Rio di

3

CALLE DELLE BECCARIE
CPLO D. BECCARIE
C.D. MAGAZEN C.D. SCARLATTO
C. D. COLORI
CALLE D. TINTOR
CALLE CANNE
FONDAMENTA DI
Canale
San Giobbe
Crea
FMTA SAVORGNAN
CALLE BISCOTELLA
CALLE DELLA CERERIA
CAMPO SAN GIOBBE
CALLE BUSELLO
CALLE CENDON
Rio di San
Rio della Crea
CALLE SECONDA D. DO CONTI
CALLE
P O N T E   D E L L A   L I B E R T A
Rio della Crea

4

CALLE PESARO
CALLE DELLA MISERICORDIA
RAMO D. MISERICORDI
CALLE PRIULI DETTA DEI CAVALLETTI
CALLE CARMELITANI
RIO TERRA
Scalzi
Ferrovia
FMTA D. SCALZI
Ponte degli Scalzi

5

Stazione Ferrovie
dello Stato
Santa Lucia
Ferrovia
FONDAMENTA SANTA LUCIA
CALLE SAN SIMEON PICCOLO
CRO D. COMARE
S Simeon Piccolo
CALLE TRAGHETTO DI SANTA LUCIA
CAMPIELLO
CALLE BERGAMASCHI
Can. d. Santa Chiara
FONDAMENTA DI SANTA CHIARA
FONDAMENTA DI SANTA CHIARA
C. VOLTO DI SANTA CHIARA
Piazzale Roma
Ponte della Costituzione
FONDAMENTA SANTA CROCE
FONDAMENTA DEI TOLENTINI
GIARDINO EX PAPADOPOLI
CORTE CASE NUOVE
CAMPO DELLA LANA
STP

A **5** B C

Street Finder Index

General Index

Acknowledgments

Dorling Kindersley would like to thank the many people whose help and assistance contributed to the preparation of this book.

Main Contributors
Susie Boulton studied languages and history of art at the University of Cambridge. She has been visiting Venice for over 20 years and is the author of several guide books on the city.

Christopher Catling has been visiting Italy for over 25 years since his first archaeological dig there while he was a student at Cambridge University. He is the author of several guide books on Italian cities and regions, including *The DK Travel Guide to Florence and Tuscany*.

Additional Contributor
Gillian Price was born in England in 1953 but grew up in Sydney, Australia. She moved to Venice in 1981 and has written nine books on walking in Italy. Gillian has been contributing to Dorling Kindersley's Eyewitness Travel Guide series since 1998.

Sally Roy first got to know Venice while at school in Rome and has been returning to the country ever since. She read medieval history at St Andrew's University, Edinburgh, and has contributed to several books on Italy.

Additional Illustrations
Annabelle Brend, Dawn Brend, Neil Bulpitt, Richard Draper, Nick Gibbard, Kevin Jones Associates, John Lawrence, The Maltings Partnership, Simon Roulstone, Sue Sharples, Derrick Stone, Paul Weston, John Woodcock.

Additional Photography
Ian O'Leary, JoAnn Titmarsh.

Design and Editorial
Deputy Editorial Director Douglas Amrine
Deputy Art Director Gaye Allen
Map Co-ordinators Simon Farbrother, David Pugh
Production Hilary Stephens
Picture Research Ellen Root
Revisions Beverley Ager, Marta Bescos Sanchez, Uma Bhattacharya, Hilary Bird, Michael Blacker, Dawn Brend, Lucinda Cooke, Michelle Crane, Felicity Crowe, Stephanie Driver, Michael Ellis, Gadi Farfour, Emer FitzGerald, Anna Freiberger, Camilla Gersh, Vinod Harish, Mohammad Hassan, Irena Hoare, Annette Jacobs, Stuart James, Jasneet Kaur, Steve Knowlden, Vincent Kurien, Erika Lang, Jude Ledger, Carly Madden, Hayley Maher, Nicola Malone, Alison McGill, Ian Midson, Sonal Modha, Gillian Price, Pete Quinlan, Steve Rowling, Simon Ryder, Sands Publishing Solutions, Azeem Siddiqui,

Meredith Smith, JoAnn Titmarsh, Janis Utton, Conrad Van Dyk, Lynda Warrington, Fiona Wild.

Research Assistance
Jill De Cet, Hans Erlacher, Paolo Frullini, Oscar Gates, Marinella Laini, Elizabetta Lovato, Fabiola Perer, Alan Ross, Sarah Sole.

Index
Indexing Specialists, 202 Church Road, Hove, East Sussex, UK.

Special Assistance
Comune di Vicenza; Arch. Gianfranco Martinoni at the Assessorato Beni Culturali Comune di Padova; Ca' Macana; Cesare Battisti at the Media Tourist Office, Venice; Curia Patriarcale Venezia; D.ssa Foscarina Caletti at the Giunta Regionale di Venezia; Jane Groom, Brian Jordan; Alexandra Kennedy; Joy Parker; Frances Hawkins, Lady Frances Clarke and John Millerchip of the Venice in Peril Fund; the staff of the APT offices throughout the Veneto, in particular Anna Rita Bisaggio in Montegrotto Terme, Stephano Marchioro in Padua; Anna Maria Carlotto, Virna Scarduelli and Christina Erlacher in Verona, Anselmo Centomo in Vicenza; Heidi Wenyon.

Photography Permissions
Dorling Kindersley would like to thank the following for their kind permission to photograph at their establishments:
Venice: Amministrazione Provinciale di Venezia (Museo dell'Estuario, Torcello); Ca' Mocenigo; Ca' Pesaro; Ca' Rezzonico; Caffè Quadri; Collegio Armeni; Fondazione Europea Pro Venetia Viva, San Servolo; Fondazione Giorgio Cini (San Giorgio Maggiore); Peggy Guggenheim Museum; Hôtel des Bains; Libreria Sansoviniana; Museo Archeologico; Museo Correr; Museo Diocesano d'Arte Sacra; Museo Fortuny; Museo Storia Navale; Museo Storico Naturale; Museo Vetrario, Murano; Arch. Umberto Franzoi and staff at the Palazzo Ducale; Procuratie di San Marco (Basilica San Marco); Santi Giovanni e Paolo; San Lazzaro degli Armeni; Santa Maria Gloriosa dei Frari; Scuola Grande dei Carmini; Scuola Grande di San Rocco.
Veneto: Arena Romano, Verona; Basilica, Vicenza; Caffè Pedrocchi, Padua; Duomo, Padua; Duomo, Vicenza; Giardini Giusti, Verona; Museo Archeologico, Verona; Museo di Castelvecchio, Verona; Museo Civico, Malcésine; Museo Civico, Vicenza; Museo Concordiese, Portogruaro; Museo degli Eremitani, Padua; Museo Lapidario Maffeiano, Verona; Museo dei Storia Naturale, Verona; Ossuario di San Pietro, Solferino; Sant'Anastasia, Verona; San Fermo Maggiore, Verona; San Giorgio, Monsélice; San Giorgio in Braida, Verona; San Lorenzo, Vicenza;

Santa Maria in Organo, Verona; San Pietro in
Malvino, Sirmione; San Severo, Bardolino;
San Stefano, Verona; San Zeno Maggiore,
Verona; Santuario di Monte Berico, Vicenza;
Teatro Olimpico, Vicenza; Università di
Padova; Contessa Diamante Luling-Buschette,
Villa Barbaro, Masèr; Conte Marco Emo, Villa
Emo, Fanzolo di Vedelago.

Picture credits
a = above; b = below/bottom; c = centre;
f = far; l = left; r = right; t = top.

Works of art have been reproduced with the
permission of the following copyright holders:
Maiastra 1912 Constantin Brancusi © ADAGP,
Paris and DACS, London 2011 134cr; *Interno
Olandese II* c.1928 Joan Miró © Successio Miró/
ADAGP, Paris and DACS, London 2011 134c;
Matisse at Venice Biennale 1992 Larry Rivers
© DACS, London/VAGA, New York 2011 256tc.

The publishers are grateful to the following
museums, companies, and picture libraries for
permission to reproduce their photographs:

ACCADEMIA OLIMPICA, VICENZA: 172tr, 173crb; ACE
PHOTO/AGENCY TORE GILL: 254b; ACE/MAURITIUS:
257t; ACTV S.P.A: 279tl, 282clb; AEROPORTO DI
VENEZIA MARCO POLO: 278cl; AIG - ITALIAN YOUTH
HOSTELS ASSOCIATION: 222tc, 225bl; ALAMY IMAGES:
AA World Travel Library 239cl; CuboImages
srl/Bluered 11bl; directphoto.bz 272br; VIEW
Pictures Ltd./Daniel Clements 51bc; FAN
travelstock/Michael Schindel 264cr; Cris Haigh
239tl; Jon Arnold Images 186; Jon Arnold
Images/Demetrio Carrasco 263cr; Michael
Juno 238cla; Aguilar Patrice 30tr; Travelshots.
com 10tc; travelstock44 10bl; ANCIENT ART &
ARCHITECTURE COLLECTION: 38c, 40br, 40tl; APT
DEL BRESCIANO: 35b; ARCHIV FÜR KUNST UND
GESCHICHTE: 26tl/c/cr, 30bl, 36, 43br, 44crb,
45bl, 45t, 46tl, 46tr, 48cla, 49clb, 50b, 54br,
130b, 131b, 131c, 132b, 133t, 30/31c; ARCHIVIO
RAIMONDO ZAGO 49cl. ARCHIVIO VENEZIANO: Sarah
Quill 29br, 51crb, 67cl, 106tr, 144t; ATV -
AZIENDA TRASPORTI VERONA S.R.L.: 286br.

BANCA POPOLARE DI VICENZA: 274cla; BAUER
L'HOTEL: 223tr; BIBLIOTECA CIVICA DI TRIESTE
(FOTO HALUPCA): 119b; BRIDGEMAN ART LIBRARY,
LONDON: *Madonna and Child and Saints*
(triptych altarpiece) by Giovanni Bellini
(c.1431–1516), Santa Maria dei Frari, Venice
27tl/tr; *The Siege of Antioch* 1098 by William
of Tyre. Bibliothèque Nationale, Paris 40cla;
Marco Polo with Elephants and Camels from
Livre des Merveilles, Bibliothèque Nationale,
Paris, 42cb; *View of Venice* by Bernardo von
Breitenbach, from Opusculum Sanctarum
Peregrinationum in Terram Sanctam,
Bibliothèque Nationale, PARIS, 8–9; *Family*

Tree of the Cornaro Family, Italian School
(18th century), Palazzo Corner Ca' Grande,
Venice, 69tr; *Salome* by Gustav Klimt (1862–
1918) Museo d'Arte Moderna, Venice, 105br;
The Nuns' Visiting Day by Francesco Guardi
(1712–93), Museo Ca' Rezzonico, Venice,
112bl; *St George Killing the Dragon* by Vittore
Carpaccio (c.1460/5–1523/6), Scuola di San
Giorgio degli Schiavoni, Venice, 118tl; *The
Stealing of the Body of St Mark* by Tintoretto
(1518–94), Accademia, Venice, 131t; *The Rape
of Europa* by Francesco Zuccarelli, Accademia,
Venice, 133c; *Marco Polo dressed in Tartar
costume* (c.1700) Museo Correr, Venice/
Giraudon, 4tr/115br; OSVALDO BÖHM: 20b,
20cl, 29bl, 41crb, 63tl, 79tl, 132c, 132t, 144c.

DEMETRIO CARRASCO: 124b, 139br, 141t, 227tr,
274t; CENTRO EUROPEO MESTIERI: 262br; CEPHAS
PICTURE LIBRARY: Mick Rock, 35cra and 238tr;
CIGA HOTELS: 70tl; CLAIRE CALMAN: 55cr; GIAN-
CARLO COSTA: 47clb; CORBIS: Stefano Amantini
266–7, Ashley Cooper 263tl, William Manning
10cr, royalty-free 146; JOE CORNISH: 15b, 209c,
216bl; STEPHANIE COLASANTI: 56, 195br.

DOLOMITI SUPERSKI: Freddy Planinschek 262tc,
264bl; CHRIS DONAGHUE THE OXFORD PHOTO
LIBRARY: 3 (inset), 5tl, 76t, 156br, 280t; MICHAEL
DENT: 82b, 252tl; DRAUGHTSMAN: 268tr.

E.T. ARCHIVE: Sala dei Prior Siena, 41tl;
Baroque Hall of Mirrors, Palazzo Papadopoli,
Venice, 64tl; *The Apothecary's Shop* by Pietro
Longhi, Accademia, Venice, 130c; ELECTA,
MILAN: 180cr, 181t/cl; ERIZZO EDITRICE SRL:
105clb; THE EURAIL GROUP: 280bl, 281tr; MARY
EVANS PICTURE LIBRARY: 7 (inset), 9 (inset), 24tl,
39clb, 44bl, 47br, 47t, 53 (inset), 58cra, 58tr,
63c, 64c, 69ca, 143tr, 159 (inset), 221 (inset),
259 (inset), 32c.

FERROVIA DELLO STATO: 272tl.

JACKIE GORDON: 273t; GRAZIA NERI: 41b, 49tl,
50crb, 50tr, 65br, 92tl, 157b, 254t; Marco
Bruzzo, 5tr, 32t, 35clb, 40tr, 166t; Cameraphoto
71tr, 115bl, 42/43c; Graziano Arici 100tr;
Roberta Krasnig 268bl; PEGGY GUGGENHEIM
MUSEUM, VENICE: 134b; THE RONALD GRANT
ARCHIVE: 50cla.

HEMISPHERES IMAGES: Maurizio Borgese 16;
ROBERT HARDING PICTURE LIBRARY: 216cl; HOTEL
EXCELSIOR, VENICE LIDO: 48crb; HOTEL ROSSI:
226tc; THE HULTON DEUTSCH COLLECTION: 38br,
38tr, 39br, 43clb, 46br, 48bc, 49br, 61tr, 66b,
66cra, 69cl, 101c, 140bl, 181br, 199b.

IMAGE BANK: Guido A. Rossi, 11 (inset); IMAGE
SELECT: Ann Ronan, 44cl. LONDRA PALACE: 226br
HUGH MCKNIGHT PHOTOGRAPHY: 71tl; MAGNUM

PHOTOS/DAVID SEYMOUR: 48tr; MARKA: 37b, L Baldissin 237bcb; L Barbazza 249br; Roberto Benzi 276cl; Enrico Cerretelli 150bl; Cristina Dogliani 262b; M Motta 277cl; Ubik 237bcla, Ubik/Pizzo 237bcar; MORO ROMA: 30cl, 48/49c; MUSEO ARCHEOLOGICO, VERONA: 38bl; MUSEO CIVICO AGLI EREMITANI: 179t/c/b; MUSEO CIVICO DI ODERZO: 39t; THE MANSELL COLLECTION: 46crb, 47bl.

NEWIMAGE S.R.L.: 33bc; Rolando Fabriani 33bc; NHPA/GERARD LACZ: 217b; NHPA/LAURIE CAMPBELL: 217c; NHPA/SILVESTRIS FOTOSERVICE: 217crb; THE NATIONAL GALLERY, LONDON: 29t.

OFFICINA: 277tl; OLYMPIA/SELECT: 34b, 51br, 51clb, 157t, 255t; OLYMPIA/SELECT/LARRY RIVERS: 256t; ORIENT-EXPRESS HOTELS, TRAINS & CRUISES: 280cra.

PALAZZO ABADESSA: 223bl; PERFORMING ARTS LIBRARY/GIANFRANCO FAINELLO: 256c; POLIZIA DI STATO, QUESTURA DI VENEZIA: 272cla, 272crb; PORTO DI VENEZIA (CAMPIONE/DEVELON.COM): 279br.

THE ROYAL COLLECTION ©1994 HER MAJESTY QUEEN ELIZABETH 11: 46/47c.

JOHN FERRO SIMS: 167t; SCALA, FIRENZE: *Madonna di Ca' Pesaro* by Titian (1477/89–1576), S. Maria Gloriosa dei Frari, Venice 27, c/cr; *Ultimi Momenti del Doge Marin Faliero* by Francesco Hayez (1791– 1881), Pinacoteca di Brera, Milan, 43t; *Banquet of Antony and Cleopatra* by Giambattista Tiepolo (1692–1770), Palazzo Labia, Venice, 60t; *Ultimi Momenti del Doge Marin Faliero* by Francesco Hayez (1791–1881), Pinacoteca di Brera, Milan, 68cra; *Crocifissione* by Tintoretto (1518–94), Scuola Grande di S. Rocco, Venice, 106c/cb; *S Michele* by Giambono (15th century), Accademia, Venice, 123b; *Il Trasporto della Santa Casa di Loreto*

by Giambattista Tiepolo (1692–1770), Accademia, Venice, 130tr; *Presentazione al tempio* by Titian (1477/89– 1576), Accademia, Venice,133b; *Intérieur Hollandais II* by Joan Miró (1928), Museo Guggenheim, Venice, 134c; *Madonna col Bambino* by Filippo Lippi (1406–69), Cini Collection, Venice 134t; *Annunciazione* by Vittore Carpaccio (1460 c.– 1526), Ca' d'Oro, Venice,144b; Pala di San Zeno by Andrea Mantegna (1431–1506), San Zeno, Verona, 200cl; SCIENCE PHOTO LIBRARY: Earth Satellite Corporation 10 (inset); SETTORE BENI CULTURALI, PADUA: 180t/ cla/ clb; SPECTRUM COLOUR LIBRARY: 28b; STUDIO PIZZI: 45cla, 47crb; TONY STONE IMAGES: 214cla, 216t, 50/51c; SUPERSTOCK: Steve Vidler 11tr.

TASTING PLACES: 262cl.

UNITED COLORS OF BENETTON: Josh Olins 51tl.

VELA SPA: 283ca, 283cb; VENETIAN NAVIGATOR: 276cla.

FRONT ENDPAPER
ALAMY IMAGES: Jon Arnold Images Ltd.; CORBIS: Ron Watts Rbl.

MAP COVER
PHOTOLIBRARY: Jose Moya.

JACKET
Front - PHOTOLIBRARY: Jose Moya.
Back - ALAMY IMAGES: blickwinkel/McPHOTO/ RUD clb; AWL IMAGES: Demetrio Carrasco tl; DORLING KINDERSLEY: John Heseltine cla, bl. Spine - PHOTOLIBRARY: Jose Moya t.

All other images © Dorling Kindersley. For further information see: **www.dkimages.com**

SPECIAL EDITIONS OF DK TRAVEL GUIDES

DK Travel Guides can be purchased in bulk quantities at discounted prices for use in promotions or as premiums. We are also able to offer special editions and personalized jackets, corporate imprints, and excerpts from all of our books, tailored specifically to meet your own needs.

To find out more, please contact:
(in the United States) **SpecialSales@dk.com**
(in the UK) **travelspecialsales@dk.com**
(in Canada) DK Special Sales at **general@tourmaline.ca**
(in Australia) **business.development@pearson.com.au**

Phrase Book

In Emergency

Help!	Aiuto!	eye-**yoo**-toh
Stop!	Fermate!	fair-**mah**-teh
Call a doctor.	Chiama un medico	kee-**ah**-mah oon **meh**-dee-koh
Call an ambulance.	Chiama un' ambulanza	kee-**ah**-mah oon am-boo-**lan**-tsa
Call the police.	Chiama la polizia	kee-**ah**-mah lah pol-ee-**tsee**-ah
Call the fire brigade.	Chiama i pompieri	kee-**ah**-mah ee pom-pee-**air**-ee
Where is the telephone?	Dov'è il telefono?	dov-eh eel teh-**leh**-foh-noh?
The nearest hospital?	L'ospedale più vicino?	loss-peh-**dah**-leh pee-oovee-**chee**-noh?

Communication Essentials

Yes/No	Sì/No	see/noh
Please	Per favore	pair fah-**vor**-eh
Thank you	Grazie	**grah**-tsee-eh
Excuse me	Mi scusi	mee **skoo**-zee
Hello	Buon giorno	bwon **jor**-noh
Goodbye	Arrivederci	ah-ree-veh-**dair**-chee
Good evening	Buona sera	**bwon**-ah sair-ah
morning	la mattina	lah mah-**tee**-nah
afternoon	il pomeriggio	eel poh-meh-**ree**-joh
evening	la sera	lah **sair**-ah
yesterday	ieri	ee-**air**-ee
today	oggi	**oh**-jee
tomorrow	domani	doh-**mah**-nee
here	qui	kwee
there	la	lah
What?	Quale?	**kwah**-leh?
When?	Quando?	**kwan**-doh?
Why?	Perchè?	pair-**keh**?
Where?	Dove?	**doh**-veh

Useful Phrases

How are you?	Come sta?	koh-meh stah?
Very well, thank you.	Molto bene, grazie.	**moll**-toh **beh**-neh **grah**-tsee-eh
Pleased to meet you.	Piacere di conoscerla.	pee-ah-**chair**-eh dee coh-**noh**-shair-lah
See you soon.	A più tardi.	ah pee-**oo** tar-dee
That's fine.	Va bene.	va **beh**-neh
Where is/are ...?	Dov'è/Dove sono...?	dov-eh/doveh **soh**-noh?
How long does it take to get to ...?	Quanto tempo ci vuole per andare a ...?	**kwan**-toh **tem**-poh chee voo-**oh**-leh pair an-**dar**-eh ah ...?
How do I get to ...?	Come faccio per arrivare a ...?	koh-meh **fah**-choh pair arri-**var**-eh ah...?
Do you speak English?	Parla inglese?	**par**-lah een-**gleh**-zeh?
I don't understand.	Non capisco.	non ka-**pee**-skoh
Could you speak more slowly, please?	Può parlare più lentamente, per favore?	pwoh par-**lah**-reh pee-oo len-ta-**men**-teh pair fah-**vor**-eh
I'm sorry.	Mi dispiace.	mee dee-spee-**ah**-cheh

Useful Words

big	grande	**gran**-deh
small	piccolo	**pee**-koh-loh
hot	caldo	**kal**-doh
cold	freddo	**fred**-doh
good	buono	**bwoh**-noh
bad	cattivo	kat-**tee**-voh
enough	basta	**bas**-tah
well	bene	**beh**-neh
open	aperto	ah-**pair**-toh
closed	chiuso	kee-**oo**-zoh
left	a sinistra	ah see-nee-strah
right	a destra	ah **dess**-trah
straight on	sempre dritto	**sem**-preh **dree**-toh
near	vicino	vee-**chee**-noh
far	lontano	lon-**tah**-noh
up	su	soo
down	giù	joo
early	presto	**press**-toh
late	tardi	**tar**-dee
entrance	entrata	en-**trah**-tah
exit	uscita	oo-**shee**-ta
toilet	il gabinetto	eel gab-bee-**net**-toh
free, unoccupied	libero	**lee**-bair-oh
free, no charge	gratuito	grah-**too**-ee-toh

Making a Telephone Call

I'd like to place a long-distance call.	Vorrei fare una interurbana.	vor-**ray** far-eh oona in-tair-oor-**bah**-nah
I'd like to make a reverse-charge call.	Vorrei fare una telefonata a carico del destinatario.	vor-**ray** far-eh oona teh-leh-fon-**ah**-tah ah **kar**-ee-koh dell dess-tee-nah-**tar**-ree-oh
I'll try again later.	Ritelefono più tardi.	ree-teh-**leh**-foh-noh pee-oo **tar**-dee
Can I leave a message?	Posso lasciare un messaggio?	**poss**-oh lash-**ah**-reh oon mess-**sah**-joh?
Hold on.	Un attimo, per favore	oon **ah**-tee-moh, pair fah-**vor**-eh
Could you speak up a little please?	Può parlare più forte, per favore?	pwoh par-**lah**-reh pee-oo **for**-teh, pair fah-**vor**-eh?
local call	la telefonata locale	lah teh-leh-fon-**ah**-ta loh-**kah**-leh

Shopping

How much does this cost?	Quant'è, per favore?	kwan-**teh** pair fah-**vor**-eh?
I would like ...	Vorrei ...	vor-**ray**
Do you have ...?	Avete ...?	ah-**veh**-teh... ?
I'm just looking.	Sto soltanto guardando.	stoh sol-**tan**-toh gwar-**dan**-doh
Do you take credit cards?	Accettate carte di credito?	ah-chet-**tah**-teh **kar**-teh dee **creh**-dee-toh?
What time do you open/close?	A che ora apre/ chiude?	ah keh **or**-ah **ah**-preh/kee-**oo**-deh?
this one	questo	**kweh**-stoh
that one	quello	**kwell**-oh
expensive	caro	**kar**-oh
cheap	a buon prezzo	ah bwon **pret**-soh
size, clothes	la taglia	lah **tah**-lee-ah
size, shoes	il numero	eel **noo**-mair-oh
white	bianco	bee-**ang**-koh
black	nero	**neh**-roh
red	rosso	**ross**-oh
yellow	giallo	**jal**-loh
green	verde	**vair**-deh
blue	blu	bloo
brown	marrone	mar-**roh**-neh

Types of Shop

antique dealer	l'antiquario	lan-tee-**kwah**-ree-oh
bakery	la panetteria	lah pah-net-tair-**ree**-ah
bank	la banca	lah **bang**-kah
bookshop	la libreria	lah lee-breh-**ree**-ah
butcher's	la macelleria	lah mah-chell-eh-**ree**-ah
cake shop	la pasticceria	lah pas-tee-chair-**ee**-ah
chemist's	la farmacia	lah far-mah-**chee**-ah
delicatessen	la salumeria	lah sah-loo-meh-**ree**-ah
department store	il grande magazzino	eel **gran**-deh mag-gad-**zee**-noh
fishmonger's	la pescheria	lah pess-keh-**ree**-ah
florist	il fioraio	eel fee-or-eye-**oh**
greengrocer	il fruttivendolo	eel froo-tee-**ven**-doh-loh
grocery	alimentari	ah-lee-men-**tah**-ree
hairdresser	il parrucchiere	eel par-oo-kee-**air**-eh
ice cream parlour	la gelateria	lah jel-lah-tair-**ree**-ah
market	il mercato	eel mair-**kah**-toh
news-stand	l'edicola	leh-**dee**-koh-lah
post office	l'ufficio postale	loo-**fee**-choo pos-**tah**-leh
shoe shop	il negozio di scarpe	eel neh-**goh**-tsioh dee **skar**-peh
supermarket	il supermercato	su-pair-mair-**kah**-toh
tobacconist	il tabaccaio	eel tah-bak-eye-**oh**
travel agency	l'agenzia di viaggi	lah-jen-**tsee**-ah dee vee-**ad**-jee

Sightseeing

art gallery	la pinacoteca	lah peena-koh-**teh**-kah
bus stop	la fermata dell'autobus	lah fair-**mah**-tah dell **ow**-toh-booss
church	la chiesa	lah kee-**eh**-zah
	la basilica	lah bah-**seel**-i-kah
closed for the public holiday	chiuso per la festa	kee-**oo**-zoh pair lah **fess**-tah
garden	il giardino	eel jar-**dee**-no
library	la biblioteca	lah beeb-lee-oh-**teh**-kah
museum	il museo	eel moo-**zeh**-oh
railway station	la stazione	lah stah-tsee-**oh**-neh
tourist information	l'ufficio turistico	loo-**fee**-choh too-**ree**-stee-koh

Staying in a Hotel

Do you have any vacant rooms?	**Avete camere libere?**	ah-**veh**-teh kah-mair-eh **lee**-bair-eh?
double room	**una camera doppia**	oona **kah**-mair-ah **doh**-pee-ah
with double bed	**con letto matrimoniale**	kon **let**-toh mah-tree-moh-nee-**ah**-leh
twin room	**una camera con due letti**	oona **kah**-mair-ah kon **doo**-eh **let**-tee
single room	**una camera singola**	oona **kah**-mair-ah **sing**-goh-lah
room with a bath, shower	**una camera con bagno, con doccia**	oona **kah**-mair-ah kon **ban**-yoh, kon **dot**-chah
porter	**il facchino**	eel fah-**kee**-noh
key	**la chiave**	lah kee-**ah**-veh
I have a reservation.	**Ho fatto una prenotazione.**	oh **fat**-toh oona preh-noh-tah-tsee-**oh**-neh

Eating Out

Have you got a table for …?	**Avete una tavola per … ?**	ah-**veh**-teh oona **tah**-voh-lah pair …?
I'd like to reserve a table.	**Vorrei riservare una tavola.**	vor-**ray** ree-sair-**vah**-reh oona **tah**-voh-lah
breakfast	**colazione**	koh-lah-tsee-**oh**-neh
lunch	**pranzo**	**pran**-tsoh
dinner	**cena**	**cheh**-nah
The bill, please.	**Il conto, per favore.**	eel **kon**-toh pair fah-**vor**-eh
I am a vegetarian.	**Sono vegetariano/a.**	**soh**-noh veh-jeh-tar-ee-**ah**-noh/nah
waitress	**cameriera**	kah-mair-ee-**air**-ah
waiter	**cameriere**	kah-mair-ee-**air**-eh
fixed price menu	**il menù a prezzo fisso**	eel meh-**noo** ah **pret**-soh **fee**-soh
dish of the day	**piatto del giorno**	pee-**ah**-toh dell **jor**-no
starter	**antipasto**	an-tee-**pass**-toh
first course	**il primo**	eel **pree**-moh
main course	**il secondo**	eel seh-**kon**-doh
vegetables	**il contorno**	eel kon-**tor**-noh
dessert	**il dolce**	eel **doll**-cheh
cover charge	**il coperto**	eel koh-**pair**-toh
wine list	**la lista dei vini**	lah **lee**-stah day **vee**-nee
rare	**al sangue**	al **sang**-gweh
medium	**al puntino**	al poon-**tee**-noh
well done	**ben cotto**	ben **kot**-toh
glass	**il bicchiere**	eel bee-kee-**air**-eh
bottle	**la bottiglia**	lah bot-**teel**-yah
knife	**il coltello**	eel kol-**tell**-oh
fork	**la forchetta**	lah for-**ket**-tah
spoon	**il cucchiaio**	eel koo-kee-**eye**-oh

Menu Decoder

l'acqua minerale gasata/naturale	**lah**-kwah mee-nair-**ah**-leh gah-**zah**-tah/nah-too-**rah**-leh	mineral water fizzy/still
l'agnello	lahn-**yell**-oh	lamb
al forno	al **for**-noh	baked
alla griglia	ah-lah **greel**-yah	grilled
l'anguilla	lahng-**gwee**-lah	eel
l'aragosta	lah-rah-**goss**-tah	lobster
arrosto	ar-**ross**-toh	roast
il baccalà	eel bahk-kah-**lah**	dried salted cod
la birra	lah **beer**-rah	beer
la bistecca	lah bee-**stek**-kah	steak
il brodetto	eel-broh-**det**-toh	fish soup
il burro	eel **boor**-oh	butter
il caffè	eel kah-**feh**	coffee
i calamari	ee kah-lah-**mah**-ree	squid
il carciofo	eel kar-**choff**-oh	artichoke
la carne	la **kar**-neh	meat
carne di maiale	**kar**-neh dee mah-**yah**-leh	pork
i fagioli	ee fah-**joh**-lee	beans
il fegato	eel **fay**-gah-toh	liver
il formaggio	eel for-**mad**-joh	cheese
le fragole	leh frah-goh-leh	strawberries
il fritto misto	eel free-toh **mees**-toh	mixed fried fish
la frutta	la **froot**-ah	fruit
frutti di mare	**froo**-tee dee **mah**-reh	seafood
i funghi	ee **foon**-ghee	mushrooms
i gamberi	ee **gam**-bair-ee	prawns
il gelato	eel jel-**lah**-toh	ice cream
l'insalata mista	leen-sah-lah-tah **mees**-tah	mixed salad
l'insalata verde	leen-sah-lah-tah **vehr**-day	green salad

il latte	eel **laht**-teh	milk
i legumi OR **i contorni**	ee leh-**goo**-mee ee kon-**tor**-nee	vegetables
il manzo	eel **man**-tsoh	beef
la melanzana	lah meh-lan-**tsah**-nah	aubergine
la minestra	lah mee-**ness**-trah	soup
il pane	eel **pah**-neh	bread
il panino	eel pah-**nee**-noh	bread roll
le patate	leh pah-**tah**-teh	potatoes
le patatine fritte	leh pah-tah-**teen**-eh **free**-teh	chips
il pepe	eel **peh**-peh	pepper
la pesca	lah **pess**-kah	peach
il pesce	eel **pesh**-eh	fish
il pollo	eel **poll**-oh	chicken
il prosciutto cotto/crudo	eel pro-**shoo**-toh **kot**-toh/**kroo**-doh	ham cooked/cured
il riso	eel **ree**-zoh	rice
il sale	eel **sah**-leh	salt
la salsiccia	lah sal-**see**-chah	sausage
le seppie	leh **sep**-pee-eh	cuttlefish
secco	**sek**-koh	dry
la sogliola	lah **soll**-voh-lah	sole
i spinaci	ee spee-**nah**-chee	spinach
succo d'arancia/ di limone	**soo**-koh dah-**ran**-chah/ dee lee-**moh**-neh	orange/lemon juice
il tè	eel **teh**	tea
la tisana	lah tee-**zah**-nah	herbal tea
il tonno	eel **ton**-noh	tuna
la torta	lah **tor**-tah	cake/tart
la trippa	lah **treep**-pah	tripe
vino bianco	**vee**-noh bee-**ang**-koh	white wine
vino rosso	**vee**-noh **ross**-oh	red wine
il vitello	eel vee-**tell**-oh	veal
le vongole	leh **von**-goh-leh	clams
lo zucchero	loh **zoo**-kair-oh	sugar
gli zucchini	lyee dzu-**kee**-nee	courgettes
la zuppa	lah **tsoo**-pah	soup

Numbers

1	**uno**	**oo**-noh
2	**due**	**doo**-eh
3	**tre**	treh
4	**quattro**	**kwat**-roh
5	**cinque**	**ching**-kweh
6	**sei**	**say**-ee
7	**sette**	**set**-teh
8	**otto**	**ot**-toh
9	**nove**	**noh**-veh
10	**dieci**	dee-**eh**-chee
11	**undici**	**oon**-dee-chee
12	**dodici**	**doh**-dee-chee
13	**tredici**	**tray**-dee-chee
14	**quattordici**	kwat-**tor**-dee-chee
15	**quindici**	**kwin**-dee-chee
16	**sedici**	**say**-dee-chee
17	**diciassette**	dee-chah-**set**-teh
18	**diciotto**	dee-**chot**-toh
19	**diciannove**	dee-chah-**noh**-veh
20	**venti**	**ven**-tee
30	**trenta**	**tren**-tah
40	**quaranta**	kwah-**ran**-tah
50	**cinquanta**	ching-**kwan**-tah
60	**sessanta**	sess-**an**-tah
70	**settanta**	set-**tan**-tah
80	**ottanta**	ot-**tan**-tah
90	**novanta**	noh-**van**-tah
100	**cento**	**chen**-toh
1,000	**mille**	**mee**-leh
2,000	**duemila**	**doo**-eh **mee**-lah
5,000	**cinquemila**	**ching**-kweh **mee**-lah
1,000,000	**un milione**	oon meel- **yoh**-neh

Time

one minute	**un minuto**	oon mee-**noo**-toh
one hour	**un'ora**	oon **or**-ah
half an hour	**mezz'ora**	medz-**or**-ah
a day	**un giorno**	oon **jor**-noh
a week	**una settimana**	oona set-tee-**mah**-nah
Monday	**lunedì**	loo-neh-**dee**
Tuesday	**martedì**	mar-teh-**dee**
Wednesday	**mercoledì**	mair-koh-leh-**dee**
Thursday	**giovedì**	joh-veh-**dee**
Friday	**venerdì**	ven-air-**dee**
Saturday	**sabato**	**sah**-bah-toh
Sunday	**domenica**	doh-**meh**-nee-kah

Vaporetto Routes Around Venice

The Vaporetto Routes

The ACTV network runs regular services around the city and out to most of the islands. Some services are circular for part of their route; others extend their routes during the high season. Full details of the different types of vaporetti *and how to use them are given on pages 282–3.*

KEY

✈ Airport	— Terminal route B	— City centre route 1
🚉 Railway station	— Terminal route O	⇥ City centre route 2 (part season
⛴ Car ferry	— Terminal route R	═ City centre route 5 (seasonal)
◯ Waterbus stop	═ Terminal route C (seasonal)	═ City centre route 8 (seasonal)
— Terminal route A	— Terminal route F	— City centre route 13